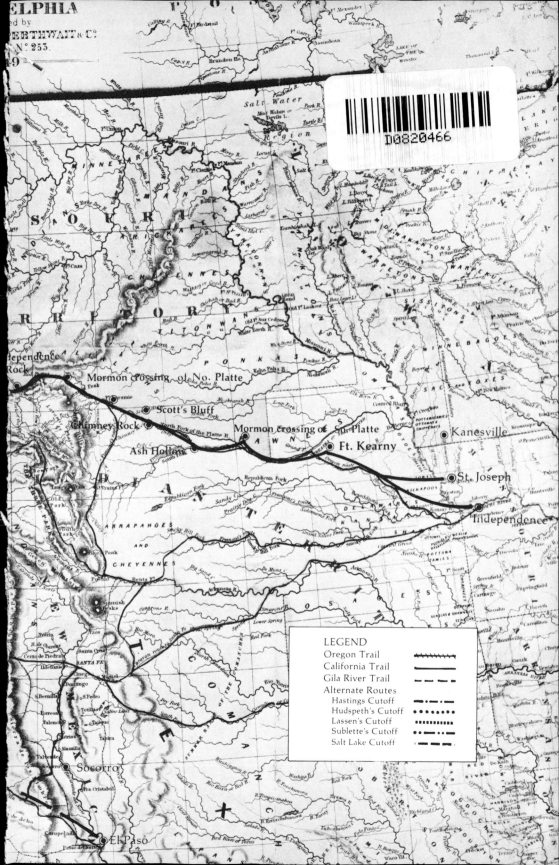

LEGEND
Oregon Trail
California Trail
Gila River Trail
Alternate Routes
  Hastings Cutoff
  Hudspeth's Cutoff
  Lassen's Cutoff
  Sublette's Cutoff
  Salt Lake Cutoff

Law for the Elephant

John Phillip Reid is Professor of Law at the
New York University School of Law. Among his
several recently published books are *A Law of
Blood: The Primitive Law of the Cherokee Nation*,
and *In a Rebellious Spirit . . . the Coming of the
American Revolution*. He has published articles
in a number of journals including the *American
Journal of Legal History*, the *New York University Law Review*, and the *Hastings Law Journal*.
The publication of *Law for the Elephant* has been
assisted by a grant from the National Endowment
for the Humanities.

Law for the Elephant
Property and Social Behavior on the Overland Trail
by John Phillip Reid

The Huntington Library, 1980

Copyright 1980
Henry E. Huntington Library and Art Gallery
San Marino, California
Library of Congress Catalog Card Number 79-26989
ISBN 0-87328-104-7

Library of Congress Cataloging in Publication Data
Reid, John Phillip.
    Law for the elephant.

    Bibliography: p.
    Includes index.
      1. Law—The West—History and criticism.   2. Property—The West—
History.   3. The West—Social conditions.   4. Overland journeys to the
Pacific.
I. Title.
KF366.R43   349.78   79-26989
ISBN 0-87328-104-7

Printed in the United States of America by
Publisher's Press, Salt Lake City, Utah
Typography by The Type Shoppe, Glendale, California

Publication of this volume has been assisted by a grant from the
National Endowment for the Humanities

for Bernard and Françoise Wuillaume of Ghent

Contents

Illustrations

The Elephant. *"If you have never seen the elephant . . . amuse yourself with a trip across the desert wilds that lay between the rocky and sierra mountains. Travel in an epidemic that is slaying its hundreds. Stand guard all night when all the elements seem to be at war while it not only rains but pours down. And you will be better enabled to realize what seeing the 'Elephant' means."*

Foreword

"To see the elephant" or "seeing the elephant" were common expressions during America's antebellum years. Although imprecisely defined, references to the elephant were generally understood. "When a man is disappointed in anything he undertakes," one contemporary explained, "when he has seen enough, when he gets sick and tired of any job he may have set himself about, he has 'seen the elephant.'"[1] More often, "to see the elephant" meant to face a particularly severe ordeal, to gain experience by undergoing hardship, to learn the realities of a situation first hand, or to encounter the unbelievable.[2] The expression was most frequently used when describing the gold rush in particular and the overland emigrations in general. To cross the continent by the overland trail was "to see the elephant." When emigrants turned back, even before crossing the Missouri River, it might be said that "they have seen the Elephant"[3] or that they were "satisfied with this view of the *Elephant.*"[4] Most travelers, however, had to journey far down the trail before encountering the elephant. "[W]e are now advanced on our trip about 200 miles and in all this trip I have not seen the 'Elephant,' " a physician wrote his wife from the Pottawatomie nation. "I am told, however, that he is ahead, and if I live, I am determined to see him."[5] "Three months today since we started and no elephant yet," another man noted.[6]

---

[1]Mitford M. Mathews, *Dictionary of Americanisms* (Chicago: Univ. of Chicago Press, 1951), p. 550.

[2]Potter, "Introduction," p. 187n1; Hannon, "Introduction and Notes," p. 114n11.

[3]Entry for 14 May 1850, Read, Journal.

[4]Entry for 1 May 1859, C. Tuttle, "Diary," p. 71.

[5]Letter of 19 May 1850, Ayres, Letters.

[6]Entry for 12 July 1852, Fox, Memorandum, p. 29.

While some emigrants saw the elephant as early as the Platte,[7] most did not find him until the Humboldt, the Forty Mile Desert, or even the Sierras. After the first hundred miles along the Humboldt, Samuel C. Plummer "began to get a glimpse of the posterior parts of the 'Elephant.' "[8] On the desert, Charles E. Lockwood, "saw tracks of the Elephant." It was not until he was standing at the summit of the Sierras that Lockwood "found the elephant, in his most formidable shape, with sundry *Horns,* and *Tusks.*"[9] Others recognized the same animal. "[T]his we found to be [the] *Elephant* and no mistake," Stephen Gage wrote of the first barrier beyond the Carson valley.[10] "Defiance seemed now to challenge our courage," John Clapp recorded while still in the valley. "Indeed, this looked considerably like the Elephant; only I did not expect to see the old fellow white-headed."[11] There were, of course, some emigrants who never saw the elephant on the overland trail, but that fact did not mean they would miss him entirely. Arriving in California in 1852, Robert Laws wrote: "I think that we begin to see the Elephant in full Uniform & I dou[b]t but we may have to ride him to water: I dont regret my going to California for I believe it to be the best thing I ever done: A young man knows nothing about this world till he goes the overland route to California."[12]

---

[7]Entry for 14 May 1850, Read, Journal.

[8]Letter of 23 July 1850, Plummer, Letters, p. 5.

[9]Letter from Charles E. Lockwood to P. H. Buren and H. A. Honey, 7 Dec. 1849 (ms., "Western Travel Papers," Missouri Historical Society, St. Louis).

[10]Entry for 27 July 1852, Stephen T. Gage, "Diary" (ts., Special Collections Department, Stanford University Libraries).

[11]Entry for 22 July 1850, Clapp, *Journal,* p. 43.

[12]Eaton, *Overland,* p. 202.

Law for the Elephant

Seeing the Elephant

1 | INTRODUCTION

There is a theme currently fashionable among historians, apparently so self-evident that it needs no proof. Premised on the assumption that Americans are a violent people, it leads to a variety of conclusions that to one degree or another can be summed up in the premise that throughout their history Americans have been more prone to lawlessness than to law.

This violence theme has recently commanded attention for several reasons. The presentism of the civil-rights and Vietnam disturbances is a major one, the American compulsion for national self-flagellation a traditional one, and the fact that non-American historians find it useful, a minor but persistent one. Comparisons with other countries, after all, can be good for the national ego. The generally colorless history of Canada gains interest and significance from the mere assertion that Canadians settled their western provinces in more orderly fashion and with less loss of life than was true for the United States. Canada's history of Indian affairs can be told in terms of comparative success; her nineteenth-century frontier appears relatively law-abiding when contrasted with the frontier that lay to the south.

In a recent use of the national-violence comparison, we are told that Canada's mining camps were more orderly than California's. The fact that Canadian authorities repeatedly warned miners that the law was to be obeyed or they would be deported from the gold fields, "coupled with the rigid prosecution of serious crimes, made the British Columbia frontier clear of the type of lawlessness so rampant in California in 1849."[1]

Apparently one need only state the proposition that America's mining frontier was lawless to prove the fact. Perhaps we are fooled by appearances or conclude that prevailing law-enforce-

---

[1] Gough, "British Columbia," pp. 269, 278.

3

ment conditions dictated the degree of law obedience that existed in a nineteenth-century American community. The discovery of gold, occurring so soon after the annexation of California, found the federal government unprepared for the rush of emigrants. There were no prosecutors, no judicial jurisdictions, and no peace officers in the California gold regions. These facts are impressive, but they only imply, they do not prove, lawlessness. The supposed propensity of Americans for violence is enough to complete the case.

The time has come to look at the record, not according to popular assumptions and familiar inferences, but by measuring "law" as lawyers define the word. Contemporaries who experienced that "rampant" lawlessness in California would have been amazed by descriptions written during the twentieth century about their society. They thought it more law-abiding than lawless.[2] It was a forty-niner who reported that in Sacramento "hundreds of thousands of dollars worth of property [was] exposed every night without a house or a guard."[3] The same was true in Stockton — surely as much a frontier town as any in the United States. "Whiskey and liquors of all kinds could be Left out-of-doors, as no man would think of touching what was left exposed," another forty-niner later recalled.[4] "Anything that is left on Shore, no matter how much exposed, is Perfectly Safe," a Bostonian landing at the height of the Gold Rush wrote of San Francisco. He reported the town "much more Peaceable than at home,"[5] while a Vermont physician thought it safer than New York City.[6]

---

[2]Entry for 5 Oct. 1849, Richard Brown Cowley, Log (ms., HM 26652, Huntington Library).

[3]Letter of 15 Oct. 1849, "Letters from George McKinley Murrell" (ms., Murrell Collection, HM 36338-36403, Huntington Library); similarly see letter of 4 Oct. 1849, Bradford, Letters.

[4]Brownlee, "Reminiscences," p. 23.

[5]Entry for 14 Sept. 1849, William W. Miller, "Diary" (ms., Western Americana Collection, S-119, Beinecke Library).

[6]Letter from Horace Pond to his parents, 12 July 1849 (ms., Western Americana Collection S-714, Beinecke Library).

What was true for the centers of commerce was true for the gold diggings. "The people here áre civil and mind their own business," a forty-niner from Michigan wrote of conditions on the middle fork of the American River. "I hear of no thefts, robberies or murders."[7] There were, in fact, very few. "Any miner," a second forty-niner said of Weaverville, "can leave his things loose in his tent, and be gone a week, or month, and come back and find them as he left them."[8] Similar statements could be quoted from such geographically scattered locations as the Yuba River, Mormon Island, Hangtown, Murphy's Diggings, and Mariposa.[9] In fact, both property and life were so secure that few men felt the need for weapons, at least not to protect themselves from fellow Americans. "Pistols and Bowie knives are laid aside & you will see the passer by armed with a pick shovel and pan," an Indianan reported from the north branch of the middle fork of the Sacramento River.[10] Joseph Warren Wood found his rifle so worthless, he had it "made into a crowbar."[11] "Almost any rifle is useless & valueless to a miner," another man wrote during the last month of the year. "Good ones are thrown away, or left with other things of equal original cost, rather than carry them."[12] On the whole, "Pistols & Dirks" were the "poorest property" a miner could possess.[13] "[T]hey laugh at the man that talks of taking a

---

[7]Letter from D. C. Downer to parents, 23 Sept. 1849, Bidlach, *Letters*, p. 33.

[8]Letter of 19 Sept. 1849 from George Mifflin Harker to the *St. Louis Weekly Reveille* in "Morgan Street to Old Dry Diggings, 1849," *Glimpses of the Past*, 6 (1939):66.

[9]Yuba River: entry for 13 Oct. 1849, McCall, *Pick and Pan*, p. 20. Mormon Island: entry for 20 Aug. 1849, Pierce, Letters. Hangtown: Letter of 13 Jan. 1850, Wells, Letters. Murphy's Diggings: James Lynch, *With Stevenson to California, 1846* (c. 1896), p. 47. Mariposa: Dawson, *Narrative*, p. 71. Isaac Jones Wistar, "Diary of Journey across the Plains" in *Autobiography of Isaac Jones Wistar, 1827-1905* (Philadelphia: Wistar Institute of Anatomy and Biology, 1914), 1:123.

[10]Letter from Allen Varner to Elias Varner, 12 Nov. 1849, Varner, Letters.

[11]Entry for 6 Nov. 1849, J. W. Wood, Diaries.

[12]Letter from S. Mathews to C. W. Adams, 13 Dec. 1849, *Benjamin F. Adams Correspondence* (ms., Western Americana Collection S-689, Beinecke Library).

[13]Letter to Eliza Mason, 18 Oct. 1849, Mason, Letters.

Pistol with him"[14] while those "that have come loaded with their weapons seem rather ashamed of them."[15] A man from Canton, New York, felt "as safe" in the diggings as "I would at home," adding that he thought "there is much more danger of a man be sick & Die than his being killed."[16]

Of course there were criminal activities during 1849 and 1850. Some property was stolen, or at least the owner thought it was. Yet even accounts published by writers critical of California life and California society conceded that "few crimes were committed" in 1849.[17] Looking back during later years, surviving pioneers recalled the orderliness of the initial period in almost idyllic terms,[18] occasionally exaggerating it beyond the believable by claiming they could not remember seeing a single fight and asserting that there "was absolutely no thievery."[19]

As time went on violence increased and some men, reversing the norm of 1849, armed themselves.[20] Yet even during 1852, the year that may have experienced the highest rate of violent crimes, miners disagreed on whether California was uniquely lawless or a tamer reflection of general American society. A New Yorker writing from the famous mining community of Angels Camp called California society "very bad" in 1850,[21] but two years later a Missourian at Auburn disagreed. "I have," he contended, "seen

---

[14]Loc. cit.

[15]Letter of 20 Aug. 1849, Pierce, Letters.

[16]Letter to Eliza Mason, 18 Oct. 1849, Mason, Letters.

[17]J. Hale, *California*, p. 33.

[18]See, e.g., Royce, *Frontier Lady*, p. 80; Cox, entry for 14 July 1849, "Reminiscences," p. 132.

[19]Pleasants, *Twice Across*, p. 102.

[20]Letters from Jesse H. Shuart to Isaac Geower, 25 March and 7 July 1852, 2 and 11 August 1853, letter from Jesse H. Shuart to his sister, 28 July 1852, Jesse H. Shuart, "Correspondence" (ms., Western Americana Collection S-746, Beinecke Library); entries for 9 Jan., 16 March, 24 April, 22 June, 26 Dec. 1851, and 6 Feb. 1852, McKinstry, *Diary*, pp. 324, 335, 342, 346, 354, 360; Potter, "Introduction," p. 71; letter from Amos P. Bradbury to his mother, 15 Jan. 1851, "Amos P. Bradbury Papers" (ms., Clements Library).

[21]Letter from Nathan Chase to Jane Chase, 2 May 1852, Nathan Chase, "Letters" (ms., Western Americana Collection S-686, Beinecke Library).

more rioting, fighting, shooting, stabbing, and all sorts of drunken debauchery in Keytesville [Missouri] in *one day*, than I have witnessed here in the two years of my stay and I have all the time been in large companies."[22]

Few reporting the change could tell why it had occurred. Some blamed a decline in morals manifested by drinking, gambling, and the absence of stable community life.[23] More pointed was the complaint that "the country is filled with broken gamblers, Sidney convicts, and desperadoes of every kind." California, it was said, had attracted "rascals from all nations."[24] In other words, the rise in violence was possibly due to foreigners and, ironically, a major part was caused by criminals from the supposedly law-abiding British Empire. "In 1849," one man later recalled, "Australia had not yet sent her convicts."[25] Thus did those who were in the gold country reverse the comparisons now being made.

Few forty-niners asked why lawfulness prevailed. True, some wondered at the paradox noted by one Californian who stated that "beyond the jurisdiction of the law they were still law-abiding."[26] Yet the topic was seldom pursued and one reason was that contemporaries, unlike twentieth-century historians, assumed that lawful behavior was the expected as well as the normal pattern.

One of the few to speculate was John M. Muscott, a man from upstate New York who arrived in California a week or two ahead of the main wave of the emigration. He thought he knew why there was so little crime to be found in the new territory. "Two

---

[22]Letter from Lisbon Applegate to Lewis M. Applegate, 25 Feb. 1852, "The Letters of George W. and Lisbon Applegate in Description of the Trip to the Gold Diggings and Life in California, 1850-1854" (ms., Western Americana Collection 9, Beinecke Library).

[23]Letter from C. N. Ormsby to his sister et al., 3 Aug. 1850, Bidlach, *Letters*, p. 46.

[24]Entry for 1 Sept. 1850, Millington, Journal. Similarly, see letter to James Kinkade, 6 Feb. 1854, John Thompson Kinkade, "Kinkade Correspondence" (ms., HM 1829-1885, Huntington Library).

[25]Brownlee, "Reminiscences," p. 24.

[26]Pleasants, *Twice Across*, p. 102.

prominent causes can be assigned for this," he reasoned, "one is that our success in the Mexican War has impressed all foreigners in the country with the idea, that the Americans have no superior in the world; — and secondly, the large infusion of law and order men from home, gives tone and character to a society here, the most heterogeneous that the world ever saw."[27]

It is the second explanation that interests us: the influx of "law and order men from home." We may be conditioned historically to doubt the assertion, but such men were in the mining camps and it is time that their presence is acknowledged. There is reason to suspect that much written about lawlessness in early California has been based on the assumption that the character of the forty-niners was formed once they reached the Sierras, not before. The legal behavior of some individuals probably was altered, but it is questionable whether such cases were numerous. We should, therefore, be able to measure the law-mindedness of the early California emigrants by looking at their conduct as they crossed the plains. After all, it was not so much on the Yuba or the Feather rivers, or in any of the legendary mining camps, as it was along that vast legal no-man's land — up the monotonous Platte, over the Rocky Mountains, and across the Great Basin — that the emigrants who traveled to the Pacific slopes in search of land and gold found themselves beyond police surveillance, free from the threat of prosecution and apparently released from the restraint of family, church, and neighborhood. What is more, they knew it.

Passing the last village beyond St. Joseph, a party of forty-niners "raised our Hats and bid adieu to civilization."[28] Next morning another company out of Independence "reached the frontier line of Missouri, which marks the separation of civilized from uncivilized life."[29] At that place, overland emigrants knew, they were leaving the United States. "My country, my country, my heart clings to thee," one man wrote. "But for a time I must be

---

[27]Letter from John M. Muscott to Ebenezer Robbins, 14 Oct. 1849, Muscott, Letters.

[28]Entry for 27 April 1849, Lindsey, Journal.

[29]Entry for 28 April 1849, William G. Johnston, "The First Wagon Train into California in '49," in *Course of Empire*, ed. Valeska Bari, p. 76.

as it were banished from civilized society."[30] The realization was not only that they were "bidding farewell to the last abode of white men."[31] More striking was the fact, as explained by a Baptist minister who three times crossed to the Pacific, they were "entering a region where there was no restraint imposed by law or usage."[32]

It was not only restraint imposed by law that overland emigrants thought they left behind, but law itself. "We were out of reach and beyond the arm of law and order," a man wrote of crossing the Missouri River, "and the only law we had was that formulated unto ourselves."[33] If thoughts such as these by unidentified individuals do not surprise us, perhaps they will when voiced by lawyers and army officers. Out on the Great Plains a Missouri attorney told his companions that they were "traveling through a country . . . influenced by no law save that which nature's God has implanted in the heart of every man."[34] Similarly, the captain of the United States regiment of mounted riflemen, writing in his official journal from the secure confines of Fort Laramie, justified putting an unruly civilian teamster in irons by noting that he was "in a country where there was neither law nor order."[35]

To find that emigrants thought there was no law on the overland trail could tell us much. If people act on their beliefs — a plausible norm of behaviorism — we should conclude that understanding law was nonexistent would have encouraged lawless conduct. If not acts of violence, it surely would have produced attitudes resulting in disrespect for other persons or for claims to exclusive ownership and possession of property. Moreover, if lawful, nonviolent behavior by ordinary citizens is

---

[30]Letter of 23 April 1850, Z. S. Tuttle, Letters.

[31]Entry for 15 May 1854, Murphy, Across, p. 1.

[32]Udell, *Incidents*, p. 111.

[33]Ellmaker, Autobiography, p. 11.

[34]"Captain James Craig's parting address on the Platte river, May 31, 1849," in McLeod, Diary, p. 50.

[35]Entry for 23 June 1849, Cross, "Journal," p. 100.

predicated upon coercive restraint imposed by the threat of government force, then also we have much to learn by observing conduct on the overland trail.

There are two facts that must be separated. The first is that the emigrants were beyond the confines of police restraint. The second is that they were conscious of the first. By saying there was no law, travelers on the overland trail were, in effect, saying they were free to act as the urgings of selfish interest and ties of conscience permitted. If we find that they did not abandon norms of legal conduct practiced east of the Missouri River, we too easily may credit either church or home. Such behavior, it could be argued, arose from the taught traditions of religious principles or from internal restraints learned while growing up in the extended families and small, law-abiding communities of antebellum America.

It would not do to reach conclusions in haste. Were we to stop guessing and look at the evidence, it could well reveal a source of social behavior previously unsuspected or deliberately ignored by historians. If the attitudes of nineteenth-century Americans toward property and ownership rights are what is to be determined, it may strike many as undissembling to seek a legal explanation. Easily overlooked is the possibility that law could be the common denominator, explaining both the definitions people shared and the conduct they followed.

To measure the law-mindedness of ordinary nineteenth-century Americans there may be no more revealing historical saga than the overland trail that stretched through an unexplored wilderness from the Missouri River to the Pacific Ocean. It is no exaggeration to describe the trail as a great laboratory for testing not merely the respect ordinary citizens showed for the rights of others but for determining the extent to which they understood law and could premise legal behavior on the expectation that strangers traveling the same route understood and respected it as well. To say there was no law on the overland trail, after all, may be to say nothing more than that there were no lawyers from whom advice could be obtained and no courts to resolve disputes.

Should evidence reveal that without attorneys to advise them, emigrants on the overland trail were able to distinguish between private, company, partnership, and other concurrent methods of property holding, we may be impressed by the legal knowledge of nineteenth-century Americans. If we find they acted on this knowledge to guide their conduct not only toward property but in dealings with fellow emigrants, then we may draw conclusions more far reaching. To a greater extent than has been thought, the habits, actions, and values of nineteenth-century American society were formed by a behaviorism based on law.

II *The Emigration*

To evaluate the evidence we must know something of those providing the testimony. The problem is that no composite can be drawn. No journal or diary was representative of all life on the overland trail, nor were the experiences of a single emigrant typical.[1] We should not even think of them fitting a common mold. "In marking the physiognomies of the emigrants for California," a forty-niner wrote long before reaching the frontier, "we at once can determine it is not confined to the young and poor only but to grey hairs as well as youth, rich and poor, literate and illiterate, halt and maimed, white and black."[2] Indeed, even the emigrations did not follow a single pattern. Before 1849, the California trail, like the Oregon trail, had generally been a family affair in which children could be almost as numerous as adults, women about as numerous as men.[3] With the gold rush the road to California became a largely grown-up, nearly all male affair —"old men young men one legged men and some that dont happen to be men," as one emigrant cryptically put it.[4]

---

[1]Introduction, *To California and the South Seas: The Diary of Albert G. Osbun, 1849-1851*, ed. John Haskell Kemble (San Marino, Calif: Huntington Library, 1966), p. vii.

[2]Entry for 22 March 1849, H. M. Price, Diary, p. 2.

[3]G. R. Stewart, *Trail*, p. 85.

[4]Letter from Ovin D. Wright to his sister, 22 April 1850 (ts., C. C. Wagner Collection, Missouri Historical Society, St. Louis).

Change may not have been as extensive as one might guess. That demographic patterns were altered did not necessarily mean the social character of emigrations was different. "The emigration is of good character," a man wrote of 1846, "entirely different from the Texas Emigrants that we knew in our Mississippi days. Good farmers and mechanics, with a small sprinkle of 'Yankee peddlers.' "[5] A physician from Michigan thought much the same about the gold rush of 1849. "With the general character of the emigration," he wrote from Independence, "I am highly pleased. With comparatively very few exceptions, they are moral, temperate, industrious and kind. True, we find a variety of grades of character — the scholar and the unlettered man — the mind rich with reflection and with study, and the brain unexperienced with either. Here we have the aristocracy of wealth and the aristocracy of intellect, but with it all we find habits of industry and moral deportment."[6] Months later at Salt Lake City, after completing two-thirds of the journey, the Michigan physician felt the same. "This emigration," he explained, "is not of the character of which it may be said, that the country can better spare it than not. My circumstances and the situation on the route, have furnished me opportunities for forming an almost general acquaintance with emigrants from every section of the country. It is composed (with some exceptions) of the honest, industrious and enterprising, male and female, old and young."[7]

If we question the physician's veracity it is because he was trying to convince folks at home that all was well on the overland trail. Even if that is true, it does not mean we should ignore his words. What the doctor wrote might be slanted but it still has the ring of contemporary testimony. If letters are less reliable than diaries, they were written on the scene and have value over memoirs composed years later. Recollections of western pioneers

---

[5]Letter from George McKinstry to Pierson B. Reading, 2 Nov. 1846, *Overland in 1846*, p. 216.

[6]Letter from C. N. Ormsby (n.d.), Bidlach, *Letters*, p. 17.

[7]Ibid., letter from C. N. Ormsby to his wife, 18 Dec. 1849, p. 37.

tend to recall moral characteristics too idealistic to be true. "The bravest of the Brave kindhearted, honest & full of energy," is how one overland emigrant remembered his companions.[8] For more balanced accounts we must go to contemporary documents such as the letter written from the Missouri border by a forty-niner: "some of the first people in the United States are a going and some of the meanest are also along."[9]

What is being said is that personal impressions depended upon the people one met and the events one saw. "A large majority of the Californians," an Illinois man wrote from St. Joseph, "are desperate fellows and they practice most all kinds of crime."[10] Four days later a Massachusetts emigrant at Independence reached opposite conclusions. "From three-fourths to seven-eights of those on the route are temperance, steady men; ministers, doctors, and all classes of respectable citizens."[11] A Mormon newspaper said much the same of emigrants starting from Kanesville, Iowa's frontier settlement. "They certainly appear to be men of character, wealth, and possess a good share of general intelligence," it commented. "We have not seen a drunken man among them."[12]

That our evidence is contemporary and personal makes more answerable the question we must ask of it: whether people who respected law and property rights at home would take the same legal behaviorism out onto the plains. There can be little doubt of the first fact. At home the average emigrant had been law-abiding.

---

[8]Harvey, To California, p. 44. See also, Applegate, "Cow Column," p. 101.

[9]Letter from David Dewolf to his wife, 15 May 1849, "Diary of the Overland Trail, 1849, and Letters, 1849-50, of Captain David Dewolf," *Transactions of the Illinois State Historical Society*, 33 (1925):186.

[10]Letter of 3 May 1849, *"A Pretty Fair View of the Eliphent"; or, Ten Letters by Charles G. Hinman Written during His Trip Overland from Groveland, Illinois, to California in 1849 and His Adventures in the Gold Fields in 1849 and 1850*, ed. Colton Storm (Chicago: Everett D. Graff, 1960), p. 11. For a more detailed account of crime in St. Joseph that week see letter from Frederick Barnard to "Larry," 6 May 1849, Barnard Correspondence (ms., Western Americana Collection 5-680, Beinecke Library).

[11]Letter from Benjamin Burt to his family, 7 May 1849, Hannon, "Introduction and Notes," p. 61.

[12]*Frontier Guardian*, 16 May 1849, p. 2, col. 3.

"I think well of the Californians as a body," a New Yorker wrote somewhere near today's Kansas-Nebraska line. "They are generally speaking, men of good sense, practical business men of good habits and some principles, disposed to observe law and order."[13] Sarah Royce, the articulate, observant, and prim mother of Josiah Royce, said much the same. "The great majority of the crowd were men," she later recalled of '49, "generally working men of ordinary intelligence, farmers and mechanics — accustomed to the comforts and amenities of domestic life, and, most of them evidently intending to carry more or less of these agreeable things with them 'across the plains.' "[14]

Mrs. Royce is telling us more than that these emigrants were likely to carry their legal values with them across the plains. She is warning us not to think of them as frontiersmen. Even before the gold rush, when most of those going overland were from the western states, they "cannot be called real frontiersmen."[15] They were not even what today we term outdoorsmen. Most were to find themselves "leading a life the whole time which at Home would have been considered as resulting almost in certain death."[16] Some "had many a laugh over the horror" their hometown folks "would have at the thought of traveling the way we have been journeying, sleeping out every night, rain or shine."[17] Others confessed that "sleeping on the ground is rather uncomfortable," and though they expressed hopes of "getting accustomed to it," many never did.[18] Inexperienced in the demands of "prairie life" and psychologically unprepared "to accomplish a journey fraught with so many obstacles,"[19] hundreds

---

[13]Letter of 20 May 1849, Muscott, Letters.

[14]Royce, *Frontier Lady*, p. 8.

[15]G. R. Stewart, *Trail*, p. 18.

[16]Letter to Father and Mother, 4 Oct. 1849, Bradford, Letters.

[17]Letter of 20 June 1849, Senter, *Crossing;* Riley Senter, "Letters" (ms., C-B 931, Bancroft Library).

[18]Entry for 26 May 1849, Batchelder, Journal, p. 9. Similarly, entry for 1 May 1858, Putnam, *Journal.*

[19]Entry for 25 May 1849, Cross, "Journal," p. 46.

returned before they had traveled many miles.[20]

The fact so many had to turn back is more than an indication of the trip's hardships. It is also indicative of the fact that many emigrants had been thrust into an unfamiliar social environment for which nothing in their past experience prepared them. To the degree that overland travelers adhered to taught legal behavior, the degree of difference in social environment makes their adherence to that legal behavior that much more remarkable.

It would be easy to underestimate the extent of change. It was more drastic than has been suspected. Contrary to general belief, overland emigrants were not "farmers' boys out on an adventure" for whom "the routine of the camp, with cattle grazing, cowbells sounding, and, on occasion, scythes swinging to provide hay for the barren stretches, was no great divorcement from the experience of an agrarian age."[21] They were not even all from rural backgrounds as has been contended.[22] Many came from urban centers; several companies of forty-niners were made up of New Yorkers and Bostonians.[23]

It may not be surprising that the appearance of an Indian in an emigrant camp created "quite a sensation." After all, many mid-century Americans "had never seen such a sight before."[24] But it should be surprising how little many of them knew about draft animals. A Michigan man purchasing a pony had to have his messmate select the animal as he had never before owned a horse.[25] A naturalized German also bought a pony and the next

---

[20]There are countless reports of returning emigrants, some of which will be noted below. See, e.g., entry for 11 May 1852, Rudd, Notes.

[21]Potter, "Introduction," p. x.

[22] Goodrich & Davison, "The Wage-Earner in the Westward Movement," *Political Science Quarterly*, 61, (19):115.

[23]"Introduction," Gray, *Off at Sunrise*, p. xii; entry for 8 Feb. 1849, John W. Audubon, *Audubon's Western Journal: 1849-1850* (Cleveland: The Arthur H. Clark Co., 1906), p. 44; entry for 4 Jan. 1850, Hayes, Diary, p. 154. See also Eccleston, *Overland; Ohio State Journal*, 2 April 1849, quoted in Giffen,"Notes," pp. 13-14; Hannon, "Introduction and Notes," pp. 37-42.

[24]Entry for 25 May 1849, Dr. T., Journal.

[25]Goldsmith, *Overland*, p. 21.

day rode it for a few miles. "I mention this," he wrote, "as being rather something great, being the first riding ever I did."[26] Even a young man from the small town of Pelham, New Hampshire, supposedly one of those "farmers' boys" accustomed to animals, did not ride until the second day on the trail. He was cautious, starting ahead of his companions at four in the morning when, it is suspected, the others were still asleep. As he explained, "This was the first time I had mounted any animal, but went on without any trouble."[27]

Other emigrants did have trouble. When we realize that some never had seen a mule before,[28] it is hardly surprising they were "at a loss to know what kind of mules to purchase"[29] or how to handle mules once bought.[30] Too often they had to take unbroken mules and were left to wonder how to tame them.[31] Even Missourians, who might be thought experienced, had difficulty. There was "considerable alarm manifested & long faces [were] very common" in a company of Missouri forty-niners when it was discovered that the mules were beginning to fail. "We are all sorry that we started with a mule younger than 5 years," a member complained.[32] Later, the animals of another Missouri train were in such bad condition the wagons had to be abandoned. "Our boys," it was explained, "not being accustomed to driving Horses we drove to[o] fast."[33]

It cannot be said the emigrants were unsuited for overland travel. Spirit, enthusiasm, and (in the case of the California trail) youth must be counted. What can be said is that they were, as a

---

[26]*Extracts from the Diary of William C. Lobenstine, December 31, 1851-1858* (New York: Privately printed, 1920), p. 18.

[27]Entry for 26 May 1849, Batchelder, Journal, p. 9.

[28]*St. Louis Weekly Review*, 16 July 1849 (ts., Missouri Historical Society, St. Louis); entry for 27 April 1849, Bruff, *Journals*, p. 6.

[29]Entry for 5 May 1849, Staples, "Diary," p. 66.

[30]Entry for 13 May 1849, Hixson, Diary.

[31]Call, Journey, p. 3.

[32]Entry for 4 June 1849, B. C. Clark, "Journey" p. 17.

[33]Entry for 17 May 1852, G. A. Smith, Diary.

group, ill adapted to frontier life. A random collection of typical Americans thrown together for a single purpose, they were, as one said, "a heterogeneous mass . . . the minister; the gambler; the merchant; the clerk; the statesman; and the clodhopper all have forsaken home, kindred, and friends for gold."[34] "[S]tore sweep Clerks and Gentlemen," a forty-niner complained, "are littel [sic] fitting for a trip of this kind."[35] Perhaps, but many not only went onto the overland trail, they continued on it to the end. By October 1849, when there was a shortage of laborers in California, Sacramento was flooded with store clerks looking for work.[36]

To discover that many forty-niners were store clerks may tell us little more than that some overland emigrants were not frontiersmen or farmers. To learn that many were physicians and lawyers reveals much about educational quality and middle-class make-up. Sacramento not only had too many clerks, it had — indeed, all California had — too many doctors and attorneys. "The great number of professional men, enlisted in this expedition," one emigrant surmised, "would seem to argue that professional labors are not well rewarded in the United States, or perhaps, that the ranks of all the professions are too much crowded."[37] A forty-niner had the same impression. "A company from Ohio dissolved," he wrote, "—cause, too many Doctors & Lawyers."[38] In fact, every type of profession was on the trail. Sixty-five members of a New York company starting from Fort Smith, Arkansas, in 1849, had previously earned their livings in thirty-eight different occupations, including jeweler, bookkeeper, engineer, pharmacist, tailor, baker, stage line proprietor, journalist, and student.[39]

The social, educational, and professional background that helps explain emigrant behavior, made adjustment to wilderness

---

[34]James David, quoted in Eaton, *Overland*, p. 32.

[35]Letter of 17 June 1849, Moxley, Correspondence.

[36]Letter from David T. McCollum to J. H. Lund, 20 Oct. 1849, Bidlach, *Letters.* p. 36.

[37]Entry for 28 April 1850, Langworthy, *Scenery*, p. 9.

[38]Entry for 8 June 1849, Decker, *Diaries*, p. 91.

[39]*Fort Smith Herald*, 14, 21 March 1849, quoted in Bieber, *Southern Trails*, p. 286n220.

ways more difficult than might be thought about nineteenth-century Americans. Some overland travelers expressed displacency at handling buffalo chips, the chief fuel of the treeless plains.[40] While several conclusions could be drawn, the point to stress is not that old sensitivities had to be discarded, but that new tasks had to be mastered. "Laid over all day," a Pennsylvania physician wrote in his diary. "Did my own washing for the first time in my life."[41] Although we may think the task not difficult, we should acknowledge that novelty was not just a matter of comfort, it could be socially jarring. If it is agreed that not only distance or changing scenery but small inconveniences could separate an individual from the familiar, then the fact that overland emigrants retained taught legal values is that much more impressive.

Education also must be considered. The level of schooling among overland emigrants was high, though too much should not be made of that fact. As we must rely on the written word, it is only the literate from whom we hear, and our evidence is colored with an erudite hue.

It would also be a mistake to put much emphasis on the fact that those who kept the records of overland life could read and write. It means they were lettered, not necessarily that they were middle class. Working men also kept diaries, several of which are extant. It is revealing that in terms of law-mindedness — in terms of their knowledge of the definitions of property and respect shown for the rights of others to property — these diaries cannot be distinguished from those of physicians, lawyers, and others of more substantial means and greater education.[42]

Whether overland emigrants were representative of the American population is a question that must be answered. What is

---

[40]Entry for 29 May 1853, McClure, Journey, p. 23.

[41]Entry for 17 May 1849, Parke, Notes.

[42]See e.g., "The Diary of Asa Cyrus Call, 1850-1852" (ts., California Historical Society, San Francisco); Murphy, Across; J. N. Lewis, Book; Thomas G. Gill, "Across the Plains in Early Days," *Stanislaus County Weekly News*, Modesto, California, 14 Aug. 1903, p. 2, cols. 4-6.

beyond question is that the legal values expressed and legal behaviorism described in overland diaries are remarkably uniform. No matter what occupations, backgrounds, or home areas, those who kept diaries and whose letters are extant shared similar legal attitudes.

III   *The Behaviorism of Habit*

When we search for evidence of legal attitudes and legal behavior on the overland trail, we are looking for what Thomas Paine and Thomas Jefferson called legal habit.[1] They used the term disparagingly. Alexander Hamilton or John Marshall would have used it with respect. Political theorists of the Jeffersonian persuasion feared that legal behaviorism stifled the free choice of elected assemblies; lawyers of the Hamiltonian tradition praised it as one of the soundest foundations upon which to rest the rule of law. That people behaved according to taught customs of their youths — even in a strange, hostile environment such as the overland trail, where those lessons might seem inapplicable — would to legal theorists of the Hamiltonian school be evidence not only of the strength of custom, but proof of its validity as law.

We may gauge the strength of legal habit by considering the strength of social habit. The young men crossing the continent to the California gold fields in 1849 belonged to the generation that would make Victorian morality the norm of conduct in American life. The religious fervor and remarkable primness they exhibited on the overland trail presaged that morality.

Two examples of what overland emigrants did not do should illustrate the point. First, no diarist ever referred to, let alone described, toilet habits on the trail. We are left to wonder about what they thought could not be mentioned. Second was their language. Only one diary has been found that uses the vulgar expression "Buffalo Shit."[2] All others tuck the unpleasant reality

---

[1] Daniel J. Boorstin, *The Lost World of Thomas Jefferson* (New York: H. Holt, 1948), pp. 204-13.

[2] Entry for 16 May 1852, W. Johnston, Diary, p. 2.

of excrement behind the euphemism "buffalo chips."

We must not assume all such conduct was habitually uncon-
scious. Many emigrants were resolved to maintain on the trail
habits learned and practiced at home. Most obvious was the
pledge of abstinence. Aware it was a frontier they were entering,
some emigrants were militantly determined not to wander from
the pledged path. "Now, boys," an elderly man told the members
of a Boston company embarking on a Mississippi steamboat,
"you must drink whiskey, or this water will kill you." Defiant in
the face of impending evil, the young men raised their right hands
above their heads and answered with one voice, "Then we shall
die!"[3] We should not be amused that they boasted of a gesture
that seems quaintly old fashioned to a later generation. We
should be impressed by their determination not to be swayed
from the ways of home.

Sunday observance fell into the same category with abstinence.
Emigrants were shocked when the day slipped by unnoticed.
"This [Sunday] almost passed without my knowledge of the
day," an Ohio forty-niner noted in his diary. "I could scarcely
believe it possible it could pass thus. Thus is man a creature of
habit." He thought he could explain the misremembrance — "To
us there is no day of rest" — and was determined it would not
again happen. "Yesterday and this day I was so engaged that I had
not time to write; otherwise this mistake could not occur, and
sincerely do I hope it will never again."[4]

To think Sunday travel only a matter of religious observance
would be a mistake. For overland travelers it was that and more
besides. It was also a matter of carrying the familiar out onto the
plains. "We shall keep the Sabbath as we would at home in New
England," a forty-niner promised his family back in Massachusetts.[5]
About to shoot a buffalo that had wandered in front of his wagon,
an emigrant was reminded by his wife that it was Sunday. "[H]e

---

[3]Hannon, "Introduction and Notes," p. 51.

[4]Entry for 16 Sept. 1849, Banks, "Diary," p. 88. See also entry for 5 Sept. 1852, Moreland,
Diary.

[5]Letter from Benjamin Burt, 7 May 1849, Hannon, "Introduction and Notes" p. 56n14.

immediately returned the rifle to its place."[6]

Companies in their constitutions or bylaws, often pledged not to travel on Sunday.[7] When compelled by circumstances to violate the Lord's day, diarists complained that it did "not seem like Sunday" and wrote of being "obliged to work" or "obliged to move forward."[8]

Being "obliged" to travel on Sunday not only disturbed, it angered emigrants. Otherwise harmonious companies dissolved over that issue alone.[9]

The discovery that few men "will keep the Sabbath when there is Sacrifice to be made" could be a shock.[10] Just as bad was learning that stopping did not bring religious meditation.[11] "Many things that would be wrong, and looked upon as highly impeachable and unchristian-like at home must be attended to by the wayward traveller."[12] There was so much work to be done while resting, "that there is full as much sin committed as in traveling."[13] Even the undeniably necessary tasks of "cooking and washing, and making hay" caused concern. "A fine example for Christian people to be setting to Indians, far in the interior of a heathen land."[14]

Our interest is not with religious zealots who cursed the sabbath-traveling majority for doing the Devil's bidding,[15] or

---

[6]Phoebe Goodell Judson, *A Pioneer's Search for an Ideal Home* (Bellingham, Wash.: Union Printing, Binding and Stationery Co., 1925), p. 33.

[7]See, e.g., "By-Laws of Lake County [Ill.] Company," Clapp, *Journal*, p. 13; "By-Laws and Regulations of the Dubuque Emigrating Company," Cooke, *Crossing the Plains*, p. 18.

[8]Entry for 10 May 1863, E. T. Adams, Diary; entry for 5 June 1853, Woodworth, Diary, p. 11.

[9]See, e.g., entry for 23 May 1852, Thomson, *Crossing the Plains*, p. 37.

[10]Entry for 24 June 1849, Burbank, Diary and Journal, p. 43.

[11]Entry for 23 May 1852, E.B.M. Hanna, "Journal," p. 33.

[12]Entry for 14 July 1850, Moorman, *Journal*, p. 44.

[13]Entry for 20 June 1852, Anable, Journal, p. 18.

[14]Entry for 1 Sept. 1850, Dowell, Journal, p. 44.

[15]Entry for 11 July 1852, "Diary of George Washington Short of Wauhesha, Wisconsin, Covering His Trip to and from California in 1852-53" (ts., State Historical Society of

wailed that "we are all so wicked that we do far more harme when we are stopt than when we are going."[16] More pertinent were those who, knowing Sunday travel and Sunday work were inevitable, regretted the need not so much for its sinfulness as for the feeling of being cut off from the institutions of their homes and their youths. "Again we pursue our wearisome way although it is the sabbath," a Michigan forty-niner wrote on the ninth day of travel down Nevada's Humboldt River. "These valleys know not the Lord's appointments or even heard the soul inspiring sound of the church going bell. But why should man forget or neglect his obligations to his God, although far away from the abode of humanity & civilization?"[17]

It was not the feeling of being cut off from the habits of home that bothered emigrants so much as being unable to retain the sense of continuity even when they tried. "It seems a strange week that has no *Sunday*," a forty-niner wrote.[18] "But for my diary I should not know when Sunday came around," another observed. "Ask any one on the road what day it is and they are unable to tell you nine times out of ten."[19] Said an emigrant of 1851, "Quite forget its being Sunday & repair my gun, while others fire at targets, run balls, mend wagons, &c."[20]

When remembered, the day was missed even more. "O what Sundays," a woman from Ohio lamented. "There is nothing that seems like the Sabbath."[21] "Oh!," a second Oregon-bound emigrant echoed, "When shall the sabbath bring to us the rest which God designed it should bring to his children."[22]

Wisconsin, Madison). See also entry for 4 July 1852, ibid., quoted in Eaton, *Overland*, p. 243.

[16]Entry for 3 July 1853, H. Stewart, Diary, p. 19. See also entry for 5 June 1853, ibid., p. 9.

[17]Entry for 19 Aug. 1849, Spooner, Diary. Similarly, see entry for 12 May 1850, Abbey, *A Trip*, p. 116; entry for 19 June 1853, Williams, "Diary," p. 199; entry for 14 May 1854, Condit, Diary; entry for 8 Aug. 1858, Putnam, *Journal*.

[18]Entry for 1 July 1849, Banks, "Diary," p. 29.

[19]Entry for 22 July 1849, Mann, Portion, p. 11.

[20]Entry for 3 Aug. 1851, Welsh, Diaries.

[21]Entry for 11 June 1854, Goodell, Crossing the Plains, p. 10.

[22]Entry for 29 May 1853, Williams, Journal.

Some trains celebrated religious services on Sunday, and those lucky enough to be there generally found their thoughts turning toward home. "[A]ttended church in a camp, about 1/2 a mile b[e]low us," a man traveling along the Platte recorded. "[I]t puts one in mind of Civilization again."[23] Listening to a Baptist minister preach to several companies reminded another emigrant "of our Sabbath spent at home."[24] "We had a good sermon," a third man agreed, "and felt as if we were again at home."[25]

There was no need to hear a sermon. Just to realize the day was Sunday brought thoughts of home and of scenes missed. "I cannot help thinking of our dear home to day," one of the relatively few female emigrants of 1849 wrote. "I think I see them going to the house of God to worship there   O! what a blessed privelege   Here on these wide prairie[s] we seldom here the voice of prayer."[26] "My thoughts run much on home," an argonaut noted that same day. What he missed was "Its temporal & Spiritual Enjoyments."[27] "It was the sabbath and my thoughts wandered back to the beloved home of my childhood," another woman recorded. "I fancied I saw them all — my young companions — with smiling faces wending their way to the loved sabbath school . . . . Oh I could wish I was with them for this one sabbath day."[28]

For some the homelonging dominated, for others the feature of home they most longed for was divine worship. "We had no church going," a man from the frontier state of Iowa noted while on the Sweetwater River. "No Church Bell, No voice of a minister, No songs of praise of the Almighty . . . . We are deprived of Sunday privileges."[29] Exactly one week later, many hundreds

[23]Entry for 5 June 1859, Chillson, Diary.

[24]Entry for 21 July 1850, Gilmore, Overland Journey, p. 16.

[25]Entry for 19 June 1853, Longworth, *Diary*, p. 24.

[26]Entry for 24 June 1849, Cecilia Emily McMillen Adams, "Journal" (ts., 1508, Oregon Historical Society, Portland), p. 8.

[27]Entry for 24 June 1849, Burbank, Diary and Journal, p. 44.

[28]Entry for 25 May 1851, Buckingham, Overland Diary, p. 2.

[29]Entry for 23 June 1850, Paschel, Diary, p. 27.

of miles away in the northeast corner of today's Nevada, another emigrant had similar thoughts. "This is again the pleasant Sabbath day of our dearly loved homes where quiet & order reign supreme, where naught is heard to mar the pleasant quiet of the bright & pleasing morning, but the sabbath school bell."[30]

For some the realization that there was no "Sunday" produced not only a sense of lost values from the past but of shame for the present. Failure to keep the Sabbath made emigrants conscious of something we might think should not trouble them on the overland trail — their reputations. "Started early & traveled 28 [m]iles passing 230 teams," a forty-niner confessed, "most of whom were laying bye for rest. I felt as if we should be doing the same & was really ashamed to meet with one even professedly keeping the Sabbath."[31] Indeed, it may surprise us, but overland emigrants were sensitive to the opinions of others. They might be traveling far from home, behaving exactly like everyone else, yet even while passing strangers they most likely would never meet again emigrants could be concerned about reputation.

A "most brutal affair took place" between two members of a Massachusetts company, and at least one of their companions sensed shame. "It commenced," he wrote, "by White pushing Ayer and kicking him. In return Ayer threw a hatchet he held in his hand at the time. It struck White on the thy and cut a gash four inches long, quite deep. Men get cross sometimes on this trip and haveing all restraint thrown off they act rash." We might think that fact excuse enough. The writer did not. "I hope," he added, "we shall not have another case of assault. It lowers us in the eyes of other Companies and ourselves."[32]

To find concern about reputation in a place where reputation, if it meant anything, had a wholly new meaning, is to find one measure of the force of social habit. The values of a Massachusetts upbringing were being carried onto the plains and into the mountains. We cannot say emigrants were reluctant to let go of

[30]Entry for 30 June 1850, Gorgas, Diary.

[31]Entry for 27 May 1849, J. A. Johnson, Note Book.

[32]Entry for 30 July 1849, Staples, "Diary," p. 150.

their past. Perhaps they gave the possibility no thought. What can be said is that previously formed behaviorism did not change once the frontier had been crossed.

Of all forces that shaped emigrant values — community, church, country, education, profession — none was more pronounced than family. Those going to Oregon quite often were whole families on the move; the argonauts of the gold rush left their families with reluctance. It is remarkable how many men got out on the plains after months of planning and hours of brave talk, only to turn back. It is even more remarkable that some "could give no reason except they were homesick."[33] Those who stayed on the trail longed for their wives, children, and parents, wishing they could be home for just a few hours and yearning for letters or some message reporting health and well being.

Memory brought back to them taught values and influenced their behavior. "[I]t does me good and softens my heart to think of my mother," a young man from Wisconsin wrote in his journal. "When I think of her, I am kind to others, and feel as though I had no enmity towards any one. May the memory of her who bore me, always, fresh, remain with me; and may I never cease to imitate the virtues of my mother."[34]

When Jim Bridger told emigrants that, having fallen into disgrace as a boy of sixteen, he ran away from home and changed his name, they understood his behavior.[35] Even the criminals of the overland trail could recall their families, exhibit shame, and win sympathy. Somewhere in the wilderness of today's southeast Idaho several suspected abactors were seized, tried, and condemned to death.

> They all went under fictitious [names] until in their examination they gave what they said were their true names, except one little fellow whose fictitious name was Badger. He declared, when asked his real name, that he would not give it even if he could have his freedom by so doing. He said his were as respectable and

---

[33]Entry for 20 May 1849, Benson, Forty Niner, p. 7.

[34]Entry for 15 June 1850, Newcomb, Journal.

[35]Ferguson, *Gold Fields*, p. 42.

respected parents as any man's, and that he would sooner die than that their name should be disgraced by him. And had it been at all appropriate, he would have been cheered to the echo. As it was, a distinct murmur of approval ran through the crowd.

It is not the taciturnity of the condemned man that furnishes our lesson but that murmur of approval. Those who were about to execute the criminal shared his values. Even the writer who helped condemn him confused family sentiment with courage and good intentions. "He certainly was a brave man and did not seem a bad one, but if not, like poor Tray, was caught in bad company and had to pay the penalty."[36]

While the bad man had to be shot, the man who sensed shame and manifested family pride stirred pathos. The emotion was not approval for correct behavior, it was nostalgia for the familiar and the missed. Similar stirrings were aroused by what an emigrant called "quite a pleasant sight." That was the appearance of "White women & children."[37] "There are but few women traveling," another explained, so when a woman was encountered the fact could be worth mentioning.[38] "To-day I saw a sight worth the while, which was a live woman on the Plains," one man wrote.[39] To see "a lady riding on horseback," another noted, was "a novel sight away here in the mountains as we have been a long time away from home and the society of females."[40] Indeed, the sight was so "novel" that even women noted the presence of other women,[41] and by the time the journey was nearing its end, the sight could be startling. "Saw white woman [sic]," someone noted on the fourth day traveling down the Humboldt River, "they looke[d] as natural as ever no mistake." Next day he was

---

[36]Burroughs, Reminiscences, p. 49.

[37]Entry for 2 July 1849, Pritchard, *Diary*, p. 105.

[38]J. E. Brown, "Gold Seeker," p. 135. "During the emigration of forty-nine, I think the average of women was about one in five hundred" (Stephens, *Jayhawker*, p. 10). Some forty-niners seem to have encountered more women. See, e.g., entry for 7 June 1849, Steuben, Journal, p. 9.

[39]Entry for 19 May 1850, Clapp, *Journal*, p. 18.

[40]Entry for 24 June 1850, Newcomb, Journal.

[41]E.g., entry for 9 June 1852, Rose, Diary.

just as surprised. "[E]ncamped with a train from Salt Lake whare we found potatoes and milk and girls a plenty which looked as natural as life they cooking & washing."[42]

Even before crossing the Missouri men traveling alone missed women. "We had an unexpected surprise," a Wisconsinite recorded in his diary while still in Iowa. "[T]his evening, as we were all gathered around our camp fire some playing the violin and others singing two Ladies suddenly appeared in our midst after we had somewhat recovered from the surprise which their sudden appearance caused us, we invited them to take a seat, which they did and after enlivening our camp with their divine presence for about half an hour, they departed leaving it doubly gloomy by the contrast."[43]

Gloom arose from thoughts of home, youth, and mother, not because the women had been untouchable and now were gone. The emigrants were recalling what they once had had; they were not coveting what they had just perceived.

"I saw the first female I had seen since I left Fort Smith," a forty-niner wrote while traveling the southern branch of the overland trail. He was referring to the wife of a soldier stationed at Socorro and, as he had passed through Santa Fe and Albuquerque, he meant she was the first non-Mexican, non-Indian woman he had seen. "[H]ad I met her in the States in all probability I would have passed her unnoticed, or not have deemed her even passable in appearance, but seeing her here I really thought her handsome."[44]

Far out on the trail men strove to retain the manners as well as the sentiments they had been taught in more stable society. Two days beyond Fort Hall in today's Idaho, a company learned that a man traveling with his wife had broken the harness on their wagon. The company sent "a committee of horsemen" back to assist and help bring them up.[45]

No matter how far out they were or how long it had been since

---

[42]Entries for 26 & 27 June 1852, G. A. Smith, Diary.

[43]Entry for 9 May 1859, C. Tuttle, "Diary," p. 73.

[44]Entry for 7 July 1849, Fouts, Diary.

[45]Entry for 2 July 1849, Decker, Diaries, p. 111.

crossing the Missouri, many emigrants could be disturbed when looks or appearances failed to conform to taught expectations or when women stepped off their pedestals. "[W]e saw a young woman packing through with two or 3 young men," an English-born gold seeker from Wisconsin mourned. "I dont think it looks hardly well of a young woman with young men so sleeping without tent or anything."[46] Tongues wagged in an Oregon-bound company when some young people went for a walk in a canyon just before the crossing of the North Platte, and were gone beyond dinner time. "This gave such offense to the termagants of the company," a member wrote, "that they did not cease growling about it occasionally until the company separated and we left them. They thought it highly improper and indecorous that young ladies and gentlemen should go into such places together without their pas and mas attending them."[47]

The standards of propriety had not changed. What had been improper conduct at home remained improper beyond the western frontier.

Not all sinners on the overland trail were female. A Missourian thought emigrant behavior so disgraceful no woman should travel without a husband. "[A] lady unprotected would be exposed to the insults of the vulgar," he warned.[48] Catherine Margaret Haun disagreed. The wife of an Iowa lawyer destined to become a California judge and United States senator, she thought the presence of women restrained male behavior in many ways, including the fact that "more attention was paid to cleanliness and sanitation."[49] A fellow forty-niner concurred. "I have not failed to observe," he wrote, "that where women are with the wagons the men are much more trim and present a much better general appearance than those who are going it alone."[50]

After arriving in California, an emigrant who had crossed the

---

[46]Entry for 11 Aug. 1852, Chadwick, Diary.

[47]Entry for 17 June 1852, Thomson, *Crossing the Plains*, p. 50.

[48]Letter to D. M. Dulany, 26 July 1850, Dulany, Papers.

[49]Read, "Women and Children," p. 9.

[50]Entry for 23 Sept. 1849, Benson, Forty Niner, pp. 70-71.

trail during the difficult year of 1850 was to write:

> Man deprived of the society of the fairer portion of the creatures of this world becomes a different being. He is taciturn & morose in his manners & the sameness of his society render it tiresome. He is careless of his speech appearance and actions, and longs for a change. Place him again in the society designed for him and the latent principles & feelings burst forth anew. I saw this Beautifully illustrated on our journey here. We left the [Council] Bluffs in Co[mpany] with 50 men & 4 ladies, and the respect that we are accustomed to pay *to* merit and virtue in the opposite sex did not forsake us here. As long as it was practible for a long company to keep together; so long we done so. [W]hen it Became necissary [sic] for us to divide in smaller co[mpanies] then we could see the difference in our society. The last part of our journey found us with the rest in a situation that was difficult to help our fellow traveler on his way. Let a woman be the sufferer and we forgot our own wants by releaveing hers.[51]

It should be understood that emigrants were not saying women's presence changed social behavior. What women changed was the appearance of behavior. The absence of females caused men to be sloppy in dress and vulgar in speech, not callous toward fellow beings.

An all-male company of forty-niners had a member dying of cholera. His companions had met the sick man less than a month before yet nursed him "regardless of comfort and expense."[52] That same year a Virginian belonging to another all-male train drowned on Thomas Fork of Green River. He could have been buried on the spot but friends refused to leave the body a prey of animals. "There was," one explained, "no timber anywhere in the neighborhood that we could get to cover over the grave to effectively protect it from the wolves, & we determined to take him with us until we reached the river again, which was distant 7 miles, where we could obtain high ground & plenty of timber. He

---

[51]California letter of M. Coleman [to Susan R. Stedman] from Auburn, California, in Description of the Overland Trip and Life in the Gold Diggings, 27 January 1851 (ms., Western Americana Collection 96, Beinecke Library).

[52]Entry for 27 May 1849, Searls, Diary (ms.).

was accordingly dressed in his best suit & put in the sick Wagon."[53]

Whether heading for Oregon to farm or California to dig gold, overland emigrants knew they were going beyond a frontier. That does not mean they thought they were crossing a pale beyond the values of their world. Even those who went for adventure — to "make the tour for the sake of the tour" as an Ohio forty-niner explained — felt the ties of home, family, and taught behavior. To leave father and siblings, he wrote, was "too much for cool regret."[54]

A New York lawyer visiting Missouri during the spring of 1849 decided, more or less on the spur of the moment, to join the emigration. If we can believe what he tells us, his sole reason was wanderlust. "I had already more than half decided upon 'seeing the Elephant,' which is but another reason for going to California."[55] He sought a change of scenery, not a change of society. After arriving on the Pacific he would mine gold, practice law, marry, raise a family, and become chief justice of California.

That lawyer crossed the frontier of law yet remained a man of law. Though he went to see the elephant, in one sense he never left home. The question to be asked of our evidence is whether he was typical of emigrants who traveled America's nineteenth-century overland trail.

---

[53]Entry for 10 July 1849, *Geiger-Bryarly Journal*, p. 142.

[54]Decker, *Diaries*, pp. 40-41.

[55]Searls, Diary (ms.), p. 1.

Providing for the Elephant

2 | THE BURDEN OF PROPERTY

Historians of the overland trail, primarily concerned with narrating a drama or writing a travelogue, have ignored the topic of property. Emigrants setting out on the trip could not afford to do so. It cost money to go to Oregon or California. "There is one continual stream of emigrants pouring into this country," the newspaper at Iowa's frontier town reported on the first day of May, 1850. "They have many fine and valuable horses, oxen and cows without number."[1] It was estimated that persons going overland from Michigan that year took with them either in money or in the value of their outfits an average of $500. Missourians and those from Iowa were believed to have averaged $350.[2] In 1846 a promoter organizing a train for California had suggested that an outfit, "including everything," could be purchased for about $125 to $150.[3] By 1849 a St. Louis newspaper, theorizing that most costs would be shared, lowered that figure to a little over $100. The total, the newspaper thought, would be no more than $1037 for ten persons.[4]

Obviously, personal choice was a key ingredient. What was taken overland depended on taste and how individuals defined necessity and luxury. The St. Louis newspaper admitted that its estimated cost would double if the emigrant wanted a riding animal. The price of one mule was about ninety dollars.[5]

Available figures indicate that many emigrants thought a limitation of one hundred dollars too spartan. Purchasing its equip-

---

[1] *Frontier Guardian*, 1 May 1850, p. 2, col. 2.

[2] *Frontier Guardian*, 15 May 1850, p. 3, col. 3.

[3] Letter from D.G.W. Leavitt to a Gentleman in Memphis, 24 Jan. 1846, in *Overland in 1846*, p. 478.

[4] Gregg, "Missourians," p. 146.

[5] Loc. cit.

ment at Independence, a company of North Carolina forty-niners "found that each man's share is $186.66, the whole outfit costing $1120.00."[6] Those costs were probably equaled by the expenses of a Wisconsin company that spent $140.69 for each member before leaving Madison.[7] Once reaching the frontier more property undoubtedly was added to the total. Similarly there was a three-man party that left Illinois with one wagon, three yoke of oxen, and one yoke of cows. The "whole cost" of its "outfit with the exception of clothing" had been $500, or $166.66 apiece.[8] Three years later an emigrant must have felt he needed more animals than that. He paid $575.79 for nine yoke of oxen and one yoke of cows.[9]

Personal taste was one factor determining what property was taken on the overland trail, personal wealth another. While some emigrants could not, for instance, afford to purchase all the livestock they felt they "should have for such a trip,"[10] a few had a good deal of money and could obtain whatever equipment they wanted.[11] Everything they needed was for sale in the outfitting towns of Independence, St. Joseph, and Kanesville.

It is remarkable how prices fluctuated in those towns. A forty-niner found oxen "very dear" in St. Joseph during the first week in May. Mules, however, were "plenty in [the] market & low."[12] Two weeks earlier a youth of seventeen reported "Every thing is very cheap here and a surplus of all things [is] on hand." He thought most items less expensive than in St. Louis; stoves, cattle,

---

[6]J. E. Brown, "Gold Seeker," p. 134.

[7]"Inventory of Equipment," *Pictures of Gold Rush California*, ed. Milo Milton Quaife (Chicago: Lakeside Press, 1949), pp. 329-30.

[8]Hall, Diary, p. 1.

[9]Entry for 29 April 1852, A. Richardson, Diary of 1852. For the best, detailed account of purchasing an outfit see entries from 13 May to 22 May 1852, Anable, Second Journal. For an itemized list of costs, both before and on the trail, see Wayman, *Diary*, pp. 104-05. See also Smedley, *Across the Plains*, pp. 8-9; letter from Thomas C. Lewis to his wife, 29 August 1852, T. C. Lewis, Notes.

[10]Entry for 20 April 1853, Welsh, Diaries.

[11]Letter of 20 May 1849, Muscott, Letters.

[12]Entry for 7 May 1849, Steuben, Journal, p. 2.

and mules were lower on the frontier than in Wisconsin.[13] "[W]e could have fitted out cheapest here," a man wrote of Independence.[14] One reason was that many would-be emigrants were selling, some because they had brought too much with them,[15] others because they had lost their taste for adventure and were backing out of the emigration.[16] By 1850 auctioneering was a major profession at St. Joseph.[17]

More significant were the people who sold because they had exhausted their funds[18] or those who would have sold could they have afforded to accept the low prices being offered.[19] When evaluating respect for property on the overland trail, an important piece of evidence to keep in mind is that a high percentage of emigrants had few or no possessions.

A large number of prospective overland travelers got as far as the Missouri River only to be forced to leave their companies, unable to meet their share of the expenses. They either turned back, hired on with trains as teamsters, or put together "inferior" outfits. One man, for example, left St. Joseph in 1850 "with a *small poor cow* harnessed to a *homemade* cart in which he had his provisions and clothes stored away — he was jeered at by the emigrants generally."[20]

It is a wonder that they jeered. With a cow to pull the homemade cart, the man was better off than many others. The year before there had been an "old grey bearded man going on foot to California from Maine,"[21] and he was not unique. While a few of those walking could afford a pack mule to carry provisions,[22]

---

[13]Letter to family, 23 April 1849, Fairchild, *Letters*, p. 10.

[14]Letter to parents, 2 May 1849, Varner, Letters.

[15]Entry for 2 May 1849, Hixson, Diary, p. 1.

[16]Letter to family, 24 April 1849, Fairchild, *Letters*, p. 14.

[17]Entry for 24 April 1850, W. S. McBride, Diary; entry for 15 May 1850, Wolcott, Journal.

[18]Entry for 4 May 1850, Newcomb, Journal.

[19]Letter to Elias Varner, 29 April 1849, Varner, Letters.

[20]Entry for 29 April 1850, W. S. McBride, Diary.

[21]Entry for 25 May 1849, Decker, *Diaries*, p. 81.

[22]Entry for 16 June 1849, Perkins, Sketches.

others started toward the Pacific transporting everything they possessed on their backs.[23] Most striking of all were those pushing wheelbarrows.[24] One emigrant had his wheelbarrow made to order at St. Joseph where "he loaded up his outfit and went wheeling up main street and down to the ferry and they crossed him over free, as they should do."[25]

We may guess that the custom-made wheelbarrow was not very expensive. Surely it cost less than a mule or the man would have packed. Money was also a consideration motivating those selecting pushcarts over wheelbarrows. Pushcarts held more and could have been taken for that reason or because several could help push. But another factor must have been that the purchase price could be shared by concurrent owners. Surely concurrent ownership was the arrangement in 1852 when a number of push-carts traveled together, eight men to each cart, four pulling at one time, the other four walking alongside.[26]

Five men, who had one cart among them, were said to be able to haul "requisites for a journ[e]y of 200 Miles" only. "I need Scarce Say this looked like Madness," an eyewitness wrote, "they must either Starve on the road or live on the Charity of their better provided neighbours."[27]

More reckless than starting with supplies for only two hundred miles was starting with the hope of getting handouts. One man of about twenty-five years, encountered beyond Fort Bridger in today's western Wyoming, "hatless, shoeless and without a coat," was said to have "borrowed, begged or appropriated a sufficient supply of daily grub to keep him in running trim."[28] He was by no

---

[23]Entry for 29 April 1850, W. S. McBride, Diary; entry for 1 June 1850, Dowell, Journal; entry for 3 June 1850, Newcomb, Journal; Mattes, *Platte River Road*, p. 45.

[24]Entry for 29 April 1850, W. S. McBride, Diary; entry for 20 May 1850, Frink, *Journal*, p. 37; entry for 1 May 1852, Frizzell, *Journal*, p. 10; entry for 13 May 1852, Rudd, Notes; entry for 16 May 1852, Crane, Journal; entry for 26 June 1852, Turnbull, "Travels," p. 182; Mattes, *Platte River Road*, p. 45.

[25]Entry for 23 April 1852, Thorniley, Diary.

[26]Entry for 1 July 1852, Verdenal, Journal, p. 20.

[27]Entry for 12 May 1850, McQueen, Diary, p. 10.

[28]Eaton, *Overland*, p. 198. See also entry for 21 July 1849, Wilkins, *An Artist*, p. 56.

means the most "reckless' of whom we know. Consider this account recorded in the diary of an 1855 emigrant:

> A destitute man came to us yesterday morning with a little girl and a small boy — the boy 11 and the girl 8. He has no money but he intends to go to California.... He and his two children were on foot; he wished us to take him to California, but we made him five or six dollars. I handed him five of the money and told him to do the best he could as we could not take him on, but he went to some emigrants not far off, [and] got them to carry his children to Fort Carny [Kearny].[29]

It would be wrong to think such emigrants belonged to the bottom of society. The man with the two children said he had been a physician and a preacher, and so we may guess had some education. Nor would it be right to classify all solitary foot travelers as destitute. Some traveled alone hoping to move faster. An example may be the man seen in 1853 loading a horse "with everything necessary" for the trip. "He said his load did not amount to 100 pounds although he seemed to have everything requisite to the journey."[30]

Packers who rode animals while leading one or two more may have been as well off. Generally young and without families, they were in a hurry to reach the gold diggings. For them a wagon was an encumbrance, not a convenience. Yet, by doing without one they paid a price that must be taken into account when evaluating social behavior of overland emigrants.

Packers lived under conditions even more removed from the comforts of home than those who went by wagon. "The pack-mule companies are a pitiful set of slaves," an ox driver is quoted as saying. "They have to sit on their mules roasting in the sun all day. If they get down to walk or rest themselves, they must be bothered leading the animals. When they stop at night, they must unpack everything. In the mornings they have to repack every-

---

[29]Entry for 15 May 1855, Bardin, Diary.
[30]Entry for 10 June 1853, Woodworth, Diary, p. 13.

thing."[31] Unable to carry many provisions, packers were compelled to move swiftly, yet were shelterless, exposed to cold, wind, and rain. Should they get sick or suffer an accident they were placed in a precarious situation.[32]

The life of a packer was too difficult for many emigrants, even after they had been on the trail for two months or more. "We had intended leaving the big wagon last night & unloaded it," a man wrote just before reaching Boise River, "but the storm scared some of us from sleeping in the tent (me particularly) & we loaded it up again & took it along."[33]

Comfort and the conditions of comfort sought by overland emigrants are not unrelated to the main theme we are considering: property and respect for property. A pertinent question, therefore, is whether the walkers, beggars, wheelbarrowers, pushcarters, and packers manifested a legal behavior different from that of their better-provisioned fellow travelers. It is not simply that such men likely came from less prosperous, poorly educated backgrounds. Also to be considered were trail conditions which some theorists surmise would make them less respectful of the property rights of others. The extreme discomfort of their mode of travel should have made them more antisocial than those in wagons, their need to cover distances every day with no margin of supplies to allow for sickness or to rest animals should have made them more desperate, and their exposed position should have made them more ruthless about ensuring survival regardless of the consequences to others. If we find they were a distinct class, less law-abiding and more violent than those traveling with families or with a wealth of property, we may attribute that fact to their backgrounds or to the conditions of the overland trail. If, however, they were not different, the conclusion must be that the legal behavior of nineteenth-century Americans was more uniform and more habitual than has previously been supposed.

---

[31]G. R. Stewart, *Trail*, pp. 107-08.

[32]Mattes, *Platte River Road*, p. 45.

[33]Entry for 27 Aug. 1853, Murray, Journal, p. 108.

II *Quantity of Property*

Depending on his employer for provisions and shelter, a hired hand started across the overland trail with no other possessions than "one double blanket, a gun, ammunition, and some clothes."[1] He was an exception to the rule. According to Lodisa Frizzell, most emigrants, in 1852 at least, owned a share in a wagon. "There is every description of teams & waggons," she noted while waiting to be ferried across the Missouri at St. Joseph, "from a hand cart & wheel barrow, to a fine six horse carriage & buggie; but more than two thirds are oxen & waggons . . . ; & by the looks of their loads they do not intend to starve. Most of the horses, mules & cattle, are the best the states afford; they are indeed beautiful."[2]

The number of persons sharing the expense of a wagon varied. In a few cases there might be only two, though the figure could go as high as seventeen if the party was packing and the vehicle used only for baggage. As a general rule those traveling without families went four to a wagon.[3] By coincidence, also on the average, there were four yoke of oxen to each wagon or four horses or four mules.[4] Despite the fact more oxen were needed (which meant more animals had to be cared for), oxen were preferred to the extent that one forty-niner counting ninety-six teams found they were all hauled by oxen "but two."[5]

Most emigrants employed oxen instead of mules, a New Yorker explained, because "they will draw heavier drafts, travel about as fast, are cheaper and will endure hunger and fatigue as well as mules, and are more manageable, and are less liable to be stolen by Indians."[6] A Virginian who took mules learned too late.

---

[1]Murphy, Across, p. 1.

[2]Entry for 1 May 1852, Frizzell, *Journal*, p. 10.

[3]Graham, Journal, p. 20; entry for 25 April 1849, "The Diary of Dr. Jonathan Clark: Across the Plains in a 'Covered Wagon' in 1849," *The Argonaut*, 97 (1 Aug. 1925), p. 3, col. 2; entry for 8 May 1850, Bourne, Diary.

[4]Entry for 10 May 1849, J. W. Wood, Diaries; letter of 27 April 1849, Muscott, Letters, p. 1; entry for 8 May 1850, Bourne, Diary.

[5]Mattes, *Platte River Road*, p. 39.

[6]Letter of 28 April 1849, Muscott, Letters.

"I have found to my sorrow, that an ox team is the way to travel to California," he wrote after crossing much of Nevada, and before losing his wagons.[7]

Many wagons were mere farm vehicles with canvas tops, but not all. "Each waggon," a member wrote of a Wisconsin company, "was furnished with one stove and cooking utensils, boots, blankets, guns, pistols, chains, ox bows, powder, lead, and other things too numerous to mention filled out the load."[8] That was in 1849. Four years later a twenty-three year old druggist set out for California with a remarkably complete kitchen.

> The wagon and harness is new. We have a supply of ropes and picket pins, & camp stools & tin table furniture . . . a table with legs, which can be taken out when we move, so as to admit of packing. We have plenty of hard bread, bacon, flour, Sugar, beans, dried apples and peaches, coffee, yeast powder, pickles, catsup, vinegar, etc. Then we have a coffee pot, camp kettle, in which to cook beans, frying pan, iron bake-oven, or skillet, tin plates and cups, water tanks, etc.[9]

Before concluding that a table and dinner ware were supernumerary in the wilderness, consider that some emigrants brought provisions worthy of formal display. "Our supply of food," one wrote, "was bountiful and of the best grade . . . consisting in part of: Cornmeal, flour, Buckwheat flour, Ham, Bacon, Sausages, Dried Beef, Beans, Peas, Potatoes, Rice, Coffee, Tea, Sugar, Honey, Syrup, Milk, Butter, Dried Fruits, Apples (Green) Walnuts, Hickory Nuts, Hazel Nuts, etc. . . . We had fresh milk twice daily, butter fresh daily; procured simply by placing milk at morning in the churn, put it aboard the wagon, at night we had the genuine article."[10] A party of forty-niners had "first rate hams, codfish herring flour hard bread, dried apples & peaches, coffee tea chocolate rice fish venison & so you see we live fine."[11]

---

[7]Entry for 13 July 1850, Payne, Account, p. 72.

[8]Brainard, Journal, p. 1.

[9]Entry for 18 May 1853, Woodworth, Diary, p. 5.

[10]Eaton, *Overland*, p. 8.

[11]Letter from David Dewolf to Matilda Dewolf, 17 June 1849, Dewolf, Diary, p. 191.

Along with good food some companies took just about everything their members could think of. A train of forty men leaving Independence on 4 May 1849, had "full provisions for six to nine months — ample clothing for two years, Indian rubber clothing — extra equipments, such as saddles, harness, shoes for the animals, axles for wagons, and all that sort of thing, to provide against accidents; we carry scythes for cutting forage — blacksmithing apparatus complete — carpenters' do., etc."[12] A company going the southern route out of La Grange, Texas, divided its one hundred members into groups of five, and decreed what had to be brought, not what was forbidden.

> Each squad of five men will be required to have a good two-horse wagon drawn by four mules or horses, with at least two extra mules for the following outfit: 2 sheets of sheet iron 30 inches wide and 6 feet long if possible; half dozen long handled shovels; half dozen spades; 2 spike mattocks; 1 weeding hoe; 1 chopping axe; 1 hatchet; 1 handsaw; 1 drawing knife; augurs; 1 frow; 1 iron wedge; extra horse shoes and nails; shoeing tools; 500 pounds of bacon; 200 pounds of coffee; 125 pounds of flour; 100 pounds of salt; 50 pounds of rice; the means of carrying at least 10 gallons of water; medicine, clothing, etc., in all making about 1600 pounds.[13]

As has been noted, the fact that an emigrant packed did not mean he went on short rations. One mess of five packers took 375 pounds of pilot bread, 115 pounds of flour, and 200 pounds of bacon besides proportionate amounts of venison, coffee, sugar, tea, and several "other small articles."[14] The Mount Washington company of packers from New Hampshire and Massachusetts even started the journey with an ambulance.[15]

---

[12]Letter of 4 May 1849, "Copies of Letters Written by Hunt, Quincy, s and d, etc. to the *St. Louis Weekly Reveille*" (ts., Missouri Historical Society, St. Louis).

[13]*Texas Democrat*, 31 March 1849, quoted in Cox "Diary," p. 213n56. For other revealing lists of property taken see Eaton, *Overland*, p. 7; entry for 23 Aug. 1852, Graham, Journal, p. 20; William E. Koch, "The Big Circle Back to Kansas," *Kansas Magazine* (1966): 57; entry for 8 May 1852, Keen, Diary, p. 13; Ramsay, "Diary," pp. 442-43.

[14]Entry for 18 May 1849, Chamberlain, Diary.

[15]Shaw, *Across the Plains*, p. 47.

All in all, the value of property with which emigrants started overland could add up to a respectable sum. A company from South Bend took a "Black Smith Shop,"[16] while the Wolverine Rangers from Michigan "had a blacksmith's wagon containing a complete supply of the necessary tools and under each wagon were slung extra tongues, axle-trees, ox bows and other articles useful in cases of breakage."[17] Other items carried by many groups were horse feed (one company took 5,600 pounds),[18] various medicines (a man from Missouri had "1 gallon of cholera medicine"),[19] and whiskey (which some emigrants understood would purify bad water).[20]

An unexpectedly high percentage of overlanders claimed they took liquor for medicinal purposes only. James Woodworth from Mississippi was the rare exception, admitting he wanted to drink it. His wagon, he boasted, "had foresight enough to order a demijon of the best old Bourbon Whiskey, just to have in case of Sickness you know, or, in time of *great drought*, so that, when the question shall be asked: 'Have we a Bourbon among us,' we shall be able to Settle the matter beyond the possibility of controversy."[21]

Although much whiskey had to be jettisoned or cached on the overland trail, it was, on the whole, not overstocked, as were many other items taken along. Emigrants, a forty-niner recalled, "laid in an oversupply of bacon, flour, and beans, and in addition thereto, every conceivable jimcrack and useless article that the wildest fancy could devise or human ingenuity invent — goldmeters, gold washers, pins and needles, brooms and brushes, ox shoes and horse shoes, lasts and leather, glass beads and hawksbells, jumping jacks and jewsharps, rings and bracelets, pocket mirrors and pocket-books, calico vests and *boiled shirts*. A full inventory would occupy pages and furnish an assortment for a variety store."[22]

[16]Entry for 1 May 1849, Lindsey, Journal.

[17]Goldsmith, *Overland*, p. 42.

[18]Eaton, *Overland*, p. 6.

[19]Hudgins, California in 1849, p. 1.

[20]Mattes, *Platte River Road*, p. 50.

[21]Entry for 18 May 1853, Woodworth, Diary, pp. 5-6.

[22]A. J. McCall, quoted in Potter, "Introduction," p. 49.

The variety of property taken on the overland trail is important. It reveals more than that the emigrants were not frontiersmen prepared to live off the wilderness, that they could afford possessions, or were reluctant to go without their customary creature comforts. As important to our tale is the remarkable fact that a large percentage started with more property than could possibly be carried to the Pacific. For them, property would become a burden.

"Many of the wagons," a forty-niner wrote, "look much as though they put in all they could think of, and hung every thing else on the out side."[23] They were, quite frankly, overloaded. Wagons started out with weights of 2500 or 2800 pounds, and one party of three brothers and a cousin left their Missouri home with 6000 pounds of provisions.[24] "[A] great evil among many before leaving home," another forty niner noted, "was to make things too convenient. Convenience should be left at home & the burden of the teams, alone consulted."[25]

The problem was weight. A knowledgeable historian of the overland trail has called 300 pounds per man "an unrealistic cargo" when eight men shared a wagon and the total was 2500 pounds.[26] A Boston company in 1849 took 300 pounds per person,[27] some New Yorkers carried 500 pounds.[28] Emigrants knew that "every pound of baggage had to be hauled thousands of miles through mud holes and heavy sand, across rivers and up steep declivites," yet they overloaded.[29]

Perhaps many were misled by guide books recommending that overland travelers take more provisions than would be needed.[30]

---

[23]Letter of 2 June 1849, Lord, Journal.

[24]Entry for 14 April 1850, Millington, Journal; entry for 8 May 1849, Farnham, Gold Rush, p. 1; Hudgins, California in 1849, p. 1. For an inventory, detailing weights and sizes, of articles taken to Oregon, see entry for 5 May 1853, Longworth, Diary, pp. 14-15.

[25]Entry for 27 May, 1849, J. W. Wood, Diaries.

[26]Mattes, *Platte River Road*, p. 52.

[27]Hannon, "Introduction and Notes," p. 62.

[28]Letter of 27 April 1849, Muscott, Letters.

[29]Potter, "Introduction," p. 25.

[30]Ibid., p. 30; Child, *Overland Route*, pp. vi-viii.

A St. Joseph newspaper of 1846 printed a letter advising that wagons be strong enough to hold from 2000 to 2500 pounds,[31] while the committee on outfits for an Iowa company of forty-niners would have placed a limit of four men to each wagon with the wagons hauling up to 2500 pounds.[32] Only one man, an emigrant from Ohio, seems to have made enquiries when on the frontier. He was told by veterans of plains travel that the safe weight to carry was "about 1800 [pounds] to six mules, in [a] not very heavy wagon."[33]

As a class forty-niners generally misjudged weight. They knew the danger of taking too much; that the definition of "necessities" depended on the realities of overland travel. "Our load will be too heavy I fear," one wrote on leaving St. Joseph, "if so we pack."[34] He at least was prepared for the worst. Others thought that if they made plans, apparently any plans, they would avoid trouble. "In laying in our provisions," a young man wrote, "we determined to lay in nothing but the real substantials of life."[35] He may have succeeded, but his "substantials" were far more than needed —600 pounds of flour for four men when 500 pounds was said to be sufficient for six persons.[36]

After crossing the Missouri it did not take emigrants long to define "necessity" from a new perspective. "We felt when leaving home," a woman almost three months out on the trail wrote, "that nothing was being taken but the merest necessities, yet we find that in our anxiety about the cattle giving out we take a different view of what we may give up without anything more than inconvenience to ourselves."[37]

---

[31]Letter from William J. Martin to St. Joseph *Gazette*, 5 January 1846, in *Overland in 1846*, p. 476.

[32]Lorch, "Gold Rush," p. 331.

[33]Entry for 22 May 1849, Perkins, Sketches.

[34]Entry for 22 May 1849, Lotts, Copy, p. 1.

[35]Entry for 27 April 1849, H. M. Price, Diary, p. 3.

[36]Keller, *Trip*, p. 48.

[37]Entry for 1 Aug. 1857, Carpenter, Trip, p. 65.

III *Destruction of Property*

It should not be surprising that overland emigrants misjudged both their needs and the weight that animals could haul. As a Rhode Islander pointed out, "what idea could a lot of merchants, counter jumpers, jewelers, doctors and lawyers have of mules and loads."[1]

If overindulgence does not surprise us, perhaps the degree to which emigrants indulged themselves will. Our best evidence is the amount of material goods they threw away. "The waste of property on this road is immense," a physician wrote as he passed abandoned wagons in the vicinity of Bear River.[2] "There is the most awful destruction of property by the emigrants that could be thought of," another man had written his wife exactly a week before. "The road is literally strewed with clothes, harness and things of every description."[3]

To a New Yorker the trail in 1849 "looked more like the route of a vanquished army flying before a host of Goths and Vandals, than the road of citizens engaged in the peaceful pursuits of civilized life."[4] The same analogy occurred to a midwesterner. "By following our track," he explained, "one would suppose, that a large army had been flying in hot haste, only careing to save their own lives."[5] A forty-niner who took the less traveled southern route across the Arizona desert thought "there has been enough thrown away on this trip to make A man Rich."[6] By comparison, a forty-niner who went by the crowded northern road saw "more property destroyed in the last seven months than would make half the people in Hempstead independent for life."[7]

---

[1]Thurber, Journal, p. 21.

[2]Entry for 20 June 1850, Parker, Notes.

[3]Letter from George Davidson to Mary Davidson, 13 June 1850, J. N. Davidson, Papers (ms., State Historical Society of Wisconsin, Madison).

[4]Letter from John Muscott to Ebenezer Robbins, 14 Oct. 1849, Muscott, Letters.

[5]Letter from Henry Page to Mary Page, 3 April 1850, Page, *Wagons*, p. 257.

[6]Entry for 18 Sept. 1849, Beeching, Journal.

[7]Letter of 20 Nov. 1849, Hentz, Correspondence.

To discover that so much worth could be worthless staggered many. "If I had" was a common thought. "If I had in gold the worth of all the property that will be lost getting to California, there would be no need of going farther," a forty-niner informed an Ohio newspaper from today's western Nebraska. "If I had in Ohio all the property thrown away & destroyed I could buy the best farm I know of at half the value of the property," another emigrant wrote in his journal three years later, shortly after crossing the continental divide. "If I had what has been wasted on the road I would not need to go to the California gold mines," a third man said after completing the overland journey.[8]

"The motto," an emigrant thought, "seems to be, to throw away, lighten up, and go ahead, and the D[evil] take the hindmost."[9] He might have added that the lightening process could start before the trip began. A party of eight forty-niners arrived in Independence with nineteen mules, three wagons, and "well loaded with provisions, clothing, firearms and ammunition." Concluding they had more weight than was "safe to tax our mules with," they disposed of two hundred pounds while still east of the river.[10]

To know the problem was not to know the answer. Criticizing others for traveling with loads of 2000 pounds, one man hoped his wagon with only 1500 pounds would make it through. Within less than three weeks his party discarded "everything that could possibly be dispensed with."[11] Most forty-niners sharing a wagon left the frontier with "too heavy a load" and "before travelling 50 miles" were throwing away "quantities" of property.[12]

---

[8]Letter from Daniel Powell, *Western Reserve Chronicle* (Warren, Ohio), 22 Aug. 1849, p. 1., col. 6; entry for 21 June 1852, Humphrey, Journal; letter of about 10 Oct. 1849, Senter, *Crossing*. Similarly, see entry for 1 June 1849, "Diary of Lorenzo Dow Young," *Utah Historical Quarterly*, 14 (1946): 169-70; entry for 10 July 1849, Clifton, Diary, p. 8; Mattes, *Platte River Road*, p. 51.

[9]Entry for 19 June 1850, Cagwin, Diary.

[10]Entries for 1 and 2 May 1849, Hixson, Diary.

[11]Entries for 27 May and 4 June 1849, Dr. T., Journal.

[12]Entry for 22 May 1849, Perkins, Sketches.

Even before reaching the Platte River, forty-niners were camping near 1000 pounds "of good bacon,"[13] or seeing "hundreds of pounds of the best, superfine flour, hard bread, beans, boxes, trunks, wagons, and portions of wagons, lie strewed by the road-side."[14]

The trouble was not that emigrants could afford only poor equipment. One man, who saw "some 40 or 50 wagons broken down & deserted" within fifty miles of the frontier, reported that they were "splendid & expensive ones but being entirely over-loaded could not stand the terrible roads."[15]

While some travelers began throwing things away as early as the second day out — "a considerable amount of clothing, a fair sized library, two bushels of beans, two pigs of lead, half a keg of nails, implements of husbandry   (a plow among the number), and a lot of mechanical tools"[16] — others tried various expedients to keep what they possessed and yet continue on. One party, for example, put all twelve of its mules to haul the wagon. "Consequently we were compelled to walk most of our time."[17]

By the time they reached Fort Kearny, some emigrants had begun to panic. "We felt that we must pass all the ox teams & some mule teams to ensure a safe passage through the country where grass & water is scarce," one man wrote, explaining why his party left seven hundred pounds of goods at the fort.[18] "We have thrown away 500 pounds of bread and bacon and large quantities of flour and beans," a forty-niner noted. "We are cooking our dinner with fuel which was a brand new wagon when we left Boston. There is more clothing on the ground at Fort Kearney

[13]Entry for 8 May 1849, McLeod, Diary, p. 30.

[14]Letter of 20 May 1849, Muscott, Letters.

[15]Entry for 22 May 1849, Perkins, Sketches.

[16]Entry for 29 April 1849, W. G. Johnston, *Overland*, p. 31.

[17]Entry for 20 May 1849, Athearn, "Log Book," p. 7. Also for discarded property before the Platte was reached, see entry for 11 May 1849, Stitzel, Diary, p. 65; entry for 21 May 1849, Gray, *Off at Sunrise*, p. 17; entry for 27 May 1849, Farnham, "From Ohio," p. 304; entry for 27 May 1850, Loomis, *Journal*, p. 25.

[18]Entry for 23 May 1849, J. A. Johnson, Note Book.

than would fill the largest store in Boston."[19]

All along the interminable Platte destruction and abandonment continued. "We had passed tons of provisions piled up on the roadside the past few days, mostly bacon," a forty-niner wrote the day after leaving Fort Kearny.[20] "This was a day of scenes of abandoned property," another wrote four days from the fort, "stoves, blacksmith tools, wagons, cooking utensils, provisions of every kind."[21] By the time they reached Ash Hollow many, realizing there was no Indian danger, began tossing away their guns.[22] Yet the prehensile trait remained dominant, and property — even useless property — was relinquished reluctantly. One company hauled a sawmill about 500 miles before throwing it out.[23]

The purpose of lightening was partly to spare the wagons but primarily to save the animals. As early as the last week in May, 1849, the skeletons of oxen, horses, and mules averaged "more than one to the mile."[24] "Seen more dead oxen by five times over than I had ever seen live ones before I left home," a forty-niner estimated.[25] Another figured that between Fort Laramie and Salt Lake two thousand head of cattle died that year. "Sometimes there would be a dozen at one camp ground."[26] A third "passed fifty five head of stock, dead & dying" in just one day.[27] Surprisingly, things did not improve over the years. "It is astonishing," an 1858 emigrant wrote, "what a number of these animals have fallen under the yoke this season, the road is literally lined with

[19]Letter quoted in Howe, *Argonauts*, p. 42. For other accounts of surplus property at Fort Kearny, see entry for 28 May 1849, Doyle, Journal; entry for 29 May 1849, Gibbs, "Diary," p. 301; entry for 31 May 1849, Parke, Notes.

[20]Entry for 22 May 1849, Hixson, Diary.

[21]Entry for 1 June 1849, Benson, Forty Niner, p. 12. See also entries for 20 and 22 July 1849, Bruff, *Journals*, pp. 48, 51; Mattes, *Platte River Road*, p. 50; Eaton, *Overland*, p. 157.

[22]Keller, *Trip*, p. 11; Mattes, *Platte River Road*, p. 304.

[23]Letter from C. N. Ormsby to his wife, 30 June 1849, Bidlach, *Letters*, p. 22. See also entry for 3 June 1849, I. Hale, "Diary," p. 71; entry for 18 June 1852, Bailey, Trip, p. 9.

[24]Entry for 28 May 1849, Batchelder, Journal, p. 11.

[25]Letter of 20 Nov. 1849, Hentz, Correspondence.

[26]Letter of about 10 Oct. 1849, Senter, *Crossing*.

[27]Letter from Henry Page to Mary Page, 3 April 1850, Page, *Wagons*, p. 257.

them . . the traveler could find his way with no other compass or guide than his nose alone."[28]

Fort Laramie, first a fur post and later a military station, was the "place of general renovating amongst travellers."[29] Knowing they were about to enter the mountains, emigrants were psychologically more receptive to the need of lightening.[30] Many had carried surplus supplies this far in the hope trappers would be buying.[31] But with so much available there was no market except for horses and whiskey.[32]

Long before the emigration of '49 had hit its crest Fort Laramie's grounds were covered with every conceivable type of property,[33] striking one man "more like a place of dessolation than like a place for protection."[34] Here dozens of wagons were simply left standing,[35] while their owners took to packing.[36] Of those who retained their vehicles, a high percentage cut them down into two-wheel carts[37] or (by sawing off a couple of feet in the rear)

[28]Mattes, *Platte River Road*, p. 41.

[29]Entry for 3 June 1849, Dr. T., Journal.

[30]Letter to uncle, 28 June 1849, S. Bradford, Letters.

[31]Entry for 14 June 1849, Spooner, Diary; entry for 14 June 1849, J. W. Wood, Diaries.

[32]Entry for 14 June 1849, McLeod, Note Books; entry for 10 June 1849, Buffum, Diary; entry for 30 May 1849, Berrien, "Diary," p. 310. Even those in the vanguard could sell only at very low prices, e.g., a wagon for $20. See entry for 28 May 1849, Breyfogle, Diary (ms.).

[33]Entry for 30 May 1849, Cosad, Journal; entry for 7 June 1849, Love, Diary; entry for 11 June 1849, Buffum, Diary; entry for 11 June 1849, Gray, *Off at Sunrise*, p. 34; entry for 15 June 1840, I. Hale, "Diary," p. 80; entry for 16 June 1849, Banks, "Diary," pp. 20-21; entry for 27 June 1849, Lord, Journal; entry for 28 June 1849, Castleman, Diary; entry for 1 July 1849, Perkins, *Gold Rush Diary*, p. 49; entry for 8 July 1849, Batchelder, Journal, p. 43; entry for 11 July 1849, Webster, *Gold Seekers*, p. 58; J. E. Brown, *Memoirs*, p. 13.

[34]Entry for 4 June 1849, Pritchard, *Diary*, p. 81.

[35]Entry for 30 May 1849, Cosad, Journal; entry for 7 June 1849, Robinson, *Journey*, p. 11; entry for 11 June 1849, J. A. Johnson, Note Book; entry for 12 June 1849, "From Waupun to Sacramento in 1849: The Gold Rush Journal of Edwin Hillyer," *Wisconsin Magazine of History*, 49 (1966): 233; entry for 6 July 1849, Staples, "Diary," pp. 125-26; entry for 28 May 1850, Thomasson, Diary.

[36]Entry for 29 May 1850, C. W. Smith, Journal; entry for 31 May 1850, Christy, *Road*; entry for 31 May 1850, W. S. McBride, Diary.

[37]Entry of 29 June 1842, Crawford, "Journal," p. 11; Lavender, *Westward*, p. 355; G. R. Stewart, *Trail*, p. 98.

Law for the Elephant

into lighter wagons.[38]

Leaving Fort Laramie, a forty-niner saw "from one thousand to two thousand pounds of bacon scattered along the road," and, if that were not enough, in the afternoon saw "two to three thousand pounds of flour and bacon thrown away, and perhaps did not see one half that was on the road."[39] We may wonder if anyone did.

Indiscriminate jettisoning continued up to the crossing of the North Platte and along the Sweetwater. Some would discard one day, only to have to discard more seven days later. Still they lost cattle and, of course, became "discourage[d]."[40]

Driving across Wyoming's Black Hills, a forty-niner noted in his journal that "thousands of Dollars worth of every thing that constitutes an emigrants out fit has been thrown away upon these Hills. Flour & Bacon by the 1000 lbs   all sorts of tools, clothing Dozens of Trucks, hundreds of wagons were here left, the owners packing."[41] Later the same emigrant wrote to his father that "the road from Fort Laramie to the South Pass was literally strewed with provisions of all sorts." Most telling is the fact that the young man could not escape thinking in the values of home. "Thousands upon thousands of dollars wasted," he lamented.[42]

There was no western terminus to the trail of jetsam. Reaching the Big Sandy in 1849, some emigrants discarded goods they still thought of in terms of monetary value when the only valid mea-

---

[38]Entry of 1 June 1849, J. A. Johnson, Note Book; entry for 4 June 1849, Dr. T., Journal; entry for 17 June 1849, Tolles, Diary, p. 30; entry for 30 June 1849, Hoover, Revised Journal; entry for 16 May 1850, Stimson, Overland, p. 37; entry for 23 May 1850, Lewelling, Excerpts, p. 7; entry for 5 June 1859, Casler, *Journal*, p. 14.

[39]Entry for 19 June 1849, Benson, Forty Niner, p. 22.

[40]Entries for 27 June and 4 July 1849, Hackney, "Journal," pp. 153, 160.

[41]Entry for 25 June 1849, Doyle, Journal. For similar comments see entry for 5 July 1849, Violette, Day Book, p. 10; entry for 18 July 1849, Dewolf, Diary, p. 24.

[42]Letter from Simon Doyle to Edward Doyle, 19 July 1849, Doyle, Journal. For other descriptions of destruction or abandonment of property on this stretch of the trail see entry for 19 June 1849, Farnham, Gold Rush, p. 11; entry for 1 July 1849, Parke, Notes; entry for 14 July 1849, Cross, "Journal," p. 137; entry for 16 July 1849, Gould, "Diary," p. 137; entry for 5 June 1850, Parker, Notes; entry for 27 June 1850, Langworthy, *Scenery*, p. 60; entry for 30 June 1850, Stauder, Memorandum, p. 22; Eaton, *Overland*, pp. 156-57.

sure was weight.[43] Ahead at the Green River that same day, "hundreds are leaving wagons, throwing away all but what they can pack."[44] Farther west the horrors both of the Gila River route along the southern trail and the Humboldt River road in the north forced many emigrants to reassess previously-made decisions about what was necessary for life and what merely convenient.[45] Even after arriving in California emigrants could be overburdened. Reaching the summit of the Sierras, three forty-niners, whose wagon had previously "been turned into a cart," found even that vehicle too heavy. It was necessary, they concluded, to "make pack saddles of the remnant and pack the remainder of the way."[46]

The historical fact of waste and destruction has often been noted by historians of the overland trail. What they have generally overlooked is the burden property imposed on emigrants. Of course much thrown away was what could, under the circumstances, be called "useless" — large feather beds, diving bells, forges, and anvils.[47] It was easy, too, for some to discard excess food by telling themselves that beans "disagree with the bowels, and are heavy freight."[48] But the overriding fact is that much was useful, like tents and warm clothing, and might even become vital, such as water kegs. Yet the useful and the vital, just as much as the excessive and the superfluous, could become a burden and have to be abandoned.[49]

The disharmony introduced into overland life by quarrels over whether concurrently owned property should be discarded, is a

---

[43]Entry for 13 July 1849, Howell, Crossing the Plains.

[44]Entry for 13 July 1849, Banks, "Diary," p. 40.

[45]Gila River road: entries for 28 Nov. and 2 Dec. 1849, Eccleston, *Overland*, pp. 215, 220; entry for 30 December 1849, Hayes, Diary, p. 141; entry for 9 April 1852, "Diary of John Cleminson" (ts., California State Library), p. 25. Humboldt River road: J. A. Johnson, Note Book, 19 - 30 July 1849.

[46]Entry for 31 July 1849, Hixson, Diary.

[47]Entry for 12 June 1849, Batchelder, Journal; entry for 17 July 1849, Bruff, *Journals*, pp. 46-47.

[48]Entry for 20 July 1849, Bruff, *Journals*, pp. 48-49.

[49]Keller, *Trip*, p. 27; entry for 23 July 1849, Bruff, *Journals*, p. 52.

topic to be developed in the following chapters. It is enough here to note that even when there was agreement among concurrent owners, they often lacked the experience on which to base sound judgment. At Fort Laramie a party of forty-niners decided to "lighten some of our waggons by cutting down the beds and throwing away some of our tools as we had quite a number of unnecessary ones." They had left the frontier thinking all their tools were necessary; now they knew better. From what is said, it appears that they intended to abandon all "unnecessary" tools. If so, their definition of "necessary" soon changed. Fourteen days later they lightened again. Among jetsam dropped on this occasion were an anvil, "a part of blacksmith tools   two guns   one hundred pounds of lead   2 Keggs of powder   several hatchets   [and] an ax or two."[50]

The burden imposed by property touched the overland emigrants in many ways. If possession of certain items allowed them to carry some of home's comforts into the wilderness, the need to abandon weight could remind them that they really were not home. A German lost in Death Valley, spent 25 December 1849 lightening his load and discarding his "best things." Despite the peril, the man did not miss the irony. "There is," he confided to his journal, "quite a difference between Christmas days in different states. In some of them you receive presents, in others you must throw things away. I hope my dear wife is having a happier Christmas day than I am."[51]

---

[50]Entries for 27 June and 11 July 1849, Castleman, Diary.
[51]Entry for 25 Dec. 1849, Nusbaumer, *Journal*, p. 44.

Fort Laramie

3 | PROPERTY AND SURVIVAL

We are interested in property for the role it played in the legal behavior of overland emigrants, and we are interested in that legal behavior for what it may tell us about the law-mindedness of nineteenth-century Americans. There are degrees and measures of law-mindedness. If we find overland emigrants respected rights of ownership to property physically possessed, we have one measure. If we find they respected not only possession but abstract rights to property, we should be even more impressed. Another consideration is the nature of property. A fact that must not be overlooked is that property on the overland trail was fluid and transitory, requiring constant repair, husbanding, and protection.

Overland property, whether draft animals, carriages, or provisions, served two primary purposes: to ensure survival and to provide a minimum degree of comfort. Men, especially young men, could pack food, clothes, and blankets on mules and ride across the continent, but to have a wagon made the trip more comfortable. For those with families, for women and children, a wagon was almost a necessity. Conversely, a wagon — or any property for that matter — meant that the journey was also more difficult, for heavy objects had to be lifted out when streams were crossed, or dried following a heavy rain, and every item needed care, repair, and, if lost, replacement.

We have seen that emigrants generally overestimated the amount of property needed on the trip and that weight created problems. It would be well to translate those problems into human terms by considering the situation of one forty-niner. He is Elisha Douglass Perkins, the Ohioan previously mentioned as the only known emigrant taking the trouble of asking what weight frontiersmen thought safe for the overland journey. Waiting at Weston on the Missouri River, Perkins read in a guidebook "that a six mule team might start with 5000 lbs beside the wagons! as the roads were good! & the load constantly decreasing." He could not believe the figure realistic and, after talking to veterans of the Santa Fe trail, decided guidebooks were "humbugs." As we have previously noted, he learned that the highest safe weight to carry was "about 1800 to six mules, in [a] not very heavy wagon."[1]

Perkins and his five companions realized that they had to plan more carefully. They had arrived at Weston with 3000 pounds in one wagon and only six mules to draw it. Besides purchasing another pair of mules and two saddle ponies, they lightened the load to what Perkins termed "the standard," by which we may surmise he meant 1800 pounds. "We find," he explained, "we have twice as much of everything as we can carry & shall sell nearly half our provisions & send most of our clothing home or round the Cape to meet us at San F[rancisco]." Now, they hoped, they would be able to "travel fast."[2]

If these six Ohioans were wiser than most forty-niners who set out on the trail overloaded, they still faced the most striking dilemma of overland travel: property was needed for survival but too much property could mean disaster. No emigrant better expressed the problem than did Elisha Perkins himself, when, a few days before reaching the Platte, he contemplated the risks during a long trip in which way stations for replenishing supplies were few and far between. Stating a desire to "go thro in from 80 to 90 days," Perkins wrote:

> I hope we may but confess I have my misgivings at times about our success in crossing this year at all. & the reflection that we may from want of feed for our animals or cold weather in the Sierra Nevada be compelled to turn part way back again, gives me no very pleasant sensations. If the thousands who have gone should find themselves in the mountains without provender or caught in a snow storm what should become of them & us? We should not find

---

[1] Entry for 22 May 1849, Perkins, Sketches.
[2] Ibid., entries for 22, 23 and 24 May, 1849.

sustinance sufficient for all at any of the stations on the road or at the Mormon settlements. & our stock of provisions could not last us back to the U.S. & I dont see how great loss of life could be avoided.[3]

The physical hardships that endangered survival on the overland trail were apprehended by Perkins and his companions. With careful planning, they believed trouble could be avoided. They had sought the advice of veterans of the Santa Fe trail, asking what weight with how many animals was safe, and then discarded almost one half of their property. Then they purchased extra mules and did so before even crossing the Missouri.

Unlike many others on the trail, Perkins's party did not quarrel. The men seem to have agreed on what had to be done and traveled with a reasonable degree of harmony, yet they did not continue as a company after Fort Laramie. The wagon was so heavy they feared it might not get beyond the Laramie mountains. They decided that it would be easier to discard expendable items if the six men parceled the common stock equally among themselves.[4] Then, free of the competing interests of concurrent ownership, each could consider only private needs.

The first plan had been to "divide our stock into companies of two & each take care of itself." To understand why this scheme was abandoned is to understand the burden imposed on many emigrants by concurrent property. Much of the evidence on this point to be developed in subsequent chapters can be summarized by considering how Perkins and his companions expected private ownership to benefit them. There would, they anticipated, be "much less work & trouble to cook for ourselves only & take care of our own goods than to do the same for the company, besides being more expeditious." Put in stark terms, Perkins's party owned concurrently too much property to continue together as a unit and hope to survive.[5]

---

[3]Ibid., entry for 8 June 1849.
[4]Ibid., entry for 1 July 1849. The "Black Hills" are today's Laramie Mountains.
[5]Ibid.

II *The Physical Problem*

The difficulties faced by John Smith, who traveled to Oregon by covered wagon in 1853, reveal a similar story, but from a different perspective. As we later must give attention to the burden of concurrent property, it would now be worth our while to consider Smith's problems in detail by following him across the continent. Like the story of Elisha Perkins, his experiences tell us much of the role played by property in the saga of the westward movement. Unlike Perkins, however, John Smith was burdened by private, not by concurrent property.

John Smith left his home in Pittsburgh, Carroll County, Indiana, on the first day of March "with 3 wagons & one carriage   7 yoke of oxen   13 Cows   one Bull & 4 Mares." He had four companions, at least two of whom were hired hands and, while passing through Iowa, picked up a nephew. That meant six persons were fed from Smith's supplies and had their personal effects hauled in his wagons until 1 August. On that date, somewhere in today's western Wyoming, one man deserted to enter the employ of another emigrant.

Also before crossing the Missouri River, John Smith bought a yoke of four-year-old oxen. That purchase gave him a total of sixteen oxen to pull three wagons. The mares drew the carriage.[1]

Even prior to leaving Council Bluffs, Smith encountered the burden of property; he learned that some types of property had to be treated differently while on the move than when at home. An item of value back in Indiana could be a hindrance in the wilderness and might have to be destroyed.

Passing through Iowa, just three days before being ferried over the Missouri, Smith stopped "on account of one of our Cows which had a Calf." It was "the fourth Calf since we started" and posed Smith's first serious property problem: it had to be cared for and could travel only slowly. "[T]he first three," he noted in his journal, "I gave away." That solution was now impossible. "[T]his one I had to knock on the head as we are traveling through

---

[1] Entries for 1 March and 4, 7 April 1853, J. Smith, Account.

an unsettled Part of the Country." Next day the event reoccurred. "[A]nother Cow had a Calf to day," he recorded. "Served it as the last one   Rather a Barberous way of using Calves but cant be helped."[2]

As he traveled westward, John Smith was to have other experiences demonstrating that property coveted east of the Missouri River could be "trouble" while on the overland trail. That was the word he used three months later when yet another calf was born at Ham's Fork of Green River. By using it, Smith was acknowledging that on the overland trail, circumstances, convenience, and necessity altered individual notions about values.[3]

Surplus or unwanted items such as weak, slow-traveling calves did not pose a major problem for property owners on the trail. As was demonstrated every day and practically every mile, whatever was not needed could be jettisoned and left to rot on the plains. The challenge was to preserve or replace implements vital for the trip.

In 1853, the year Smith made the journey, draft animals were a key source of worry. Grass had begun to appear late in the season and when it came, one man noted, it was "barely sufficient for our animals to get a subsistence." He even thought that "the farther we advance the poorer the grass gets," and some discouraged emigrants were said to have turned around and gone back east for no other reason that that grass was so poor.[4]

A second difficulty, afflicting an unusual number of cattle during the first hundred or so miles of the march that year, was lameness. With little moisture it is possible the ground was hard, damaging the animals' legs more than most years.[5]

During the early stages of the trip, John Smith does not seem to

---

[2]Ibid., entries for 28-29 April 1853. Similarly, entries for 4 and 24 May 1853, Murray, Journal, pp. 20, 41.

[3]Entry for 25 July 1853, J. Smith, Account.

[4]Entries for 8 and 13 May 1853, McClure, Journey, pp. 2-3, 5.

[5]Letter of 17 July 1853, E: N. and J. W. Taylor, Letters. Four days before reaching Ash Hollow an emigrant wrote: "Cattle getting Lame Principal Disease was the Foot Evil" (entry for 7 June 1853, G. N. Taylor, Diary, p. 10).

have been troubled by grass shortages or cattle lameness. The reason may be that he came via Council Bluffs, an easier route to the Platte River than through Kansas.[6] Smith's first indication of danger was the "Very bad Alkali ponds of which if Cattle would drink much it would kill them."[7] He wrote these words while at Independence Rock, on the Sweetwater River in central Wyoming, and, had he known it, might have counted himself fortunate. Emigrants could be troubled by alkaline water as early as the crossing of the South Platte in western Nebraska, and during some years dead animals were seen along the road for more than a hundred miles prior to arriving at Fort Laramie.[8]

Conditions varied from emigration to emigration. A physician crossing the year before Smith noted peril even along the Platte. "The water of Plat[te] R. is very muddy but the best tha[t] can be got," he explained; "as the water in the slews is badly impregnated with alkali."[9] A drover traveling about two or three weeks behind Smith encountered the problem near the confluence of the North and South Plattes. "A great deal of alkali water in pools injurious to sheep, lost 3 head on account of drinking it."[10]

After crossing the South Platte more emigrants began to notice the alkali and its effects. In 1859 a man estimated there were 2000 dead oxen between the South Platte and Fort Laramie, although we cannot be certain all died that season.[11] Noting that "the greatest quantity of bones I have seen anywhere is on the South

---

[6]Though grass was scarce and feed so expensive, "many persons not able to buy were letting their animals run out & starve" (entry for 27 April 1853, Murray, Journal. p. 15). Others were forced to start early, without waiting for friends (entry for 10 May 1853, Pengra, Diary, pp. 15-16).

[7]Entry for 5 July 1853, J. Smith, Account.

[8]Entries for 27 June and 4 July 1859, J. E. Brown, Journal, pp. 24, 27. For difficulties during 1853 see entry for 15 June 1850, Starr, Tour of West.

[9]Entry for 8 June 1852, Dalton, Diary, p. 11.

[10]Entry for 1 July 1853, Thomas Flint, "Diary" (ts., "Fort Laramie Journals," Fort Laramie Historic Site, Fort Laramie, Wyoming), p. 5. Similarly, entry for 8 June 1853, Murray, Journal, p. 52.

[11]Entry for 6 July 1859, J. B. Brown, *Journal of a Journey*, p. 29.

Platt[e]," a traveler four years later referred to the dead animals as the " 'Fallen heroes' of '49."[12]

By the time the emigration passed Ash Hollow alkali was found "every day."[13] At Scotts Bluff one man wrote of "the strongest bed of alkali I have seen yet" and two days later "passed 57 head of dead cattle."[14] Between Scotts Bluff and Fort Laramie both "[t]he water and grass was strongly empregnated [sic] with alkalia."[15] It was so bad, in fact, one forty-niner believed that "to travel cattle through this [region] when wet will cause their hoofs to come off."[16]

Once beyond the North Platte, the situation became critical. During the drive to the Sweetwater, a trip taking two or more days, only a few running streams provided potable water, and occasionally even that was barely drinkable.[17] "Look at this — look at this!," a notice at the Mormon ferry warned in 1849, "The water here is poison, and we have lost six of our cattle. Do not let your cattle drink on this bottom."[18]

The ponds, puddles, and sloughs "were coated with a thick alkali resembling carbonate of soda or saleratus."[19] One forty-niner, whom the terrain reminded of ice, thought the saleratus "a very superior article."[20] Another noted that "a deposit of tolerably pure carb[onate]. potash can be picked up on the banks" of any stream.[21] The water had "a strong taste of alkali,"[22] but even

---

[12]Entry for 30 Aug. 1863, Yager, "Diary," Part 5, p. 28.

[13]Entry for 30 May 1850, Ingalls, *Journal*, p. 22.

[14]Entries for 14 and 16 June 1859, Chillson, Diary.

[15]Entry for 23 June 1849, Clifton, Diary.

[16]Entry for 10 June 1849, Farnham, Gold Rush, p. 7.

[17]Entry for 2 July 1852, Rudd, Notes; Yager, "Diary," Part 2, p. 37n45; Child, *Overland Route*, p. 24; Eaton, *Overland*, pp. 155-56; entry for 8 May 1850, C. W. Smith, Journal; letter of 9 July 1847, Ingersoll, *Overland in 1847*, p. 27.

[18]Entry for 18 June 1849, Delano, *Life*, p. 86.

[19]Entry for 20 June 1849, H. M. Price, Diary, p. 7.

[20]Entry for 3 July 1849, Andrew Lopp Murphy, "Diary" (ts., 2723, State Historical Society of Missouri, Columbia), p. 20.

[21]Entry for 16 July 1849, Perkins, *Gold Rush Diary*, p. 65.

[22]Entry for 8 July 1849, *The Diary of a Pioneer, and Other Papers, Being the Diary Kept*

Boiling Springs. *"the fallen heroes of '49"*

though humans did not have "much inducement to drink as both the smell & taste is very disagreeable,"[23] "the stock are very fond of it,"[24] "requiring the greatest Vigilence on our part to save our stock."[25]

Apparently their "Vigilence" was not very great. The road from the North Platte to the Sweetwater, an emigrant wrote, was "strewn with dead carcasses."[26] A forty-niner counted thirty-four

---

by *Niles Searls on His Journey from Independence, Missouri, to California* (San Francisco: Pernan-Walsh Printing Co., 1940), p. 45.

[23]Entry for 23 June 1849, *Geiger-Bryarly Journal*, p. 113.

[24]Entry for 28 June 1849, Spooner, Diary.

[25]Tate, Letter. Some of Smith's fellow 1853 travelers had similar problems. "Had a great deal of trouble to keep the stock from drinking the poison or alkali water. It is almost sure to kill man or beast who drink it" (entry for 14 June 1853, Knight, "Diary," p. 44).

[26]Tate, Letter. For dead cattle in this area in 1853 see entry for 15 June 1853, Luark, Later Diary, p. 19; entry for 26 June 1853, Handsaker, Journal, p. 13.

dead oxen in one day and twenty-five the next, a second counted thirty-seven, a third between thirty and forty, and a fourth claimed to have seen one hundred fifty in a stretch of fifty miles.[27]

The next year, 1850, one of the earliest travelers "saw many skulls of oxen that died last season from the effects of this water."[28]

---

[27]Entries for 18 and 19 July 1849, Gould, "Diary," pp. 138-39; entry for 24 July 1849, Hall, Diary, p. 8; entries for 21 and 22 July 1849, Littleton, Journal, pp. 31, 32; letter from Simon Doyle to Edward Doyle, 19 July 1849, Doyle, Journal. For other accounts by forty-niners see entry for 24 June 1849, *Geiger-Bryarly Journal*, p. 116; entry for 26 June 1849, Spooner, Diary; entry for 28 June 1849, Farnham, Gold Rush, p. 13; entries for 28 and 29 June 1849, Benson, Forty Niner, p. 26; entry for 1 July 1849, Doyle, Journal; entry for 6 July 1849, Cross, "Journal," pp. 118-19; Loring, "Report," p. 333; Evans, "Letter," p. 40; "Letter from Henry R. Wiman to Parents, Brothers, and Sisters, 25 October 1849" (ms., "Robert H. Miller Papers," Missouri Historical Society, St. Louis).

[28]Entry for 15 June 1850, Read, Journal.

Although one man wrote that the ground looked as if covered with "flour,"[29] most thought of scenes of winter. The soda, an emigrant said, was "like drifted snow."[30] "The wheels and horses' hoofs," another claimed, "break through the crust as if it were ice."[31] By way of contrast, a Missourian wrote of entering the "ante-chamber of Hell."[32]

What these physical problems meant to a traveler between the North Platte crossing and Independence Rock where Smith first wrote of the danger and the trail struck the Sweetwater, was that the emigrants "had to pay strict attention to Our stock in order to keep them from getting the water."[33] That fact demanded more effort to preserve property; even more should the cattle get sick. A second Oregon-bound settler, about three days ahead of Smith, saw people feeding their cattle bacon grease and vinegar to neutralize the poison.[34] The captain of an 1859 company, who had crossed the plains before, advised that, when traversing an "Alkali region," emigrants feed their cattle "a small piece of pork every night."[35]

What this information tells us is that emigrants had to expend

[29]Entry for 25 June 1849, Mann, Portion, p. 2.

[30]Entry for 22 June 1850, Langworthy, Scenery, p. 57. See also entry for 26 June 1849, McCall, Wayside Notes, p. 44.

[31]Entry for 17 June 1850, Frink, Journal, p. 53.

[32]Entry for 16 June 1850, Wallenkamp, Diary, p. 3. The emigration of 1850 is important because, as will be argued in chapter nine, it was the one that experienced the greatest suffering and shortages. For other 1850 descriptions of the perils of the alkali poison between the North Platte and Sweetwater, see entry for 19 May 1850, Millington, Journal, p. 28; note to entry for 22 May 1850, Stimson, Overland, p. 56(6)-57(7); entry for 6 June 1850, C. W. Smith, Journal; entry for 3 June 1850, L. Sawyer, Across the Plains, p. 40; entry for 6 June 1850, Keck, Journal; entry for 15 June 1850, Ingalls, Journal, p. 25; entry for 23 June 1850, Gilmore, Overland Journey, p. 10; entry for 23 June 1850, Gundlach, Minutes; entries for 24 and 25 June 1850, Chalmers, "Journal," p. 43; entry for 1 July 1850, McKinstry, Diary, p. 151; entry for 11 July 1850, Bennett, Overland Journey, p. 25.

[33]Entry for 17 June 1850, Paschel, Diary, p. 24. See also entry for 2 June 1852, Keen, Diary, p. 32; entries for 5, 6, and 7 July 1852, Yeargain, Diary, p. 7; entry for 12 July 1864, Merrill, Diary, p. 18. For the description of an emigrant traveling a few days ahead of Smith, see entry for 29 June 1853, Goltra, Journal, p. 12.

[34]Entry for 1 July 1853, McClure, Journey, p. 65.

[35]Entry for 12 July 1859, J. B. Brown, Journal of a Journey, p. 31.

great physical effort just to retain property. Even if bacon and vinegar were common items on the overland trail, their use as antidotes for alkali meant that an emigrant forced open an animal's mouth just to pour the grease down its throat. That overlander traveling a few days ahead of Smith wrote that the camping ground just beyond Devil's Gate "presented rather a strange spectacle, some drenching, some boreing cows horns and some stuffing them with fat bacon." [36] Three weeks later a third Oregon-bound emigrant was on the Fort Hall road when it was discovered that all the horses and oxen were sick. "We found we had camped on alkili grounds. We commenced pouring the lard and vinegar down them and they soon seemed better."[37]

Bacon used as medicine was not only hard to administer, it was not very effective. Worse, bacon was weight adding to the very problem it was supposed to cure. One reason the animals became weak was excessive loads and a heavy part of those loads was bacon. If that dilemma was not discouraging enough, overlanders soon discovered that the Sweetwater River did not always live up to its name. There were emigrants who rushed by other streams only to find the Sweetwater as bad as those they had avoided.[38] "[S]o strongly impregnated with alkili that it is hardly fit to use," was how it was described by one of Smith's fellow emigrants of 1853.[39] As a result, animals continued to get sick, and the bodies of dead horses, mules, and oxen stretched from Devil's Gate to beyond the Big Sandy.[40]

There is no need to elaborate further on the physical problem. It is enough to say that the alkali threat did not end until the journey was completed. It continued along the Sweetwater,

---

[36] Entry for 1 July 1853, McClure, Journey, p. 65.

[37] Entry for 21 July 1853, Goltra, Journal, p. 19.

[38] Entry for 25 June 1849, Ramsay, "Diary," p. 450; entry for 27 June 1850, Gundlach, Minutes; entry for 30 June 1850, Lampton, Diary, p. 14; entry for 4 July 1850, McKinstry, *Diary*, p. 157; entries for 21 and 24 June 1852, Frizzell, *Journal*, pp. 27-29; entry for 9 July 1852, Moore, Journal of Travails.

[39] Entry for 3 July 1852, Goltra, Journal, p. 14.

[40] Entries from 12 to 24 July 1850, John R. Shinn, "Crossing the Plains to California, 1850" (ms., photostat, Bancroft Library); entry for 5 July 1849, J. W. Wood, Diaries.

through South Pass, across the Big Sandy, Green, and Bear rivers, on even into California.[41]

On the Oregon trail, the route taken by John Smith, we might expect conditions to improve once the Snake was reached. Surprisingly, they did not, nor had emigrants learned that a good deal of the poison was not visible. Consider the following account written by a man traveling to Oregon the same year as Smith. He was, it must be stressed, a physician. If any emigrant was able to recognize poison water it might be thought he could. Instead, after his animals had died, the man did not even know what had killed them.

> [W]e camped one night, on a small crick, about 20 miles east of the south pass," he wrote, "& we had 27, of our horses poisoned in less than 2 hours. [T]he water was beautiful, & the grass appeared very good, & another train camped within 40 rods of us, & their horses fed with ours, & yet there was none of theirs Poisoned in the least, but they did not water where we did.[42]

Many emigrants that year were puzzled about why their cattle died.[43] The mystery made the problem more difficult to deal with. We may gain a deeper perspective of John Smith's frustrations by considering some excerpts from the diary of Elizabeth Goltra, who traveled up the Snake River road the same month as Smith.

The Goltra company had been forced to divide in the Bear River valley "on account of grass."[44] They left two wagons

---

[41]Area of South Pass: letter from Mr. Hardenstein to Harriet E. Hardenstein, 24 June 1849 (ts. "Fort Laramie Journals," vol. 2, Fort Laramie Historic Site, Fort Laramie, Wyoming); entry for 28 June 1849, Delano, *Life*, p. 112; entry for 30 June 1849, *Geiger-Bryarly Journal*, p. 130; entry for 4 July 1849, Spooner, Diary; entry for 9 July 1849, Benson, Forty Niner, p. 32. Rivers: entry for 17 June 1850, Keck, Journal; entry for 16 July 1850, McKinstry, *Diary*, p. 184; entry for 25 June 1849, Stitzel, Diary, p. 141; entry for 23 July 1849, Mann, Portion, p. 12. To California: entry for 22 July 1849, Breyfogle, Diary (ms.); entry for 10 Aug. 1849, Merrill, Diary, p. 15; letter of 23 July 1850, Plummer, Letter, p. 6; entry for June 1852, G.A. Smith, Diary.

[42]White, "Letter," p. 14.

[43]Even before reaching the Snake (entry for 3 July 1853, Knight, "Diary," p. 45).

[44]Entry for 19 July 1853, Goltra, Journal, p. 18. The entries quoted in the text are all from this journal.

carrying seven men, one woman, and four cows which meant (as the Goltra's single wagon had four yoke of oxen) that the grass was not sufficient for three teams and four cows to remain together. Hence it is not surprising that by the time Elizabeth Goltra reached the Snake River ferry on 9 August, the draft animals were in a weakened condition. Yet she was as puzzled by their sickness as was the physician near South Pass.

9 August 1853 (after crossing the ferry): "[D]rove out about 1 mile and one of our oxen laid down and died. Saw a great many dead cattle along the road to-day. Some attribute it to swimming the river."

11 August 1853: "This morning some of our cattle are sick and we hardly know what is the matter. They are not poisoned. Many have died around us during the night and this morning. It is the prevailing opinion that swimming the river so choked up with dust causes irritation of the lungs as they bleed very freely at the nose and mouth just before they die."

12 August 1853: "Lost 2 oxen belonging to our train last night and they are dying off all around us. Destruction stares us in the face."

14 August 1853: "Some of our neighbor's cattle died last night, but we lost none. They seemed to be well when they turn them out and in the morning find them dead."[45]

15 August 1853: "Again some of our neighbor's cattle died during the night. We find them lying along the road sometimes within a few feet of each other and two or three together."

21 August 1853 (heading toward the second ferry on the Snake): "Lost one ox and one cow last night."

---

[45]Of travel along the Snake that year another woman wrote: "[I]t was every day and every night someone had lost an ox,   we lost four in one day and two nights   when we got up in the morning we wemon [sic] got the breakfuss and the men went after the cattle, and we tho[ugh]t at last that we could not dare to see them come back for they always came back minus someones cattle" (letter of Elizabeth Stewart Warner, pp. 3-4 (ts., reproduced by Lane County Pioneer-Historical Society, 1959).

1 September 1853 (today she buys "a good light wagon" and at night arrives at the Powder River valley): "[W]e start out again in a team of our own as we had joined teams with another man and threw our wagon away until we could get a lighter one."

Other emigrants taking the Snake River branch of the Oregon trail lost cattle. Unlike Mrs. Goltra, many attributed these deaths to poison.[46]

When his first animal died, John Smith did not know why. It was an ox, apparently, lost at Big Sandy.[47] He was, however, certain that poisoned water killed one of his cows in Bear River valley, and probably was the cause of an ox dying along Thomas Fork the next day. It is not certain that the last ox was Smith's property but that same day he did purchase his first replacement.[48]

By then, it must be noted, John Smith had moved out of the alkaline desert of Wyoming and was traveling what was believed to be the more fertile trails of southern Idaho. He was still not in the region where the Goltras would lose their stock. For Smith the worst was yet to come.

Emigrants were warned of danger to cattle when they began to lose the core of their horns. Debility in oxen and cows was attributed to the hollowness of the horns. The name John Smith

---

[46]Poison of a "herb": entry for 5 Aug. 1853, Washburn, Journal, p. 26. Poison of alkali: entry for 5 Aug. 1853, *Dinwiddie Journal*, p. 10. Poison of a scorpion bite: entry for 15 Aug. 1853, Murray, Journal, p. 100. Poison "by some noxious weed": entry for 8 Aug. 1854, Ebey Diary p. 238. One man did an autopsy on a cow and "found an unusually large gall nearly a quart and the melt swoolen bloodshot or purple and upon cutting it it seemed nearly putred   The blood a bad color   Not hunger   hallow horn nor murram and if poison whether vegetable or mineral I cannot tell" (entry for 1 Sept. 1852, Cornell, Description, p. 58). For most it remained a mystery. "I do not know what ailed him" (entry for 29 Aug. 1854, Ebey, Diary, p. 39).

[47]It is not clear if the ox was his property although the best guess is that it was. Smith was not as precise about events as we would like. "We had to leave one of Calvins Black oxen at Big Sandy," he wrote, not indicating whether Calvin was a hired man driving one of his wagons or was the owner of a wagon who was traveling in Smith's party (entry for 21 July 1853, J. Smith, Account).

[48]Ibid., entries for 26 and 27 July 1853.

gave to the disease that would cripple his animals was the hollow horn.[49]

"[O]ur cattle are getting very much reduced," Smith noted as he traveled up the Snake River, a day before reaching the ferry at Salmon Falls. "[A] great many of them are getting the hollow horn which I suppose to be oc[c]asioned by the dust." Horses as well as cattle were suffering, and that very day "one of my Bulls gave out" and had to be left behind. Three days later another of Smith's cows died, "poisoned with something she Eat or drank it was not over an hour from we discovered she was ailing till she was dead." Soon a second cow died, and Smith must have experienced the frustration of being the victim of forces he could not combat. "[I]t is now thought," he noted, "that the Excessive dust has a great deal to do with causing the death of so many cattle." Even more depressing was the realization that conditions were deteriorating. "Since we started we have not saw so many dead Cattle as we have since crossing the [Snake] river for the same distance."[50]

III   *The Financial Problem*

John Smith's misfortune was to lose his cattle on the Snake. While still on the more populous part of the road[1] — the eastern half where the Oregon and California trails were one — he had replenished dead or injured draft animals by purchasing fresh oxen from traders.

During a seven-day period when traveling between Bear River

---

[49]So did others. See entry for 12 July 1853, Murray, Journal, p. 75; entry for 26 June 1852, Frizzell, *Journal*, p. 30; entry for 21 July 1849, Benson, Forty Niner, p. 37.

[50]Entries for 14, 17 and 19 Aug. 1853, J. Smith, Account. For "dust" as the cause of death see Goltra, Journal and entries for 29 Aug. and 1 Sept. 1853, Murray, Journal, pp. 109, 111.

[1]That year may have been an exception for in early June the register at Fort Kearny indicated that most of the emigration was going to Oregon (entry for 4 June 1853, Hines, "Diary," p. 93). Three months later, 3600 emigrants and 780 wagons were already recorded in Oregon (entry for 2 Sept. 1853, *Dinwiddie Journal*, p. 12). Later 5789 persons and 1729 wagons were registered (entry for 17 Sept. 1853, G. N. Taylor, Diary, p. 25).

and Fort Hall in today's Idaho, Smith bought at least three.[2] To raise money to pay for them, he sold some of his surplus provisions.

On that very fact, that out in the middle of the wilderness, hundreds of miles from any market, Smith had food for sale, hangs a good part of the story we seek to learn about legal behavior on the overland trail. It also constitutes a major part of John Smith's own tale of woe.

There are two facts to be digested, though the first need not be considered now. That Smith thought it safe to carry extra provisions — that he expected others to acknowledge both his ownership of surplus and his right to dispose as he saw fit of what he "owned" — is a theme to be developed in subsequent chapters. The second, Smith's tale of woe, has to do with the burden of property. For together with the poisoned water and the hollow horn, a cause of Smith's losing his animals was that they were overloaded.

We may be reasonably certain John Smith, on his way to Oregon in 1853, was aware of the perils overburdened wagons created for gold seekers in '49. The destruction of property on the overland trail had been well publicized through the midwest. So also had the famine of the following year when, as will be discussed later, emigrants heeded the warnings of forty-niners and took far too few supplies, facing starvation before even reaching today's Nevada. Once again newspapers had reported suffering on the plains, this time caused not by losing worn-out animals but by human hunger.

Smith does not seem to have taken caution from the warnings. Unquestionably he was overloaded. We do not have precise figures, but from the perspective of survival they do not matter. Forcing his animals to drag many pounds of unneeded provisions, Smith made the burden of property a daily reality.

At Peoria, Illinois, when Smith still had the entire state of Iowa to cross before reaching the start of the Oregon trail, he

---

[2]Entries for 27 July and 1-2 Aug. 1853, J. Smith, Account.

purchased twenty-eight pounds of bread. At a Sioux village beyond Scotts Bluff on the north side of the North Platte, he traded some hard bread — he does not say how much it weighed — for six pairs of "mockisans." The sale occurred almost two months after and many hundreds of miles west of the purchase.[3]

Passing through the town of Burlington, Iowa, immediately after crossing the Mississippi, Smith added to his freight fifty pounds of coffee, fifty-three pounds of bacon, and fifteen pounds of light bread.[4] Four months later, during a seven-day period spent traveling from the Thomas Fork of Bear River to Fort Fall, he sold to various traders 496 pounds of flour and 228 1/2 pounds of bacon: over 724 pounds of provisions not needed for his own consumption but which had been hauled by his animals over hundreds of miles of difficult terrain.[5]

As he progressed over the trail, John Smith continued to sell. We cannot be certain that his diary reports every sale, but it tells enough to substantiate the story. In one forty-eight hour period, for example, Smith disposed of another 105 pounds of bacon. These transactions occurred fifteen days after he had sold the 724 pounds of provisions. What this fact means is that during those fifteen days, if Smith traveled an average of twenty miles a day, he hauled 150 pounds of unnecessary weight an additional 300 miles.[6]

Unquestionably, Smith considered these transactions profitable. From the perspective of accumulating pocket money, perhaps they were. He bought, for example, fifty-three pounds of bacon in Burlington, Iowa, for $4.24, and sold fifty pounds in Bear River valley for $12.50. But money could not compensate him for the

---

[3]Ibid., entries for 19 March and 18 June 1853.

[4]Ibid., entry for 29 March 1853.

[5]"I . . . sold him 100 *lbs* of flour for $15.00 and 50 *lbs* of Bacon for $12.50" (ibid., entry for 27 July 1853). "I sold to Capt[ain] Grant at Soda Springs 67 lbs of Bacon at 20 cts 13.40 & 196 lbs flour 15¢ 29.40" (ibid., entry for 30 July 1853). "I . . . sold him 100 *lbs* of flour for 15.00 & 50 lbs Bacon for 12.50. Sold 6 1/2 lbs Bacon to Mr. Wingart for wagon grease at 20 cts" (ibid., entry for 1 Aug. 1853). "Sold to the Trader 100 lbs flour for 15.00 & 55 lbs Bacon for 13.75" (ibid., entry for 2 Aug. 1853).

[6]Ibid., entry for 18 Aug. 1853.

wear and tear upon his animals. It was dangerous to haul so much unnecessary weight. Although physical problems such as alkaline water and the hollow horn contributed, they alone were not responsible for Smith's difficulties. As much to blame were his own carelessness and parsimonious tenacity.

Reading between the lines of his diary, it is apparent that John Smith realized he had excess weight and desired to lighten the burden on his animals. Financial considerations, not miscalculations, made him reluctant to jettison items worth money east of the Missouri. When his oxen were relieved of some of the weight they had been hauling, it was usually because Smith sold, not because he threw property away.

It would not do to judge in haste. The obvious conclusion is that in seeking money Smith took unwise risks to acquire a commodity of relatively little benefit before reaching Oregon. Emigrants knew otherwise: money was necessary on the overland trail. That point may be asserted with confidence despite the fact that some thought it more valuable for psychological than for practical reasons. "Booth," an Ohio physician wrote of a companion about twenty miles before entering South Pass, "met with a slight accident yesterday in losing his purse containing all the money he had. It, however makes but little difference as landlords here do not make any charge for keeping us over night. A man however feels better with a little money in his pocket even if he does not wish to use   it."[7]

Money was needed for more than "feeling better." A young man who crossed the continent to Oregon during the summer of 1852, advised a brother coming in a later year to have "perhaps twenty-five or thirty dollars" before venturing onto the overland trail.[8] A Michigan newspaper in 1849 warned that a prospective

---

[7]Entry for 7 June 1850, Parker, Notes.

[8]Thompson, Across, p. 4. "[I]t was generally supposed this year, that after we left the frontier, money was of no use; it is the greatest mistake possible; I know of no part of the world where money is of more use than in crossing the Plains, and where a man is more helpless without it. No man ought to leave home without at least two hundred dollars" (Shepherd, Journal, p. 44).

emigrant should "have $100 in his pocket."[9] Five years earlier, James Frazier Reed, planning to cross with the Donner party, had been told to take "all the mon[e]y you can [for] money is good any wheere in the World."[10]

Once out beyond the frontier, emigrants found money more easily missed than forgotten. Certainly it was anything but unnecessary. "[H]aving been strap[p]ed for a month or so [I] was relieved by finding a $5.00 gold piece," a fifty-niner observed while camped at the South Pass.[11] "I have traded of[f] my Camanche mule for A smaller one," an emigrant on the Gila trail wrote ten years earlier, "getting $15 to Boot w[h]ich furnishes me with A little pocket money w[h]ich by the by I kneeded [sic] very much."[12]

We will never know why that particular man needed "pocket money." We can only be certain that other emigrants understood that neither need nor equity created claims on overland property. A lawyer made the point when — with gross exaggeration — he charged "that here on the prairies you might starve if you had no money & having it you must pay it all for a bite."[13] He wrote these words on the very day he crossed the Missouri, hardly enough time to appraise conditions on the trail. With experience the lawyer might have reached a somewhat different conclusion: that in times of acute shortages, money could not buy what was not available. "I find it very hard to arouse the sympathies of the people," one man wrote during August 1850, the period of greatest suffering in the history of the trail. "[M]oney, a man's

[9]*Washtenaw Whig*, 24 Jan. 1849, quoted in Bidlach, *Letters*, p. 10.

[10]Letter from James M. Maxey to James Frazier Reed, 10 Nov. 1845, in *Overland in 1846*, p. 475.

[11]Entry for 12 July 1859, Alden Brooks, "Grand Trip across the Plains" (ms., photocopy, Fac 223, Huntington Library).

[12]Entry for 17 Sept. 1849, Beeching, Journal.

[13]Entry for 15 May 1849, Charles Benjamin Darwin, "Journal" (ms., HM 16770-16771, Huntington Library).

best earthly friend, is no inducement for men to part with bread, on this trip."[14]

If money could not always buy food, it was still useful for purposes almost as important. Economic independence, emigrants soon learned, made progress both easier and faster. An example to become clearer in subsequent chapters is that money permitted emigrants to break free of the burden of concurrent property. By buying the property interests of obnoxious partners, an emigrant with money could separate from them. "When you start over these wide plains," an 1846 Oregon guidebook advised, "let no one leave dependent on his best friend for anything; if you do you will certainly have a blow-out before you get far."[15]

John Smith was not burdened by concurrent property, everything he possessed was privately owned. If that fact freed him from dependence on others, it increased his personal financial problem. Just six miles after paying toll to be ferried across the Missouri, Smith learned that even out beyond the line of settlement, money was needed if one was to get to Oregon. Some local Indians had constructed a "Brush bridge" over "a small stream" and charged him thirty cents to cross.[16] Two days later it cost him fifty cents to go over a second Indian-owned bridge at Papea Creek.[17] The sum was apparently negotiable, and it seems that the amount Smith paid was for all his stock, three wagons, and one carriage. Five days later when the proprietors asked twenty-five cents a wagon, another emigrant bargained them down to nine cents per vehicle.[18]

It would be premature to discuss Indian ownership at this point. It might, however, be noted that property and personal

---

[14]Entry for 24 Aug. 1850, "Diary of John Wood," printed in *The Great Trek*, ed. Owen Cockran Coy (Los Angeles: Powell Publishing Co., 1931), pp. 179-80.

[15]Lavender, *Westward*, p. 364.

[16]Entry for 11 May 1853, J. Smith, Account. To cross the Missouri at Council Bluffs cost five dollars a wagon that year. See entry for 29 April 1853, Washburn, Journal, p. 8; entry for 29 April 1853, Handsaker, "Journal," p. 1; entry for 9 May 1853, *Dinwiddie Journal*, p. 4.

[17]Entry for 13 May 1853, J. Smith, Account.

[18]Entry for 18 May 1853, Belshaw, Journey, p. 5.

contract set the pattern for most encounters with Indians on the overland frontier. Not military action or violent confrontation but economic enterprise characterized Indian-emigrant relations. As a general rule, the Indians sold and the emigrants bought. Smith not only purchased "mockisans" from the Sioux, but on at least two occasions — like many other emigrants facing the swift waters of the Snake River — "paid the Indians for swimming over my cattle & horses 60 [cents]."[19]

Crossing rivers and creeks on the overland trail could be expensive. Anyone hoping to reach the Pacific with wagons and wishing to avoid unnecessary risk to life or property, paid to be ferried across the swifter, deeper streams. As most ferries could not handle animals, a property owner might also have to hire Indians or fellow emigrants to swim over the cattle.

Ferries will be considered again. Their existence tells us much of how emigrants defined ownership and the degree to which they respected property. For the moment we are interested only in expenses incurred by individuals on the overland trail and, unfortunately, John Smith does not tell us what ferriage cost him at each river crossed. Generally he listed the total toll charged, not the itemized amount paid for each wagon or each animal.

It is likely that Smith does not mention every ferry. Another emigrant going to Oregon that same year reported that up to the Bear Mountains there had been ten toll-charging ferries.[20] John Smith lists only three. One reason is that he did not use as many as did emigrants coming via Missouri. Starting at Council Bluffs, Smith was on the north side of the Platte River and avoided the expensive bridge at today's Casper, Wyoming.

There are, however, some tolls Smith had to pay that are not mentioned — at Bear River for example. Other emigrants that season paid fifty cents per team at Thomas Fork[21] and up to one

---

[19]Entry for 2 Sept. 1853, J. Smith, Account.

[20]Letter of 17 July 1853, E. N. and J. W. Taylor, Letters.

[21]Entry for 9 July 1853, Washburn, Journal, p. 21; entry for 11 July 1853, Allyn, "Journal," p. 412; entry for 14 July 1853, Pengra, Diary, p. 39.

dollar a wagon at Smith Fork.[22] John Smith does not tell us what these crossings cost him, although he does reveal enough of expenses at other places to provide a rough idea of ferriage paid for the entire trip.

At the Elkhorn, where two ferries were in operation, Smith says the toll was three dollars a wagon.[23] The total charge may have been even more than he indicates. Six days later another Oregon pioneer reported paying three dollars per wagon and one dollar per head for horses, mules, and oxen.[24]

As just noted, since Smith came through Iowa, he traveled along the northern banks of the Platte rivers, avoiding tolls at Fort Laramie or across the new bridge over the North Platte which charged six dollars per team.[25] There was, however, no avoiding Green River, where Smith "paid $24.00 for crossing my 3 wagons & carriage & $1.00 for my 3 horses." As the rate was six dollars a vehicle, his carriage was charged the same as a wagon, besides which he had to swim his cattle, a task both difficult and dangerous.[26]

Along the Snake River there were at least two places at which Smith paid to be ferried.[27] The first, at the Salmon Falls, cost five

---

[22]One dollar: entry for 25 June 1853, Welsh, Diaries; entry for 3 July 1853, Knight, "Diary," p. 45; entry for 8 July 1853, Washburn, Journal, p. 20. Twenty-five cents: entry for 9 July 1853, Zilhart, Diary, p. 9.

[23]Entry for 14 May 1853, J. Smith, Account. Similarly: entry for 8 May 1853, Washburn, Journal, p. 11; entry for 12 May 1853, Longworth, Diary, p. 16; entry for 14 May 1853, Pengra, Diary, p. 19.

[24]Entry for 20 May 1853, Allyn, "Journal," p. 389.

[25]Entry for 1 July 1853, J. Smith, Account. Actually, the rates varied from five to eight dollars a wagon: entry for 20 June 1853, Zilhart, Diary, p. 6; entry for 24 June 1853, Bradway, Journal; entry for 3 July 1853, H. Stewart, Diary, p. 19.

[26]Entry for 18 July 1853, J. Smith, Account. For other costs and the dangers at Green River in 1853 see "Replenishing the Elephant," p. 78. See also entry for 21 June 1853, Welsh, Diaries; entry for 13 July 1853, Owen, My Trip, p. 20; entry for 16 July 1853, Hines, "Diary," p. 103; entry for 28 July 1853, Williams, "Diary," p. 211. Some emigrants were charged eight dollars at Green River ferry. See entry for 29 June 1853, Knight, "Diary," p. 45; entry for 1 July 1853, Washburn, Journal, p. 20; entry for 9 July 1853, Pengra, Diary, p. 37.

[27]Entries for 15 Aug. and 1 Sept. 1853, J. Smith, Account. Other emigrants report a "pole toll bridge" during July on the Portneuf River, prior to reaching the Snake. See entry for

dollars a wagon and two dollars fifty cents for three horses.[28] Again the cattle were swum. If guided across by the skiff, Smith probably paid for each animal. A week earlier it cost another emigrant "50¢ a head for swimming cattle by the side of the boat."[29]

The crossing at Fort Boise was even more expensive. Down to only two wagons and his carriage, the eight-dollar toll meant Smith paid a total of twenty-four dollars if, as before, his carriage was assessed at the same rate as a wagon.[30] Finally, while crossing the Columbia watershed, Smith had to take a ferry over the De Schutes River. Besides being charged three dollars a wagon, he again had to hire an Indian to swim the stock.[31]

All along the road to the old Oregon Territory Smith incurred expenses. Just beyond the ferry at Salmon Falls, he "bought some Salmon from the Indians," as had other emigrants from the earliest days of the Oregon trail.

When needing repairs requiring skills he lacked, such as blacksmithing, Smith hired fellow emigrants. On the North Platte, for example, he paid a man named Enos Kenneday "for setting 3 prs horse shoes 75 [cents]." Even more costly were prices at the numerous trading posts along the trail. One farrier charged Smith more than three times what he paid Kenneday. Similarly products cheap at home became more expensive as emigrants moved west from the Missouri River. At a post in

23 July 1853, McClure, Journey, p. 110; entry for 25 July 1853, Belshaw, Journey, p. 15. Earlier, on the Sweetwater near Independence Rock, earlier arrivals paid two and three dollars a wagon to cross "a rickety bridge" that "must soon break down." See entry for 10 June 1853, Welsh, Diaries; entry for 15 June 1853, Knight, "Diary," p. 44; entry for 23 June 1853, *Dinwiddie Journal*, p. 7.

[28]Entry for 15 Aug. 1853, J. Smith Account. Other reported prices were four dollars: entry for 30 July 1853, *Dinwiddie Journal*, p. 10. Six dollars: entry for 10 Aug. 1853, Hines, "Diary," p. 110. Two dollars fifty cents: entry for 1 Sept. 1852, *The Journal of James Akin, Jr.*, ed. Edward Everett Dale, *University of Oklahoma Bulletin* n.s. no. 172, University Studies no. 9 (Norman, Okla., 1919), p. 25.

[29]Entry for 8 Aug. 1853, Longworth, Diary, p. 39.

[30]Entry for 1 Sept. 1853, J. Smith, Account. Similarly, entry for 13 Aug. 1853, Pengra, Diary, p. 51.

[31]Entry for 28 Sept. 1853, J. Smith, Account.

today's Idaho, Smith "bought 4 lbs Tallow of the trader for wagon grease at 25 cts per lb."[32]

Smith's heaviest expenditures — the ones made directly and purposefully to save property he wanted hauled through to Oregon — were for fresh draft animals to replace those he had lost. On 27 July, at Thomas Fork of Bear River, a trader sold Smith an ox for forty-five dollars. Six days later he got a second for forty-five dollars and fifty cents, and the following day a third for forty-six dollars.[33] What these transactions meant to him in terms of comparative contemporary prices may be gauged by the fact that at Independence, during the height of the 1849 gold rush, when argonauts were driving up the cost of draft animals, a yoke of oxen may never have gone higher than sixty-five dollars.[34]

The significant aspect of John Smith's purchase is not that he had to pay $136.50 for a mere three oxen. The salient point is that the sales occurred in the vicinity of Fort Hall, just before the junction where the Oregon and California roads separated. After leaving the California trail it would become increasingly difficult for John Smith to acquire fresh oxen no matter how much money he offered.

IV *The Preservation Problem*

There was a basic difference between the Oregon and California sections of the overland trail. With different objectives, emigrants took different attitudes toward preserving property. Anxious to get through and commence digging gold, the average Californians put the journey above other considerations and would be willing to discard property that jeopardized their chances or slowed their pace. When the best ox belonging to one mess of forty-niners

---

[32]"Replenishing the Elephant," p. 79.
[33]Entries for 27 July and 1-2 Aug. 1853, J. Smith, Account.
[34]Unruh, The Plains Across, p. 166.

died, the mess threw away 300 pounds of weight. Determined "to sacrifice everything, except provisions," one of them wrote.[1]

The average Oregon pioneers would have been more reluctant to "sacrifice." They were settlers, not argonauts. They wanted to get their milch cattle, bedding, and household goods through. To the Oregonian, wagons and oxen were not expendable, but necessary — vital to success on the trail and useful later in his new home. Yet, once the Oregon trail separated from the California road, property became more scarce, not only because the number of travelers had been sharply decreased, but also because less was being abandoned. Now emigrants were protecting what they could, cherishing every mule and horse, and to get the most out of each, were willing to travel at the pace of the slowest animal still able to draw a load.

Once his train reached the Snake River and shortages became more acute, a change occurred in John Smith's relationships with fellow emigrants. Self reliant and apparently socially independent while on the more crowded section of the trail, he found that he now needed assistance to survive and was forced to associate with others.

Four days beyond Fort Hall, probably in the vicinity of the fork where the Oregon road, swinging north, left the California trail, Smith's diary began referring to another emigrant identified as "Mr. Davidson." That day Davidson "broke an axeltree," damaging his wagon to such a degree he had to saw an end off, converting it into a cart "which does not do well." Davidson owned more than one wagon and probably did not need the cart for survival. There can be little doubt, however, that he hoped to save whatever property the vehicle had been transporting. When the abbreviated cart proved to be inadequate, he purchased a substitute wagon from a fellow emigrant.[2]

Smith and Davidson then began traveling together. Just why is not explicitly explained in the extant diary, but one fact appears

---

[1] Entry for 27 June 1849, Gray, *Off at Sunrise*, p. 47.
[2] Entries for 8 and 9 Aug. 1853, J. Smith, Account.

obvious from what is said: the property possessed by the two men was complementary. Smith had a supply of food, while Davidson had strong teams hauling his wagons.

Companionship was often determined not only by property but the condition, strength, and durability of property. If one emigrant had a supply of meat and no horse, he might be welcomed into a pack company with extra mules but little "grub."

The year before Smith and Davidson were drawn together, a company of twenty-four men and one woman started from Monroe, Michigan, for California with eight wagons, forty-four head of horses, and a sufficient number of mules. Although they were careful not to push their animals, the company began to lose its horses in the region of the Sweetwater due to alkali. Beyond South Pass the company divided. "Some of our wagons were pretty nearly worn out," a member explained, "and, as we had but little in them, there were sixteen men who that night decided to give up their five wagons and resort to 'packing.' Consequently the remaining three wagons . . . bade us goodby and pulled out in the morning."[3]

Our lesson is that the condition of property — flagging animals and "worn out" wagons — helped determine the course of events. Sixteen of the original twenty-four male members of the Monroe company left the wagons to pack because of the state of their property. In time some would return for precisely the cause that had persuaded them to leave. Beyond Goose Creek in today's northeastern Nevada, just before reaching the headwaters of the Humboldt, the packers overtook the three wagons from which they had departed near the South Pass. "Some of our boys whose stock was nearly worn out," one of the packers wrote, "concluded that they would join the three wagons and take more time to get through."[4]

---

[3]Cole, *Early Days*, pp. 13-15, 66, 69.
[4]Ibid., p. 88.

The significance of property and the role it played in the lives of emigrants becomes ever more controlling the more closely we examine the evidence. Later the theme will be developed that ownership of property often determined a person's companions as well as the comfort, safety, and speed of travel. In the case of the Monroe company we see the same factors being determined by the condition of property. Because the hauling animals were stronger than the packing animals, wagon travel, despite its slower pace now had greater appeal for the men who left the packing party and rejoined the wagons.

The decision could be quite complicated, for the condition of other property might qualify the attractiveness of strong hauling animals. A fact not to be overlooked was that the Monroe company crossed the continent in 1852, a year of relative plenty on the overland trail. Had it been 1850, a season of starvation along the Humboldt, the decision could have been different. Then the most salient condition of property — the shortage of food — might have made the speed of packing, even with uncertain animals, more attractive than the slower-moving wagons, despite their stronger oxen.

John Smith was drawn to Davidson for much the same reasons the Monroe packers had rejoined their wagons: the strength of his draft animals. Before they had proceeded very far, the condition of their property was drastically altered and Smith found companionship less attractive than he had hoped. Deadly poison had not been left behind on the Sweetwater. It reappeared on the upper Snake. In addition, due to changing terrain, travel became progressively more difficult.

We may gain some idea of the perils of this section of the Oregon trail by considering the diary of Sarah Sutton, who came overland the year after Smith and Davidson. Back at the Green River ferry her party must have felt their animals were likely to last the trip, for they sold a yoke of oxen for fifty-five dollars.[5]

---

[5]Entry for 26 June 1854, Sutton, Diary, pp. 13, 17. They also sold "two lame cows for $15 apiece" and purchased one pony also for fifteen dollars two days before crossing the

Less than a month later, on reaching the Snake, they began to experience the burden of hauling too much property.

12 July 1854 (at the American Falls): "One of T. Cooks oxen died tonight of Murrin."[6]

18 July 1854: "Here we left one of Tom Cook's calves. It went down to drink and was too weak to return."

20 July 1854: "Came on five miles to the ferry . . . . Thomas Cook bought a yoke of oxen for $100."

22 July 1854: "One of our cows gave out and others are very near it. Here is a killing on wagons and team[s]. The wagons are broke down banging over the rocks and mountains, and the cattle give out worrying over the rocks and mountains and are left to die."

23 July 1854: "Our cow that gave out yesterday could not be found dead or alive this morning. We refitted our wagons and left a good many things to lighten our load, which we would be happy to have at home."

24 July 1854: "One of our yearlings has died here in sight since we stopped . . . . One of our largest and best oxen died today, and just before he stopped he ran into the team, as it was going, at the place where he had worked for months. It was hard to get him out, just to have it said that he died at his post, making three that have died in two days. One of Mr. Chapman's died at the same time, that makes 14 that we have lost since we started."

27 July 1854: "Had to leave another one of our oxen to die this morning and our team, part of it, is about to give out, as it is half cows."

North Platte. It may be that the cows were not draft animals (entry for 9 June 1854, Sutton, Diary, pp. 9-10). Another company that year lost ten oxen in eighteen days (entries for 1 to 18 Aug. 1854, Condit, Diary).

[6]Murrin was also spelled Murrim by Mrs. Sutton. "One of Joe Carters oxen died of Murrim this morning" (entry for 24 June 1854, Sutton, Diary, p. 12).

28 July 1854: "We have lost four yoke of oxen and are now working eight or ten cows. Our case is somewhat discouraging at present, but hope for his blessing to rest upon us."

29 July 1854: "Yoked up our teams this morning to start and discovered one of our cows was sick; turned her out, put in another and started. We had not got far when we saw one of Mr. Cook's oxen was sick and could not work. Turned him out and gave them both a dose of lard and pepper and they both died in two hours. One of Mr. Chapman's died at the same place yesterday, very sudden. Mr. Cook has paid $100 on Snake River for his oxen, a few days ago. Only worked him two days. The Lord only knows what we are to do if we lose any more. It is all we can do to get along, but we have the promise if we will but trust in him he will help us out of our troubles."

John Smith says nothing about relying on Mrs. Sutton's "promise." He did, however, suffer from Mrs. Sutton's problem. More precisely Davidson, with whom Smith had started to travel, did the suffering. Two days after crossing the Snake River by ferry, the place where Thomas Cook had paid one hundred dollars for a yoke of oxen, the Smith-Davidson train drove its wagons up a high hill. "Just as we got to the top," Smith wrote in his diary, "one of Mr. Davidsons oxen dropped down in the yoke & died in about an hour   he was poisoned by something he Eat or drank. We traveled about 18 miles & camped without reaching water   on the way I had a cow to Die . . . She was poisoned with something she Eat or drank   it was not over an hour from we discovered she was ailing till she was dead   Mr. Davidson had a steer to give out on the way & had to leave him."[7]

Next morning the two owners awoke to find Davidson had lost another ox. "Died same as the others," Smith noted. The double loss put Davidson in desperate straits. Another day's drive convinced both men that the remaining animals could not haul Davidson's load much further. He would, Smith thought, be

---

[7] Entry for 17 Aug. 1853, J. Smith, Account.

"obliged to leave a wagon unless he can get aid in the way of oxen from some one." By noon the next day they had accepted the inevitable. "Mr. Davidson left a wagon," Smith wrote. It was a step alleviating but not solving the survival problem. "[P]rospects seems rather gloomy on account of so many Cattle dieing   almost every one is loosing more or less."[8]

Smith was correct. Others were "loosing" cattle. On the same day that Davidson's first ox died, another Oregon emigrant lost one purchased at Soda Springs, just before reaching the Snake.[9] "The emigration is very large," a second 1853 overlander wrote just beyond Fort Boise, "and the cattle is dying like rotton sheep   they have opened some and their Melts is rotton   some of them bleeds at the nose and dies in a few minutes after working through the day."[10]

Davidson had no choice but to stop and Smith stayed with him. Their purpose was "to rest our Cattle & see whether Mr. Davidson can procure aid," which he did. "Mr. Davidson bought an ox this Morning at $50, he also sent back to our last Encampment & had his wagon brot. on."[11] Next day, while they continued to rest, waiting for the wagon to be retrieved, Davidson lost a cow and one of Smith's oxen died. "[T]here is the greatest fatality amongst the Cattle that I ever saw," Smith lamented. "Cause not know."[12]

---

[8]Ibid, entries for 18 and 19 Aug. 1853.

[9]Entry for 18 Aug. 1853, McClure, Journey, p. 151. The day before (two days beyond the crossing of Salmon Falls River) another emigrant wrote: "Here commenced the sickening among the stock, 2 of our oxen, a cow and 2 calves died here." See entry for 17 Aug. 1853, Diary of Joseph Hite Family (ts., 1508, Oregon Historical Society, Portland).

[10]Entry for 24 August 1853, Belshaw, Journey, p. 23. This emigrant "counted 190 dead animals along a 321 mile stretch of Snake River in 1853" (Unruh, The Plains Across, pp. 218-19).

[11]Entry for 20 Aug. 1853, J. Smith, Account.

[12]Ibid., entry for 21 Aug. 1853. That same day a twenty-one-year-old girl wrote that "we hear often of people losing all their cattle and we ought to be grateful" her wagon had lost none. Four days later, four of her oxen were dead. Entries for 21 and 25-26 Aug. 1853, "The Diary of Agnes Stewart" (ts., reproduced by Lane County Pioneer-Historical Society, 1959), p. 20.

Though he had acquired a new ox and recovered an abandoned wagon, Davidson believed he lacked resources sufficient to carry his property to Oregon. While the small train was encamped "a Mr. Mann," apparently rich in animals, came in. Davidson struck a bargain either to rent or borrow all or part of Mann's surplus oxen.

A question that we seek to answer is whether legal behavior on the trail was the same as law east of the Missouri River. Here we encounter evidence indicating that in one respect it was: when a person owned property another wished to use, the owner of the property set the terms.

Davidson, possessing wagons, was short on oxen. Mann, with spare animals, refused to sell. Moreover Mann did not "wish a large company" and would "not let anyone have any of his Cattle to work unless they travel with him."[13] We must guess, but it seems a reasonable supposition that, with so many oxen dying, Mann insisted that Davidson travel in his company so the bailment could be terminated should he need the animals. All we know for certain is that Davidson agreed, and as he and Smith now parted, whatever arrangement had existed between them was terminated.

Again it is important to recall that we are looking at John Smith because he traveled the Oregon Trail, on which objectives (and therefore the role of property) were somewhat different than on the road to California. Had Davidson been on his way to the gold diggings, he probably would not have bothered making a contract with Mann. Most likely he would have put what he could on the backs of his surviving animals and packed the remainder of the way. That he did not do so is a good indication he either was traveling with a family or transporting property he believed he needed in Oregon. Whatever contractual arrangement Davidson made with Mann, he was (at least for the moment) successful in accomplishing his purpose. He kept his wagons and perhaps the remainder of his property.

---

[13]Entry for 22 Aug. 1853, J. Smith, Account.

Contracts for the use of property were common on the overland trail. Emigrants unable to purchase stock or other equipment to replace things lost or damaged, frequently negotiated leases permitting them to rent other people's property. Commonly, the practice was to combine sets of complementary property as, for example, Davidson hitching Mann's spare animals to his own wagons. A similar case occurred later that year, as noted earlier, where Mrs. Goltra "joined teams with another man and threw our wagon away until we could get a lighter one."[14]

A variation of the Davidson-Mann bailment occurred when a family possessed animals but had lost its wagon. Hiram Spencer, his wife, and child found themselves in that predicament while crossing the plains during 1859. They were traveling in a wagon accompanied by Spencer's brother when part of their team gave out. Forced to abandon their wagon, the couple joined the wagon of Lorin Sykes and his family, former neighbors from Michigan. The brother was taken in by the mess to which another young man from Michigan, J. A. Wilkinson, belonged. There was reluctance to accept him, apparently because he "was driving his way through" and had only labor to contribute as his share of the common assets. Hiram Spencer, on the other hand, put his remaining oxen to work hauling the Sykes's wagon.

"The Sykeses," Wilkinson noted in his journal, "are Rushers, and by the looks they have been driving to[o] hard." Their animals were being worn out and Spencer, having already lost some of his, apparently did not care to risk the remainder in reckless haste. Besides, he and his wife did not get along with their new companions. In ten days they quit the Sykes's wagon and joined Wilkinson's mess. There was less reluctance to take them than there had been with the single man. Wilkinson's mess had lost two oxen and Spencer's property would help insure they could get their wagon through to California. Wilkinson explained

---

[14]For a discussion of overland contracts see "Binding the Elephant." Mrs. Goltra: entry for 1 Sept. 1853, Goltra, Journal, quoted p. 66 above.

the pact in terms of two sets of privately-owned property joined in an arrangement of mutual assistance — a contractual but not a property partnership. "Hiram Spencer and Family have become dissatisfied with their treatment in the Sykes train and we have taken them with us," he wrote. "They have one good yoke of oxen that are able to work and a Stag that is sore footed, and a nice little cow that is giving milk and broken to work. This gives us 3 yokes to work and 2 Sore footed ones bringing up the rear with the cow."

As events turned out, the joinder of property aided both parties. Spencer received transportation for his wife and child, while Wilkinson's mess obtained the use of stock they would badly need. Before reaching California they lost two more oxen, while "Spencer got through with 3 oxen and a Cow."[15]

John Smith, hoping to carry specific property to Oregon, would have gained less than he needed from a sharing contract such as Spencer made with Wilkinson's mess. He had to keep his own wagons drawn by his own animals if he was to arrive on the Columbia with the things he thought necessary to begin life in Oregon. That necessity became his problem now that after leaving the California part of the trail there were fewer trading posts with goods for sale and fewer emigrants disposing of excess weight or discarding wagons. Besides, Smith encountered a new problem. He ran short of cash, making it more difficult to purchase from an ever-decreasing market.[16]

Five days after saying goodbye to Davidson, Smith had to abandon a wagon. "[M]y team," he explained, "is getting so reduced that I cannot take it." On that same day he counted thirty-seven dead cattle, the day before it had been forty-five, and soon his own became part of the grim statistics.

Four days beyond the Fort Boise ferry, Smith lost an ox. It was one that he had "Bought this side of the Soda Springs for

[15]"Replenishing the Elephant," pp. 83-85.

[16]Smith did not say he was cash short. That supposition is inferred from the fact he will have to purchase on credit (entry for 29 Oct. 1853, J. Smith, Account).

46.00   he had the hollow horn & was a good deal stubborn & when he got tired [would] not be drove. I left him not far from where we last past Snake River."[17]

That was 6 September. On the tenth another ox was lost. "Died with the same Complaint that so many has been dieing with," Smith explained. "Cattle are lieying dead as thick along the road as they have been at any time yet."[18] Smith met one company that lost fifty head of cattle between the two ferries on the Snake River and "had to leave 6 wagons." It was a fate he could not avoid. In the valley of the Grande Ronde he lost another ox and had to abandon one of his two remaining wagons. The best chance of getting the last wagon into the settlements was to obtain fresh oxen. That was what Smith did — by gambling on strength over numbers. "I sold the Traders here 8 head of worked down oxen . . . for $25.00 Each," he explained, "& bought two yoke of oxen from him for 300.00 one yoke of which he bought of emigrants last year   they are fat Cattle   the other yoke he has had about 2 months   they are large cattle & in tolerable order."[19]

Smith's words indicate confidence. He had been forced to abandon a wagon, probably giving up some property he had hoped to have in Oregon. But he still had one wagon and his carriage, and by trading eight jaded oxen for four that were fresh, he had stronger animals to haul that one wagon. He could reasonably expect to get through. Then, the very next day, disaster struck.

"Started up the Blue mountain," Smith wrote in his diary. It had been necessary "to double team." "[J]ust after getting to the top of the Mountain one of my wagon wheels crushed down   here

---

[17]Ibid., entries for 27, 29 Aug. and 6 Sept. 1853.

[18]Entry for 10 Sept. 1853, J. Smith, Account. Next day, also on Grande Ronde River, an emigrant noted "dead Cattle In Large quantities" (entry for 11 Sept. 1853, G. N. Taylor, Diary, p. 24). Earlier, after taking a ferry across the Salmon Falls River, a woman "found the smell of carrion so bad that we left as soon as possible. The dead cattle were lying in every direction. Still there were a good many getting their breakfast among all the stench" (entry for 22 July 1853, Knight, "Diary," p. 47). In a manuscript version the last word was not "stench," but "fago" (entry for 22 July 1853, Knight, Journal, p. 32).

[19]Entries for 10 and 14 Sept. 1853, J. Smith, Account.

then I had to leave the last one of my three wagons." It is difficult to escape the conclusion that it had been too loaded. Just a few miles back his party had sold to some Indians "forty or fifty dollars worth of old bed quilts & others things so as to reduce our load as much as possible." They had, in fact, gotten rid of so much that, "when the wagon broke down there were not over 1500 lbs in it." Smith implies that 1500 pounds was not heavy, but considering all the food he had sold and the fact he had been feeding five people, it seems a remarkable amount for one wagon still to be hauling so late in the trip. It was only three hundred pounds lighter than the advised limit when leaving the frontier with six animals, and all Smith had to pull it were four oxen.[20]

Smith sold the broken wagon to a trader "for about $6.00 worth of Beef." The trader, however, had no substitute to sell him in exchange, or at least none that Smith could use. Thus the loss of the wagon might well have marked the end of Smith's efforts to save his property had not another emigrant, a "Mr. Hite," been present. He owned four wagons. "I had to get the use of one," Smith wrote, and he did — apparently on credit.[21]

Smith's deal with Hite was the usual solution employed by emigrants to insure that their property survived — a transfer of title by bargain and sale. He did not attach his oxen to another person's wagon as had Hiram Spencer. Whatever goods Hite was transporting probably were shifted to his other three wagons and Smith's 1500 pounds put in the fourth. Nor did Hite bail the vehicle, as apparently did Mann when he lent animals to Davidson. In the remaining entries of his diary, Smith referred to the wagon as his own. When at the Dalles, the company made arrangements to be carried to the Cascades. Hite paid for three "wagons" and Smith paid for two — the one he got from Hite and the carriage he had driven all the way from Indiana.[22]

---

[20]Ibid., entries for 14 and 15 Sept. 1853. He had been feeding six persons up to 1 Aug. when a hired man left his employ.

[21]Ibid., entry for 15 Sept. 1853.

[22]Ibid., entries for 4 and 8 Oct. 1853.

It would seem that Smith increased the chances of getting his property to the Oregon settlements by also purchasing animals. He was now able to hitch two yoke of oxen to the carriage "as my horses have hauled it all the distance since we started & are pretty well worked down." We are not told where he obtained the four oxen; probably from Hite.[23]

Smith's diary does not state the precise terms of his arrangement with Hite. From what he says — or fails to say, as he usually noted a cash transaction — it is unlikely that he paid for the wagon at the time he acquired it. He had made over a hundred dollars exchanging his eight tired oxen for the four fresh ones, but he needed money now that they were in Oregon Territory. Many emigrants signed notes on the trail, often payable upon reaching a designated destination rather than on a date certain.[24] It is possible Smith and Hite executed a promissory document on the trail. More likely, however, they waited until reaching their destination — Albany, Oregon — and after studying the state of the local economy were better able to agree on a mutually acceptable price.[25]

John Smith's troubles were not quite over when he purchased the fresh oxen in the valley of the Grand Ronde and then obtained a wagon from Joseph Hite. He was destined to lose at least one more ox as well as a cow that he apparently had been using as a draft animal.[26] But for all intents and purposes he had accomplished much of his goal. He had left Indiana with three wagons and a carriage. Nineteen days after acquiring Hite's wagon, Smith and his party were at the Dalles, buying tickets to be transported down the Columbia to their new homes.

---

[23]Ibid., entry for 15 Sept. 1853.

[24]Entry for 15 Aug. 1849, Gray, *Off at Sunrise*, p. 81; entry for 23 June 1849, Powell, Diary, p. 52; entry for 26 Jan. 1850, Bruff, *Journals*, p. 698; entry for 26 May 1850, Parker, *Notes;* entry for 30 May 1852, Crane, Journal. For a promise payable both at a place and a date certain see entry for 26 May, Parker, Notes.

[25]Once at Albany, Smith purchased from Hite a wagon for $150.00 (entry for 29 Oct. 1853, J. Smith, Account).

[26]Ibid., entries of 18 and 19 Sept. 1853.

It cannot be said that the experiences of John Smith were typical of the Oregon trail. Starting with three wagons and ending with one, he probably managed to save more than a third of the property he had hoped to carry to Oregon, perhaps almost a half. Much of the early weight, after all, had been food, and by the time he reached Grande Ronde valley this had been either eaten or sold. Smith was typical, however, in the fact that to preserve property he had to replenish property.[27] By purchasing fresh oxen and acquiring a wagon he did manage to bring through perhaps as much as 1500 pounds of private property.

Another Oregon emigrant who replenished the elephant that year was Enos Ellmaker. He, his wife, five children, and three hired men, traveled in two wagons that had been ironed "with careful exactness" in Iowa. One of the wagons was taken through to Oregon, the other had to be abandoned on the plains. Like Smith, who purchased from Hite, and Davidson, who made a contract to use Mann's animals, Ellmaker replenished his lost property. The wagon was replaced when he "hitched on to another one, which was much lighter, [and] had been left by some person whose team had died or given out."

What could not be picked up free of charge, Ellmaker had to buy. "I purchased twenty six head of the largest, and finest, steers that I could find in Iowa — two of which died from alkali water," Ellmaker recalled some years later. "I also exchanged two yokes, on the Plains for two yokes of fresh, and fat cattle that had been kept at tradeing poasts on the Plains. I having to pay $50 a yoke and giving a yoke, costing me for two yokes of Fresh cattle $100 dollars and two yokes of cattle."[28]

---

[27]Another "typical" solution was to abandon property to preserve property. Thus an 1853 emigrant, traveling with his wife and children, abandoned his wagon and buggy "as the horses were getting so poor that I feared we would lose them" (letter from Joseph Lyman to his mother, 11 Nov. 1853, "Esther and Joseph Lyman Letters: About 1853 Lost Wagon Train" [ts., Fac 587, Huntington Library]). The day after crossing the Salmon Falls, another man wrote, "I have seen [abandoned] at least [$]1,000.00 worth of wagons and irons of every description used in teaming the last few days and great number of dead stock a perfect boneyard" (entry for 21 July 1853, Luark, Diary, p. 47).

[28]Ellmaker, Autobiography, p. 10.

Ellmaker paid a higher price than did Smith for the two yoke of cattle purchased in the valley of the Grande Ronde. But he received a better return for his money. Ellmaker's oxen did not die in the harness and one of Smith's new animals did. Economic success on the trail should not be measured by the bargain struck. It is best ascertained by the quality of property obtained from a seller and the quantity of property carried through to the settlements in Oregon.

If John Smith can be criticized for any fault, it was that he thought of property in eastern terms. He overloaded three wagons and then failed to lighten them as quickly as he otherwise might had he not measured the value of property by money instead of norms of survival. True, prices had been high at Council Bluffs,[29] but the overland trail was not the place to recoup losses or seek a profit. Smith does not say what he paid for flour east of the Missouri River,[30] but after carrying it for better than two months he sold 200 pounds for $30.00, or $7.50 for 50 pounds.[31] Near Portland, in Oregon, he paid $6 for 50 pounds.[32] Smith may have counted the difference as a profit, but the wear of hauling 200 unneeded pounds on animals bloated with alkali made monetary figures unrealistic.

---

[29]See, as examples for 1853, entry for 2 May 1853, *Dinwiddle Journal*, p. 4; entry for 9 May 1853, Compton, Diary, p. 12; entry for 10 May 1853, Pengra, Diary, pp. 15-16. One emigrant, however, found prices on the Iowa frontier "on the whole as reasonable as we expected" (entry for 9 May 1853, Murray, Journal, p. 26).

[30]At Kanesville "We got flour at $7.00 pr bbl" (entry for 9 May 1853, Murray, Journal, p. 26).

[31]Entries for 1-2 Aug. 1853, J. Smith, Account.

[32]Ibid., entry for 12 Oct. 1853.

Trading the Elephant

4 | THE DYNAMICS OF TRANSFER

The fact that John Smith and his fellow emigrants found numerous traders located along the overland trail should not be passed over lightly. It tells us much, not only about property on the overland trail, but about attitudes toward property in antebellum America. In searching for and measuring those attitudes, none is more striking than the sense of confidence manifested by people vending property on the trail.

We might think trading on the overland trail a high-risk venture; contemporaries did not. Those who brought goods into the wilderness for sale realized the dangers posed by nature, but seemed unconcerned with human threats — either from Indians or thefts. As early as 1841, the famous mountain man Joseph Reddeford Walker met the tiny emigration of that year in Green River Valley and offered for sale California horses and mules.[1] Four years later, "a number of traders . . . from the neighborhood of Taos, and the head-waters of the Arkansas," were at Fort Bridger, with "buckskinshirts, pantaloons, and moccasins, to trade with the emigrants." Even at that early date Edwin Bryant thought the emigrant trade "a very important one to the mountain merchants and trappers."[2] When the gold rush began, many frontier hunters and fur men, some famous like Kit Carson, sold animals at a variety of places such as the last crossing of the North Platte.[3] "There were a number of traders here, mountaineers and

---

[1]Unruh, The Plains Across, p. 353.
[2]Entry for 17 July 1846, Bryant, *Journal*, p. 123.
[3]Entry for 13 June 1850, Ingalls, *Journal*, p. 25.

Mormons," a forty-niner wrote at the last crossing of the Sweetwater. "They had lots of ponies, ranging in price from $75 to $130. They sell some, as more or less mules get lame, and some of the men who have money, traveling with uncongenial partners, buy a pony and leave their companions with the ox teams."[4]

Although most of these stockmongers were trappers already living in the mountains, who stationed themselves near the trail to do business with overlanders, a few may have come from east of the Missouri. Passing the same area eleven days later, a second emigrant "Saw a bulletin" by the side of the road, "stating that oxen & horses were for sale in a hollow nearby & on our going down there we found a lot of traders from Arkansas."[5]

By the second decade of overland travel, trading posts were located all along the trail. "Traders buying & selling everything a person wants to eat all over these mountains," a young man from Wisconsin noted while crossing the Sierras in 1852.[6] "For the last three weeks we have been passing trading posts nearly every day," an Indiana emigrant wrote just after Devil's Gate on the Sweetwater.[7]

Stations along the Platte River were not very numerous until later years, probably because it was so close to the Missouri that emigrants were still well supplied with necessities.[8] Also, from 1849 on, there was competition at Fort Kearny.[9] One company, well ahead of the main emigration that year, was able to buy "500 lbs of flour at the fort, and several other articles that we needed from the sutler."[10]

---

[4]Entry for 17 June 1849, Hixson, Diary.

[5]Entry for 28 June 1849, Gray, *Off at Sunrise*, p. 48.

[6]Entry for 14 Aug. 1852, Turnbull, "Travels," p. 216.

[7]Entry for 20 June 1854, McCowen, Journal and Notes, p. 31.

[8]Entry for 25 June 1863, E. T. Adams, Diary.

[9]Mattes, *Platte River Road*, pp. 50, 204.

[10]Ibid., p. 175.

During the gold rush, trading posts were not encountered until after leaving the Pawnee nation and crossing the South Platte. At Ash Hollow, near where the emigration struck the North Platte, there were occasional temporary lodges of white traders, even a few Sioux traders.[11]

The first permanent establishment of any note most emigrants saw was owned by a member of the fur-trading Robidoux family and located at Scotts Bluff in far western Nebraska.[12] By 1850 two blacksmith shops were there in addition to a store where Robidoux had "a neat assortment of dry goods & somewhat of a general assortment of goods — buys or trades a great deal of Furs from the Indians & sends them [down] the Missouri River."[13] There also at times were "a few Sioux" at Scotts Bluff with "excellent & finely decorated robes for sale."[14] Their ponies, however, were either not of the same quality or else the Sioux drove an unusually stiff bargain. "[W]e made an exchange with them" an emigrant complained, "and got badly cheated."[15]

That same year, 1850, there was at least one trading post between Robidoux and Fort Laramie.[16] By 1852 there were several in the last ten miles alone,[17] and the next year one man counted "probably 25 establishments for trade with emigrants" within twenty miles of the fort.[18]

---

[11]Entry for 6 June 1849, J[oshua] H. Drake, "Diary, 1849-1851" (ms., microfilm 580, Huntington Library); entry for 12 June 1849, Howell, Diary 9; entry for 30 May 1852, Thorniley, Diary; Mattes, *Platte River Road*, pp. 307-08, 415.

[12]Fairchild, *Letters*, p. 31; entries for 18 and 19 June 1852, Hampton, Diary (ts.), p. 4; Mattes, *Platte River Road*, pp. 35-36, 438, 448.

[13]Entry for 26 May 1850, Thomasson, Diary; entry for 25 May 1850, Gorgas, Diary.

[14]Entry for 29 May 1850, W. S. McBride, Diary. Three years later, just beyond Scotts Bluff, Nez Perce traders were encountered, though they may have been trading with Sioux, not with emigrants. See entry for 10 June 1853, *Dinwiddie Journal*, p. 6.

[15]Entry for 5 June 1850, Payne, Account, p. 39.

[16]Entry for 13 June 1850, Stauder, Memorandum, p. 16.

[17]Entry for 12 June 1852, Anon., Diary, pp. 5-6.

[18]Letter of 17 July 1853, E. N. and J. W. Taylor, Letters, p. 138. See also entries for 17 and 28 June 1853, Hines, "Diary," pp. 97-98.

At Laramie itself, the sutler had little to sell, except at very high prices, but often there were independent traders in the area and, during the gold rush at least, emigrants overhauling their outfits at the fort peddled everything but draft animals.[19]

What could not be purchased at Laramie might be available at the crossing of the North Platte. A blacksmith shop generally was located there. So too were grocery stores — three during 1859, one of which was "filled with several thousand Dollars worth of goods."[20]

Along the Sweetwater, starting at Independence Rock, there were scattered trading posts, generally owned by mountain men.[21] "[T]he traders are here," one emigrant observed, "principally to buy lame stock which they keep on good feed untill they recruit, and then sell or trade them to emigrants. Some of these traders are very rich and own big droves of cattle and Indian horses."[22] Louis Vasquez, partner of Jim Bridger, was there in 1849.[23] To do business with emigrants, Bridger, back in 1843, established a trading post in the southeast corner of today's state of Wyoming. Settlers bound for Oregon, Bridger had observed, "generally" were "well supplied with money but by the time they get there, are in want of all kinds of supplies. Horses, Provisions, Smith work, &c, brings cash from them."[24] That first year, Dr. Marcus Whitman estimated that emigrants spent two thousand dollars at Fort Laramie and Fort Bridger, both of which, it should be recalled, were private concerns, not military

---

[19]Entry for 12 June 1850, Abbey, *A Trip*, p. 127; Eaton, *Overland*, p. 112.

[20]Entry for 12 June 1859, Wilkinson, Across the Plains. See also entry for 22 June 1849, Spooner, *Diary;* entry for 1 July 1852, Hampton, Diary (ts.).

[21]Entry for 18 June 1849, Dr. T., Journal; entry for 6 July 1849, Burbank, Diary and Journal, p. 55; entry for 22 June 1852, Anon., Diary, p. 7; entry for 22 June 1852, Kitchell, Diaries, p. 27; entry for 14 June 1854, Sutton, Diary, p. 11.

[22]Entry for 21 July 1859, J. B. Brown, *Journal of a Journey*, p. 37.

[23]Entry for 10 June 1849, W. G. Johnston, *Overland*, p. 93; entry for 20 June 1849, Pease, Diary to Oregon, p. 16.

[24]Letter from James Bridger to P. Chouteau & Co., 10 Dec. 1843, quoted in Unruh, The Plains Across, p. 353.

establishments.[25] By 1849, due to the recent opening of several cutoffs, the bulk of the emigration bypassed Fort Bridger. That is why Vasquez, "accompanied by a considerable party of trappers," went to the Sweetwater: to recapture some of Bridger's lost trade.[26]

Gold-rush travelers who took the old route and stopped at Fort Bridger found a prosperous enterprise, "composed of several log houses & a small enclosure,"[27] with the appearance "of one of our country farm yards."[28] Besides a store filled with buffalo robes priced at five dollars each, there were plenty of horses for sale but no oxen.[29]

If Jim Bridger guessed wrongly about the future of this trail, Pegleg Smith, another mountain man, did better when he located near present Dingle, Idaho. The bulk of the gold rush passed his post with its ample stock of goods. Praised for his hospitality — "a liberal hearted old fellow, with only one leg" and "a jolly but one-legged man" — Smith was described in 1849 as "a fat, high strung good liver [who] makes $100 per day now."[30]

Although there were, from year to year, numerous trading posts on the banks of both the Green[31] and Bear rivers,[32] the most

[25]Lavender, *Westward*, p. 378.

[26]Entry for 10 June 1849, W. G. Johnston, *Overland*, p. 93.

[27]Entry of 17 June 1850, John William Watts, "Diary Written while Crossing the Plains in 1850" (ms., California Historical Society, San Francisco).

[28]Entry for 7 July 1849, Gray, *Off at Sunrise*, p. 56.

[29]Entry for 17 June 1849, W. G. Johnston, *Overland*, p. 107. See also entry for 7 July 1849, Robert Chalmers, "Diary" (ms. California State Library); Eaton, *Overland*, p. 195.

[30]Hospitality: entry for 16 July 1849, I. Hale, "Diary," p. 92. "Liberal hearted": entry for 13 July 1849, Mann, Portion, p. 9. "Jolly": entry for 24 July 1849, Boyle, Diary, quoted in D. L. Morgan, "Notes to Pritchard," p. 158n57. "Stock of goods": entry for 26 June 1849, Hixson, Diary. "Good liver": entry for 24 June 1849, Decker, *Diaries*, p. 106.

[31]Entry for 25 July 1849, Castleman, Diary; entry for 7 Aug. 1849, Bruff, *Journals*, pp. 76, 78; entry for 14 June 1850, Parker, Notes; entry for 30 July 1857, Carpenter, Trip, p. 65; entry for 25 June 1859, Wilkinson, Journal, p. 82. At Green River in 1860 a woman wrote: "I am astonished at the number of trading stations along this road often as many [as] three in the space of a mile" (entry for 20 July 1860, M. C. Fish, Daily Journal, pp. 16-17).

[32]Entry for 27 June 1850, Loomis, *Journal*, p. 62; entry for 6 July 1851, "Daily Journal of Susan Marsh Cranston" (ms., P-A 313, Bancroft Library).

Fort Hall

permanent establishment after Smith's was Fort Hall, belonging to the Hudson's Bay Company. Not far from the American Falls of Snake River, its chief stock in trade during the gold rush was "splendid Horses of all sorts and colors."[33] Some emigrants found the fort's butter and cheese its most memorable feature, others were joyed just to be there.[34] "It was quite a picnic to saunter

[33]Entry for 11 July 1850, Paschel, Diary, p. 38. See also entry for 9 July 1849, Buffum, Diary; entry for 30 Aug. 1843, "Journal of Pierson Barton Reading in His Journey of One Hundred Twenty-Three Days across the Rocky Mountains from Westport on the Missouri River, 450 Miles above St. Louis, to Monterey, California, on the Pacific Ocean, in 1843," ed. Philip B. Bekeart, *Quarterly of the Society of California Pioneers*, 7 (1930): 175.

[34]Entry for 24 June 1849, Cosad, Journal; entry for 30 June 1849, Hixson, Diary.

around the fort for a few hours," one forty-niner told his diary.[35] "It was the most human place we saw since leaving the States," a second wrote home. "A live Yankee had established a dairy, had 40 cows, sold cheese and butter to the emigrants at 25 cts. per pounds."[36] The Yankee was probably one of "a lot of Mormons" there to do business with emigrants.[37] While the fort remained in private hands, its employees were mostly British subjects.

During the first decade of the overland trail — until about 1852 or 1853 — there were few trading posts beyond Fort Hall until reaching either the Carson or Truckee rivers. Later, especially after government stations were established, some businesses located along the Humboldt, most notably at the Meadows and the Sink.[38]

As will be seen when the concept of ownership is discussed, there were even traders on the Forty-Mile Desert. Due to the harshness of the terrain, they could not long remain, going out in the evening to sell to emigrants, returning during the day to the shade trees and cool waters of one of the rivers. The scene was constantly changing. One woman crossing the Forty-Mile Desert in 1852 counted seven or eight trading posts between the Sink and the Carson. Next day a man counted ten.[39]

At both the Truckee and the Carson there always were some businesses. "Groceries for sale here," an 1850 emigrant wrote on reaching the Truckee. "Flour $1 per pound, everything that can be weighted is one dollar per pound."[40] At Ragtown, on the Carson, there was more activity. "Here we found a village of traders," a man from Wisconsin noted that same year, "perhaps twenty in

---

[35]Entry for 30 June 1849, Hixson, Diary.

[36]Letter from C. Truesdale to Joseph Truesdale, 13 Aug. 1849, *Western Reserve Chronicle* (Warren, Ohio), 24 Oct. 1849, p. 2, col. 5.

[37]Entry for 30 June 1849, Hixson, Diary.

[38]Humboldt: entries for 20 July and 1 Aug. 1853, Welsh, Diaries. Meadows: entry for 13 Sept. 1857, Carpenter, Trip, p. 104. Sink: entry for 21 Aug. 1852, Chadwick, Diary; entry for 11 Sept. 1852, Hosley, Journal.

[39]Unruh, The Plains Across, p. 402.

[40]Entry for 22 Sept. 1850, Stine, Letters.

number, living a tent life and speculating off the destitute emigrants."[41] By 1852, there were as many as fifty pole-and-canvas tents lined along the banks of the Carson at Ragtown selling goods to California-bound travelers.[42]

Beyond the rivers, particularly beyond the valleys where Reno and Carson City now stand, emigrants with money generally could obtain supplies. "No more worries about food from here on," a forty-niner recalled, "met speculators (scalpers) with food and all kinds of provisions, twice a day."[43] He was referring to the numerous individuals who came out from California with, as one gold-rusher put it, "provisions and liquors, beef &c, &c., all at a very exorbitant price, all to strap the poor starving emmigrant."[44] Remarkably prevalent were men speculating in animals. By 1852 hundreds were on the trails from California, some meeting emigrants as early as one hundred and thirty miles northeast of the Humboldt Sink.[45]

II *The Emigrant Salesman*

To learn that men made a business of hauling goods onto the trail or recruiting animals for resale to emigrants, reveals but half a tale. The fact that emigrants were vendors as well as buyers also must be examined. As a woman noted in 1852, "people trade all along the road selling brandy, hardbread, flour, bacon, sugar &c."[1]

It should be emphasized that circumstances determined prices — not overland custom, demands of survival, or taught traditions of Christian charity. As at home, the law of supply and demand controlled the market place. "Bought a light waggon of [the]

---

[41]Entry for 20 Aug. 1850, Newcomb, Journal.

[42]Unruh, The Plains Across, p. 402.

[43]Scheller, Autobiography, p. 5.

[44]Entry for 30 July 1850, Christy, *Road.*

[45]Unruh, The Plains Across, p. 403.

[1]Entry for 16 June 1852, Frizzell, *Journal*, p. 25.

Madison Co[mpany] for 55$," a forty-niner noted. "Sold our large waggon, about 200# [*i.e.*, pounds of] bacon and 100# lard for 10$ which is about par with other sales."[2]

The price should not surprise us. It did not surprise the forty-niner. He had left the Missouri overloaded and before traveling very far along the trail had been compelled to put all his mules on one "large wagon." Forced to sell, he expected the buyer to be in control. Moreover, the economics of the local market was as much a factor as it would have been east of the Missouri. The transaction occurred at Fort Laramie, where the grounds were strewn with wagons, tons of bacon, and other provisions.

Forced sales on the overland trail were probably as common as desperation purchases. Perhaps the chief cause was overloading. "[P]eople," the woman of 1852 explained, "do not charge very high for whatever they have to spare, for they do not like to haul it."[3] Lying by on a Sunday, only nineteen days from Independence, a company of forty-niners took inventory of its stock. "We overhauled our loading," one member wrote, "and found we had more provisions on hand than we would be likely to use, and the roads being so fearfully bad we concluded we would dispose of some more flour and bacon. It was of the utmost importance to save our mules in every way we could, for on them we depended to get to our journey's end."[4] Four months later, at the other side of the overland trail, on Lassen's cutoff near Mud Lake, a physician also found he had too much weight. "Sold some things at a sacrifice," he mourned.[5] In truth, he was probably better off. "They are wealthy," a man explained, referring to a company forced to sell excessive weight. "[B]ut on the plains, the man who has the lightest load and the best team is the most independent."[6]

---

[2]Entry for 15 June 1849, Athearn, "Log Book," p. 9.

[3]Entry for 16 June 1852, Frizzell, *Journal*, p. 25.

[4]Entry for 20 May 1849, Hixson, Diary.

[5]Entry for 5 Sept. 1849, McLane, "Leaves," 2:1270.

[6]Entry for 12 June 1864, Katherine Dunlap, "Journal" (ts., photostat, P-I 109, Bancroft Library), pp. 12-13. See also, for forced sales, entry for 1 June 1849, B. C. Clark, "Journey," p. 16; entry for 15 June 1849, Castleman, Diary.

Quality and condition were other familiar economic realities determining the price of goods. Damaged property lost value on the overland trail just as it did east of the Missouri, an economic principle qualified by the fact that a higher percentage of buyers were in need and had to accept what was available. An emigrant from Ohio, traveling through the southeast corner of today's Idaho, sold a horse for fifty-five dollars. He had purchased the animal at Council Bluffs for forty-five dollars, and, despite the fact that his profit was only ten dollars, called the transaction "a very good sale." The reason was that the horse had become "very thin" and he "had expected to leave her ere this."[7]

The seller was traveling in a packing company and, after disposing of his animal, had to put his packs on a horse that was not his property. It belonged to a companion. Despite the fact he was now dependent on another person, the man thought that with the cash he was better off than if he had kept the thin animal. It would be useful to know something about the buyer. Most likely, he had no companions to pack his provisions and concluded he needed the horse no matter how reduced. The dynamics of the overland market are important not because they are surprising but because they are familiar. The more adverse the circumstances the better a product looked to a buyer.[8] Conversely, emigrants wishing to travel faster by packing, sold perfectly good equipment at low prices or simply abandoned it.[9]

Some of the problems encountered by men deciding to pack, yet unwilling to abandon what they no longer could carry, can be gathered from the account of John A. Johnson, traveling with the eight-member Fort Stephenson company from Ohio in 1849. By the time they arrived at Fort Hall on 9 July, some of the party were urging that they pack. A majority apparently refused and a

---

[7]Entry for 30 July 1850, Wheeler, Diary.

[8]On the barren banks of the Humboldt, a "much reduced" horse fetched twenty-five dollars. See entry for 29 July 1850, Kitchell, Diaries, p. 50. On the Forty-Mile Desert cows that had "gave out" were purchased (entry for 9 Sept. 1852, Udell, *Incidents*, p. 75). See also entry for 13 July 1849, Bruff, *Journals*, p. 42; entry for 10 July 1852, Egbert, Record.

[9]Entry for 8 Aug. 1849, Gould, "Diary," pp. 158-59; entry for 22 June 1849, Tolles, Diary, p. 31; Call, Journey, p. 9.

compromise was struck. "[W]e shall probably throw away one wagon first & try that." With extra animals available for hauling the remaining vehicles they might move faster.[10]

The plan succeeded for awhile. The Fort Stephenson company continued on into today's northeastern Nevada, traveling with two other groups whom Johnson referred to as "Captain Titus's" and the "Tiffin Boys." Then, somewhere along the Humboldt River, twenty-one days after the Fort Hall compromise, a majority voted to pack. After cutting up Captain Titus's wagon for lumber to manufacture packs

> we advertised by the roadside wagons, provisions & clothing *for sale*. During the day while our packs were being rapidly constructed we sold to ox teams who wanted lighter wagons our remaining two & the Tiffin's Boys for $10 each and also sold out our clothing & other articles that could not be packed at about the same destruction [sic] rates; except provisions which commanded exhorbitant prices for instance — bacon & flour sold for 25 cts a pound & sugar for 50 cts to $1.00 per pound & we was offered $1.25 per pound but had none to spare even at that price. Money in this trip seems to have lost its charm; and articles necessary or desirable for the completion of our journey *only* are deemed *valuable*. A good healthy mule could scarcely be bought for $1000. We thought we would try & pack the whole of our provisions through although we had more coffee, bacon, flour & rice than we need for the trip.[11]

Titus's men and the Tiffin Boys numbered eleven. Added to the eight of Fort Stephenson, that was a total of nineteen making, Johnson believed, "probably the largest [company of packers] now on the road except [Edwin] Bryants some days ahead who packed from the States." It is possible that, due to its size, the combined party had more surplus property than most groups preparing to pack. Faced with a choice of abandoning, giving away, or selling, Johnson and his companions decided to sell. Arriving at Humboldt Meadows three days later, it was decided

---

[10]Entry for 9 July 1849, J. A. Johnson, Note Book.

[11]Ibid., entry for 30 July 1849.

to drive over on to the river & get as good grass as possible & lay by that day & the next in order to prepare our animals for the stretch [the Forty-Mile Desert] & also to sell or throw away every article of provision & other property not absolutely necessary to this journey into California (excepting such light articles of clothing as each one felt safe in risking on his riding mule [)]. I was left on the part of our company at the Slue with some coffee, bacon & rice to sell & the rest passed over to the river, Fox remaining with me to sell for the company & the Tiffin boys.

Johnson succeeded in disposing of all he had for sale at what he thought favorable prices: bacon for twelve and a half cents a pound, rice for between ten and twelve cents a pound, and coffee from twelve and a half to fifteen cents a pound. More noteworthy for a theme to be developed in a later chapter, was the fact that the three companies, though making joint traveling decisions, did not mingle their property. Johnson sold for the Fort Stephenson group, Fox acted for Titus and the Tiffin Boys, although it is not said whether he kept one or separate accounts.[12]

Much depended on good fortune — being at a certain place at an opportune moment. A chance encounter could mean the difference between a hungry night and a full stomach. Just after crossing the Truckee River for the last time, in the vicinity of today's California-Nevada line, a young pharmacist from Saint Louis halted for the night. "One train with 9 or 10 encamped close by and they told us that they had nothing but jerked beef and coffee to eat for three day[s]. Mr. B[owman] sold them 5 lbs of flour for $2.50."[13]

Three months earlier, the pharmacist had met a company herding a drove of sheep said to contain ten thousand head. "Bought a sheep and dressed it," he reported.[14] Without commenting, he was saying something about the role pure chance played on the overland trail. Just to be in an area where an animal was

---

[12]Ibid., entry for 2 Aug. 1849.

[13]Entry for 6 Oct. 1853, Woodworth, Diary, pp. 51-52.

[14]Ibid., entry for 2 June 1853, p. 10.

killed could mean fresh beef. "We passed the Batavia and an Illinois Company," a forty-niner wrote, "[the] last had killed an ox, and we bought some meat of them."[15]

Similar good luck occurred when meeting persons who, for one reason or another, were returning to the states; they often sold cheaply.[16] It was just as fortunate to be near someone possessing a needed product and willing to sell. While a few emigrants carried "suitable running gears" with them,[17] it is surprising how many ventured onto the overland trail without spare parts. More surprising was the number able to buy what they needed on the spur of the moment. "Just as we got into Goose Creek," a forty-niner wrote in his diary, "we broke the axel tree that we put in a few days ago. We got it out of the wagon and in a few minutes a man came along with an extra one, and we bought it."[18]

Not only the availability of goods, but prices depended on where an emigrant was at a particular moment. At Fort Kearny and Fort Laramie, where wagons were sold at one-quarter their cost, for as little as two dollars and fifty cents, or just abandoned,[19] an emigrant might find no market for goods worth considerable money at home. During 1849, for example, flour at Fort Kearny was being offered at a dollar a hundred pounds. Much of it could not be sold and was left to rot on the ground.[20] Later that year, on Lassen's cutoff, a District-of-Columbia company needing flour

---

[15]Entry for 6 Oct. 1849, Bruff, *Journals*, pp. 207-08.

[16]Entry for 27 May 1849, Staples, "Diary," p. 87; entry for 31 May 1849, Cosad, Journal; entry for 20 May 1853, Allyn, "Journal," p. 389.

[17]J. Hale, *California*, p. 6.

[18]Entry for 3 Aug. 1849, Armstrong, "Diary," p. 56. For similar purchases see: entry for 15 June 1849, Pritchard, *Diary*, p. 91; entry for 22 June 1849, Graham, Journal, p. 11; entry for 14 Aug. 1852, C.E.M. Adams, "Crossing the Plains," p. 306. A similar type of purchase occurred when a needed item was found. Just a few miles beyond where the axletree was purchased in 1849, "One of Anabel's company broke the axletree of his wagon. Having passed two broken wagons about one mile back, they returned and obtained one that was made to answer a very good purpose" (entry for 26 Aug. 1853, Williams, "Diary," p. 217).

[19]Entry for 24 May 1849, I. Hale, "Diary," p. 65; letter of 24 Aug. 1849, Senter, *Crossing*; entry for 28 June 1849, Castleman, Diary.

[20]Hannon, "Introduction and Notes," p. 109.

had to pay thirty-five cents a pound.[21] "Money does not here represent the value of property," a forty-niner theorized. "If one man has a thing that another wants, he will give twenty times its value in something he does not want. There is a great deal of trading done in this way. . . . "[22]

Perhaps the most remarkable fact is not prices, but what could be purchased on the overland trail. This was especially true of animals which, after stampeding, were often irretrievably lost. In 1846, for example, the cattle belonging to a train of about thirty wagons were stampeded at night, supposedly by buffalo. Even when the company searched for a week, one hundred and twenty head were missing, of which sixty-two were oxen. One might think that three years before the crowds of the gold rush, the owners had no chance to obtain replacements. The expected, however, was not always the rule on the overland trail. "[T]hey managed to buy some cows from other trains, and by working those and what cows and oxen they had, they were enabled to proceed on their journey."[23] Similarly, during a year even more sparse, 1848, one company spent three days far down the Platte searching for thirty head of cattle without finding them. "A trying time," a woman wrote in her diary. "So many of us having to get teams, had to hire, borrow, buy, just as we could. Had to take raw cattle, cows, or anything we could get. Some had to apply to other companies for help; at last we moved off."[24]

It must not be thought that everything needed could be obtained. In the area of the Sweetwater, just before arriving at South Pass, Charles Gray, a forty-niner from New York City, who investigated the bulletin by the side of the road mentioned earlier, was anxious to purchase an ox. He went to the place, but found the stock either inferior to his needs or too dear for his

---

[21]Entry for 16 Oct. 1849, Bruff, *Journals*, p. 225.

[22]Entry for 28 June 1849, Wilkins, *An Artist*, p. 48. He was at Fort Laramie. Also at the fort on 7 June that year, another emigrant purchased "a Boat wagon that cost in the states 175 Dol[lars] and I got it for 25 Dol and sold ours for 2 Dol" (Robinson, *Journey*, p. 11).

[23]Elam Brown, quoted in D. L. Morgan, "Introduction and Notes," p. 390n28.

[24]Entry for 2 July 1848, Geer, "Diary," p. 158.

pocketbook. The animals "were good for nothing & the price very great." Continuing on, he took the longer route by Fort Bridger, hoping there "to buy a yoke of cattle, a horse, a coffee mill, & a buffalo robe, all of which I succeeded in getting except the cattle."[25]

It may not be what we would anticipate finding in the wilderness, but the notice Gray spotted near South Pass was not unique. Emigrant vendors often advertised. Going along Goose Creek a forty-niner saw an announcement, "written in a fair hand," and stuck on a stick by the side of the trail. "Public Sale," it proclaimed. "Will be sold, on Sunday, 2d Sept. on the head of Mary's [Humboldt] River, Stores, and a lot of merchandize. Emigrants in the rear will do well to be there, as great bargains will be sold." The notice was dated five days before the proposed sale and signed "Wm Mullin & Co."[26]

Sometimes rumors circulated along the trail that "a company a few miles higher up, in the valley, had flour to spare," and a party would dispatch members to buy what they could.[27] Better still was to stumble upon one of the very rare caravans selling goods as it moved westward. An example was "Pomeroys train," encountered near Pacific Springs during the third week of July 1849. "Pomeroys," explained an emigrant who purchased "some cheese & liquor" from it, "is a train of 40 waggons, he & his brother are traders taking goods & groceries to California, & they supply the emigrants with liquor & groceries."[28]

With provisions and liquor — especially liquor — the Pomeroys had the merchandise that, aside from animals, was most salable

---

[25]Entries for 28 June and 7 July 1849, Gray, *Off at Sunrise*, pp. 48, 55.

[26]Entry for 31 Aug. 1849, Bruff, *Journals*, p. 159. For advertising see also entry for 13 Aug. 1849, J. W. Wood, Diaries.

[27]Entries for 8 Aug. and 14 Sept. 1849, Bruff, *Journals*, pp. 78, 174.

[28]Entry for 18 July 1849, Lotts, "Copy," p. 5. A similar, if more specialized, enterprise was reported the next year. "James Philly was a prominent tobacco grower, and, knowing well that the average tobacco chewer would rather go without his bread than his tobacco, he loaded a wagon with it, for which he paid twenty cents per pound, and long before he reached Fort Laramie, ... he was selling it at one dollar per pound" (Thissell, *Crossing the Plains*, p. 34).

on the overland trail. Emigrants frequently mentioned buying whiskey or brandy from passing trains.[29] Costs could be high: eight dollars a gallon paid in 1849 for brandy,[30] sixteen dollars a gallon offered in 1850.[31] According to one forty-niner, what he called the "Missouri whisky cart" sold some rather inferior stuff. The proprietors, he claimed, watered the alcohol, "and with dried apples, peaches, &c. manufacture all kinds of liquors. They sell a dilute whiskey at 50¢ per pint, and expect that on the route, and in California they will realize a fortune from the proceeds: but I doubt much that they will ever get a gallon of it into California."[32]

The impression must not be left that anything labeled "whiskey" was a certain seller. "On the River Bank opposite me," an Indiana judge wrote in his journal while resting near the Sweetwater, "sits a young man with some boxes and kegs about him and a sign up 'Whiskey & Soda Water' but I have not observed since here that he has many customers. Saw one young man pay him 15¢ for a glass of *soda,* which I judged to be simply a foam made with 'Saleratus' and some cheap acid."[33]

The young man had the right idea if the wrong product. When the article was genuine, profits could be great, although a high price did not always persuade an owner to sell. Troops stationed at the forts were the best customers. It was a soldier who in 1850 had offered sixteen dollars for a gallon of brandy.

An Englishman going overland described the garrison at Fort Kearny as "a most unsoldierly-looking lot." Writing for publication and well aware of the prejudices of his British readers, he dwelled upon the troops' appearance — "unshaven, unshorn, with patched uniforms and lounging gait" — and saw no reason to explain how so decrepit a group possessed spending money. "Both men and

---

[29]Entry for 16 June 1849, Chamberlain, Diary; entry for 17 July 1849, Castleman, Diary.

[30]Entry for 6 July 1849, Burbank, Diary and Journal, p. 55; entry for 23 July 1849, *Geiger-Bryarly* Journal, p. 163.

[31]Entry for 30 May 1850, C. W. Smith, Journal.

[32]Entries for 6 Aug, and 17 July 1849, Bruff, *Journals,* pp. 73, 47.

[33]Entry for 21 June 1852, Crane, Journal.

officers were ill off for some necessaries, such as flour and sugar; the privates being more particular in their inquiries after whiskey, for which they offered one dollar the half-pint; but we had none to sell them even at that tempting price."[34]

[34]William Kelly, *Across the Rocky Mountains, from New York to California: With a Visit to the Celebrated Mormon Colony at the Great Salt Lake* (London: Simms and M'Intyre, 1852), p. 78.

Selling the Elephant

5 | THE CONTOURS OF TRANSFER

That soldiers stationed at Fort Kearny in 1849 offered extraordinary sums for whiskey may for an Englishman of that day have confirmed some preconceived notions concerning the United States Army. For those not sharing his prejudices, the same fact reveals something concerning the nature of property rights and respect for ownership in antebellum America. Attitudes of military men are not different from those of overland emigrants. Craving whiskey, the soldiers, by offering to purchase, acknowledged it was private property. Also accepting the economics of a seller's market in which the owner set the price, they were prepared to bid high.[1]

The law of sales cut both ways. Prices were less favorable when emigrants unloaded surplus weight at military stations. Then a buyer's market prevailed. A merchant from Liberty, Missouri, for example, stopped at Fort Kearny "and sold 900 pounds of flour and bacon at two cents a pound — pretty cheap for such goods, after hauling them so far through the mud, but our purchaser was sutler to Uncle Sam's soldiers, of course he had to make a few hundred per cent."[2]

Emigrants probably received better prices at private trading posts when dispensing provisions like flour, beans, rice, salt, soap,

---

[1] Army officers adhered to the same code. They did not requisition from emigrants what they needed for the service without compensation. A forty-niner was on Lassen's cutoff in northern California when he met a party of United States engineers. "I sold them one ounce of quinine for twenty dollars," he noted in his diary much as if it were an everyday occurrence (entry for 13 Sept. 1849, I. Hale, "Diary," p. 129).

[2] Entry for 21 May 1849, Hixson, Diary. "Good wagons here bring from 4 to 30 dollars, mules from 100 to 150 dollars," another forty-niner wrote of private traders at Fort Laramie. "That is you sell your waggons to the traders at the Fort and buy from them their mules. Everything you buy cost four times as much as it is worth and everything you sell bring perhaps one tenth its value" (entry for 3 June 1849, Dr. T., Journal).

and whiskey. At least diaries seldom complain about buyers driving too hard a bargain. Of course, as traders were located along the trail hoping to sell high, it is not surprising they sometimes paid what emigrants asked. They were dealing with the very class to which they planned to resell what they purchased. Mountain men, on the other hand, could have taken a radically different attitude toward overland travelers. It might be thought they would be less inclined to respect the property of emigrants who, after all, were intruding into their domain and threatening to disrupt the Indian peace upon which the fur trade depended.

That emigrants, as a general rule, felt their property safe in the presence of mountain men, and expected that if mountain men wished to acquire it they would pay the asking price, is a telling fact. Indeed, some of these men even sought out emigrants to make purchases. Philander Kellogg was a trapper transporting seven hundred dollars worth of fur in 1846 when three of his mules and two horses were taken by Indians. As the raiders were said to be Apache, the incident probably occurred far south of the Oregon Trail. Yet Kellogg rode north to meet the emigration and buy new horses.[3] Thirteen years later six young men started for the Pike's Peak gold rush with two years' provisions. Before getting to the junction leading to Colorado, they heard discouraging news about Pike's Peak and decided to go to California — now overloaded with food and dry goods no longer needed. At a branch of Green River, Jack Robinson, saying he had been a mountain man with Kit Carson, rode over to their camp to inquire if they had anything to sell. The young men spent the next day bargaining with the old trapper, selling him supplies "to the amount of $500.00 in cash and cattle." In the extant account of this transaction, there is no indication that the mountain man contended that because the six emigrants did not need the goods and he did, their ownership rights were compromised by his equitable

---

[3]Letter from B.F.E. Kellogg to Preston G. Gesford, 5 July 1846, printed in *Overland in 1846*, ed. D. L. Morgan, p. 580.

claim of necessity. The bargaining seems to have been conducted much as it would have been back in the young men's home state of Maine: between a legal owner and a person who wished to become a legal owner.[4]

There is a second point to be marked about that sale: the six young men received both cash and cattle from Robinson. Mixing money and goods was a common method of payment on the overland trail. So, too, was straight barter. Animals were swapped one (or more) for one (or more), as in 1849, when a company "traded a mule for a horse"[5] or in 1862 when a party of emigrants "traded a yoke of large fat oxen that were footsore" to a train of government wagons "for a yoke of sinewy long horned oxen that were better able to stand the hardships of the trip."[6] On a single day the Washington City Company crossing the alkaline barren between the North Platte and the Sweetwater exchanged first with a party planning to pack "a couple of indifferent common saddles for a fine wagon," next "made a similar bargain with another company," and finally "[g]ave a bag of indian meal to a neighboring company, for about 2 bushels [of] biscuit."[7]

Despite the large amounts of money circulating on the overland trail, the importance of barter cannot be exaggerated. It was used to transfer just about every type of property. An example is the packer from Michigan who owned some meat and balanced his diet by bartering. Meeting a wagon on Lassen's cutoff during 1849, he "struck up a trade with its owner; for one of the ribs of beef he got some flour, a red pepper and the use of a camp-kettle."[8] Ten years later an emigrant on the Platte "traded a watch for some groceries"[9] and nearby another fifty-niner "swap[p]ed a

---

[4]William Whitney, "His Reminiscences, 1909-1924, of an Overland Journey to California from Iowa in 1859" (ts., California Historical Society, San Francisco), p. 12.

[5]Entry for 21 May 1849, Cosad, Journal.

[6]J. G. Fish, Crossing, p. 4. For similar barter of an animal for another animal or a rifle for an animal see entries for 11 June and 21 July 1859, Chillson, Diary.

[7]Entry for 22 July 1849, Bruff, *Journals*, pp. 51, 123-24.

[8]Goldsmith, *Overland*, p. 81.

[9]Entry for 16 May 1859, Chillson, Diary.

pair of leather Boots to a trader for one pair of shoes and two pair of moccasins."[10]

A feature of these exchanges deserving special notice is the bailment of the camp kettle. The wagon owner bartered its use for some of the Michigan packer's meat. Here is another overland clue to property and ownership concepts in mid-century America. The owner was not using the kettle at the moment, yet did not lend it to the borrower, he rented it for a portion of the beef.

There is a related case illustrating the same point, and though its theme is premature, as it must be considered later in detail, the facts may be mentioned now as it involved barter. It shows the exclusiveness to which overland travelers regarded rights to private property. Even an item easily lent at no loss to the owner had to be purchased or bailed at a price accepted by the owner or its use could not be demanded. The tale is told by Lorenzo Sawyer, a lawyer and future member of the California supreme court. He was traveling in 1850 down the Humboldt River, the time and place of the most severe shortages in overland history. "We are offered," he noted in his journal, "a dollar a pound for flour by an Ohio company, but we could not spare any even at that price." Sawyer and his companions soon learned that, due to the doctrine of exclusive ownership, they would have to part with what they could not afford to be without for far less than the paper profits they had been offered. The Ohioans, asserting the same exclusive rights in property that Sawyer had asserted when refusing to sell them flour, drove a hard bargain. "Having no sythe, and finding one necessary to procure grass from the miry bottom, we were obliged to purchase one of the Ohio company. They would not sell for money, so we paid twenty pounds of flour which we would not for money, each wagon paying its proportion."[11]

---

[10]Entry for 1 June 1859, John Wesley Powell, "Book to California" (ts., C-F 127, Bancroft Library). A company of West Virginians bartered with a "Government train" powder for whiskey — "a canister of powder for a canteen of whiskey" (entry for 31 May 1849, *Geiger-Bryarly Journal*, p. 91).

[11]Entry for 29 June 1850, L. Sawyer, *Across the Plains*, p. 76.

We may regret that Sawyer did not comment on the transaction. As a lawyer he might have told us much about how his fellow emigrants viewed property and exclusive rights to ownership. Perhaps his silence, suggesting that he took the Ohio company's right for granted, tells us more than any analysis. Fortunately, there is no need to make the same complaint concerning overland business practices. We are able to learn something about them because many emigrants were interested enough to comment on their dealings with traders.

The chief stock in trade of overland merchants was draft and riding animals. Though they sold some provisions and a small variety of Indian-manufactured goods, such as buffalo robes and moccasins, traders anticipated making their money on horses, mules, and oxen. They bought animals from emigrants, recruited them, and sold them back at a profit. A representative transaction occurred when a man from Koscuisko, Indiana, passing by a Sioux village in far western Nebraska, "traded a jaded broken down horse with a French trader taking in exchange an American animal which had been obtained from a last years emigrant."[12] In 1852, another man, near a village of Shoshoni at Soda Springs, exchanged "even up" with a trader a "lame horse" for "a small native mule." Everyone benefited. The emigrant's new mule proved the best riding animal in his company and the trader recruited the "lame horse" into a substantial piece of property. "I afterwards," the emigrant wrote, "saw the horse I had traded for the mule in Sacramento, hitched to a dray. His owner valued him at four hundred dollars."[13]

It appears both these transactions were straight exchanges. Swapping between emigrants and traders occurred occasionally as when an Ohio forty-niner "traded two oxen for one to a

---

[12]Entry for 25 May 1850, W. S. McBride, Diary.

[13]Cole, *Early Days*, pp. 78-79. Passengers wishing to leave the slow-moving Pioneer Line exchanged their tickets of passage for an outfit shortly before the South Pass (*Notes Preparatory to a Biography of Richard Hayes McDonald of San Francisco, California*, comp. and ed. Frank V. McDonald [Cambridge, University Press, 1881], pp. 65-66).

Mormon,"[14] or, as a companion may more accurately have explained it, "traded two lame for one not very sound ox."[15] As a general rule, however, even when animals were bartered something additional changed hands — usually cash. "[T]he best ox in our team died this A.M. W.D. traded his mate for a cow and some money," was a more typical entry in overland diaries.[16] In fact, the sum demanded was generally fixed. "We could exchange almost any kind of a horse with them by giving $30. difference," was the way a forty-niner described doing business with traders from Fort Bridger.[17]

From what diarists say it seems these traders did not bargain. They had a flat rate or what one emigrant called "the accustomed $10."[18] In some cases they asked ten dollars, in others twenty, and some, like those from Fort Bridger in 1849, wanted as much as thirty dollars for each transaction. Dealing with French traders at the Big Sandy, one man gave "a little cow and 10 dollars for a three year old steer in very good order." (His father-in-law, purchasing "one immensely large ox," but apparently not swapping an animal in exchange, paid fifty dollars.)[19] At Scotts Bluff another emigrant "traded both his horses for a mule giving ten dollars besides."[20] Similarly, at a trading post just beyond Fort Laramie, an 1852 company "traded our lame ox for another and gave $20 dollars."[21]

Obviously, the condition of property being transferred was generally immaterial. "These mountain traders do not care much about the kind of animal they get," a forty-niner explained, "but must have at least $10 to boot." He had traded to Pegleg Smith a

[14]Entry for 21 July 1849, Armstrong, "Diary," p. 46.
[15]Entry for 21 July 1849, Banks, "Diary," p. 47.
[16]Entry for 5 July 1859, Chillson, Diary.
[17]Dr. T., quoted in D. L. Morgan, "Notes to Pritchard," p. 155n46.
[18]Entry for 30 June 1849, Hixson, Diary.
[19]Entry for 26 July 1857, Carpenter, Trip, p. 60.
[20]Entry for 20 June 1853, Woodworth, Diary, p. 17.
[21]Entry for 27 May 1852, W. Johnston, Diary, p. 4.

mule, "which had become somewhat jaded, for a span of four-year-old halfbreed, iron grey horses," plus the "accustomed" ten dollars. "This was the slightest mule we had. We called her the race filly, but it would have been the same had we proposed to trade the best mule we had, we would have had to pay $10 difference."[22]

Without direct testimony from overland traders, we must guess why they charged emigrants a set amount when exchanging animals, rather than dealing for the highest profits from each transaction. It may be they were lazy and saving themselves trouble. Put in commercial terms, however, it seems a reasonable surmise that they were collecting a fee for doing business. After all, it is not far fetched to analogize these traders to brokers. They served as a clearing house for horses, mules, and oxen between successive waves of emigration.

II The Sale of Services

We well might wish emigrant diarists were as revealing about their own notions of valid transfer as about the business practices of overland traders. Hardly anything, for example, is said concerning whether they thought a warranty of soundness ran with property sold. The fact is not surprising when we consider that the question may seldom have arisen due to the pattern of life on the overland trail. A seller might be encountered only once along the route. Before a defect in the animal or wagon sold became known, he could be many miles away, either ahead or behind, never to be seen again even if he acted in good faith and believed the product sound in all respects.

Although no hard-and-fast rules can be expounded or general principles distilled, one clear case has come to hand suggesting, if little else, that "buyer beware" was not the legal norm. As nothing is said about expressed promises, the evidence is inconclusive, but what we have indicates that a warranty of soundness might be

---

[22]Entry for 26 June 1849, Hixson, Diary.

implied on the overland trail, at least in the sale of animals. "Bought a yoke of Oxen today for $60," a purchaser writes, "and found come to use them one was lame and of no use to us returned them and got our money again."[1]

Although extant diaries and letters tell us little about warranty of soundness, they are replete with evidence concerning another aspect of sales: the transfer of services. One rule was immutable — on the overland trail an individual's skills, profession, and time were private property to be disposed of as the owner saw fit, for whatever price he was willing to accept.

The service convertible into saleable property that was most indigenous to the overland trail was knowledge of the road. It was a commodity especially valuable during the early years before the trail was well marked or guidebooks available. It should be recalled that the first emigration to cross the continent to California — in 1841 — knew nothing about the route except that it lay westward. The tiny party, therefore, waited for the veteran mountain man, Thomas Fitzpatrick, who was guiding Father Pierre Jean De Smet and two other Catholic priests to the Flathead nation. He conducted the emigrants as far as Soda Springs and then, while Fitzpatrick went north with those to whom he had leased his services, the California-bound travelers, thirty-two in number, wandered blindly toward the setting sun, trusting fortune rather than knowledge of geography to bring them through.[2]

As time went on fewer and fewer companies wanted a guide, but those that did knew they had to negotiate agreements for the purchase of services. It is a surprising fact that during the early days of overland travel, these sales often occurred beyond the line of settlement. The California emigration of 1843, for

---

[1]Entry for 28 May 1850, Pomroy, Diary, p. 14. For an example of an emigrant who could not exercise a warranty even if expressed because of the dynamics of travel consider the following: "Traded a cow and calf today for a steer to yoke up with the odd one. And find after using him half a day that we have been cheated as he can't stand it to travel" (entry for 6 July 1853, Knight, "Diary," p. 45).

[2]Bidwell, *Echoes*, pp. 23-39.

example, had gotten as far as Fort Bridger when it met Joseph Reddeford Walker. Having explored with both Bonneville and Frémont, he was one of the most knowledgeable mountain men of that day. The emigrants hired him as guide for $300.[3] Another company that same year had to settle for Indian guides,[4] while in 1844 the Stevens party, also far from the Missouri River, retained the famed trapper Caleb Greenwood.[5]

During the gold-rush era there was less need for guides. The trail was well rutted and fear of Indian hostilities had more or less dissipated. A guide's chief value was his ability to recognize potable water, his familiarity with poisonous grass, and his knowledge of the best methods for fording streams and crossing deserts, information that by 1849 was supposedly available in several guidebooks. As a result, most companies in that and subsequent years did not bother to retain a guide. Those that did paid lower fees than might have been expected. The large Washington City and California Mining Association voted to hire a young man, compensating him with "the use of a good riding horse, and equipment, exemption from guard duty, and $75 cash when we *got in*."[6] At the same time, by way of contrast, a one-wagon partnership of six members retained a guide hoping he would be an inducement luring other parties to join them in a traveling company. In return "for his board with us," he was to be their "pilot" "across to California." In other words, for services rendered each day, he was paid a daily ration of food from the

---

[3]Helen S. Giffen, *Trail-Blazing Pioneer: Colonel Joseph Ballinger Chiles* (San Francisco: J. Howell, 1969), pp. 39-40.

[4]Entries for 10, 12, and 17 Oct. 1843, Reading, Diary, pp. 24, 25, 27. Also in 1843, another Oregon-bound party lost its guide on reaching Fort Hall. The emigrants took up a collection, raised four hundred dollars, and purchased the services of Dr. Marcus Whitman as guide (Lavender, *Westward*, p. 379). During 1849 three separate traveling companies in which today is New Mexico combined resources and offered one thousand dollars to "an old trapper comrade of [Kit] Carson, to pilot us through . . . to Southern California" (Hudgins, California in 1849, p. 5).

[5]G.R. Stewart, *Trail*, p. 57.

[6]Entry for 2 May 1849, Bruff, *Journals*, pp. 7, 442n33.

mess and perhaps given a corner of the wagon for his blankets and a few personal items.[7]

There were other vendible services more or less indigenous to the overland trail. Some more properly belong with a discussion of contracts for hire than the transfer of service. One example is road building,[8] another is guard duty.

A few impoverished emigrants may have started overland depending on such work. One was a "little Irishman," walking to the Pacific from Utica, New York, with no baggage except an old shirt in which he carried "about a dozen cakes of *hard bread.*" When questioned, the man "said he oftentimes stood guard half the night in order to procure some provisions."[9]

More specialized services for which men were paid included swimming cattle across swift, deep rivers,[10] tracking missing cattle,[11] carrying letters back east,[12] and hunting for fresh meat.[13]

---

[7]Letter of 27 April 1849, Muscott, Letters. There were, of course, 1849 guides who sold their services for cash compensation only. See Webster, *Gold Seekers,* p. 21; Shaw, *Across the Plains,* p. 12; entry for 15 May 1849, McCall, *Wayside Notes,* p. 20. Among those forced by circumstances and inexperience with frontier conditions to hire a guide was a party of Cherokees (Bieber, *Southern Trails,* p. 341).

[8]During 1852, three emigrants, aged twenty-two, twenty, and sixteen, decided to build a new road beyond Bear River and "hired some men to assist for a day or two, to cut brush" (entry for 18 July 1852, Egbert, Record, p. 35; Eaton, *Overland,* p. 228). The task may have taken longer than anticipated. Five days later a man recorded that he had stopped to work "for an Emigrant that is making a road around the mountains." He was paid "$2.00 per day" (entries for 23 and 24 July 1852, Hampton, Diary [ts.]). Similarly an Ohio company hired slaves from another train to wash clothes (entry for 7 April 1850, Lane, Diary).

[9]Entry for 15 June 1850, W. S. McBride, Diary. One emigrant, who insisted that guard duty was the most disagreeable task on the trail, says men took the job for pay. "[S]ome of the boys are hiring Peter Calibaugh to stand guard for them   Calibaugh is a Du[t]chman and would do anything for money his fee for standing guard is 50 cents" (entry for 17 May 1852, Keen, Diary, p. 21).

[10]Entry for 7 May 1853, Owen, My Trip, p. 7; entry for 27 July 1853, Washburn, Journal, p. 23; entry for 8 Aug. 1853, Longworth, *Diary,* p. 39; entry for 10 Aug. 1853, Hines, "Diary," p. 110; entries for 2 and 29 Sept. 1853, J. Smith, Account; entry for 3 July 1862, "Journal Kept while Crossing the Plains by Ada Millington," ed. Charles G. Clark, *Southern California Quarterly,* 59 (1977): 150.

[11]Entries for 13 and 14 July 1848, Geer, "Diary," p. 159; entry for 15 Oct. 1849, Powell, Diary, p. 139.

[12]Entry for 11 July 1850, Loveland, Diary, p. 27; entry for 30 May 1852, Thorniley,

Philander Kellogg, the trapper whose mule and horses were taken by Apaches in 1846 and who came up to the trail to buy new animals, was hired by the emigrants to do a job at which they were not skilled — kill buffalo.[14]

Many trades, professions, and services marketable at home were equally merchantable on the overland trail. Just as emigrants brought the law of the east out into the wilderness, so they brought the economy of the east, and diaries tell us of druggists being paid for filling prescriptions,[15] wheelwrights for setting tires,[16] farriers for shoeing horses,[17] and blacksmiths for a variety of work from repairing wagons to making screws.[18]

The picture may be given flesh by considering the profession most in demand and most frequently retained on the overland trail. Emigrants had no need for lawyers, but there were times when physicians were more essential than draft animals. Fortunately for the sick, there were many of them. "Doctors," a forty-niner wrote, "are more numerously represented among the emigrants in proportion to their number among the inhabitants of the country than in any other part of [the] community."[19]

Although most of the large joint-stock organizations had at

Diary; entry for 7 June 1852, A. N. Graham, Journal, p. 9.

[13]Entry for 5 May 1849, Decker, *Diaries*, p. 66.

[14]Letter from B.F.E. Kellogg to Preston G. Gesford, 5 July 1846, printed in *Overland in 1846*, ed. D. L. Morgan, p. 580.

[15]Entry for 19 June 1853, Woodworth, Diary, p. 16. See also entry for 2 July 1849, Caldwell, "Notes," p. 1256.

[16]Entry for 15 Sept. 1849, Gray, Passage; entry for 17 July 1851, Welsh, Diaries.

[17]Entry for 12 July 1851, Welsh, Diaries.

[18]Entries for 12 to 23 May 1849, B.C. Clark, "Journey," pp. 11-12; entry for 8 June 1853, Abraham Hite, "Diary of a Trip across the Plains; March 28-October 27, 1853" (ts., California State Library), p. 4. Some companies not only had a smith, but carried a forge and a complete set of tools. Occasionally the smith would stop, set up shop, and sell his services to passers by (entry for 2 July 1849, Lord, Journal; entry for 12 July 1851, Welsh, Diaries). See also entries for 17 to 19 May, 1850, Cagwin, Diary. However, most smith work was probably done at trading posts. For example: entry for 8 July 1852, Conyers, "Diary," p. 461.

[19]Letter of 2 May 1849, quoted in Potter, "Introduction," p. 85n20.

least one physician as a member,[20] the smaller companies — especially the traveling companies formed on the border — could neither obtain nor afford one. Consequently, as a Wisconsin emigrant said, "[o]ur surgeon has frequent calls from other trains." During the height of the cholera epidemic of 1849 along the Platte, physicians were said to "pass in both directions, in full speed to visit some poor sufferer."[21] Emigrants needing medical help generally assumed they could obtain it.[22] Finding a packer who had accidently shot himself near the Humboldt, a company from Iowa confidently "stationed a man by the roadside, who asked the passers by for a doctor, finally got a doctor, from across the river."[23]

Few commercial incidents are more frequently recorded in diaries than accounts of companies without surgeons seeking physicians from other companies,[24] or of doctors from one train going to attend sick people traveling with a second train.[25] It was not always an easy physical task. One physician wrote of

---

[20]"Binding the Elephant," pp. 292-93. Some organizations elected "surgeons," and the elected captain of one of the forty-niner companies from the Cherokee nation has been called "a credit to the medical profession." Read, "Diseases," p. 261.

[21]Entry for 9 June 1849, Howell, Diary, p. 7.

[22]Though they were not always successful. See, e.g., entry for 6 June 1852, Hickman, *Overland Journey*, p. 8.

[23]Haight, Trip, p. 28.

[24]Entry for 14 June 1846, Bryant, *Journal*, p. 68; entry for 7 June 1847, "Diary of Loren B. Hastings: A Pioneer of 1847," *Transactions of the Fifty-First Annual Reunion of the Oregon Pioneer Association* (Portland, Ore.: F. W. Baltes, 1926), p. 14; entry for 16 May 1849, Gould, "Diary," p. 76; entry for 19 June 1849, Pattison, Diary, p. 14; entry for 21 June 1849, McCall, *Wayside Notes*, p. 40; entry for 11 Aug. 1849, Dewolf, Diary, p. 33; entry for 28 June 1850, Steele, *Across the Plains*, p. 79-80; entry for 23 May 1851, Welsh, Diaries; entry for 5 July 1852, Graham, Journal, p. 14.

[25]Entry for 10 July 1849, Parke, Notes; entry for 14 July 1849, B. C. Clark, "Journey," p. 28; entries for 21 and 22 May 1850, Maynard, Pocket Diary; entry for 20 June 1850, W. S. McBride, Diary; entries for 1, 4, 9, 10 and 13 June 1852, C. L. Richardson, Journal, pp. 43-60; entry for 11 July 1852, Wayman, *Diary*, p. 69; entry for 14 Aug. 1853, Bradway, Journal. There were even professional consultations between medical men, especially when diseases were encountered for the first time. Seeing a case of mountain fever, one doctor "got alarmed and called in another Physician" (Evans, "Letter," p. 41).

traveling six miles to treat several sick people,[26] another went nine miles, [27] a homeopath fifteen miles over "our hardest road,"[28] and David Maynard had to travel so far he eventually moved in with his patient. "Left the comp[any] of Distress[e]d," he wrote, "the widow ill in Body as well as mind at 1/2 past 4 in the morning with a Light Encouragement of returning to & assisting them along. & overtook our Comp[any] at 20 miles at Noon. Returned & met them in trouble Enough & traveled with them till Night & Left & overtook our Comp[any] 3 miles ahead. Made arrangements & was ready in the morn[ing] to shift my Duds [to] the widow's waggon when they came up."[29]

It has been claimed that overland physicians charged nothing or very little. There is some evidence supporting this assertion.[30] One allopath, at least, said he "made no charges for advice or medicine" until selling twenty-five cents worth of opium while camped at Devil's Gate.[31] Also, a forty-niner reported sending for a physician who "declined to accept anything for his trip or for the medicine although I urged him." Earlier that morning, by contrast, the same forty-niner paid a different doctor "two five franc pieces for the trip."[32]

On the whole, however, there is no doubt physicians regarded their services as private property and expected anyone seeking their aid to pay compensation much as if visiting their offices at home. One even left cards "freshly written in bright red keel" by the roadside announcing that, should a doctor be needed, he

---

[26]Entry for 4 June 1852, Dalton, Diary, pp. 10-11.

[27]Entry for 21 June 1849, Lord, Journal.

[28]Entry for 30 June 1850, Shepherd, *Journal,* p. 18.

[29]Entries for 8 June and 28 July 1850, Maynard, Pocket Diary. Occasionally a company might travel so much in the vicinity of a physician, the members came to think of him as theirs. "6 or 7 of us are very sick. We think we have a splendid Doctor who is near us most of the time, sometimes he is ahead of us sometimes behind. Today he gave medicine to 16 of our company at one visit" (entry for 2 Aug. 1852, Wigle, Copy, p. 14).

[30]Unruh, The Plains Across, p. 204.

[31]Entry for 2 July 1849, Caldwell, "Notes," p. 1256.

[32]Entry for 9 June 1849, Benson, Forty Niner, pp. 17-18.

could be found in a train ahead.[33] How well they did monetarily is another matter, but the fact that they did charge fees is significant as far as it bears on the question of professional services and professional knowledge as private property on the overland trail. A few sums have been recorded and can be mentioned, but perhaps only two physicians left a summary of overland finances or commented on professional expectations and disappointments.

An 1850 emigrant, referred to as "doctor" and who may have been a dentist (though not an educated speller), "puld one tooth to knight and administered Cloriform charged 100 dollars kiled the nurve of one tooth." He undoubtedly meant one dollar, not a hundred. That was his fee for pulling a second tooth ten days later.[34] In 1852, a physician who made two visits and furnished medicine said he charged a patient $1.25.[35] Maynard, four days before reaching the South Platte crossing, examined three persons "ready to Die." For that service he received one and a half pints of brandy and $2.20. Next day he attended "some sick with cholera. One Died before I got there & 2 Died before the next morning." It does not seem his services were very beneficial, yet Maynard collected $8.75.[36]

To put these figures into some perspective, consider a young man passing Fort Kearny in 1865. While unyoking a bull his left eye was struck by a horn. The army surgeon treated him "and," the young man wrote, "only charged me *$2.00* for his services." The injured emigrant may have been sarcastic, but more likely he was saying that two dollars was a reasonable fee for medical services.[37]

No matter what their patients thought, some overland physicians thought themselves poorly rewarded. "I was in the thickest of the fight all the time," William Allen, a Missouri allopath who crossed

[33]Entry for 24 June 1857, Carpenter, Trip, p. 32.

[34]Entries for 5 and 15 May 1850, Thomasson, Diary.

[35]Entry for 4 June 1852, Graham, Journal, p. 8.

[36]Entries for 6 and 7 June 1850, Maynard, Pocket Diary.

[37]Entry for 30 Aug 1865, E. M. Lewis, Route.

in 1850 wrote his brother, "attended over 700 cholera patients and strange to say, while other doctors lost nearly every case, I lost none that I got to in anything like a reasonable time after attacked. If these fellows had been returning from the mines, I would have made a fortune. As it was that few had money,   I just got paid for the medicines I used. Was paid in money say $150." Accepting his figures, Allen averaged less than twenty-two cents a patient.[38]

Samuel Matthias Ayres, also a Missouri physician who crossed to California in 1850, seems to have fared even more poorly than Allen. He had to barter his horse for a mule, Ayres wrote his wife, because he had ridden the animal "too hard practicing in the midst of the sickness so that he was fast failing . . . I have had more calls than I could attend to, being half sick myself." Ayres had not, however, become rich from his extensive overland practice, though he did not complain. "I have made some money and have considerable owing to me, some of which I will get and some I will never get."[39]

It is evident that both Allen and Ayres, like all overland physicians, expected professional knowledge to be as much property beyond the Missouri River as at home. It was universally accepted that physicians and patients, blacksmiths and customers, wheelwrights and wagon owners, all shared the same legal tenets: professional expertise was property and professional service rendered was a transfer of property.

No extant diary or letter hints that due to the perils of overland travel, individuals in need had a claim on the services of others. Those who engaged blacksmiths knew they should pay. If they could not compensate a physician, they might have to forgo professional treatment. Should they receive help despite being unable to pay, they attributed that care to generosity, they did not call it their right or say that conditions of the trail made it their due.

---

[38]Allen, Letter.
[39]Letters of 15 and 21 June 1850, Ayres, Letters.

One final point merits discussion. Dr. Ayres was not indulging in wishful thinking when he told his wife he yet might collect fees owed him by fellow emigrants. Credit was not uncommon on the overland trail. Just as bank notes were freely accepted by emigrants far out in the wilderness, so were negotiable instruments and demand receipts.[40] Encountering the traders whom Jim Bridger had sent out to meet the emigration at the Sweetwater, a company of forty-niners exchanged "some bacon, and a lot of beads, trinkets, etc., and a mule for a horse." The transaction was executed even though the traders had no horse to transfer. Stock was being sent by Bridger and the forty-niners were told to select from what they met on the road or "from that at Fort Bridger, we being furnished an order to that effect."[41]

The realities of the trail often shaped the terms of an instrument. Knowing something of the route ahead, but moving on an unpredictable schedule, overland emigrants made notes payable on arrival at some way station or at the ultimate destination, rather than due by a date certain.[42] "[O]ur boys have lent 100 lbs of flour and 12 lbs of bacon to Mr. Downer as he is all out and will pay us at the [Humboldt] Sink," a cabinet maker from Massachusetts recorded in 1852.[43] Charles Gray, from New York City, "Bo[ugh]t of three brothers & a Mr Whitlocke (the brothers nam[ed] Owens) 126# nett of flour to be *paid pound for pound in California*, which I did not like to do preferring & offering to buy it out & out, but could get it upon no other terms."[44]

Other notes were less sui generis to the overland trail and followed the conventional pattern of being payable by a specified date. Interestingly, one of the few lawyers to leave extant a

---

[40]For an example of bank notes see entry for 26 Jan. 1850, Bruff, *Journals*, p. 698.

[41]Entry for 10 June 1849, W. G. Johnston, *Overland*, p. 94.

[42]Entry for 4 Oct. 1849, Castleman, Diary; entry for 21 July 1850, Gorgas, Diary; entry for 5 Oct. 1852, C.E.M. Adams, "Crossing the Plains," p. 322. Also below, there is an account of a note, with security, given on the southern branch of the trail and "payable at Santa Fe" (see p. 208).

[43]Entry for 5 Sept. 1852, Hosley, Journal.

[44]Entry for 15 Aug. 1849, Gray, Passage.

reasonably detailed diary thought in terms of a time certain. Tired of walking when less than a month out on the trail, Judge Addison Crane "purchased a fine bay mare for $90 *on a credit of three months* of an emigrant with whom I have become acquainted on the road." Crane was delighted. "So you see," he exulted, "my Credit is good even among strangers."[45] Some emigrants anticipated not being known. A Canadian forty-niner, for example, took a letter of reference with him on the trail, testifying that he was "a man of good character and standing in this Community and in good Circumstances as to property."[46]

It may be contended that the extending of credit on the overland trail reveals less about law than about the moral judgments of nineteenth-century Americans. Emigrants, one could plausibly argue, trusted fellow Christians perceived as honest, God-fearing men. There is no reason to quarrel with that chain of thought as long as the legal perspective is given consideration. All that need be asked is an acknowledgment indisputable by our evidence: when emigrants made that judgment, the premises upon which they relied assumed more than that those they trusted shared their moral principles. They also were saying they defined in common the meaning of a legal as well as a moral obligation.

---

[45]Entry for 30 May 1852, Crane, Journal; Eaton, *Overland*, p. 133. For other instances of credit extended till a date certain see entry for 26 May 1850, Parker, Notes; *Overland in 1846*, p. 401n10.

[46]J. H. Johnson, Journey (insert).

6 | DISTINGUISHING PROPERTY RIGHTS

We are asking about behavior but we are also asking about law. Many questions concerning American legal history can in part be answered from the extant diaries, memoirs, and letters written by those who passed over the trails to Oregon and California. Ironically, the most obvious topic — how emigrants dealt with acts of violence and punished delinquents within their ranks —may not be the most revealing. It tells us that they imitated the remembered criminal process and what they remembered was hardly surprising.[1] More valuable would be questions about the less familiar, about knowledge of rules governing rights to property, for example. It is on this point that the uniqueness of overland documentation should yield some of its richest dividends.

There may be no better material available for discovering to what degree average middle-class Americans understood legal principles governing the acquisition, control, and disposition of property than that furnished by our overland evidence. Moreover, if proper questions are asked, the same material could answer whether emigrants, far from the advice of lawyers, the guidance of courts, and the coercion of police, could distinguish between various types of ownership, keep the rights associated with different interests in property separate and distinct during negotiations, and conduct their affairs confident that those with whom they dealt applied the same legal definitions and conformed to the same legal principles.[2]

We have already seen that it would defy calculation to place a value on the possessions of the emigrants who traveled the

---

[1]"Prosecuting the Elephant," pp. 327-50.

[2]Sections of this and the following two chapters were published previously as parts of the following articles: "Knowing the Elephant," "Sharing the Elephant," and "Dividing the Elephant."

overland trail during the 1840s and 1850s. It has also been contended that the property they owned — wagons, draft animals, and provisions — was vital to survival. The point that now must be emphasized is that this property was held in a variety of legal arrangements. Some, of course, was private, much belonged to companies organized as joint-stock ventures, and a surprising proportion was owned concurrently by members of partnerships or messes.

Distinctions need not be drawn between the Oregon and California trails. The same types of property and the same legal maxims prevailed on both. There was, however, a difference. Most emigrants going to Oregon traveled in private wagons and depended on personally-owned animals to haul their personally-owned property. On the California section of the overland trail, gold seekers heading for the diggings more often joined an organization: either as shareholders of joint-stock corporations,[3] partners in a mess, clients of passenger lines,[4] hired hands working as teamsters, contractees bound to an underwriter by stipulated obligation,[5] or personal-property owning members of traveling companies.[6]

The historical fact is identical with the legal fact: on both the Oregon and California trails emigrants generally distinguished between five main types of property holding. Three of the five were mess property, partnership property, and company property. The other two were really not different types, but deserve separate classification because each reveals so much concerning law-mindedness on the overland trail. One was property owned personally by individuals going alone, in small groups, or in

---

[3]Leslie D. Shaffer, "The Management of Organized Wagon Trains on the Overland Trail," *Missouri Historical Review*, 55 (1961): 361; Howe, Argonauts, pp. 3-45; Potter, "Introduction," pp. 213-22.

[4]Reid, Diary, p. 3; L. H. Woolley, *California, 1849-1913, or the Rambling Sketches and Experiences of Sixty-Four Years' Residence in That State* (Oakland, Calif.: DeWitt & Snelling, 1913), p. 3; Unruh, The Plains Across, pp. 148-56; Reid, "Letter," p. 225; Mattes, *Platte River Road*, p. 33.

[5]"Tied to the Elephant," pp. 140-46.

[6]"Knowing the Elephant," p. 641.

traveling companies. The other was property owned personally by members of large joint-stock concerns; in other words, private property within concurrent-property-holding organizations.

II *Partnership and Mess Property*

One reason the overland trail has been ignored by legal historians is that few have realized how much can be learned, partly because they have asked the wrong questions. It is easy, especially for those trained in law, to be led astray. Seeking to decipher emigrant definitions of property and property rights, the test must not be how much the notions of travelers on the overland trail matched those of lawyers. More relevant is how consistently they applied uniform concepts when dealing among themselves.

There were three types of property interests that all Americans on the overland trail took for granted — private property, mess property, and partnership property. The first was thought so elementary it seldom was noticed as a legal entity. What was known to all did not have to be explained. Diarists assumed everyone understood private property and what it meant. Stories were told without elaboration or without even realizing law was being discussed. At Thomas Fork of Bear River an aged man, traveling with his younger wife and two children, lost a horse. The family still had one horse and was able to salvage its wagon by slicing it into a cart. To haul what provisions they had left, however, the old man needed another animal. Emigrants observing his predicament are not reported to have discussed priorities based on necessity or equity or even to have weighed the special needs of women and children. Knowing the best chance of that husband and father to obtain a second horse was by buying it, they took up a collection "from the result of which, sufficient money was given to him to purchase a horse, wherever an opportunity should be presented."[1] The passing stranger record-

---

[1] Entry for 17 June 1850, Clapp, *Journal*, p. 30.

ing the event, and writing for publication, thought there was nothing of interest to relate except the family memberships, the loss of the horse, the reduction of the wagon, and the collection. His silence about law tells us more than would any discussion concerning the perils or inequities of personal ownership. That alternatives might exist probably never occurred to him.

Diarists also assumed everyone understood partnership property, its meaning and its consequences. The term "partnership" came readily to the lips of those who took the trail west. Indeed, even some for whom English was not a native language used the word to explain overland relationships. "I am in partnership with two other Germans; with 2 waggons and 6 horses," a Bavarian immigrant informed his mother.[2] A man from Illinois, waiting at Independence to begin the trip, wrote of receiving "a letter in pardnership" with two friends.[3] Lawyers might object that a legal term was used too loosely, but most people knew what was meant. Surely a second emigrant thought there was no ambiguity when reporting that he and a traveling companion had "purchased a horse in partnership." He may not have known the legal meaning of the word "concurrent," but he was saying that the horse was concurrently owned by them both.[4]

When considering partnerships we are also considering the topic of contracts. Most partnerships were created by the exchange of promises. Occasionally elaborate agreements would be negotiated, reduced to writing and signed. More commonly, though, a chance meeting led to an arrangement more assumed than stated. "They were queer affairs, those partnerships of that day," a forty-niner recalled many years later. "Two entire strangers would meet, and without preliminaries go to work, living and toiling together for weeks and even months, trusting each other with their joint earnings, and dividing the same without trouble; never perhaps learning any more of each other

---

[2]Letter of 1 March 1850, Kuhliwein, Letters, p. 16.

[3]Entry for 4 May 1852, Graham, Journal, p. 5.

[4]Letter from Quincy Adams Brooks, 7 Nov. 1851, quoted in Mattes, *Platte River Road*, p. 44.

than simply the Christian name."[5] He was writing about miners in California, but except for the comment about sharing earnings he could have been referring to partners on the overland trail.

In the majority of cases, overland partnerships were so informal they were concluded without reducing the terms to writing. In the typical situation, a man with funds to buy but part of an outfit, or one who was alone and sought company, would join other emigrants to form a "mess," generally of four or five members. There was no need to draft an instrument of ratification as everyone understood the legal principles involved in private and concurrent ownership.

It is revealing that one of the few extant partnership contracts negotiated on the frontier and reduced to writing was never signed. A trio of young men arrived at Council Bluffs in 1854 with an equal amount of funds but no outfit except a yoke of oxen owned by one of the three. Pooling their money they "bought a shackly, light two horse wagon for $45.00, [and] a pair of wild steers that had never been handled for $60.00." This business arrangement, they believed, was a partnership for that was the word used to describe it in their written agreement. They did not, however, think it necessary to indicate what they meant by "partnership." Even more revealing, the implications of concurrent ownership were not defined. It was assumed that such matters were mutually understood by all three, and the contract dealt only with the division of property on dissolution. "Made May 29, 1854," the instrument read. "We the undersigned having entered into a partnership for the better accomplishment of a trip to California do hereby agree to divide the joint stock or proceeds thereof among each other in proportion to the amount invested by each. Such division to take place as soon as convenient after our arrival at our destination." The contract, one of the partners later wrote, was "Agreed to by all, but never signed — but Executed to the letter."[6]

---

[5]H. Degroot, "Six Months in '49," *The Overland Monthly*, 14 (1875): 321.
[6]McCowen, Journal and Notes, pp. 3-5A.

One more case deserves attention. It is offered not so much to explain what overland emigrants meant by "partnership," as to illustrate the extent to which they took partnership and concurrent ownership of property for granted. A day beyond South Pass three young packers discovered and appropriated to their own use an abandoned mule. Less than a week later, they "went snooks" and paid twenty dollars for a horse. Next day they found a buyer for both animals. "Sold the two for $95.00," one of them recorded in his journal, "which we divided among the three of us." The diarist did not elaborate. There was no need to explain the obvious: he and his friends had owned property concurrently, had sold it, settled accounts, and now no longer were partners.[7]

Another species of overland ownership was mess property. At first glance it appears to be but another word for partnership. In many cases it was, for the word "mess" was often used in a way indicating that it was considered synonymous to "partnership." For example, a small traveling party was formed in Salt Lake City. One member called the arrangement a "partnership." Another termed it a "mess."[8]

Although in many if not most overland cases the words were interchangeable, there are two reasons for placing "mess" in a category separate from "partnership." One is that emigrants saw a difference. Even if a mess was a partnership, it was a partnership peculiar to the overland trail and therefore distinguishable. More important, as emigrants knew, not every mess was legally a partnership. A mess might be formed by contract only, not by pooling property, or, if a partnership, it could be a partnership between two or more emigrants to which others were admitted by contract. The partners would own concurrently the mess's property. Those who joined by agreement, not by capital contribution, would have a contractual right to share, not a proprietary interest in the property owned by the partnership. The relationship was much like that between a hotel and its

---

[7]Entries for 5, 11 and 12 Nov. 1865, E. M. Lewis, Route.

[8]Entry for 23 Sept. 1850, Stine, Letters, p. 26; entry for 23 Sept. 1850, Littleton, Journal, p. 60.

guests. "[W]e have a young man traveling with us this week," a Wisconsin emigrant noted, "he paid us 4 dollars this morning for his board."[9]

Payment did not have to be in specie. Usually it was not. Labor was a common form of payment,[10] or a contracting member of a mess might contribute the use of private property that remained private and did not become mess property. For example, an emigrant would hitch his oxen to the partnership wagon and by contract become a member of the mess, though not of the partnership.

Whether a contractee mess member furnished money, labor, or property, the legal emphasis was never on contractual rights (for the person was always contracting for an equal share of whatever was distributed each day), but upon ownership. This matter will be touched on again, but it should clarify concepts now if the diary of Elisha Douglass Perkins is quoted. "John Huntington's funds which he expected at Independence not reaching him, we supposed he would be obliged to turn back," Perkins wrote of one of his Ohio neighbors whom he had expected to be a partner in his overland mess. "Today however we concluded to carry him through for 110 dollars which he could muster & he not to own any thing but go merely as a passenger, of course helping when needed & standing watch in his turn."[11]

There is no need to read between the lines. What concerns us is not the terms of the contract but the property arrangement Perkins has described. He is telling that he, his partners, and John Huntington, their contractee, had no difficulty distinguishing between a mess that was a property partnership and a mess that was not.

Take one more example. Three forty-niners from Wisconsin owned a wagon in partnership. After crossing the Missouri at St. Joseph these three "joined in a mess with 4 others." That made a

---

[9]Entry for 19 Aug. 1852, Chadwick, Diary.

[10]Eaton, *Overland*, p. 197; Ghent, *Road*, p. 115.

[11]Entry of 25 May 1849, Perkins, Sketches.

total of seven men who remained together as a traveling group until after reaching California. They were not a partnership of seven owners of concurrent property, but two separate partnerships — one of three members, the other of four — joined in one mess of seven members. When the partnership of four divided some of its concurrent property into private property, the three partners from Wisconsin had no rights to assert for they had no interests in the property of the other partnership. After reaching the end of the trail, one of the Wisconsin partners wished to go to Sacramento. The other two wanted to get to the diggings, as did the four men in the second group. It was now the turn of the partners from Wisconsin to divide. The man going to Sacramento was given the wagon and "2 of the best pair of cattle." His two former partners put their share of the provisions in the wagon belonging to the other four. Regarding that property they were now a partnership of two, but had no proprietary interest in the wagon hauling it. Though still members of the mess, they were traveling with that wagon as guests or contractors, not as owners.[12]

It must not be inferred that the word "mess" was used with etymological exactness or legal precision. Five men leaving Warren, Ohio, for California "make what they call a mess," a local newspaper reported.[13] On the morning of the seventh day of travel down the Humboldt River, a young emigrant from Hannibal lost his horse and was unable to go on. Two other Missourians, an onlooker wrote, "took him into their mess."[14] It was possible that both accounts were describing the same type of property ownership. It is just as possible they were not.

In truth, "mess" was a vague term that obtains legal definition only in those individual cases for which we have sufficient information to understand the contractual, property, or partnership arrangements involved. Sometimes, for example, "mess" was used to indicate a small party that took all meals from a

---

[12]Entries for 6 May, 29 July, and 6 Sept. 1849, J. W. Wood, Diaries.

[13]*Western Reserve Chronicle,* (Warren, Ohio), 25 April 1849, p. 2, col. 6.

[14]Entry for 14 Aug. 1850, Stauder, Memorandum, p. 97.

common store. That was an "eating mess." On other occasions it meant a group that traveled with one or more wagons — a "traveling mess." Usually the implication was clear: the provisions or wagons were concurrently owned. Yet there was a certain amount of ambiguity connected with the word "mess," rendering it too inexact for lawyers to have used without adding some clarifying definition. An emigrant could speak of an "eating mess" and a "traveling mess" yet say "partnership" when referring to the ownership of concurrent property. Writing home to Rome, New York, a forty-niner reported that he and six companions had formed an "eating mess" and had "two wagons in our mess, and four yoke of cattle to each wagon." He did not, however, speak of mess ownership when reporting what they possessed concurrently. "Our provisions, our common stock," he wrote in the same letter, "are held in partnership among us."[15]

It is possible the New Yorker used words loosely. More likely he did not. He had reasons to distinguish between "mess" and "partnership." A lawyer in his situation would have done so. There had been seven men in the mess, only six of whom owned a share of the concurrent property. The seventh man was their guide. For "his board with us" he had been hired "to pilot" the other six "across to California."[16]

Emigrants did not have to be lawyers to understand that the boarder guiding the New Yorkers had a contractual claim on the mess, but owned no interest in the partnership property. A company from North Carolina got as far as Knoxville, Tennessee, before dissolving. John E. Brown, a member, sold his share and continued alone. Aboard a steamboat he and three Tennesseans formed what he called a "mess." Arriving at St. Louis they met two more emigrants whom they brought into the mess "on equal shares." Finally, after getting to Independence, the six men took inventory and discovered that only four had money. One of the two who did not left the group. The other, H.M. Atkinson, was

[15]Letter of 27 April 1849, Muscott, Letters.
[16]Loc. cit.

135

apparently popular or valued as a likely companion on the overland trail. The four possessing funds "agreed to furnish Atkinson with an outfit." He was a member of the mess but had no property claims on it. When they reached Fort Laramie, Atkinson decided to go home. "We regretted seeing him return on foot," Brown wrote, "but he did not own any interest in the Company, and we could not spare him a mule."[17]

When the departing member of a mess was a partner with a share in concurrently-owned property, it was more difficult to effect separation. He could not be dismissed with a handshake as could a nonproprietor like Atkinson. Unless it had been stipulated that anyone leaving the mess forfeited property rights, the man had to be compensated. Just beyond the Missouri during 1849, an emigrant became very ill. The date was 28 May, quite late to be starting across the plains if the Sierras were to be reached before snow blocked the passes. The sick man's companions feared they might be delayed beyond the margin of safety. "We all joined in urging his return home," one of them wrote. The man agreed and the "mess bought out his share which reduces our pocket again."[18]

III   *Company Property*

The words just quoted tell us much — the "mess bought out his share." More precisely, the "mess bought out his share of the mess." Thus in one sentence the term "mess" has two meanings. It would, however, be a mistake for historians to disparage the word because of its vagueness. Lawyers would never do so. "Mess" was an operative legal term and like many other legal terms regulating the affairs of people is far less susceptible to precise definition than many academicians, such as anthropologists or jurisprudents, insist is necessary when writing about law.

A similar example from overland history is the word "company." It was employed daily by emigrants to describe important social

---

[17]J. E. Brown, *Memoirs*, pp. 3-6, 13-14.

[18]Entry for 28 May 1849, William Brisbane, "Journal of a Trip or Note of One from Fort Levenworth to San Francisco, via Sante Fe in 1849" (ms., Princeton Univeristy).

and legal relationships, yet they used it even more loosely than "mess."[1] Sometimes "company" referred to joint-stock organizations to which each member contributed equal amounts of capital. Wagons, draft animals, and other property purchased by a joint-stock company were held concurrently, belonging to the entire organization. At other times the term meant a group journeying together, whether organized informally or under a set of popularly-adopted rules such as a constitution.[2] In the parlance of the overland trail, a "traveling company" usually did not own common property. If it did, emigrants were more apt to use the term "partnership" than to say "company," though in some cases the words "company" and "partnership" were synonymous. "Quite a number of persons are selling their interests in companys and returning to the *States*," a forty-niner noted in his diary.[3] By "companys" he could have meant joint-stock companies or partnerships; he did not mean traveling companies.

Loose legal terms may well have caused loose legal concepts. "We have joined the Peoria Pioneers and have a Boat that will carry a wagon and load over any stream," another forty-niner wrote his wife. "The Pioneers got divided at St. Joseph and part took the road to Santafee which reduced their numbers so that they admitted other teams by each person paying $3 which makes us joint owners in the boat and 3 yoke of oxen that drew it and if our team should fail, the Company are bound to see us through to California."[4] Unless a very unique agreement had been signed and sealed, the writer was assuming an incorrect legal result. The reason for error was that he gave too much credit to the word "company." There was no way the Peoria Pioneers could have been "bound" to see that he and his messmates got through to California.

---

[1]Perhaps the loosest connotation of "company" was when used to describe a number of wagons gathered in one camp or vicinity, having no organization or direction, but which could act together for defence should Indians attack. See entry for 30 July 1849, Foster, Journal, p. 60.

[2]"Governance of the Elephant," pp. 421-27.

[3]Entry for 31 May 1849, Parke, Notes.

[4]Letter of 27 May 1849, Wells, Letters.

Remarkably, such misconceptions of law were more rare than we might think. When legal distinctions were meaningful, emigrants were capable of drawing them. That forty-niner furnished an example when defining the property relationship between his mess and the Peoria Pioneers. By paying three dollars, he and his partners became what he called "joint owners" in the Pioneers' boat and the oxen hauling it. Thus they had two sets of concurrent property. First, they owned their wagon, team, and provisions, in which the Peoria Pioneers had no interest. The second was the boat and oxen tying them to a limited extent to the fortunes of the Pioneers who surely retained the majority interest.

It was a simple legal relationship that emigrants easily understood. They might not have asked or thought it worth considering whether the partnership had purchased a proprietary share in the boat or nonproprietary right to its equal use, but no one would have suggested that the members of that partnership had become members of the Peoria company. True, strangers passing them on the trail, seeing them travel together, and employing common overland parlance would have referred to them all, boat owners together with the Pioneers, as one company. They would not, however, have meant that the total party was a "company" in the same sense that the Pioneers were a company. Those joined together merely for traveling purposes were not confused with those united by concurrent ownership. Assuming that the Peoria group was a joint-stock organization, they were a company held together by corporate property. The larger body was closer to a traveling company sharing some relatively unimportant pieces of concurrently-owned property.

It is best to allow the emigrants themselves to define terms. It will be recalled that eight men from Ohio arrived on the Missouri in 1849 already organized as the Fort Stephenson Mining Association. On the plains they joined, for purposes of travel, eleven other men. As Fort Stephenson was a joint-stock company it is evident that the original eight owned some property concurrently. The larger group of nineteen did not own property concurrently. It was referred to by one of the Ohio emigrants as a "traveling company."[5]

Ownership of property or of rights to property was the operative criterion used by almost all emigrants. A forty-niner provided some evidence of this fact by distinguishing between his joint-stock company, the traveling company within which the joint-stock company journeyed, and an individual who traveled with but was not a member of either group. When going through the South Pass he noted in his diary the existence of three wagons which, he said, were "all that belonged to our Joint Stock company." In addition to those three there was another wagon "that had traveled from one days travel t[h]is side of St Jo[seph] with us this making four waggons that belong to our company." About three weeks earlier, the four wagons had been joined by a man who was "riding a government horse but was dressed in citizen dress so we suspected him for being a deserter which he did not deny   but after we heard his pitty [sic] tale we told him he could get some thing to eat and could travel with us but that he could not join us as one of the company for we did not want any dif[f]iculty on his account."[6]

The writer referred to two different groups as "our company," yet distinguished between them because they were, in fact, not the same but separate. They were not separate for reasons of overland social patterns but due to legal considerations: they were two groups owning separate property. Interesting too, though somewhat puzzling as to the legal premises upon which it rested, was the belief regarding the status of the deserter. It would seem that these emigrants thought that they — whether one of two units of property owners or as one united traveling company is not clear — could escape the consequences of sheltering an army deserter if they did not admit him (certainly) to membership in either property-owning group or (apparently) to the traveling company even though he traveled with them.

We may wonder what liability they feared might attach to the

---

[5]Entry for 30 July 1849, J. A. Johnson, Note Book.

[6]Entries for 19 July, 27 June 1849, Castleman, Diary.

members of a traveling company for the prior sins of one of their associates. It is possible not many emigrants would have shared this worry. Most thought of traveling companies as social or quasi-governmental units, not as corporations capable of bearing collective responsibility. The same was true of property-owning companies. They were seen as economic or legal groups. Our evidence even suggests that many emigrants thought that a company owning property, especially a joint-stock company or mess in which the food was concurrently owned, stood in relationship to that property very much as did an individual owning private property. There is some indication that members of a company could contract debts that the company, as the property owner, would have to pay.[7] In the reverse situation, if others damaged or destroyed company property, it was the company that was reimbursed.[8]

Should we count the references to company property in the literature of the overland trail, we would find most related to the burden of concurrent property and the division of concurrent property, topics discussed in the next two chapters. Very few companies journeyed from the Missouri to the Sierras without either total division or drastic alterations in number or management. The ironic lesson, as we shall see, is that a major cause of dissension within companies was disputes over the very thing that was supposed to unite them: the concurrent property.

IV Personally-Owned Property Within Companies

It could be misleading to stress disputes about property without noting a pertinent distinction. Though emigrants often argued the use or disposition of concurrently-owned property,

---

[7] A crowd attending a religious service on Sunday was caught in a sudden rainstorm and, to escape, the women filled a nearby tent in which the owner "had placed my biscuit and jerked buffalo meat." The women "soon found it out and that was the last of it, their company however repaid its loss" (entry for 14 July 1850, Stine, Letters, p. 17).

[8] "Layed by to go back after our boat . . . and some of the emigrants cut the boat up and spoilt it   we caught some one at it and made them pay for it ten dollars (entry for 10 June 1853, Compton, Diary).

140

they seldom questioned whether specific items were personally or concurrently owned, whether by a mess, partnership, or company. It is surprising how uniformly nonlawyers on the overland trail acted on legal concepts. Oddly, one of the few emigrants to become confused between various rights to property was Addison Crane, a lawyer and judge from Indiana, on his way to California, where he would for many years preside as a trial judge of Alameda County.[1]

Crane was traveling up the North Platte toward the Mormon ferry at today's Casper, Wyoming, when an event occurred that he later recorded in his diary:

> Mr Merriweather (one of our Co.) gave me a sack of flour to day (100 lbs) he having more than they could use. He would take no pay for it — quite generous, as it could have been sold for $12. to $15. I believe however it is considered out of character for any one to *sell* any provisions to any person in the same train, but if he has any over it is considered common property.[2]

As both a lawyer and a judge, Crane should not have made so mistaken a guess about wagon-trail law. Moreover, what he called "our Co[mpany]" was not a joint-stock organization with members pledged to assist one another throughout the trip, but a traveling company so loosely organized it almost mocked the name: a collection of carts and wagons whose owners had little in common except that they were proceeding together. There was no elected leadership, no popularly-promulgated rules, no mutual contracts, and no concurrently-owned property. Yet Crane supposed that mere companionship was sufficient to convert surplus private property into concurrent property or transfer title from the over-supplied to the needy.

The one or two other diaries providing even a hint that such a legal principle existed are too vague to serve as convincing legal authority or positive historical evidence. A forty-niner who had eight oxen killed between the North Platte crossing and Inde-

---

[1]Addison Moses Crane, "Memoir Written by Himself," in Myron W. Wood, *History of Alameda County, California* (Oakland: M. W. Wood, 1883), pp. 865-69.

[2]Entry for 13 June 1852, Crane, Journal; Eaton, *Overland*, p. 152.

pendence Rock was furnished a substitute team by the train to which he belonged. "Many of them," an observer wrote of overland companies without specifying whether he was referring to partnerships, traveling companies, or joint-stock organizations, "are bound to aid and assist each other to their journey's end."[3] A similarly inconclusive comment was made that same month by the secretary of the Holt County Missouri Mining Company. That group had been formed for the sole purpose of traveling to California. It was not a joint-stock corporation and its members did not plan to remain together on reaching the gold mines. One day while on the Platte, two men of the Holt Company returned from hunting "with their saddles well loaded with buffalo and antelope, causing them to be hailed with delight, since all game is generally considered a sort of common property, or rather those who procure it make it so."[4]

These two statements are the closest found supporting Crane's suggestion that surplus private property, owned by a member of a "company," could, by customary law, be converted into company property or into personal property over which fellow members of the company to which the owner belonged might exercise demand rights. All other evidence clearly demonstrates that there was no such rule.[5] Two cases should serve to illustrate the correct legal doctrine. They are especially useful, as the first involved a long-lived traveling company, the second a well-organized joint-stock company.

Bryan McKinstry and his three messmates, concurrent owners of a wagon, team, and provisions, had journeyed to Council Bluffs with a second wagon from their home in McHenry County, Illinois. At Council Bluffs the men from both wagons

---

[3]Entry for 27 June 1849, Banks, "Diary," p. 27.

[4]Entry for 1 June 1849, McLeod, Note Books.

[5]With the possible exception of a rule, also concerning property obtained by hunting, which acknowledged the personal nature of game killed, by providing for compensation when requisitioned. A small party in 1850 "had an understanding that any food procured [through hunting] by any member of our company should be considered 'joint stock,' and that when we reached the mines he [the hunter or "owner"] should be reimbursed to the extent of the value of the property exchanged" (Abbott, *Recollections*, p. 72).

joined with others to create a traveling company, known as the Upper Mississippi Ox Company. The larger company traveled as a unit only for a limited time, but three wagons — McKinstry's, the other from McHenry County, and a third — remained together, forming a new, smaller traveling company. The three wagons reached the Humboldt River during the second week of August, 1850 — the time and place of the most severe starvation on the overland trail. On reaching the river, McKinstry and his messmates killed a horse that had become lame. They sold half the meat to the mess traveling in the third wagon, some at five cents a pound to the second McHenry County mess, some to strangers for six or eight cents a pound, "& some we hauled along."[6] They had surplus food that others in their company needed. Those others, it is true, obtained a share, but not by exercising a demand right. Like the strangers, they paid for it.

The same rule of law prevailed in one of the best organized and most tightly-run joint-stock companies to cross the plains during 1849. "One member of the Company," the captain wrote in his diary, "offered another $5 for a flour biscuit, & [was] refused."[7] The time of that incident is also significant, as it occurred during another period of shortage on the overland trail. The Washington City Company was on Lassen's cutoff in northern California, the spur of the road where the largest number of forty-niners experienced the greatest suffering. Two days later the same captain recorded that "certain men and messes in the company had purchased flour, and were well provisioned, but most of the men had scarcely sufficient to take them in [to the settlements]."[8] These emigrants had traveled as a paramilitary organization from the District of Columbia to California, intending to mine together and then divide all profits into equal shares. If any group had developed a custom of demand rights upon the excess goods of companions, we would expect it to have been they. They had not. What they owned as individuals was as absolutely personal as

---

[6]Entry for 10 Aug. 1850, McKinstry, *Diary*, p. 249.

[7]Entry for 20 Oct. 1849, Bruff, *Journals*, p. 332.

[8]Ibid., entry for 22 Oct. 1849, p. 236.

143

any property protected by police and courts east of the Missouri River. Even in times of famine, except for what was concurrently owned there was no common grainery.

The evidence is clear and unambiguous. It indicates there was no item of private property that an owner had to share with his company. Even water (which, we shall see, could be private, vendible property on the overland trail) might within companies be husbanded for exclusive, personal use. It was a rule of law explaining, for example, why, when a company of forty-two men and eleven wagons reached the Green River in western Wyoming after crossing a long desert, some teams arrived in better condition than did others. "I had the precaution," one member explained, "to fill our water cast this morning, which gave our mules each an advantage of water over the rest of the train."[9]

Horses and mules were the most frequently mentioned kinds of private property held by persons who were members of companies. Just because a man belonged to the same company as you gave him no right to take your horse.[10] If borrowed, horses had to be returned,[11] and few owners were willing to see their property worn down to keep the company moving.[12]

Hasty conclusions should not be drawn. It would be fair to say that within companies private interest was equal to — perhaps enjoyed precedence over — public interest only if we keep in mind that the law of ownership was the determinative factor. And being law, it played a neutral role in the allocation of resources. The preference given private ownership must not be equated with individual benefit. Change the circumstances and

[9]Entry for 20 June 1849, Dr. T., Journal.

[10]"A young man of the company, as reckless as unprincipled, backed by several scoundrels, attempted this morning to take my horse, prompt determination frustrated them" (entry for 21 Sept. 1849, Bruff, *Journals*, p. 183).

[11]Two men in a company of forty-two lost their horses on the Platte. "[O]ne of the Horses belonged to our mess . . . . We borrowed 2 Horses and started them back in pursuits with directions not to return until they had found them" (entry for 22 May 1849, Dr. T., Journal).

[12]Two draft horses pulling a mess's wagon became weak and had to be rested. One member, it was then said, "grumbles because he has to put his horses on [the] heavy wagon" (entry for 29 May 1850, Cagwin, Diary).

by the same law the winner becomes the loser. Andrew Orvis was a forty-niner traveling in a company of ten packers, each with a riding and pack horse. Beyond Bear River on the cutoff north of Great Salt Lake, one of Orvis' horses became sick. The company moved on, the horse died, and Orvis was alone. "It is ev[e]ry one for him self," he commented, resignedly accepting the consequence of depending on private property even though the member of a "company."[13]

"Another wagon left the train this morning," a woman emigrant noted in 1852. "The man's horses were poisoned by eating a weed and the company thought them unable to travel . . . so the train started on."[14]

Perhaps this evidence repeats what was said about sales: luck had much to do with how an individual fared on the overland trail. But if we speak of luck and ownership, we must keep in mind the fact that the luck was in the condition and durability of the property, not in the ownership. Ownership was an absolute, not a variable.

Joseph Stuart was one of many emigrants who understood that ownership and its rights were constant. A forty-niner traveling with the Granite State Company, he carried the law of New Hampshire onto the plains where yet there were no courts and judges. Some of his companions shot a buffalo and he wanted to go back for the meat. The company's officers objected, in part because they "were opposed to the extra travel for company horses." Stuart went anyway, saying that "riding a private horse I was independent as to animals."[15]

During the famous migration of 1841, in which the first strain of American settlers crossed the Sierras and entered California, the

---

[13]Andrew M. Orvis, "Journal of an Overland Trip . . . and Life in the Mines" (ms., Western Americana Collection 367, Beinecke Library).

[14]Entry for 1 June 1852, Algeline Jackson Ashley "Diary of Crossing the Plains in 1852" (ts., Newberry Library). See also "Diary of Mrs. Algeline Ashley Jackson Crossing the Plains in 1852" (ts., HM 16773, Huntington Library).

[15]Entry for 22 July 1849, Stuart, *Roving Life*, 1: 40. A month later another forty-niner was crossing the Forty-Mile Desert with his seven-member mess. They had lost their wagons and were packing. One of the mess-owned horses died and some messmates took the remaining animal, which was personally owned. "I at once," the owner wrote, "flew to the

wagons were abandoned in the western region of today's Utah. Going down the Humboldt, at least half of the party was on foot. Almost out of food (their few remaining oxen were the only available source), "a portion of the company who had the best horses, about nine of them, parted from the others, and said they were going to travel faster, and get in before they became exhausted." Taking advantage of their stronger private property, they departed, leaving behind the less well equipped.[16]

Eight years later, along the same river, Oliver Goldsmith and a messmate were able to leave the slow-moving Wolverine Rangers in part because they had "our faithful Indian ponies."[17] Had other members of the Wolverine Rangers lost their cattle to the local Diggers or because they drank poison water, they would have had no claim on the horses of Goldsmith and his friend. Company losses fell on all, private losses were not shared.

It would be wrong to leave the impression that the law of property governed all decisions within groups. It did not for Ananias Pond, a forty-niner crossing the Sierra Nevada. He was traveling in a company of two wagons, one member of which was sick. Just as the party passed the summit the cattle became so jaded that only one wagon could continue. The decision was made to leave the second wagon with a guard. Pond was asked to stay and another man volunteered to remain with him. Thinking in terms of property and ownership, Pond recorded surprise that he should be requested to wait. His cattle had survived best and on that basis, he thought, he should have been the one to go on. The two men who did continue, however, were brothers of the sick man being carried to the settlements. They argued that they should accompany him. Pond acquiesced. What interests us is not

---

rescue, and with my knife cut the cords that lashed the burden and let the packs all tumble to the sand. Not one of them uttered a word" (entry for 29 Aug. 1849, McCall, *Wayside Notes*, p. 76).

[16]Bidwell, *Echoes*, pp. 45, 52-55; Josiah Belden, "Statement of Historical Facts on California" (ms., 1878, Bancroft Library), p. 10.

[17]Goldsmith, *Overland*, p. 57.

that an argument of kinship prevailed over the argument of property but that Pond thought the matter should be settled in terms of property rights.[18]

v *The Transmutation of Property*

The conclusion is almost too obvious to draw: emigrants on the overland trail understood and utilized the legal concept that within a single company some wagons could be concurrently owned while others were personal property. When mentioning such arrangements they saw no need to elaborate about legal distinctions.[1]

Emigrants also understood the consequences of investing personal funds in concurrent property. "I had not a dollar in the world," one forty-niner wrote on leaving his company without reimbursement. "[T]he property that we had was Joint stock and I had nothing that was my individual property but my clothes blankets &c. [S]o I selected a few of the best and two blankets and struck out on foot."[2]

The legal sophistication of these nonlawyers is but part of the tale. What must not be overlooked is that pressures against traditional concepts were great on the overland trail — no police, no social permanency, strangers passing never expecting to meet again, stalked by fear of hunger, fear of exposure, and fear of being left behind. Yet if we search the records, there is but one indication that the emigrants may have departed from common law and formulated customary law. Ironically, it may underline, not disprove, the theory that behavior was determined by remembered rules. It was the possible alteration of company property into personal property by prescriptive use.

---

[18]Entry for 29 Sept. 1849, Pond, Journal.

[1]See, e.g., letter from Charles G. Moxley to Emily Moxley, 24 May 1849, Moxley, Correspondence.

[2]Entry for 23 Oct. 1849, Castleman, Diary.

Only a few companies held property in common. This type of ownership occurred when the use of draft and saddle animals depended on need, or they were assigned in rotation.[3] As a rule, concurrent property on the overland trail, like communal property everywhere, tended to take a hue more private than common, more personal than corporate. Generally, company-owned horses, mules, and oxen were assigned to individuals or to wagons either by lottery or at the direction of the elected captain.[4] In companies where mules were used in common, they usually were sold when the company disbanded, or divided among individual members as private property.[5] But where a mule was exclusively ridden by one person, there came a time when it was thought of as the property of that person.[6]

As a case in point, consider a packing company that drew mules from a common pool. We might expect its members to experience equal comforts and hardships during the trip. Equality, after all, is a purpose of common ownership. Instead, the strength and endurance of each animal created differences between individuals, much as if they were owned as personalty. And it was at the very beginning — at the draw, before either the right of use could emerge or a foundation for prescriptive claim could be laid — that luck played a role. "This evening," a forty-niner explained, "we drew lots for the choice of riding animals. Mr. Washington

---

[3]"We have 17 horses in our company which we take turns riding" (*Western Reserve Chronicle* [Warren, Ohio], 22 Aug. 1849, p. 1, col. 6).

[4]Goldsmith, *Overland*, p. 14; entry for 11 May 1849, Gould, *Diary*, p. 65; letter from George Winslow to his wife, 12 May 1849, Hannon, "Introduction and Notes," p. 68; entry for 16 May 1849, Batchelder, Journal; entry for 17 May 1849, Staples, "Diary," p. 78.

[5]Entry for 18 Oct. 1849, Batchelder, Journal.

[6]It is revealing that the same principle of prescription may have been exercised within proprietorship trains in which the teamsters were hired hands working their way over the trail, not shareholders. On starting, one such teamster stated that he owned only "one double blanket, a gun, ammunition, and some clothes." He did not buy a mule but did ride two while herding cattle belonging to his employer. Near Goose Creek, in today's northeastern Nevada, he "commenced to drive an oxteam, having to take the place of another man, as the roads were very rough; the man was driving cattle with my mules, which the Captain of the train took away from him and he had to walk" (entry for 16 Aug. 1854, Murphy, Across, p. 9).

was fortunate in getting first pick, and chose a large, fine, bay stallion. Following all others, by getting the last choice I had left to me a Mexican horse, not prepossessing in appearance, and of doubtful parts."[7] The luck of the draw, therefore, could determine how the journey went for an individual.[8] A good animal, after all, made progress easier than a lame or stubborn one.

When company property devolved upon individuals, they assumed the burden of personal ownership as well as its benefits. In one company all mules, although concurrently owned, were assigned to specific wagons. Early one morning, two were found missing. "As they were my & my partner's mules it devolved upon us to hunt them," wrote a man riding in the wagon to which the missing mules were assigned.[9]

The Granite State Company, which packed all the way to the gold fields in 1849, also acted on the premise that the horse a man rode, even though purchased by the company and assigned by lot to that man, was his personally-owned property. After arriving in California, "[e]ach man had the privilege of retaining the animal he had ridden, or to take his chance of drawing a better one" from among the packing mules.[10] But title did not transfer from the company to the individual when the choice was made. It had occurred long before California. Two months earlier, while in the vicinity of the Wyoming-Idaho line, a member of Granite State dropped his rifle, it accidently discharged, and the ball struck a pack mule in the knee, severing the artery. The owner of the rifle

---

[7]Entry for 26 April 1849, W. G. Johnston, *Overland*, p. 25.

[8]A joint-stock company from today's West Virginia purchased a double-barrel shotgun for each of its eight members. It "bought seventy-seven of one kind and three fine ones that cost $40.00 each. We drew for these guns and I was fortunate enough to get one of the $40.00 ones" (Edward Washington McIlhany, *Recollections of a '49er: A Quaint and Thrilling Narrative of a Trip across the Plains, and Life in the California Gold Fields during the Stirring Days Following the Discovery of Gold in the Far West* [Kansas City, Mo.: Hailman Printing Co., 1908], p. 15).

[9]Entry for 27 July 1850, Moorman, *Journal*, p. 53.

[10]Entry for 18 Oct. 1849, Stuart, *Roving Life*, 1:76-77.

"gave up his [riding] horse to be packed by the men having charge of the mule, and walked ever after."[11]

What happened in Granite State and other companies[12] assigning corporate property to individuals for their exclusive use, was that title eventually transferred from the company to the assignee by some rule defining "ownership" analogous either to adverse possession or prescriptive right. Surely that was the understanding of another forty-niner packer who had been assigned his riding animal by lottery. "[T]he last 7 or eight miles is sandy & heavy," he wrote of the Truckee River route across the Forty-Mile Desert. "[A]s soon as Tylers mule reached this Sand he gave out so far he had to get off & lead him: the same was the case with two or three others. My mule unexpectedly carried me through."[13]

The writer is not as specific as we might like. The words "my mule" and "Tylers mule" can have more than one meaning. Nineteenth-century Americans did not limit use of the possessive pronoun to describing only what they owned. They could call a horse they possessed, borrowed, or bailed "my horse" as readily as a horse to which they had title. But the best reading of this account implies (if it does not assert outright) that the writer thought the mule his property. Little else can be made of his words except that the company's mule, concurrent property when first purchased, had become personal property either by assignment as personalty to its rider or by exclusive use amounting to a prescriptive right.

VI *A Representative Case*

Perhaps the evidence proves the case so well that it does so to our detriment. We could wish that nineteenth-century Americans traveling the overland trail to the Pacific had been less familiar with the various methods of owning property. Had diarists not taken legal concepts for granted, they might have told us more of

---

[11]Ibid., entry for 15 Aug. 1849, 1:53.

[12]For similar transfer of title in 1850 see Bourne, Diary.

[13]Entries for 3-4 Aug. 1849, J. A. Johnson, Note Book.

their theories and of how they defined terms. A rare exception to the general rule was an emigrant from Ohio who recalled how he paid one-fourth the cost of an outfit in 1852 by purchasing a pair of oxen. "They were to be my one-quarter interest in the team," he explained. "If they died, it was to be my loss; if they got through, to California, they were to be my team."[1]

What appears at first to be a purchase of one-fourth the con-currently-owned property of a mess, becomes on explanation a more complicated arrangement. Personal property was combined with other personal property or with mess property to perform a joint task while the owners of each set of property retained both the risk of personal loss and the potential for personal profit. If others had been as revealing about ownership arrangements as was this 1852 emigrant, we might be able to judge whether what he described was sui generis or common on the overland trail. As matters stand, the best guess is that it was less than typical, but not unique.

More exemplary of the details generally furnished by overland accounts is the journal of Robert Beeching, a forty-niner who went to the gold fields of California via the southwestern trail through Texas, New Mexico, and Arizona. He was a member of a New York joint-stock organization that collectively purchased and concurrently held title to all of the wagons and oxen transporting the company. Before starting on the long stretch of wilderness between San Antonio and El Paso, Beeching "purchased an excellent Horse . . . w[h]ich I purpose taking to California useing him as my own."[2] That remark, "as my own," was as close as most emigrants came to explaining the distinction between methods of holding property. Beeching did not specifically state that the horse was his own risk and its loss would be his loss or its sale his profit. But even if he is more vague than the emigrant just quoted, Beeching does not force us to guess. One only has to read a bit between the lines to realize that he acknowledged at least two

---

[1]Stephen T. Gage, "Reminiscences, 1852-1862" (ts., Special Collections Department, Stanford University Libraries), p. 4.

[2]Entry for 22 April 1849, Beeching, *Journal.*

types of ownership within his train: concurrent ownership in the wagons and in the cattle belonging to the joint-stock company, and his own personal ownership in the horse.

More revealing is the diary of Charles Gray who distinguished among four types of ownership while crossing to California. On the evening his train left Independence and crossed the Missouri, Gray slept in "the common stock wagon." That was the first type of ownership he identified: concurrent ownership or, as Gray phrased it, "the common property of the Co."[3]

The second type of ownership identified by Charles Gray was partnership property and, like the personal property Beeching had purchased in Texas, it was a saddle animal. Gray found the overland trail fatiguing. As he was apparently unused to physical hardship, the trip proved demanding on his strength. Within a week, Gray attempted to buy a horse from passing Indians.[4] Failing that, on the twentieth day out, he and at least one other man purchased a horse for seventy dollars from a messmate. That horse was partnership property.[5]

The partnership did not last very long. A little over a month later Gray regretted having "sold my share in our horse some few weeks ago." Because the best ox in the team had died and the remainder were jaded, he was "obliged . . . to walk all the time."[6] It was more physical exertion than his constitution could tolerate. "A very heavy sandy road," Gray complained during the third week of June. "I walked all day behind the train, driving a yoke of lame cattle; never did I remember wishing more earnestly for night (quite as bad as Wellington at Waterloo!) which came at last, but tired, worn & fatigued."[7]

---

[3]Entries for 1 and 10 May 1849, Gray, *Off at Sunrise*, pp. 3, 9, 12. We must guess, but it is almost indisputable that Gray's company was a joint-stock enterprise. Goods purchased in New York had been shipped ahead to California, a common practice among eastern joint-stock concerns intending to mine gold as a company. See ibid., entry for 20 Aug. 1849, p. 83.

[4]Entry for 7 May 1849, Gray, *Passage*.

[5]Ibid., entries for 22 and 30 May 1849.

[6]Entry for 30 June 1849, Gray, *Off at Sunrise*, p. 50.

[7]Ibid., entry for 21 June 1849, p. 42

At Fort Bridger Gray purchased another animal. "I found the constant walking had made my feet so sore," he wrote, "that I should be obliged to have a horse at all hazards & was compell'd to pay $81 for an old, broken down horse & saddle, but our folks think he will recruit."[8] This horse and saddle were personal property.

Charles Gray soon learned that personal ownership did not necessarily solve property problems on the overland trail. Under certain circumstances it compounded them. The responsibility and risk of exclusively owning a horse could be a heavy burden for a New Yorker. "I found him too much trouble to take care of," the city-bred man wrote, "& also some what dangerous to take along as he may break his leg or my neck, or be stolen by the Indians."[9] Perhaps for these reasons — the unwanted risk of personal financial loss and because the horse stepped in a gopher hole, threw him, and hurt his leg — Gray traded the horse and saddle for a yoke of oxen.

The oxen were also personalty and that too posed a problem. Unlike the horse they could not be ridden. To be useful they had to be attached to the mess wagon as Gray well knew. Despite this fact he expected to benefit from their ownership in at least two ways. First, as owner he could set the terms for the animals' bailment. By permitting his messmates use of the oxen, he bargained for the right to "ride all the time" in the wagon — a safer, more comfortable way to travel than jogging on the back of a horse. Second, Gray was speculating, hoping to turn a profit and earn some pocket money. The oxen were "powerful & large, too much so in fact, as I am somewhat fearful of their going through, however if the emigrants on the Fort Hall road dont want them & at a good profit to me also then I'm mistaken very much."[10]

Gray was referring to emigrants taking a different route than he was. Bypassing Fort Bridger and Salt Lake City, they had gone directly west into today's Idaho before turning south into

[8]Ibid., entry for 7 July 1849, p. 55.
[9]Ibid., entry for 16 July 1849, p. 66.
[10]Loc. cit.

Nevada. His idea was that with fewer opportunities to acquire fresh animals than if they had gone via the Mormon settlements, they would be paying higher prices.[11]

Gray succeeded in only half his goal: he sold the animals, but at a loss. "Traded off my large oxen for a smaller pair by giving $10 to boot," he wrote. Still, he counted himself better off than had he found no buyer. Although he had not realized the anticipated profit, the new, "smaller pair" of oxen made him "confident of going through safely."[12]

It would be too much to hope that the new confidence made Charles Gray content. He still felt the burden of overland property. The new oxen may have been better than the former yoke, but the type of ownership bothered him — he had not wanted exclusive personal title. Gray would have preferred the animals held in that fourth type of overland ownership — not as company, partnership, or personalty but as mess property. "My mess," Gray complained, "who have all along refused to buy a yoke with me, permit me however to invest *$100 for their benefit*, which I consider perfectly mean & contemptable."[13]

The remaining oxen drawing the wagon in yoke with Gray's pair were mess property. In fact, Gray purchased his animals to replace an ox that had died just beyond Devil's Gate of alkaline poisoning. "He belonged to my mess," Gray explained.[14] Later, in the Sierras, some "Indians eluded the guards & seized 11 head of cattle." Gray apparently did not have any of his private stock taken — "as the devil would have it they seem[e]d to have selected the best" — but that did not mean he was unaffected. "[O]ur mess looses two," he lamented.[15]

---

[11]Gray also may have been anticipating a much larger group to whom to sell. A year later James Abbey also went via Salt Lake. "Before arriving at the junction of the roads," he wrote on rejoining the main emigration, "we appeared to be almost alone, but now we have any amount of company" (entry for 10 July 1850, Abbey, *A Trip*, p. 145).

[12]Entry for 19 July 1849, Gray, *Off at Sunrise*, p. 68.

[13]Loc. cit. .

[14]Ibid., entry for 26 June 1849, p. 46.

[15]Ibid., entry for 8 Sept. 1849, p. 97.

The mess owned other property. Brandy is an item we know about because one afternoon some of Gray's messmates treated the general traveling company to a spree, much to his annoyance.[16] What else was possessed as mess property is not indicated in Gray's journal. We may, however, be certain there were some items of value for when the New Yorkers reached California it was necessary to settle two different sets of accounts. One was mess business, the other company affairs. In fact Gray negotiated transactions for three different categories of property. First he sold his personally-held animals for substantially less than he had paid for them, underlining the word "my" when recording the transaction as if to emphasize the fact he had sold his own property. That same day Gray disposed of "the common stock wagon & its implements for $250 (about one third of its cost)."[17] The next morning he negotiated an agreement settling mess ownership. "Drew up an article of dissolution between our mess & we all signed it," Gray wrote,[18] giving us no specifics but making it clear that mess property and mess business were not mixed with company property or company business. The affairs of the larger, joint-stock company were more complicated. Gray himself was next day "busy *a long time in making out the* shares & *dividing the gold dust which we received for our common stock wagon & tools, & apportioning it among so many made a long & delicate job of it.*"[19]

---

[16]Entry for 9 July 1849, Gray, *Passage*.

[17]Entry for 7 Oct. 1849, Gray, *Off at Sunrise*, p. 125.

[18]Ibid., entry for 8 Oct. 1849, p. 126.

[19]Ibid., entry for 9 Oct. 1849, p. 126. A year later James Abbey, arriving in California, also dissolved his overland partnership. "This forenoon was occupied in deliberation, and it was concluded to have a division of the mess; consequently we had an auction of a portion of our goods. I bought a sharp pointed shovel for $13.00 and a pick for $4.50. The mess was then dissolved in 'Friendship, Love, and Truth,' as the Odd Fellows say." He might have made it in friendship, love, truth, and law (entry for 20 Aug. 1850, Abbey, *A Trip*, pp. 160-61). Indeed,companies separating at the terminus of the overland trail had no arguments about how property should be divided. Emigrants knew the "owner" because they agreed about the law. "I sold our waggon and mules for $700 reserving the mule I bought on the road in which my partner has no interest" (entry for 15 Aug. 1849, Berrien, "Diary," p. 351).

When that task was completed, Charles Gray and the men with whom he had traversed the overland trail no longer held shares in company or mess property. There was only personal property and, if any two or more men now negotiated agreements to work together in the mines, there may also have been partnership property.

7 | THE BURDEN OF CONCURRENT OWNERSHIP

Too much must not be claimed for the tale so far related. A study of concurrently-owned property does not tell the story of the overland trail. Still, an assertion that is both a criticism and a boast may be made: an understanding of the role played by ownership and of how emigrants viewed types of ownership reveals more than has been suspected by historians of the American West. Indeed, so taciturn have they been concerning the subject that it is not unfair to wonder if historians have suspected anything about what property — or law for that matter — could tell them concerning life, values, and decisions on the frontier. Enough has been said to show that law did play a role on the Oregon and California trails and that it did so because property dominated overland life and by its very nature property is a legal subject. Property, as a concept embodying rights, cannot exist in a state of anarchy, only in a state of law.

Any lingering doubts about the significance of types of property ownership on the overland trail should be dispelled by recalling that property not only determined how an emigrant fared, but whether he undertook the journey. Here concurrent ownership played a major role. Combining resources was the technique by which a large percentage of travelers crossing the plains obtained the means to make the trip. Many, possibly most of the single men and small groups leaving the Missouri River might never have started had they been unable to share the elephant.

It is symbolic of the role played by concurrent ownership that the California trail was opened by two emigrants pooling their property. John Bidwell, who became a leader of the first train of American settlers to scale the Sierras, arrived in western Missouri to find himself alone. Unfavorable publicity caused his would-be companions to change their minds and abandon the quest. With a

157

wagon but no draft animals, Bidwell might have remained behind, had not a young man from Illinois come along. His arrival "seemed almost providential," Bidwell thought. "He was pretty well dressed, was riding a fine black horse, and had ten or fifteen dollars. I persuaded him to let me take his horse and trade him for a yoke of steers to pull the wagon and a sorry-looking, one-eyed mule for him to ride."[1]

What has been said is more significant than one might think. The migration of 1841 was not only epoch making, but its participants were usually poor. Several members of the small band straggling into California late that November could not have undertaken the trip without understanding and acting upon principles of concurrent ownership. Nicholas Dawson, for example, had traded his "horse for an mule." With the money, Dawson "bought an interest in Bartleson's wagon and team" and, after paying his "share of the provisions," he "had seventy-five cents left."[2]

The lesson to be stressed is that John Bidwell, who was destined to achieve national fame in California, and Nicholas Dawson, who was destined to remain but a few months, were able to undertake their historic journey because of partnership arrangements. As the theme of this chapter stresses the burden that concurrently-owned property placed on emigrants rather than its benefits, it is well that the precedents of 1841 not be forgotten.

To maintain a proper perspective it should be kept in mind that concurrently-owned property could bind as well as divide. This fact was not only true when the trip was being organized but also out on the trail. Driving up the North Platte in 1850, a small party of Germans "resolved to devide [sic] all our possessions and leave it to the individual to find his own way, but by evening decided to

---

[1]Bidwell, *Echoes*, p. 21.

[2]Dawson, *Narrative*, p. 9. Others made their arrangement not by purchasing partnership rights but by contract. A young man became a member of the same mess that way. He "joined us after we had started, and begged to be allowed to pay his way by driving our wagon, as he could furnish nothing" (ibid., p. 10).

stick together till we reach Fort Laramie and sell our wagon there." It was a common interest in concurrently-owned property, therefore, that kept this group, even though "desperately depressed," united — at least for the time being.[3]

A second point qualifying the picture of concurrent ownership as a source of divisiveness is that if concurrently-owned property could not be divided it might remain a source of unity, shaping and even defining the social contract. Arriving at Fort Hall in 1849, two physicians "had a fuss" about how one should "tie his mule." As a result, they "concluded to dissolve [the] partnership," which blended both personal and concurrent property. One doctor had title to the wagon and team, the other to the mule, and probably he had also contributed a share of the provisions, all or some of which were concurrently owned. After agreeing to separate, the men encountered two unexpected difficulties. First, they "could not get scales" with which to divide their medicines. Second, the physician who owned the mule attempted "to get a conveyance, but could not." Unable to divide part of their concurrently-owned property or to find alternative transportation for the one who had no ownership claim on the wagon, the physicians "did not dissolve." They remained together until death took one on Lassen's cutoff, just before the end of the trail in northern California.[4]

Concurrently-owned property could be as decisive a factor in uniting large companies as small. Indeed, as often as not it was the binding force of government within joint-stock companies. That is a conclusion we may be inclined to resist but again overland reality departs from the anticipated. Were students of human behavior asked what factor caused some companies, in defiance of an almost universal rule, to cross the overland trail without division, the most likely answer would be leadership. Strong leaders, social theorists might say, held groups together, weak leadership permitted groups to flounder. It is astonishing, but

[3]Scheller, Autobiography, p. 2 (7 June 1850).
[4]Entries for 28-29 July 1849, Caldwell, "Notes," p. 1259.

when the empirical evidence is examined there can be no other conclusion than that leadership played a minor role. The two most significant factors perpetuating organizations were concurrent ownership and contractual obligation.[5]

Concurrent ownership, to a large degree, was the controlling consideration. It was not just a matter of the obvious — that creation of dependent property relationships determined the makeup of traveling groups or the patterns of companionship. Besides furnishing social cohesiveness, concurrently-owned property was a source of legal coercion. Proof comes from the Granite State Company of 1849. At the very time it was being pulled apart by the pressures of concurrently-owned property it was held together by property that members owned concurrently.

For a packing company, the Granite State organization owned a large amount of property, much of which some members considered not only useless but dangerous, as it was excessive weight wearing down the animals.[6] Any suggestion that loads be lightened, however, was resisted by those fearful of abandoning a single article. Add to that controversy the belief of some that the company was "too large to travel in one body" and it is evident why there were members thinking of dividing. Yet Granite State did not divide and the reason it did not was the same as that pulling it apart: concurrent ownership of property. The company was "so situated," it was said, "it cannot well be dissolved." Granite State, a member explained, "would have been dissolved long before it reached California had it not been for the beef

---

[5]"Binding the Elephant," pp. 301-10; "Tied to the Elephant," pp. 153-59.

[6]Granite State was a joint-stock company that subdivided its concurrent property among messes. It is interesting, therefore, to find that contention over property concurrently owned occurred within some messes as well as the larger company. A week before arriving at Fort Kearny, dissenting members of one mess overhauled their packs and tossed away "all of the axes, picks and shovels not needed on the route." When a member opposed to lightening saw what had been done, he threatened a "courtmartial" unless they repacked everything. The minority refused. "We offered to take our share of the mess weight [i.e., provisions], but more we would not [carry] any longer." The matter was dropped, and the weight not needed for the trip was left behind (entry for 10 June 1849, Stuart, *Roving Life*, 1:29-30).

cattle, which were the means of holding it together. They were their principal dependence for food, and it was not practical to divide them among small squads, as they would have been little benefit to them." Unable to divide the concurrently-owned property, the company itself could not divide.[7]

ii *Mess and Partnership Property*

In an effort to balance the picture of concurrently-owned property on the overland trail we may have been led too far astray. The emphasis should not be on concurrent ownership as a unifier, but as a divider. Concurrently-owned property was as much a burden on the overland trail as it was a necessity.

The experiences of John Hale in 1849 are illustrative. Arriving in Independence from his native New York, Hale "joined funds with three men to purchase a team and outfit for a journey to California." About sixty miles out on the trail the newly-formed partnership, with its concurrently-owned wagon, team of seven mules, and single horse, encountered four men returning to Independence. They reported that they had traveled three hundred miles and that it was impossible to get across to California. The New Yorker became worried. "[T]hey looked like men of good strength, courage, and intelligence," he reasoned. "I thought they had come to a wise conclusion and felt desirous to follow their example; but I could not persuade my company to return; consequently was obliged to proceed on the journey." He was "obliged" to go west because the property in which he owned a share was going west. At Fort Kearny, the partnership fell in with a government supply train traveling to Fort Hall. Again Hale began to worry. The teamsters crawled along at ten miles a day, half the pace he thought necessary if California was to be reached before November. Hale's three partners refused to

---

[7]Entries for 18 June, 24 July, and 19 Oct. 1849, Webster, *Gold Seekers*, pp. 49, 63, 96. Although beef held Granite State together, individual messes within the organization divided, while remaining corporate parts of the larger company (entry for 24 July 1849, Stuart, *Roving Life*, 1:41).

leave the train, however, because the teamsters kept night watch "which relieved them of the trouble."

Reaching Fort Laramie after long delays, Hale concluded he had to leave his three partners or risk never getting across the Sierras before snow blocked the passes. He demanded that the concurrently-owned property be redistributed as severalty. "They refused to let me have it," he wrote, and so Hale appealed to the commander of the military garrison. "[H]e decided that I should have a division, which was effected at the Fort; we then had seven mules which were sold at auction. This gave the men the advantage of getting the best mules, as I was limited in funds, consequently I was obliged to bid off the two poorest."[1]

Hale had been both in and out of luck. His misfortune in not having the money to bid on equal terms with his partners was balanced by the fact that the government had purchased Fort Laramie a few days before from a fur company and stationed a garrison there. It was rare for an emigrant to have a government official to whom to appeal for assistance. Until you reached the end of the journey in either California or Oregon, there was no place on the overland trail at which you could conduct a law suit except Salt Lake City. The experience of C. W. Smith was more common: out in the wilderness and wanting to leave his partners, he had no choice but to take what was offered and walk away. On the Humboldt River in today's Nevada, Smith became impatient with the pace of travel. Making the best he could of the bargain, Smith "sold out my share in the team, and in company with another of our party who sold out his team also, proceeded ahead of the wagons, carrying our provisions upon a pony."[2]

The facts should be understood. Smith wished to travel faster

---

[1] J. Hale, *California*, pp. 5, 8-10, 14.

[2] Entry for 18 July 1850, C. W. Smith, Journal. Others unable to appeal to third parties for judgment and, unlike Smith, unable to sell, were forced by concurrent ownership to remain in their situation. A company, for example, divided over the issue of Sunday travel. Those wishing to journey on Sunday moved on. "Githens wished to go, but Lewis would not consent and they could not agree in [sic] a division, so he gave it up" (entry for 23 May 1852, Thomson, *Crossing the Plains*, p. 37).

162

but was restrained by concurrent ownership. To make better time and escape that burden he "sold out" his share of the partnership property. To do so he had to be willing to pack his provisions on a horse and walk the remainder of the way from the Humboldt into California.

Dissatisfaction over the pace of travel was only one cause for partners and messmates feeling the burden of concurrent ownership. Another was the clash of personality. Concurrent property bound individual owners one to another and if a co-owner was disagreeable, antisocial, or a slacker, his companions might have to give up some of that property to be free of him.

A few days beyond St. Joseph, a mess from what is now West Virginia discovered that one of its members, "of a stubborn quarrelsom[e] disposition," was unwilling to take his turn at camp chores. During "his week to cook," for example, he "left the tent and was cooking his Solitary breakfast without troubling himself about the rest of us." A burden on his messmates, he posed a threat to social harmony that could be removed only by purchasing his share of the property. "We concluded," a member of the mess wrote, "the best thing we could do was to buy him out and let him go which accordingly we did by paying him one hundred doll[ar]s."[3]

When money, or sufficient dividable property, was available the burden of concurrent ownership might be easily eliminated. A good illustration is the negotiation conducted by one man terminating a partnership by bartering away claims on concurrently-owned property. It is of special interest because the emigrant no longer able to tolerate his companion and wanting to end their connection was both a lawyer and a judge. He had purchased two-thirds of the outfit and knew that had a court been available to adjudicate the dispute, his obnoxious associate might have been found to have a claim on no more than one third of the property. Perhaps because he was so anxious to be free of the

---

[3]J. S. Wilson, "A Trip across the Plains" (ms., Western Americana Collection, Beinecke Library), pp. 7-8.

man — "the lowest and most degraded human being I have ever met with" — the lawyer did not quibble. "I willingly gave him all he asked for his one third interest in the concern, one yoke of oxen and the pair of cows, keeping three yoke, the wagon, and all the provisions (which I [had] bought myself)."[4]

The implication is that the lawyer surrendered a larger share of the partnership property than the other man would have received had they settled their business east of the Missouri River. The reason the lawyer did so was because his partner, as one-third owner, had rights not to a specific third of the partnership property, but a one-third interest in all the property. Those rights could be terminated only by mutual agreement or by judicial action. Had a court been available the lawyer might have sought a legal or equitable division. Unable to do so, he had to accept a higher price than a jury might have imposed.

Even if everyone was social, cooperative, and industrious, emigrants could become unhappy with concurrent ownership. For some it was just not worth the effort. That was why Elisha Perkins and his messmates dissolved their partnership. As he explained, they anticipated "so much less work & trouble to cook for ourselves only & take care of our own goods than to do the same for the company."[5]

Messmates sometimes quarreled over mess purchases[6] or became angry at the use or misuse of things belonging to the mess.[7] The same was true for personal property. Mess members like Charles Gray felt imposed upon when incurring costs others

---

[4]Entry for 30 June 1852, Crane, Journal.

[5]Entry for 1 July 1849, Perkins, Sketches.

[6]Some members of one party, authorized to purchase animals, traded "a favorite dun mule for two other animals. Great fault was found at this barter by some members of our mess, and was the occasion of a bitter quarrel this evening; one never afterwards healed. Cordial relations, I regret to say, were severed" (entry for 18 April 1849, W. G. Johnston, *Overland*, p. 20).

[7]"[S]ome of the company cut up our chair and bench for to make warm water for Foster [sick with cholera] which caused a great row and ended in a seperation" (entry for 13 June 1849, Hoover, Diary).

did not share, such as purchasing oxen for the common wagon. "Ames," an emigrant wrote of a companion, "grumbles because he has to put his horses on [the] heavy wagon."[8]

In messes the wagon or team might be the personal property of one member or the partnership property of more than one, but generally provisions were concurrently owned by all. The fact is significant. By its very nature, at least in times of shortages, food and concurrent ownership of food contained the seeds of conflict. Indeed, there did not have to be famine for concurrent owners to suspect that others might be taking advantage of them. "There was a considerable wrangling about mess no. 1 helping themselves to bread," a forty-niner wrote. The date was 21 May, when the emigration had been on the trail for less than three weeks and food was being discarded by the ton at almost every camp site.[9]

At other times, when food was scarce, not only hunger but fear of hunger bred suspicion that a messmate was eating more than his share of the common "grub." During 1856, a German and an American who had worked their passage to Salt Lake City and then packed, were relieved of most of their possessions by Indians. Virtual strangers, in the middle of a hostile desert, without horses, and with scanty provisions, whatever mutual trust previously existed between them soon dissipated. One became convinced the other was eating too much, a situation that surely would precipitate violence, even homicide, if it occurred in a work of fiction about the overland trail. Real life was different. Each man respected the other's right to property and,

---

[8]Gray: Chapter 6, p. 154. "Ames grumbles": entry for 29 May 1850, Cagwin, Diary. Conversely, emigrants whose property was contracted to serve a mess might have to take steps to preserve it by providing substitutes. A forty-niner, for example, owned an ox that was obliged by agreement to help haul a wagon. The ox became sick. "There was a cow in the company," owned by a partnership of two men. To save his oxen, the forty-niner purchased the share of one of the owners of the cow and, with permission of the other owner (his new partner), put the cow in yoke, "and drove my ox before the train" permitting it to recruit. Entry for 1 July 1849, Delano, *Across the Plains*, p. 50.

[9]Entry for 21 May 1849, Farnham, Gold Rush, p. 3; Farnham, "From Ohio," 21 April 1849, p. 303.

despite different national backgrounds, they shared an understanding of concurrent ownership. As a result, these emigrants did not resort to force, they reached a settlement. The two "parted company," the American wrote, "and divided our little share of 'grub;' my share was six pints of flour, and one of coffee; no meat!! I am very glad of the separation, for he had been stealing the little bread left after satisfying *lightly* our *crawling* appetites."[10]

On no occasions did emigrants more keenly show their appreciation of the implications of concurrent ownership on the overland trail than when acknowledging its potential for internal conflict. One mess, for example, discovered that its sugar was being consumed faster than planned. Rather than impose rationing or end the partnership, the mess divided the common stock of sugar. Each man received the same portion, and it was for him to decide how quickly his share would be consumed or how carefully it would husbanded.[11] By converting concurrent into personal property, the mess avoided one of the burdens inherent in mess ownership — quarrels about unequal consumption.[12]

III   *Joint-Stock Company Property*

When a mess was not traveling alone but was part of a company, it could be easier to adjust differences between

---

[10]J. R. Brown, *Across the Plains*, p. 93.

[11]Entry for 19 May 1850, Parker, Notes. It is interesting to note that Parker was not a partner in the mess. He was a passenger who had paid one hundred thirty dollars to be taken overland. Yet, when the sugar was divided he received a share equal to that given the concurrent owners. This practice was customary on the overland trail.

[12]Bernard Reid described a similar division: "For a good while back our rations of sugar had been growing small and at our frugal board some were given to complain that others were taking more than their share. This led to unpleaseant bickering and, to avoid its continuance, I proposed to make a little muslin purse or sugar bag for each of the mess, into which the sugar ration was to be equally distributed when served to the commissary every fifth day. Then each man could help himself at meal time out of his own stock and no one could complain. This was assented to, and I was appointed to spoon out to each man his equal modicum of sugar. It worked like a charm, and there was no more bickering from that cause" (entry for 26 July 1849, Reid, Diary, p. 44).

messmates who feared too much was being eaten or that they were not receiving their fair share of the common provisions. If their company was a joint-stock concern, disagreements might readily be adjusted by subdividing company property into mess property or by moving an unhappy man from one mess within the organization to another.[1] Should he be reluctant to switch and if there was no bylaw compelling him, the problem might have to be solved by private consideration. "This morning," an 1852 emigrant wrote, "Giles & Morton fell out because the grub was nearly gone and G always thought M took more than his share. To get rid of [Morton] Giles proposed to give Morton the last five dollars he had to leave his mess & join another. He accepted and barefooted Bill fell in with us for the balance of the journey."[2]

Compensation might also be needed to shift messes in traveling companies. After all, the most notable mark distinguishing traveling from joint-stock companies was that traveling companies were not property owners. Unlike joint-stock organizations, therefore, members did not concurrently own the provisions and messes were legally autonomous. For a member to shift from one to another required negotiations and occasional compensation.

Because traveling companies owned no concurrent property it may be thought they were unburdened by it. Oddly enough, this is not true, or at least it is not true that they were free of the burden of property. Within traveling companies, however, most problems were created by personal, mess, or partnership property rather than company-owned concurrent property. The topic can be summarized by considering events that occurred during the early days of the Oregon Trail. The 1842 emigration, for instance, experienced a number of squabbles over individually-owned property. One involved the difficult matter of balancing private rights to personalty with the need for public order. The train was

---

[1]"We voted to divide the company into five messes, as there was contention among the members concerning our mode of traveling" (entry for 23 June 1849, Sedgley, *Overland to California*, p. 28).

[2]Entry for 27 July 1852, Diary John Clark, quoted in Eaton, *Overland*, pp. 213-14.

not far out on the trail when, a diarist noted, there was "much excitement in camp about Dogs: 22 dogs shot." An unusually high percentage of the party had brought along dogs, and those who had none were irritated. The arguments against dogs are not important: the frivolous, that they would go mad on the plains, or the serious, that their barking would frighten away game and attract Indians. What is significant is that the traveling company divided on the legal issue of the right of members to own a certain species of personal property. Following debate, a majority apparently voted to eliminate the dogs. Acting much as if they were abating a nuisance, nonowners started shooting the animals. Owners, also carrying onto the plains theories of American law, in this case the right to preserve and defend personal property, armed themselves. The crisis was resolved when both sides, seeking compromise, agreed on new leadership.[3]

Later, at Green River, the emigration again quarreled over personal property. One faction favored abandoning the wagons for packhorses. Others, generally family men, wanted to take their wagons into Oregon. This time the company divided permanently. Those keeping their wagons continued on as a unit, while the packers pushed ahead.[4]

Next year, 1843, occurred the most famous dispute over property in the history of the Oregon Trail. Some members of that emigration started overland with "from 50 to 100 head of [personally-owned] cattle." Demanding that obligations of mutual security be pushed to their logical limits, they insisted that guard

---

[3]Entry for 18 May 1842, Crawford, "Journal," pp. 7-8; Ghent, *Road*, p. 59; Ray Allen Billington, *The Far Western Frontier, 1830-1860* (New York: Harper & Bros., 1956), p. 96. Twenty-two years later a somewhat similar incident occurred. "[H]ad a stampede broke 2 wagons and tore off some horns caused by a dog in the evening had a split on the dog question leaving 25 wagons in our train the dogs and from another train the Major wanted all the dogs killed" (entry for 15 Aug. 1864, "Life and Memoirs of A. P. Flory from Date May the First, A.D. One Thousand Eight Hundred and Sixty-Four, to July 31st, A.D. One Thousand Eight Hundred and Sixty-Eight" [ts., Washington State Historical Society], p. 5).

[4]Lavender, *Westward*, p. 357.

duty be mandatory upon all men in the traveling company. Those with just draft animals or only one or two family cows saw no reason for being required to stay awake keeping watch over other people's property.[5] It is hardly surprising that the company divided. Overland historians, generally more interested in the picturesque than with substance, have often told how sixty-one wagons belonging to families owning no more than three cows went in one company, twenty-five wagons belonging to cattle owners went with the so-called cow column made famous by its captain, Jesse Applegate.[6] What has not been noted is that the division resulted when emigrants were unable to resolve the conflict between private interest and corporate responsibility.

Similar events took place during the 1850s. A common occurrence was for traveling companies to divide should one or more wagons stop for repairs. Some or all of the other members of the party would roll on. As with messes and joint-stock organizations, a major cause of dissension within traveling companies was the rate of speed. Unlike messes and joint-stock concerns, however, the controversy within traveling companies generally related to the inferior condition of someone else's personal property.[7]

Not all distinctions turned on the type of ownership. Messes, partnerships, and joint-stock organizations all were owners of concurrent property. But joint-stock organizations, unlike messes

---

[5]Entry for 31 May 1843, Reading, Diary, pp. 3-4; Ghent, *Road*, p. 71; Lavender, *Westward*, p. 369.

[6]Lavender, *Westward*, p. 370; entry for 8 June 1843, Reading, Diary, p. 6; Applegate, "Cow Column." For a similar event in 1846 see D. L. Morgan, "Introduction and Notes," p. 92.

[7]Conversely, although more rare, the high quality of some private property could set owners socially apart and create such jealousy that no one would be sorry when the traveling company split apart. For example: "Ten wagons had horses only, which made their owners our 'aristocracy.' They would not conform to the rules, would not stand guard, and made themselves very disagreeable. The ladies dressed in their merinos, white collars, chains, rings, and brooches. They had their crockery ware instead of tin and late into the night they danced and sang and fiddled, so hardly anyone could sleep for the noise they made. Soon they found it too slow to travel in a train with oxen, and left us, expecting to gallop into California" (Lydia Milner Waters, "Account of a Trip across the Plains in 1855," *Society of Southern California Pioneers Quarterly*, 5 [1929]: 62).

or small partnerships, were generally oversupplied with provisions and seldom dissolved because of suspicion that some members were eating more than their share of the common food. That fact does not mean that among the large or wealthy groups consumption of common provisions posed no problems. Joint-stock companies occasionally experienced difficulties when items had peculiar appeal, such as sugar or brandy.[8] To say these were minor irritants, however, might be nothing more than acknowledging that property important to one category of owner had less significance to another. For when we look at the record, it does seem that although joint-stock companies had few quarrels about food concurrently owned, they often quarreled because of other property they owned concurrently. In fact, the three chief causes for the disbanding of joint-stock companies on the overland trail all related to ownership of property. The three were: (1) dis-

---

[8]The problem of sugar has been referred to previously. Problems posed by company-owned whiskey were generally less serious than might be thought. The physician of a forty-niner company from Cincinnati, finding much of the common brandy gone and no members admitting they drank it, was more amused than troubled. "Our brandy," he noted, "was taken along for medicinal purposes the company being organized under the titotal abstinence principle, but that *Brandy* was a very popular preventive and of course was *all* used medicinally" (Farnham, Gold Rush, p. 303). J. Goldsborough Bruff, the captain of the Washington City Company was more disturbed when some malcontents in his organization raided the medicine chest. "At night the disaffected gang, or 5 of them, stole the wine, reserved for medicinal purposes," he complained. "They turned the bung of the keg down and swore the wine leaked out, though I noticed great laughter & hilarity in their wagons at night." (Bruff, *Journals,* pp. 195-96). Although consumption of food caused most dissension, the implication must not be left that concurrent ownership of items such as brandy did not create difficulties for messes as well as for joint-stock companies. It has already been noted that Charles Gray became annoyed when his messmates treated the general traveling company to a spree with their brandy (see p. 154, above). "One of our mess this afternoon," Gray mourned, "with a very ill judged liberality took out our brandy demijohn & about half the camp got in a spree, all being in first rate humour." Gray had reason to be unhappy as he had use for the brandy. Due to "violent attacks" of "rheumatism," he suffered much pain. His "*only* remedy," one he employed several times while keeping his diary, was "a large dose of brandy [which] put me in a comparatively insensible state, thereby giving me a little comfort." Once when sick, Gray passed "a tolerable night by the aid of a lot of whiskey." "This brandy," he lamented on the day the camp drank it, "is certainly the best 'pain extractor' extant" (entries for 9 July, 10 June, and 4 Aug. 1849. Gray, *Off at Sunrise*, pp. 57, 33, 75).

satisfaction with the pace of travel; (2) arguments over retaining property necessary for the trip; and (3) fear animals were burdened with too much weight.[9]

Little need be said about speed. A caravan could travel only as fast as its slowest part and that fact meant trouble no matter how well organized it was or how close knit its members.[10] More deserving of careful attention is the matter of weight. For joint-stock organizations it created more complicated questions than did speed of travel, and posed the most serious problems connected with concurrent ownership of property. "None of the emigrants," a Michigan forty-niner observed, "know how to fit out for their journey. They are all split upon the same rock."[11] The statement was especially relevant that year to joint-stock companies. Most planned to dig gold together in California and left

---

[9]There were, of course, other reasons, not related to concurrent property ownership, for joint-stock companies dividing on the plains. Personality clashes were a cause, politics another. Men aspiring for office were suspected of being agitators (entry for 24 July 1849, Read and Gaines, "Introduction," p. 500n210). "I have seen enough on this trip," Israel Hale wrote, "to satisfy me that a co-partnership or stock company will not do. The reason is: men do not think alike" (Potter, "Introduction," p. 38). Put another way, a second emigrant explained that "there is too much legislation on the plains, which invariably results in disagreement" (entry for 13 June 1850, C. W. Smith, Journal). When his wagon left their "original company," another man thought of pursuing "our journey without further entangling alliances with foreign nations or companies" (Ferguson, *Gold Fields*, p. 54).

[10]For example, in one forty-niner company, emigrants with fast wagons and strong yokes complained "because some of the messes had bad teams" (entry for 25 May 1849, Decker, *Diaries*, p. 272n62). Another cause of dissension, dividing messes, partnerships, property-owning companies, and traveling companies, was the issue of Sunday travel. See, e.g., entry for 28 July 1850, Loomis, *Journal*, p. 103; entry for 30 May 1852, E.B.M. Hanna, "Journal," p. 37. It is a revealing commentary upon the importance of ownership on the overland trail that quarrels about resting on the Sabbath not only divided property owners , they created sectarian property-owning groups. "This morning we had another division of our company. Our captain and two other families left us, making in all 4 wagons and a carriage. They wished to travel on the Sabbath. The company took a vote on it. All the rest wished to remain, so they left. Now we are reduced to 5 wagons and our carriage. Our captain was not a professor of religion, nor any of the others excepting his wife. We are still a Presbyterian colony! The owner of each wagon left is a Presbyterian" (ibid., entry for 4 July 1852, p. 59).

[11]Mattes, *Platte River Road*, p. 51.

the Missouri River burdened with weight not needed until the end of the trip. The Iron City Rangers from Pittsburgh, for example, "loaded down with shooting irons of various kinds," started for the west coast with an experienced chemist, "all necessary mining equipment," and provisions for nine months.[12]

Valuable property of this type was expected to hold a company together. As often as not it was a source of division. Those who thought of cost viewed concurrently-owned posses- sions from one perspective, those who worried about the animals from another. Before leaving New England the Granite State Company purchased trunks especially made for packing. For about a month after crossing the Missouri, some members urged "the company to break them up and make bags from the leather covering," only to be "laughed at by the majority." The more cautious also wanted the company to stop hauling heavy iron spades, picks, and shovels. Had these items been personalty, the owner could have done as he pleased. Concurrently-owned property was less easily discarded. "There are," a New Hampshire member explained, "such a large number in the company that are so bitterly opposed to leaving any such article that they will defeat any such measure proposed; and even call all foolish who believe it would be wise to lighten the loads of our poor mules in such a manner."[13]

"[W]e k[n]ew," another forty-niner wrote, "that we must either loose a great deal of our property now by throwing it away or loose all our teams soon with provisions clothing and every thing else if we did not do something to help our horses so we all agreed to throw away everny [sic] thing that we did not actu[a]l[l]y stand in need of and there were several who wanted to throw away all the tools but this was opposed [by the captain and the company physician] . . . so we overhalled our waggons and threw away a great many things that we thought might be disposed of but was still compel[le]d to hall 2 or 300 lbs of tools and castons

[12]*New York Herald*, 22 April 1849, quoted in Giffen, "Notes," p. 275n88.
[13]Entries for 9 July and 18 June 1849, Webster, *Gold Seekers*, pp. 57, 49.

which never was worth having even when they wer[e] first made."[14]

To elicit a legal theory from this account, we must surmise that in some companies an individual's right to his share of the concurrently-owned property was so absolute that one or two members could prevent company-owned property being destroyed. This fact probably would not be true if the controversial weight consisted of convertible commodities in the nature of res fungibles. Another point is apparent. When the minority blocked the will of the majority, the majority did not have to thwart openly the minority's property rights. They could simply redistribute loads among the wagons, and leave behind what was not wanted.[15] The same tactic was even more true in companies where the majority ruled and a minority of members wanted to lighten. By acting covertly they did more than avoid forcing their opponents to confront them. By not raising the question they made their action less illegal than it would have been had there been a public scandal. That was the method used by some members of the Granite State Company to unburden themselves of useless concurrent property. One of the animals was packing a patent "filter" they suspected would not work even if taken all the way to the gold mines. It weighed thirty pounds, quite a bit to be carried "on the sore backs of mules" for two thousand miles. Somewhere between the North Platte crossing and Independence Rock the man having it in charge discreetly left it by the side of the road.[16]

In some organizations, the majority seems to have been able to

---

[14]Entry for 14 Sept. 1849, Castleman, Diary.

[15]Entries for 23 and 24 Aug. 1849, Lord, Journal.

[16]Entries for 18 June and 20 July 1849, Webster, *Gold Seekers*, pp. 49, 61. The point should be made that even when there was no strife about whether to discard property, concurrent ownership could still be divisive. What remained, after all, was still company owned. After lightening, for example, one company sold a wagon, but kept possession of the four mules that had been hauling that wagon. The members then started to squabble about how those four mules should be employed and how to redistribute the load that had been carried in the wagon they were selling (entry for 4 June 1849, Decker, *Diaries*, p. 88).

dispose not only of concurrently-owned property but of property personally owned by individual members.[17] At Fort Kearny one company of forty-niners held a meeting and decided to equalize "the private baggage — disgarding [sic] a great deal of superfluous weight."[18] It is not clear, however, what could have been done if owners of personalty objected.[19] Possibly the safety of concurrently-owned wagons and draft animals had priority over personally-owned excess weight. A majority of the Boston-Newton Company, in which the mules, vehicles, and provisions were owned by the organization, "voted that no member should carry more than 100 lbs. unless he paid 25 cts. per pound for all extra." In a passenger train, by contrast, it was the owners of the personalty rather than the corporate property who made the decision.[20] The Pioneer Line was a hundred miles beyond South Pass when the passengers concluded that they had little chance of getting through with what they were carrying. "We accordingly agreed," one wrote, "to sacrifice our baggage and lighten up the train. Each man was limited thenceforth to 75 pounds, everything included. I threw away, consequently, more than half my outfit, which was considerable loss."[21]

One of the heaviest property burdens individuals encountered as members of joint-stock companies was the rule, contained in many articles of agreement, that no one could withdraw from the

---

[17]Entries for 16-17 July 1849, Staples, "Diary," pp. 137-38.

[18]Entry for 17 June 1849, Bruff, *Journals*, p. 23.

[19]For example, the same company that "equalized" the private baggage, later ran into contention over personally-owned weight. "Here," the captain wrote on Lassen's cutoff, "the selfishness of some of my men was exhibited to such a degree, in reference to the baggage of 2 of their comrades, that I had to interfere in a peremptory manner" (ibid., entry for 24 Sept. 1849, p. 189).

[20]Entry for 7 July 1849, Gould, "Diary," p. 129. The Granite State Company, for all its difficulty with concurrent property, had no trouble limiting personally-owned weight, probably because everyone was bound by majority decision. At Fort Kearny, "The clothing of each man was limited to 50 pounds *and weighed*" (entry for 18 June 1849, Stuart, *Roving Life*, 1:30).

[21]Reid, "Letter," p. 228. For more details, see entry for 11 July 1849, Reid, Diary, pp. 36-37.

association without approval of a specified percentage of the membership. The usual penalty for doing so was forfeiture of property rights.[22]

The Wolverine Rangers from Michigan apparently had such a rule. When they arrived on the Humboldt River in 1849, Oliver Goldsmith and one of his messmates could no longer tolerate either the slow pace of travel or the mosquitoes. When they announced they were leaving, however, the Rangers sought to dissuade them by voting

> to give us each five pounds of hard bread for our interests. We thought that rather a small amount of food to carry a man through a journey of three hundred miles — which we supposed was the distance to the summit of the Sierras, though it proved to be nearer seven hundred miles by the route we took — still we were determined to go and accepted the offer. When they saw we were fully decided, the different messes contributed five pounds of coffee and three pounds of sugar for us.[23]

Enforcement of the forfeiture rule sometimes took an ironic twist. As the Wolverine Rangers demonstrated, emigrants who worried about friends' safely getting through on their own could try discouraging them by proportioning less than equal shares of the concurrently-owned provisions. Troublesome or quarrelsome men, on the other hand, found it easier to have rules suspended. An example is provided by a couple of members of the Washington City Company. Termed by the captain "2 of the most obnoxious men in the company" they wanted to move ahead of the wagons and asked the others to "grant them the 2 lead mules of their wagon, (mediocre animals) 6 days rations of bread, and a full discharge from the company." The chief

---

[22]Rule: e.g., "No member shall be allowed to withdraw from the Company, without the written consent of two thirds of all the members." Article 18, Constitution of the Sagamore and California Mining and Trading Company, Lynn, Massachusetts (1849) (Library, California Historical Society, San Francisco). Penalty: Article 1, section 2, of the Constitution just cited; also, Agreement of Monroe Michigan Association, printed in Coy, *Great Trek*, p. 100. See also "Tied to the Elephant," pp. 147-48.

[23]Goldsmith, *Overland*, pp. 57-58.

opposition seems to have been based on a remarkably legalistic argument that was overcome by an answer equally legalistic. "Some members were opposed to it at first, as a bad precedent, but when I told them how cheaply we should thus rid ourselves of these troublesome fellows, and that it must be a peculiar case, expressly for that, and no other occasion, it unanimously passed, with 3 cheers."[24]

If members wishing to withdraw were not as unpopular as these two, opposition to rule changes could be substantial. Ironically, to get permission to leave, they might have to threaten to make themselves social misfits and perhaps even cause trouble.

The tactic did not always succeed, as Albert Thurber discovered. He was a Rhode Islander who joined a joint-stock company of forty-four members chiefly from Boston and Roxbury in Massachusetts. Before they had traveled very far onto the plains, Thurber wanted to resign — even at the cost of losing most of his investment. "At night," he explained, "a meeting of the company was held when I proposed that if they would let me have one mule (cost $34) and 100 lbs. of provisions that I would make over to the co. all my interest amounting to $275.00. They would not do it. I told them that I loved peace and had made the proposition in order to have it, but if they would not grant for me to leave I should take the liberty of freely expressing my opinion at any and all times." The company, Thurber concluded, was so excessively overloaded it "would never see California." He even "[g]ave a lecture on freighting west iron gold washers, [and] an enormous amount of India rubber hose, picks, spades and shovels," but to no avail. The majority was not persuaded and his request was denied.[25]

Thurber was unable to convert a share of the company's concurrently-owned property into personal property freeing him to move at his own pace until he had traveled the length of today's

---

[24]Entry for 27 Sept. 1849, Bruff, *Journals,* pp. 195-96.

[25]Thurber, Journal, p. 21.

Nebraska and arrived at Fort Laramie. The organization to which he belonged was one of the many that year to disintegrate there. "[T]he dividing fever raged," he wrote. "[W]e divided into 4 messes and here the company was virtually broke up and we divided [the] animals by lot."[26]

iv   *A Representative Case*

At about the time Thurber and his fellow stockholders were terminating their concurrently-owned property holdings, the Cincinnati Mining and Trading Company was also at Fort Laramie reorganizing itself from a joint-stock to a traveling company. Following its fortunes across the plains, and considering how it shed the burden of concurrent ownership, will serve both to summarize the contents of this chapter and introduce issues to be considered in the next.

The Cincinnati Mining and Trading Company had a capitalization of $25,000 and a membership of fifty, separated into messes of five men each. To accommodate the ten messes, Cincinnati owned ten mule teams, one ox team, "and a large Santa Fe wagon."[1]

Even before reaching Fort Kearny, members of Cincinnati Company, like so many other forty-niners, discovered that their wealth was not a source of strength. It was, instead, a burden: a source of disharmony, dissension, and division. In his diary, a member explained why:

> Our teams are beginning to be a good deal jaded, our wagons being much too heavily loaded. At noon called a meeting of the company and at which meeting resolved to abandon a part of our property as it was considered impossible almost to take it through. A committee, composed of two others and myself, was appointed to select out the property to be abandoned and in accordance to said duty commenced designating the articles which should be left

---

[26]Ibid., pp. 21-22.
[1]Entries for 23, 25, and 26 April 1849, Nixon, Journal.

and among the proscribed articles was a coining ap[p]aratus which had cost the company between 5 & 600$, but to this sacrifice of property this is of said aparatus, there was quite a good deal of dissatisfaction, consequently the committee had to consent to let it go.[2]

The dispute about the coining machine bears close attention. Embodied within it are all three major reasons for the dividing of joint-stock companies: unhappiness with the rate of travel, fear that the wagons were hauling more weight than was safe, and doubts about the necessity of retaining certain kinds of property.

The victory of the niggardly could at best be temporary. As the draft animals declined and fears arose in proportion, the alarmists were certain to become more vocal. One day beyond Fort Kearny and eight after voting to keep the coining machine, Cincinnati Company appointed a second committee "whose duty should be to have a general supervision over the property of the Co[mpany] and make such sales purchases or disposition of property as they might deem proper to expedite our movement towards the end of our journey."[3] The committee contracted with a stranger emigrant to carry the controversial machine to Sacramento for one hundred dollars. Whether many members expected to see the "Aparatus" in California is doubtful. As one who had wished to discard it observed, the carrier was "not bound to deliver the coining Aparatus at the [Sutter's] Fort if he fails to get his wagons through." The question, however, is immaterial to our theme. What is significant is that an amiable compromise had been ironed out. One faction saved face by not discarding the machine; the other accomplished its goals of relieving the draft animals of excessive weight.[4]

---

[2]Ibid., entry for 10 May 1849.

[3]Ibid., entry for 18 May 1849.

[4]Ibid., entry for 23 May 1849. Unbonded contracts of this nature were not as unusual as might be supposed. In some instances it is even possible the machinery was delivered. Such may have been the case for a small Tennessee joint-stock company transporting quartz crushers. Down to one wagon, their mules jaded, and crossing the treacherous Hastings cutoff, "we negotiated with a man who had an ox team to haul our mortars through — six in number — for which we gave him one; — thus making our wagon much

Restoration of good feelings proved only temporary. Some members of the company continued to worry about the weight being hauled, others insisted nothing more be thrown away. At Fort Laramie the inevitable occurred when it was discovered that so much property was being abandoned by overloaded emigrants that it was impossible for the company to sell its surplus as apparently had been planned. The men were now "much dispirited as our animals were beginning to give out. Many were in favor of dissolving the company and dividing the property equally among the messes."[5]

With fifty members, much property worth thousands of dollars in the States but valueless on the middle reaches of the North Platte, Cincinnati Company could not thresh out a negotiated settlement or call in arbitrators to settle personal grievances. If a dissolution was to occur, there was little alternative to the proposal of "dividing the property equally among the messes."

A meeting was held, and a committee appointed to draft "a set of resolutions to be submitted to the Co[mpany]." Regretably, we are not told the specifics of the "ten or twelve" proposals eventually adopted. The missing details may not be significant, however, as their general import has been recorded and we learn enough to understand what had been decided. "They provided for an equal distribution of the property only leaving the dis[s]olution of the company to the vote of another meeting."[6]

Two days later the men gathered for the last time as members of a joint-stock enterprise. "Another meeting was called when a resolution was adopted dissolving the company. Also a set of resolutions [was] adopted for the reorganization of the company

---

lighter. He would, also, travel along with ours and assist in getting it over bad places" (entry for 6 Aug. 1850, Moorman, *Journal*, p. 60). The evidence is not clear, but it is possible the machines were delivered (see entry for 19 Oct. 1850, Moorman, *Journal*, p. 85).

[5]Entries for 3-4 June 1849, Nixon, Journal. The supposition about the intention to sell is based on the fact that back on the Platte the diarist had been appointed to a committee to "make such sales purchases or disposition of property as they might deem proper to expedite our movement toward the end of our journey" (ibid., entry for 18 May 1849).

[6]Ibid., entry for 5 June 1849.

for traveling purposes." The men then rolled out of Fort Laramie and up the Platte "in fine spirits."[7]

Concurrent ownership, rights to concurrently-owned property, and the threat to safe travel that rights in concurrently-owned property sometimes held for emigrants on the overland trail determined not only how but why Cincinnati Mining and Trading Company dissolved. There was little animosity between the men. They did not intend to separate socially. They only changed their method of property ownership by converting from a joint-stock company to a traveling company. As members of a traveling company, the men from Cincinnati were now free of the heavier burdens arising from concurrent ownership.

Traveling companies were formed for convenience, for safety, and for companionship. People joined a traveling company and left it at will. Members were not restrained by property interests to remain with disagreeable individuals or slow-moving teams. Before another month, the former shareholders of Cincinnati Company would be largely dispersed along the trail, traveling alone, in small groups, or with wholly new companions.

While the problem that the Cincinnati forty-niners had faced was resolved by converting company property into personal or mess property, it must not be overlooked that, but for concurrent ownership and its legal implications, the problem would not have arisen. The members owned their wagons, their cattle, and their provisions in common stock and that arrangement of ownership had been their undoing. Men who were impatient to get to the gold fields, or fearful that the oxen were overloaded, fretted at the restraints placed on them by concurrent ownership. That method of holding property forced every member of the company to travel at the pace of the slowest wagon. Transferring title from the corporate group to individuals or to mess partnerships did not change the physical attributes of what was transferred; it removed the restraint concurrent ownership had imposed. Emigrants could push ahead, stay and rest their weary

----

[7]Ibid., entry for 7 June 1849.

mules or judge for themselves what weight was indispensable and what provisions were expendable.

A desire for freedom and fear that overburdened animals would never reach California led to the dissolution of Cincinnati Company. By altering their method of ownership, its members altered their rate of progress toward the Pacific, and, by making it possible to depart at will, restored harmony to the group. And if there is legalism where we may not expect it, there is also irony, for that very harmony insured the company's eventual disappearance as a social as well as a legal entity.

Dividing the Elephant

8 | THE SEPARATION OF CONCURRENT PROPERTY

Ideas tell us even more than facts. What the actions and words of overland emigrants reveal about the nineteenth-century American legal mind is to be found in attitudes as much as in behavior. To learn that they honored the property rights of each other says much about their respect for legality. If we find that they not only respected but understood the distinction between various types of ownership we may learn even more about the average American's knowledge of law in the middle decades of the nineteenth century.[1]

So well did nineteenth-century Americans on the overland trail understand the legal consequences of concurrent ownership that the presence of lawyers or the availability of law courts would probably have made little difference in the resolution of disputes. Let us look at some typical cases of conflict. Disagreements between partners and demands to dissolve the partnership contract are, after all, the cutting edge upon which common-law rights and obligations of concurrent ownership were shaped and given recognition. To find that intrapartnership squabbles were settled by applying principles similar to those that would have been followed by legal institutions in the populated areas of the United States demonstrates more than a respect for law. It indicates a knowledge of that law; an intuitional rather than educated knowledge perhaps, but a working knowledge commonly shared and consistently drawn upon to guide disputants to a mutually agreeable settlement.

Admittedly there were special circumstances controlling dissolution of concurrent ownership of property. Unless they were callously inhumane, companions could not discard a partner in

---

[1]Sections of this chapter were previously published in "Sharing the Elephant" and "Dividing the Elephant."

the middle of a wilderness. That reality aside, law determined the course of negotiations. Absence of legal institutions of adjudication and enforcement had far less impact on events than might be expected.

Our topic is one of conflict and of how individuals resolved conflict without resorting to violence. The impression must not be left, however, that without the guidance of an innate or culturally-taught legal intuition, disputes over concurrently-owned property would have led to violence. Many were amicably settled because the participants were reasonable persons. Arriving at Fort Laramie on the first day of July, 1849, Elisha Perkins and his three messmates "determined to leave our wagon here, divide our stock into companies & each take care of itself." Their reason for dissolving the partnership summarizes much of the material discussed in the last chapter concerning the burden of concurrent ownership. "For some time we have been talking of making up our minds to do this," Perkins explained. "We find our wagon so heavy & so much load[ed] that we dare not try the Black Hills as we are, & though we cannot see any thing to throw away as a company, yet when divided the whole weight can be much reduced."[2]

It could be wished that other overland diarists were as specific and as clear as Elisha Perkins. Without ambiguity or qualification he tells us that he and his messmates knew that the burden of concurrent ownership was the cause of their division. Unable as a "company" to agree on its disposition, they realized it had to be distributed either as personal property to individuals or as concurrent property to partnerships of two members each. Only after the decision-making unit was reduced to the smallest size could, as Perkins said, "the whole weight be much reduced."

The best explanation for the amicable division of the Perkins mess is that they knew their problem was concurrent ownership, not personal animosity or the suspicion that some members had been taking more than a fair share of the common provisions. Realizing that concurrent ownership was the difficulty also made

[2]Entry for 1 July 1849, Perkins, Sketches.

184

it easier to divide. After the mules were disposed of, they "proceeded to weight out our provisions &c equally & other things were then portioned out as each could agree with the others." That evening they took their "last supper together as a company & had of course the best that the ingenuity of its members could invent, & few suppers at home tasted better."[3]

II   *Company Property*

We will never know if amicable settlements were the norm of partnership divisions on the overland trail. Perhaps the negotiations between Perkins and his messmates were not typical. What can be said with certainty is that as a general rule the dissolution of messes and partnerships created thornier legal problems and spurred greater personal animosities than the separation of concurrent property owned by joint-stock companies. For that reason it would be best to consider how the larger organizations were disbanded before returning to messes and partnerships.

Less than a hundred miles out on the trail from Fort Smith, within the jurisdiction of one of the five civilized nations, a company from upstate New York disbanded. "[C]ompleted our division after a great deal of difficulty," one member wrote, "by selling to the highest bidder."[1]

The New Yorkers adopted a method of division frequently employed by both small partnerships and large companies. Since they were dealing with property and, as a measure of property is value, they proportioned it by determining its value, and they did that by selling to themselves. Joint-stock companies dissolving in California often used this technique.[2] It might be argued that out on the overland trail the plan was harsh on those without funds. If so, the fact demonstrates again a point that cannot be too often repeated. Emigrants acknowledged individual rights to each

---

[3]Ibid., entry for 2 July 1849.

[1]Foreman, *Marcy*, p. 322.

[2]For a detailed discussion of a company dissolution in California see letters to Eliza Mason, 26 Feb., 31 March, and 23 April 1850, Mason, Letters.

according to his means, not according to his needs.

It was possible to leave property rights uncompromised yet provide for those without money — at least those who had no assets except membership claims on the concurrently-owned property. One company that did so dissolved somewhere in the area of El Paso, Texas. What had been company property was redistributed in three steps. First, every member who contributed to an "extra assessment or any part of it" was reimbursed from cash on hand. Next, "such property as could be divided" was parceled out in individual shares. Finally, the balance was sold and the proceeds handed over to the stockholders. "The reason," one member explained, "was to give each one the chance of getting through the best way he could, as the funds were not sufficient to buy a proper supply of animals and provisions for the route." The proposition may be accepted, but although the idea was to distribute funds among the general membership, it must not be overlooked that the determinative criterion was ownership, not need. The man already in possession of a riding horse, or even more, got just as much as the man possessing nothing but clothing.[3]

The Sagamore and California Trading and Mining Company from Lynn, Massachusetts, did not anticipate dissolving. Expecting to remain a going concern at least until its members became rich on California gold, it printed its constitution in pamphlet form.[4] The first signs of internal pressure occurred on the Platte River. Grumbling about the weight produced a vote reducing "personal baggage to 80 lbs per man." While loads were equalized, a member noted with some satisfaction, "good order prevailed."[5] Two more weeks filled with arguments over the

[3]Entry for 19 July 1849, "Diary of David D. Demarest" (ts., microfilm, Bancroft Library), pp. 12-13.

[4]There is a copy of the Constitution of the Sagamore and California Trading and Mining company in the library of the California Historical Society, San Francisco.

[5]Entry for 14 June 1849, Churchill, Journal p. 25. "Our wagons," another member explained, "being heavily loaded, we were obliged to reduce the weight about twenty-five hundred pounds, by leaving all articles that we could dispose with" (entry for 14 June 1849, Sedgley, *Overland to California*), p. 24.

pace of travel and need for Sunday rest, and the company was ready to dissolve. It did so, but still good order or — more accurately — constitutional order prevailed. Unhappy as some members may have been, they had to proceed with legal caution. The constitution imposed a penalty for withdrawal; forfeiture of all interest in the company and its property. It is not surprising, therefore, the members acted cautiously — a legal caution reflected in the regularity of the procedure they followed. While Sagamore Company was traveling up the North Platte, members of a mess wanting to move faster circulated a petition "the purport of which was a dissolution of the company," someone belonging to a different mess wrote. "[I]t took us by surprise but after a few moments spent in deep thought we thought it best to have a meeting called to try a vote of the Company to see if they were willing that No. 1. mess, and all the others, who wished to, withdraw from the Company, might have the privilege & receive equal shares with the other members of the company. Voted in the affirmative and the meeting adjourned till 6 the next morning."[6]

From what is said it appears that those wishing to divide did not question the legality of the forfeiture proviso. They sought a legal solution to a legal dilemma: a constitutional amendment. Certainly there is no doubt what the writer thought. Mess number one, he wrote, was asking a "privilege," not asserting a right.

The next day "a meeting was called according to adjournment" and "a motion was made for division no 1 & all others who might see proper to withdraw to receive their shares of all the company property & travel as they see or thought best." With most members coming to the conclusion that large organizations were not the most feasible way to cross the plains, the motion carried. By legislating that corporate ownership of property could be terminated at will, "a general withdrawal from the Co[mpany]" became legally permissible. The political reality was constitutionally acknowledged by "calling a second meeting" that voted to dissolve "the old original Sagamore Company of Lynn Mass."

[6]Entry for 22 June 1849, Churchill, Journal, p. 30.

The members, preparing for new social and legal relationships, formed "themselves into 5 messes, each mess to retain their former teams." By "teams" apparently was meant wagons, not animals, for the next step adopted was the selection of

> proper officers...to divide the newls [mules] and all other property that could be divided   the wagons were unloaded & the provisions stacked up in a pile   the committe[e] then commenced dividing them out equally among the 5 messes which they continued to do through the day   there was another committe[e] appointed to divide the teams which they accomplished to the satisfaction of all   those things that could not be divided were sold at auction & the funds divided among the members.[7]

As there was extensive trading and shifting of money back and forth between messes, negotiations were somewhat complicated. One mess, for example, paid to the company eleven dollars owed by one of its members, purchased four dollars worth of company property, and received "$41.15 cts after the money was divided." Legal details were accorded the same close attention: after getting their money "all signed a bill to show [that] the old Sagamore Co[mpany] was extinct."[8]

The legal tactics followed by the Sagamores reveal one reason some joint-stock companies disbanded with relative ease. Before dividing the property the men first divided themselves into five new messes — four of ten members each and the fifth of nine. The company's property, therefore, did not have to be separated into forty-nine equal parts. It was parceled out not to individual owners but to new units also holding concurrently.[9] As another member expressed it, "We voted to divide the company into five messes." What he meant was that five smaller organizations took the place of a single large one.[10]

The Sagamore Company seems to have had an unusual arrangement. Provisions apparently had been carried in supply

---

[7]Ibid., entry for 23 June 1849, pp. 30-31.

[8]Ibid., entry for 24 June 1849, p. 31.

[9]Ibid., entry for 23 June 1849, p. 30.

[10]Entry for 23 June 1849, Sedgley, *Overland to California, p. 28.*

wagons, not by individual messes. As a result, before distribution to the five new messes, everything had to be taken out and stacked in piles. Within most companies, even joint-stock concerns from New England, each mess was responsible for its own food which it carried in its own wagon. On dissolution, property could be divided by leaving it where it was, merely assigning ownership rights from the defunct larger organization to the mess, which now became the holder of title. Surely this scheme was what dissentient members of the Columbus Ohio Industrial Association had in mind when they talked of "separating our company & have messes travel as they wish."[11]

It is likely that in many cases property was not distributed to accommodate existing messes; rather messes were formed to facilitate the distribution of property. Why else did the Sagamore members form into uniform units of equal size, each taking at least two wagons? If so, we see another manifestation of the control that ownership of property exercised over the social affairs of overland emigrants.

The Steubenville Ohio Company of 1849 provides a striking instance of how ownership, rather than personal preference, could determine the membership of the smaller parties into which larger organizations dissolved. Steubenville was hardly out on the trail — waiting to cross the Kansas River — when its members, as one explained, "having become impressed with the conviction that small trains could travel much faster than large ones, and other circumstances being favorable to a dissolution, a meeting of the company was called, and a resolution adopted to dissolve into companies of tens, making an equitable division of the general stock on hands."[12]

There were sixty members in the Steubenville Company and, most likely, messes of tens were created for convenience. True, ten was also the unit adopted by Sagamore, but it was at least twice the size of the average mess, a fact both the New

---

[11]Entry for 14 July 1849, Decker, *Diaries*, p. 118.

[12]Entry for 8 May 1849, Dundass, *Journal*, p. 13.

Englanders and Ohioans surely knew. Moreover, for one mess from the former Steubenville organization, ten members soon proved too large. Beyond the Sweetwater, in what is today Wyoming, one of these new "companies" decided on a second redistribution of the property. "To effect this object," the same member wrote, "we divided our stock into three shares or messes, or rather into individual shares, and afterwards formed three messes. Rudy and Ream formed one mess, McConnel and myself another, and our remaining companion[s] the third mess in question."[13]

What seems to have happened is that the social and ownership arrangements had been decided by property, not by personal preferences. The original Steubenville Company had sixty share-holders and twenty-six wagons. When it divided into six ten-member partnerships, each mess could have been assigned four wagons, a factor making the assignment of ten men to each group a somewhat arbitrary attempt at equal distribution. Possibly the party dividing beyond the Sweetwater had had only three of those four wagons left, and split into three units for that reason. It is more likely, however, that four wagons remained because two new units were of two members each and the other of six. Had there been only three wagons, the large mess of six probably would not have agreed to so unequitable a division. Four vehicles made the plan more reasonable. Thus it was property, not social choice, that determined the eventual make up of individual messes because it is the perspective of property ownership, and property ownership only, that gives the word "reasonable" meaning.

Perhaps lawyers see more than historians. But surely even to laity, the methods adopted and procedure followed for dividing Steubenville's concurrently-owned property are revealing. When the original joint-stock organization of sixty members dissolved, there was no mention of individual ownership. The property was parceled by assigning it to traveling units possibly already in existence, but more likely created for the purpose of receiving

[13]Ibid., entry for 3 July 1849, p.33.

190

ownership. Executing the second division, the smaller group found it possible — perhaps even necessary — to abandon concurrent ownership. It will be noted that the diarist said "we divided our stock into three shares or messes, or rather into individual shares, and afterwards formed three messes." Put in legal phraseology, the men, in order to accomplish their purpose, first transmuted the common stock from company or partnership property into personal property. Then, by negotiating contracts, goods they had held briefly as individuals were converted back into partnership or mess property. Finally, as just mentioned, property may have been the determinative factor influencing the path of division, for the split into three messes seems to have been an accommodation to practicalities.

The argument may be misunderstood. It must, therefore, be emphasized that property not only shaped the form division took, it often caused the division. The majority of the members of Sagamore voted to dissolve, not due to social animosity or political discord, but because when one mess sought permission to leave, others saw an opportunity to hold property in smaller ownership units. Except for that one mess, these units planned to continue together — no longer as a joint-stock organization but as a traveling company of four partnerships each holding separate parcels of concurrently-owned property.

Perhaps the most unusual cause for dissolving a joint-stock organization was reported on the Truckee River in 1849. The Kingsville Company from Ohio was resting there on the day its constitution mandated that new officers be elected. After a meeting was called, the members "found the constitution of the company missing." Due to some unexplained theory of extreme legalism, "this [discovery] prevented the Election of our officers whose terms had expired & the company by mutual consent conclude[d] to divide the money that was in the treasury." The company was dissolved, but the men had no intention of separating. "[T]he provisions," one wrote, "we agreed to consume together & divide the rest when we get through."[14]

[14]Entry for 6 Aug. 1849, Tinker, "Journal," p. 82.

191

It would be a mistake to attempt to decipher this statement. Whether the provisions remained the concurrently-owned property of the disbanded company, now transformed into a partnership, or were owned in severalty though stored in a common grainery, is a distinction that probably did not trouble these otherwise remarkably legalistic forty-niners. What we are told is that in the midst of an all too concrete reality, legal abstractions fashioned conduct. Dissolving to satisfy imagined requirements of law, and except for dividing among themselves the funds held by the treasury, these men separated in legal theory only, remaining in physical reality and social composition just as before.

Of course there were joint-stock companies that dissolved for more serious reasons than constitutional sensibilities, and the bitterness causing the division sometimes carried over into negotiations when concurrently-owned property was being reassigned as personalty. From a legal perspective the most fascinating instance occurred at Fort Laramie in 1849 and was described by James A. Pritchard, leader of the Boone County Company, named for a Kentucky county of which he once had been sheriff. "I[n] consequence of the disagreement among several of the members of our company," he wrote, "we were here driven to the necessity of dividing it."[15]

Historians of the overland trail owe much to Sheriff Pritchard. His detailed discussion of how Boone County's members settled their differences and divided the concurrently-owned property is the best available account of the dissolution of an emigrant joint-stock organization. While not unique, it is a rare document: a case study of average nineteenth-century Americans settling an important property dispute without resort to a court of law. Moreover, to accomplish their objective, these forty-niners created a sui generis institution, an arbitration forum or tribunal to which they submitted legal and factual issues they otherwise could not resolve.

---

[15]This and the following quotations describing the dissolution of the Boone County Company are from entry for 4 June 1849, Pritchard, *Diary*, pp. 81-84.

We learn much about the role of property on the overland trail when we realize that this settlement, the most complicated and one of the bitterest on record, involved a small group of men. Two inferences can be drawn from this fact. One is that members of large organizations, often transporting property and food to be used in California as well as along the trail, were better able to compromise and treat one another with generosity than were emigrants dividing one or two wagons, a few animals, and provisions intended for the trip alone. The second inference will become more apparent when we consider the separation of mess and partnership property: the smaller the party the more likelihood that the division was forced by personal conflict and social animosity. When there was only one vehicle, a member unable to tolerate his messmates could not be shifted to a different wagon. Either he found new companions or the group dissolved. In the meanwhile, daily friction was unavoidable, occasionally making final separations rather nasty affairs.

When it arrived at Fort Laramie, Boone County was both a traveling and a joint-stock company. Of nine men journeying together, eight held equal shares in the property. They were aligned in two rival factions — three opposed to five. Sheriff Pritchard was the leader of the minority group. The other side elected Samuel Hardesty to be its negotiator.

Some matters were settled immediately, probably without discussion. The ninth man was ignored. As Pritchard explained, he "was not one of the Company proper, he was attached mearly to travel across the country." Rephrased from a legal perspective, Pritchard was saying that the man was a contractee who had purchased a mess privilege, not an ownership interest. Not being a particeps, he had no property rights to be considered.

As the ninth man sided with Pritchard, it would have been to the sheriff's advantage to have included him. That the point was apparently not even raised is instructive. Pritchard, after all, could have contended that since the original company had accepted the ninth man as a paying passenger, all members were responsible for him and any division of the animals as well as the provisions had to take the man into account. That Pritchard did not mention this obvious argument is indicative of a lesson to be stressed later: overland emigrants were not equity-minded, they were property-minded. Whatever rights the ninth man had were contract rights, not property rights. Principles of equity were not employed to convert nonproperty rights (such as here, contract rights) into property rights. So far as is known, in no division between owners of concurrent property on the overland trail was any rule employed except legal ownership.

Most issues between Pritchard and his adversary resolved themselves due to mutual understanding of the law involved. They did not need a lawyer to know that property that was not "company" but "private" was "to revert back to its proper owner." Other matters were quickly settled by the simple process of counting heads. "In the division of the wagons & provisions there was no disagreement," Pritchard explained. "As there were 5 to 3 we gave them the large wagon, and 5/8 of the provisions were conceded to them." Trouble developed over the mules. "There was 8 men & 10 mules — 8 of the mules were old work mules & 2 young unbroke[n] ones" — too few to go around and not of equal quality. Distribution by lottery, the procedure larger companies often followed, would have entailed risks for either side.

Pritchard was willing to gamble. "My first proposition," he explained, "was, to put the name of each of the 8 old mule[s] on a blank piece of paper and let the men draw and take the mule he drew and then fix the division of the 2 young one[s] afterwards. That proposition was rejected. I then proposed to give them first choice . . . and I the next till we had drawn 2 each — and then give him 2 next time, and I one — and he the next which would have given, us 3 and he 5. He would then [have] had first choice of the first four, I the 2nd, he the 3rd, I the 4th, then of the next four he would have had the first choice of 2, I the 3 choice & he the 4 choice, the young mules afterwards to be divided."

Hardesty was either unwilling to leave anything to chance or had been instructed by his colleagues not to accept a lottery. "There was 2 large mules that were considered to be worth a

194

good deal more than any other 2, and he said that he would not divide unless he could get both of those." Pritchard was agreeable "if he would give me choice of the next 2, and he the 5th I the 6th & he the 7th & 8th." Again Hardesty rejected the proposal. His side demanded the six best mules and a cash settlement of seventy-five dollars.

Pritchard became indignant.[16] There were, he replied, considertions of equity deserving some weight: the company had been his creation while the dissolution was the demand of Hardesty's cohorts.

> I . . . told Hardesty that under the circumstances I considered the proposition, not only ungentlemanly but dishonorable. I had been at all the trouble of makeing the outfit. I had spent my time, and part [of] my own personal funds without one cents charge to the company. And not one member of the company had been to one cents expence or one hours trouble, except to put into the Treasury the amount due the company to make the outfit. And not only that — that I was doing this thing of seperating because Wilkie & Hardesty could not agree with Youell & Stephens. . . . I rema[r]ked to Hardesty, Thus you see Squire, I am driven to the exceedingly unpleasant necessity of seperating with you and Wilkie entirely for your sakes and on account of others not for myself.

Hardesty withdrew from the negotiations, replaced by his ally Wilkie who said that his side also had an equitable claim. The ninth man, the passenger traveling with the company, owned two mules and a horse. As personal property they were not part of the division. The owner had elected to join Pritchard's mess, a fact that meant those traveling with the sheriff would obtain use of the animals. Wilkie wanted his faction compensated for the loss. That was why they asked for seventy-five dollars.[17]

Aside from the money, matters were eventually adjusted. The

---

[16][W]e were left the little black mule, the wild untameable yellow mare mule & the 2 unbrok[en] 3 year olds . . . the little wagon & 3/8 of the provision[s]" (loc. cit).

[17]The legal theory upon which this demand was premised must be surmised. Considering it to be "unjust," Pritchard did not bother to explain it. He does, however, say that Wilkie claimed the money "because Abbott joined our mess to travel with us across the plaines and therefor[e] his mule would be put to our wagon" (loc. cit).

difficulty stalling the negotiations had apparently concerned the value of property, not assignment of items. Rather than arguing about which side took what animals, Pritchard proposed that they put a price on all their property, "Mules & wagons &c &c," and then divide everything according to worth at a ratio of three to five. Wilkie agreed and they apparently had no difficulty pricing the animals. "In that way," Pritchard wrote, "we very soon effected a division of everything. If I wanted anything I paid to him the worth [of] it. If he wanted anything (that could not be divided) he paid the worth of it to me."

The only matter still in dispute was the demand for seventy-five dollars, and on that question there could be no compromise. "I considered it unjust," Pritchard explained. Unable to resort to a court of law, the litigants created a close equivalent: an arbitration proceeding.

The question whether Pritchard's side owed the money was submitted for judgment "to 3 disinterested men one to be chose[n] by him, one by me, and they 2 to select the 3rd person." The parties even drew up a stipulation of facts for the guidance of the referees.

> About the 3rd of May 8 men with 2 waggons & 10 mules overtaken by W. W. Abbott & his 2 mules & his white horse with about 200 lbs of baggage, and provisions & proposed to those 8 men to give them his provisions and the use of his 2 mules to work in the waggons, and the use of his poney when we wanted to chase buffalo upon only — and to carry his baggage to California and he to be as one of us in the mess. Now we want to divide the company into 2 parts and each of us origional 8 men mutually agree to a dessolution 5 men in one mess, and 3 in the other — Abbott joining the 3 members of the former company. Now these 5 men claim money from the 3 men for the use of the 2 mules of Abbott's, from this to California.

While Wilkie, Hardesty, and their three partners may have believed they had a legal right to compensation for the loss of Abbott's mules, it is more likely they were thinking in terms of fairness and equity. They had helped carry Abbott this far, contributed to his share of the mess, and now the other group alone would reap benefit from his animals.

Whether law or equity, the referees saw no merit in Wilkie's argument. Happily for us they submitted a written opinion to the parties, a unique document on the overland trail and surely one of the earliest non-Indian judicial decisions in the legal history of the state of Wyoming.

> [W]e can see no just cause why the mess of 3 men Should pay anything to the mess of 5 men. It being . . . a mutual and simul aneous agreement to desolve the origional contract. The fact that Abbott joines in with the 3 men does not alter in our opinion the matter of the case — for the dessolution being mutually agreed upon, all the parties Stand in the Same relation to each other which they did, before any contract was entered into. And Abbott might or not just as he chose unite with either party. If he chose to unite with neither party, then clearly neither could claim of the other. If he united with a foreign party then who could think of claiming any thing of such a party.

There is no way of knowing if any of the referees were lawyers. The fact may not matter, as it is likely the decision would have been the same regardless of available legal talent. Except for the unique wealth of details recorded by one of the parties, and the resort to arbitration, there is nothing unusual about this settlement. Like all others of which we have accounts, it was resolved by legal principles. Pritchard had not wished to divide, yet received no consideration for that fact. Nor did he get credit for having organized the company or for putting into it more money than the others. Their joint-stock contract apparently acknowledged only equal contributions and when the property was divided it was placed in equal eighths because all the partners were equal owners. By the same standards the referees rejected Wilkie's demand for seventy-five dollars. Only the original contract, the contract with Abbott, and the dissolution contract guided their decision. Finding nothing in three agreements to sustain the claim, they refused to compensate the claimants for lost expectation. Legal rather than equitable rights determined this verdict.

III *Mess and Partnership Property*

Because of the company's small size — only eight property-owning members — division of Boone County's concurrently-owned property seems more typical of mess or partnership breakups than of the larger joint-stock companies. With little property to go around, each mule was important. Although Sheriff Pritchard did not mention the fact, one reason for this undoubtedly was that neither side involved in the controversy had money with which to buy out the other's property rights.

When money was available, property concurrently owned by dissolving messes and partnerships could often be divided with as much ease as that of joint-stock companies overloaded with surplus provisions and animals. The partner with funds would buy out the other, who then purchased his way into another mess, got an animal for packing, or started walking.[1]

When there were divers partners, all did not have to purchase from the separating member. Four messmates traveled from Illinois to the Carson River where one decided to leave. Two of the remaining three paid him twenty dollars for his claim on the team. The fourth man, not a party to the transaction, retained his one-fourth interest, apparently unaffected by the sale except for the fact he now had only two partners, both of whom owned a theoretically larger share than he in some, but not all of the property.[2]

---

[1] A forty-niner from Lexington, Kentucky, provides a case in point. Slow progress of his company made him fearful of being caught in Sierra snows. On reaching Salt Lake City, he "sold out and packed through on mules" (letter to parents, 4 Oct. 1849, Bradford, Letters). Three years later, when at least one hundred miles out on the plains, a man and woman quarreled with their partner. Selling to him, they returned to St. Joseph "to get another outfit, and take a fresh start (entry for 11 May 1852, Crane, Journal). That same year, on the Humboldt River, a mess bought out an obnoxious partner with whom they had been having trouble for almost two months (since 8 June). They paid him cash —"fifty-eight dollars and a few cents" (entry for 2 Aug. 1852, Hickman, *Overland Journey*, p. 17).

[2] The vendor must not be thought to have sold his interest in the partnership. He sold only his rights to the team (and perhaps other property), and kept his claim on the food, which then was converted into personalty, for he is said to have walked off with "his share of provisions on his back" (entry for 2 Sept. 1850, McKinstry, *Diary*, p. 287.)

Money could even serve as the common divider when all parties possessed it and were willing to buy the concurrent property. Distribution arguments could be avoided by putting everything up for auction and giving members an equal chance to bid. Even indivisible partnership property could be turned into personalty if there was money on both sides. Bernard Reid from Pittsburgh and an acquaintance with whom he was traveling in a passenger train had purchased a pony in St. Louis. Before the trip was completed Reid concluded that his partner "was not quite the person to suit me" and "resolved to separate from him quietly before reaching California." Both apparently wanted the pony for packing and had money to purchase it. Unable to divide the property into equal shares, they left the matter to chance. "We valued [the] pony and trappings at first cost and drew lots for him," Reid wrote his sisters, "the winner to buy out the other's share and also to carry on the pony, to Sutter's Fort, an equal share of baggage for each."[3]

No legal transaction was more common in overland experience than partnership dissolutions. They occurred not only on the trail and after arriving in California, but even before crossing the Missouri. When rumors reached Nebraska City that the Pike's Peak gold rush of 1859 was a "bust," perhaps more partnerships were dissolved than on any other single occasion in overland history. "Walk along by their camps," an eyewitness wrote, "and you will see them busily engaged overhauling their *traps* and dividing their things   one will get the frying pan another the coffee pot while the third likely will have the oven. [S]ometimes one will sell out his share to the others and then start home a foot or on the Boat. Sometimes the whole co[mpany] will sell off at auction and dividing the proceeds each man will take his own course."[4]

Partnerships surviving the tensions of overland travel and reaching their destination also had to divide concurrently-owned property. "The whole proceeding was very laughable," a member

---

[3]Reid, "Letter," p. 228.
[4]Entry for 31 May 1859, J. B. Brown, Journal, p. 10.

of a German mess from Milwaukee wrote after converting goods from partnership property into personalty. "Each packed his things in a given spot, and he who had the least was really better off, because he had less to carry."[5]

Although the German was in Downieville, California, his words provide a clue as to why many overland partnerships divided with relative ease. Having suffered from the burden of property, emigrants were willing to surrender claims they might have clung to tenaciously anywhere else but on the trail. Of course, the opposite was also true; the trail could make property of relatively little value elsewhere so indispensable that one had to retain possession of it. Then partnership divisions could become quite complicated, especially if the items in controversy were indivisible.

Before considering the legal implications of difficult partnership divisions, a qualification should be made. Again it must be pointed out that the extreme was not necessarily indicative of overland behavior. At least as many dissolutions of partnerships were negotiated amicably as with rancor. In order to maintain a proper perspective, it would be well to keep in mind the experiences of some emigrants who left Ohio with two wagons: one or two men in one, three in the other. About sixteen miles from South Pass they "concluded to join teams." One of the two wagons, therefore, was abandoned. A month later, at the meadows of Humboldt River, the three whose wagon had been abandoned became discontented, "believing that by taking their portion of the team & packing they could get along eiser [sic] & through sooner." The matter was resolved almost as quickly as the decision had been made. "[A] division of the eatables took place without delay, & in less than one hour from the time the seperation was proposed we were all upon the road again."[6]

---

[5]In Downieville, California (entry for 18 Sept. 1852, Charles G. Schneider, "Memorandum, 1852" [ms., with ts. English trans. from German, State Historical Society of Wisconsin, Madison].

[6]Entries for 9 June and 12 July 1850, Gorgas, Diary; letter of 9 Sept. 1850, Gorgas, Letter. For other accounts of partnership dissolutions apparently resolved with equal ease, see entry for 17 May 1845, Snyder, "Diary," p. 225; entry for 27 June 1849, Fouts, Diary, p. 2;

One reason for the ease of dissolution was that the three departing men were planning to pack and could take little with them. Another was that they knew their property rights, and what they owned was easily identified. The three that had joined their team to the second wagon were leaving as a new partnership (or reconstituting the old one that had existed before discarding their wagon) and simply took out the property they had contributed to the amalgamated partnership now being dissolved. A third reason matters were quickly settled was that they were anxious to be off. Other emigrants surrendered interest in property to make greater speed or, less frequently, to be rid of a partner whom they could no longer abide.[7]

Much depended on circumstances and upon the amount of personal rancor that had developed between dividing partners. If the dissatisfied party was unable to pack, did not dare to, or thought the distance too great, the division could become currish unless he found another mess with which to travel.[8]

When tempers were raw, negotiations over dividing were not always conducted rationally. A partner refusing to surrender his claim to the wagon might drive a stubborn bargain more harmful to himself than to those from whom he separated. "There was an amusing scene on the side of the road this day," a forty-niner from Missouri noted less than a month into the trip. "Three men owning two yoke of cattle and a wagon had a disagreement, and they determined to separate. So they stopped by the roadside, ten miles from anywhere, and divided their effects. Two took a yoke

---

Leeper, *Argonauts*, p. 54; entry for 20 June 1852, Keen, Diary, p. 44; entry for 8 June 1863, A. Howard Cutting, "Journal of a Trip by Overland Route to California" (ms., HM 652, Huntington Library).

[7]It is possible, but not certain, that three messmates, to be free of a fourth, had to surrender to him the partnership wagon. That is implied by the following entry in a diary written at Pacific Springs. "Messrs. Beal, Otzman and Hinkley, who had become very much dissatisfied with Mr. Sweazy, purchased three yoke of cattle of another company today, joined Mr. Bolton in his wagon, took their proportion of the provisions and left the train" (entry for 22 July 1850, Bennett, *Overland Journey*, p. 28).

[8]"Moses Beck and Sam Hayes divided their outfit and Hayes went with the gambling wagon" (entry for 28 May 1850, C. W. Smith, Journal).

of oxen each, and the other the wagon. Those having the oxen had the right to hitch onto another team, but what the poor fellow was to do with his wagon, I could not see, for wagons were not much in demand in these parts without stock."[9]

If the man taking the wagon was so angry at his partners, and so intent on not packing, that he ignored the dilemma of having a vehicle without a team to draw it, he was unique. Other emigrants in his situation wanting a wagon for shelter yet realizing the uselessness of a stationary vehicle, pushed the principle of concurrent ownership to its ultimate enforcement by dividing the wagon along with other property.

During 1850 a "mess divided the wagon and oxen — sawing the wagon bed in [the] middle, 2 taking the fore wheels & 2 yokes of cattle, the other two the hind wheels & 2 yoke & so on."[10] Two years later an emigrant "saw an instance where two men were equal partners all around, in four horses, harness and wagon. They seemed to have quarreled so much that they agreed to divide up and quit traveling together. They divided up their horses and provisions, and then measured off the wagon-bed and sawed it in two parts, also the reach, and then flipped a copper cent to see which should have the front part of the wagon. After the division they each went to work and fixed up his part of the wagon as best he could, and drove on alone."[11]

Overland literature is filled with such incidents[12] and it would be wrong to see them, as some historians have, as representing breakdowns of social ties on the frontier. For lawyers these cases demonstrate the opposite. No matter how angry individuals

[9]Entry for 2 June 1850, Hixson, Diary.

[10]Entry for 26 June 1850, Lampton, Diary, p. 13. A month earlier two partners "not being able to agree, made a division, sawing their wagon in two and making each a cart. Each taking a horse" (entry for 26 May 1850, Lane, Diary).

[11]Cole, *Early Days*, p. 49.

[12]In 1850, a Missourian was amused on encountering two Irishmen who owned a wagon and two yoke of cattle. "[O]ne wanted to go to Oregon & the other to Cal[ifornia]   they talked loud & threatened each other with their coats off. finally on[e] got a handsaw & proce[e]ded to saw the Bed into [in two] in the middle so that each of them could have [a] cart" (Harvey, To California, p. 47). See also Stephens, *Jayhawker*, pp. 11-12; Mattes, *Platte River Road*, p. 36.

might become, personal rights in concurrent ownership of property were respected to a remarkable degree on the overland trail. Every diary reporting a partnership dissolution tells of either an outright sale or that the property was divided.

An even bolder assertion can be made: negotiations were guided by notions emigrants shared concerning property, ownership, and vested rights. The institutions of law may have been hundreds of miles away, yet law controlled the business affairs of people. The pattern of legality held true even during moments of extreme bitterness, although on at least one occasion churlishness so blinded the parties that the method and spoils of the division made more comedy than sense.

> Two brothers quarrelled about the exact spot in which to place their wagon and had to part. They divided everything they had. The yoke was sawed in two and each took an ax and half in yoke; the wagon next had to be divided, and a long quarrel ensued whether it should be halved lengthwise or sidewise. They left it to chance, and chance said lengthwise; so they sawed their wagon from the end of the tongue to the hind gate, and even the tent was cut in two and the poles.[13]

While few divisions of concurrently-owned property were so foolish, many were legally complicated, but even then law, not emotion or violence, was the common denominator. Legal terms were even employed by emigrants — or what they thought were legal terms. "Passed receipts with A.W. Phelps," one man wrote of two partners from whom he was separating, "but Vail acted abusive and would not pass receipts although he had agreed to do so."[14] Others, caring little for the language of lawyers, took a

---

[13]J. R. Brown, *Across the Plains*, p. 98. It was rare but not unknown for brothers to quarrel. One other case is of interest as it indicates that public opinion and voluntary action were sometimes utilized to support rights in concurrent property on the overland trail. "[T]wo brothers wished to join our train. They had been with us but a few days before one had taken their team and left his brother behind. Two of our company went forward in pursuit, and caught up with a train which he had joined, demanding his return. The company refused to let him go without a trial of the case between the brothers which resulted in both returning to our train" (Rowe, Ho for California, p. 5).

[14]Entry for 17 June 1852, Fox, Memorandum, p. 20.

lawyer's attitude by emphasizing the consequences of divisions as much as the division itself. A good example is Jefferson Drake, who started across the trail with two messmates. "Before leaving here," he wrote at Fort Kearny, "we have agreed to seperate and di[s]olve our partnership which we are to do this day. Audrain & McCoy are to take the two horses, wagon, & harness, leaving me with my three horses and the lead harness and & all belonging to my horses and divide our provision[s] groceries &c. equally betwixt us, leaving me my blankets cloak and every thing brought by each is to held by each as his own." Up to this point, one might say Drake was doing only what hundreds of other emigrants had done: making certain personal property was not confused with partnership property. Next, however, he added a sentence, placing the emphasis not on the division but on its legal consequences. He and his former partner, Drake explained, "divided in a way that neither of us was indebted to the other" and, as a result, "my horses and every thing else, as well as myself are entirely distinct from the two gentlemen partners."[15]

iv *Two Representative Cases*

By separating personal from partnership property before dividing what was concurrently owned, Jefferson Drake and his "two gentlemen partners" avoided legal problems. It was a procedure not everyone could employ — as when contributions to partnership or company property had not been equal or the dividing process got down to an item either indivisible or that could not be set off by property of comparable value. Trouble was further compounded if owners, agreeing about facts, disagreed about what those facts meant in law.

An instructive division of concurrently-owned property involved H. M. Powell who, in 1849, traveled the Santa Fe route to California. He had started with a train of nine men. In addition to three personally-owned wagons, there was partnership property

---

[15]Letter of 26 May 1850, "Letters from Jefferson A. Drake to Abigail Drake" (ms., Missouri Historical Society, St. Louis).

to which each member contributed goods of equal value. One of the party, a Dr. Park, furnished his assessment by borrowing bacon from Powell.[1]

An early dispute deserves mention as it sheds light on the management of overland partnerships. "Before starting," Powell explained, "Dr. Burchard and Detrich insisted on the shares of the Company being divided in 11 parts instead of 9 so that the two boys [sons of Powell and Park] should have a share in the risk of loss. This gives Dr. Park and myself the onus of paying for 2 shares and double losses if anything happens to the waggon or Teams. I agreed to this on condition that the boys had a vote in the council; which was agreed to." Many traveling and joint-stock companies had councils, but this is the only partnership to mention one. We must regret Powell did not say something about its functions — whether limited to making policy decisions or convened several times daily to legislate routine decisions such as when to march and when to halt. Powell does reveal enough to add an unexpected dimension to our story of property on the overland trail. Unlike some traveling companies, the franchise in this one was based on ownership. It was by contributing property to the common whole that the boys claimed the right to vote.[2]

Besides Park, there were two other physicians in the party, but despite an abundance of medical expertise three men died of cholera. Park was one of the victims and after his death, with the company smaller and the remaining men drawn into closer contact, Powell discovered he could not abide the surviving doctor. After they had a "fuss," Powell decided to "take what is

---

[1]The fact of individual ownership is evident from what Powell said. He had been sleeping outside but, finding nights colder than expected, he ordered out someone who had been sleeping in the wagon, told him to sleep outside, and from then on Powell slept in the wagon (entries for 13-15 April 1849, Powell, *Santa Fé Trail*, pp. 2-3).

[2]Ibid., entry for 27 April 1849, p. 6. From what Powell says, a lawyer might conclude that the organization was a joint-stock company. He himself referred to it as a partnership, and facts subsequently revealed make that term appear reasonably accurate. Another question not answered, is what sort of "losses" members were promising to share. One guess is that the contemplated "losses" were not losses in company-owned concurrent property, but individual losses: a sort of overland insurance policy with the risk spread among eleven rather than nine.

mine & quit the company."[3]

One day, with "all my copartners seeming to be in an amicable and easy state of feeling," Powell announced that he wanted to divide and the others agreed.

> [W]e at once went to work to close our accounts and make a partition. They peremptorily refused to allow me the debt that Dr. Park owed me; would not even allow me for the bacon I let him have, which he had placed to his credit as part of his capital stock in the Company, and which they still have, and which they will either use or sell at Santa Fé and make a great profit on. They cannot allow me for it but they can use it or sell it themselves. Nice casuistry this: the difference between "tweedle dum and tweedle dee." I raise it on my farm and put it in the concern. They do not pretend for a moment to deny the justice of the debt, but still they have a scruple of conscience either to allow me for it or let me take it back; but no scruple of conscience to use it themselves or sell it, and remit the proceeds when they choose to. And thus I am deprived of about $62.00, a serious matter in settling accounts. By transfer of property on the Cimarron I take the waggon I put with the concern at $90.00; my 2 yoke of cattle at $100.00; with such provisions as they in their benignity choose to let me have.[4]

It is evident that Powell and his former partners disagreed less about facts than about law. There was apparently no argument as to who had contributed and in what amounts to the original arrangement. They disputed legal issues. Powell thought he should be credited for loans made to Dr. Park; certainly for loans that went directly toward paying the dead man's share of the partnership property. The others disagreed. Their theory has to have been that Park died owing a personal obligation to Powell. No matter how Park had utilized the borrowed property, the partnership had not incurred a debt. Legal questions of this sort

---

[3]Death: entries of 17 & 27 May 1849, Powell, Diary, pp. 27-28. Surviving doctor: "He is the most sullen, morose, jealous & overbearing man I ever knew in my life. His habits, ways, and manners are every way repulsive and disgusting. He has come out plainly as an Infidel also . . . . Sorry am I I ever had anything to do with him" (ibid., entry for 17 June 1849, p. 47). Decision to separate: ibid., entry for 10 June 1849, p. 40).

[4]Entry for 21 June 1849, Powell, *Santa Fé Trail*, p. 53.

206

were settled by vote, and Powell's interpretation of the law had no chance of being sustained with all five of his surviving partners opposing him. To escape, he, like many other emigrants caught in the vise of concurrent property, had to pay a price.

Powell had not been alone, nor had he been negotiating without support or friends to advise him. He and his former partners had met a company from Missouri and had been traveling with it for some time before the division of property. Anticipating that Powell would be looking for new companions, the captain of the company had told him he was welcome to join them should he wish.[5] Just four days later Powell did so. Avoiding tying himself down economically or again being compelled to tolerate men he could not stomach, Powell joined the company for protection only and did not buy into it. "My heart was light, " he wrote on leaving his former companions. "I have no persons whims to study & no one to find fault with me, thanks be to praise I am free, free."[6] He was free not of men, but free of men with whom he shared concurrent ownership of property.

Powell attached himself as a boarder to a member of his new traveling company named Snelling. This arrangement, one of contract rather than property, meant that he and his son took their meals with the Snelling family. "I, in consequence got my cup of Coffee at Mr. Snellings tent this morning," Powell noted the day he separated from his former partners. For a few hours he traveled in formation with them until they closed "accounts" and then "left...and passed over to the rear of Mr. Snellings four wagons, as I wish to incorporate myself with him, & detach myself from them at once."[7]

Snelling was something of an overland lawyer. He gave Powell legal advice on how to get back at his old partners, perhaps even promising to support him physically if necessary. Snelling's

---

[5]Entry for 17 June 1849, Powell, Diary, p. 48.

[6]Ibid., entry for 22 June 1849, p. 51.

[7]Loc. cit.

suggestion was that Powell delay payment, probably the only retaliatory step most emigrants would have thought "legal." The day after the division, Powell explained,

> my old partners, who by refusing me my just dues, had, as they thought, brought me in debt for $29.00, sent Fuller to me to demand security for it. They modestly claimed a bill of sale of cattle, waggon etc., as security. This outrage I resisted and determined to pay them, but was dissuaded by Mr. Snelling. I went to them, however, and came to a final settlement of everything when lo! they found all the claim they had against me was $15.66, for which I gave them my note with Mr. Snelling's name as security, payable at Santa Fé. I again wished to pay them and have done with it, but Mr. Snelling said that as they seemed to desire to persecute me, he would not gratify them by paying until the latest moment.[8]

Lawyers might conclude that Powell did very well. Like most emigrants on the overland trail, he had not anticipated leaving his partners and their agreement had contained no provision for termination. Yet he managed to end it on terms he could accept. Had an attorney been consulted before the original contract was executed, a clause for dividing the concurrently-owned property probably would have been included. It is, however, doubtful if conventional law would have made much difference. No matter the provisions drafted, events anticipated, or rights defined, the future simply could not be foretold. Conditions of life on the overland trail were unique, defying social soothsaying and probably prior legal solution.

As evidence demonstrating the difficulty of foreseeing partnership problems, we may conclude this investigation by considering the case of an 1852 emigrant from Wisconsin named Samuel Chadwick. He anticipated that he might have a dispute with his companions, although most likely he was thinking of the final division once they reached California, rather than a termination on the trail. Chadwick insisted that the contract be put in writing, yet events occurred which he did not expect and the final disposition of the partnership property was determined as much

[8]Entry for 23 June 1849, Powell, *Santa Fé Trail*, p. 55.

by prevailing circumstances as contracted rights.

Chadwick left Wisconsin in company with Jonas Boyer and Frank Aldrich. Their property was personally, not concurrently owned. Chadwick possessed two oxen, the only wagon in the group, and had $25 in cash. Boyer and Aldrich owned three yoke of cattle. In addition, Aldrich's wife was a member of the party. Their business arrangement seems to have been informal, for, after they arrived at Kanesville, someone decided it should be defined with precision or, as Chadwick said, "we had A set[t]ling up me and my partners."[9]

As owner of the wagon, Chadwick sought credit for its use, probably because Mrs. Aldrich rode in it and (quite likely) slept in it with her husband. Aldrich wanted the matter postponed until they were in California. Thinking "we should have to have a split up," Chadwick told Aldrich "I could not trust him for the wagon till I got to California   he might take his team of[f] my waggon if he could not pay for it." Aldrich may have had little choice but to agree. "[T]o rec[k]on up our accounts," Chadwick retained a local storekeeper, "and so he [Aldrich] paid the bill some 20 d[ollars]."[10]

The agreement between Chadwick, Boyer, and Aldrich was not uncommon. As we have seen, many emigrants pooled equipment while retaining personal ownership of the items contributed. What complicated the arrangement among these three men and created concurrent ownership was the fact that they made a contract with a fourth individual to take him overland to California. While waiting to be ferried across the Missouri, they met a man who "had had some difficulty with his partner" and "wanted to go through with us." His name was Samuel Fox and he owned two yoke of cattle. As one of Boyer's oxen had recently gone lame, the three Wisconsinites had need of his property. Fox proposed that the cattle be his fare; their use paying for a share in the provisions and probably a place in the wagon to store his clothes. Chadwick, Boyer, and Aldrich,

---

[9]Chadwick, Travels.
[10]Ibid.

however, desired more than two oxen before consenting to take him along. The matter was resolved when they "aggreed like this   he [Fox] was to sell his oxen to us for 140 and give us what he had towards his outfit and we take him through for 60 dollars and pay to him 80 dollars when we got through to California and we have a chance to dispose of the cattle. he paid us the 60 dollars by the way of the cattle   he turned out the cattle to us at Kanesville before we started and we paid a part of the 80 dollars in Kanesville."[11]

If Chadwick, Boyer, and Aldrich had previously not owned property concurrently, they did now. Fox was their passenger, and they shared title to what had been his oxen, for which they would not fully pay until after delivering him in California.

Once across the Missouri, Chadwick's party of four men, one woman, and a single wagon, joined a company of about twelve wagons and thirty men. Within a month, six men died of cholera, one of whom was Samuel Fox. Due to the delays and dangers arising from sickness the three partners left the train and pushed on alone. Just beyond the Pacific Springs they overtook the Badger Boys, a company from their home state of Wisconsin. Chadwick and Boyer decided to travel with this train, partly because they had recently had "a little fus[s]" with Aldrich. He, or so Chadwick complained, "wanted to boss us around to[o] much so we are a trying to divide of[f] and let him go alone."[12]

The strain of travel had become too much for Aldrich. When carelessness on Chadwick's part caused them to be delayed one morning — left alone while the Badger Boys rolled on — Aldrich's temper snapped. The abusive words he heaped on his two companions "did not suit" either Chadwick or Boyer. "W[e] came pret[t]y near fetching on him," Chadwick wrote, "we had a regular jaw   well we aggreed to divide of[f] with him so and so and when it came to it he would not do it so we got started again in

---

[11]Ibid., entries for 18 June and 11 May 1852.

[12]Ibid., entries for 17 May, 17, 18, and 21 June 1852; entry for 7 July 1852, Chadwick, Diary.

210

perfect hatred as neither the old man nor I liked his company"[13]

A quarrel, somewhat typical of the overland trail, had destroyed the partnership. The men agreed to separate until Aldrich realized his predicament and backed down. Personal ownership of property determined the course of events. They were alone in western Wyoming. Chadwich owned the wagon. Had the partnership ended then, Aldrich and his wife would have been left with only their oxen to carry whatever goods they possessed. Because of the woman, Aldrich had to insist that the original agreement remain in force.

Traveling along, they overtook the Badger Boys later that same day at the Big Sandy River. The captain of the company, a man named Condy, had a surplus light wagon which he bailed to Aldrich. With the dilemma of how to convey his wife solved, Aldrich again demanded that the partnership be terminated and this time did not have to change his mind.

> [W]hen we got to the river frank comes up with another wagon and says lets divide the provisions I am going with Condys Company   but we told him to hold on   he had got to settle with us first but he fetched condy up and was going to take things out of the wagon   but we told Condy that he was not a going to takeing things out of our waggon   we told him we thought he was more man than that so he said he wanted nothing but what was right so we showed him our accounts and we had some considerable due us.

It would appear that Captain Condy and perhaps his entire company were prepared to support Aldrich. Had the question of ownership come down to the word of both sides, Aldrich might well have prevailed. Chadwick's insistence on keeping a written record saved the situation for himself and Boyer. If they were unable to prove the ownership of individual items, they at least had evidence of personal debts owed them by the Aldrich couple. Like every emigrant we have encountered so far, even those seen with only a fleeting glance, Captain Condy's conduct

---

[13]Entry for 7 July 1852, Chadwick, Travels. For the nature of the quarrel and abusive words, see "Sharing the Elephant," p. 218n61.

was guided by an innate respect for property rights. The wagon belonged to Chadwick. No emigrant would have said that because they had depended on that conveyance, the Aldriches had a claim on it. Not even the fact one was a woman altered the law. Again we have evidence that property rights, not sentiment, shaped behavior on the overland trail.

In fact, the partnership encountered little difficulty dividing the property because, as is often the case, the human factor played a role. Boyer, the third partner, was so tired of Aldrich he told Chadwick "he would call it even if I would." As a result, the two yoke of oxen purchased (or inherited) from their former passenger, Samuel Fox, were divided unequally. Aldrich got one yoke, Chadwick and Boyer the other.[14]

It would be incorrect to judge events on the overland trail by what lawyers might have done. In law Aldrich was entitled to one third of the concurrently-owned property. He received one half. Although it is true he needed at least one yoke to draw his light wagon, legal, not equitable, considerations determined the division. He still had a claim on his partners. When saying "he would call it even if [Chadwick] would," Boyer showed that he was aware of the relevant law. By taking two oxen and not insisting on absolute rights, Chadwick and Boyer voluntarily paid a small price to be free of an obnoxious companion.

v *Conclusion*

Americans have long been conditioned to think of violence when the frontier is mentioned. It is a perspective that distorts the true picture. Even a revisionist legal historian contributes to the illusion when asking how well and how uniformly law operated under stress. To find the answer it is necessary to focus attention upon quarrels and their resolutions. By its very nature, the evidence tends to emphasize conflict rather than result, human failure rather than legal adjustment. It is not enough

---

[14]Entries for 9-10 July 1852, Chadwick, Travels.

merely to state what the facts prove. We must also insist that they do not prove something else.

The time has arrived to give law its due and restore a balance to our frontier perspective. If the story of partnerships and concurrent ownership of property on the overland trail reveals cantankerous Americans unable to agree when removed from familiar social surroundings, it also reveals law-minded Americans able to adjust claims according to their understanding of legal rights and their willingness to respect the property rights of others.

The push to the Pacific was a tale of sharing more than of dividing, a time of accommodation rather than discord. Far removed from lawyers and courts, the concept of concurrent ownership proved to be one of legal strength, not of legal failure, promoting social peace, not internal disharmony. The overland trail was not a place of conflict. More accurately, it was a place of settlement.

The generality just made is sweeping and must be kept in perspective. We have not been considering the respect nineteenth-century Americans had for rights to property as exemplified by the conduct of emigrants on the overland trail. That is a topic to be examined at the conclusion of this study. We have, rather, been considering several forms of concurrent ownership, how well they were understood, and how they shaped the course of events beyond the frontier where law is often said to have ended and lawlessness begun. In truth, these may not be two topics or, if they are, they should not be rigorously separated. To assert that the emigrants who traversed the continent on the overland trail respected rights of mess, partnership, or joint-stock property, may be the same as saying that the meaning and implications of these types of property holding were being acted upon and by being acted upon were understood.

The question of violence must be given close attention. It would be well, however, not to ask about the degree of violence or why violence was not employed, for these questions have been misleading American historians for too long. When Oliver

Goldsmith of Michigan sought a private share of the common provisions so he might leave the slow-moving Wolverine Rangers, he did not ask for a right but an accommodation. He was aware that the company could deny him what he sought, for the property was concurrent, not personal. By seeking to terminate his contract and depart prematurely, he was begging an indulgence from the majority. It was his companions, not he, who had the "right." What they voted him, he called "a offer." It was, he said, an offer he "accepted."Goldsmith knew he had been asked to accept or reject a contract.[1]

Of course there were some emigrants, caught in the vise of concurrent ownership, who thought of using violence to escape their dilemma. Albert Thurber, the Rhode Islander not permitted by the Congress and California Joint Stock Mining Company to convert his "share" of concurrent property into personalty, found two other members wanting to leave. At Fort Laramie they agreed that if the majority did not divide, "we would take our armes and walk out and take all the animals we needed and the best in the company." The significant fact is that they did not do so because they did not have to, nor did any other recorded emigrant have to resort to force in order to effect a settlement of concurrent property. As Thurber wrote, "the dividing fever raged" at Fort Laramie. His fellow New Englanders were also chafing under the restraint of concurrent ownership.[2]

There were, of course, occasions when violence was not only contemplated; it was threatened and actually employed. Evidence to be presented below will show that even in such situations law often continued to play a role. Legal principles might furnish the excuse justifying counter, or what some would call "police violence,"[3] and legal realities might be factors underscoring the

---

[1]Goldsmith, *Overland*, pp. 57-58; see p. 175 above.

[2]Thurber, Journal, p. 22; see p. 177 above.

[3]For example, in a case to be considered again in a different context, "law" was said by the reporting emigrant to be on the side of one partner threatening the other. Several members of a traveling company concurrently owned a wagon. For all except one who owned several horses the wagon was indispensable. The horse owner, for some reason not

214

wisdom of restraint.[4]

The point is not that violence was avoided and property divided peacefully. The lesson is that because the average emigrants understood the legal concepts with which they were dealing and knew that their adversaries understood the same principles, they were able to dissolve according to rules of property law rather than the rule of force. For that very reason — that law was not a mystery to nineteenth-century Americans — there was less need for violence in the American wilderness than has generally been assumed.

---

explained, "sulked, raised an axe to chop up the rear wheel of the wagon, claiming it was his share of it." A messmate stopped him by threatening to shoot at his heart at the first blow of the axe. The messmate, we are told, "as a matter of law was right" (Harris, Account, p. 104).

[4]In a second case of known force, three partners owned a wagon and oxen. Two of them had a quarrel, one took the wagon, the other the oxen, and the third was left at Salt Lake City without transportation. He explained: "Sam (I mean Mr. McFadden) took away 2 yoke of Oxen without saying by *you[r] leave sir* but said to Doct[or] Downer he would either have them or my life   not wishing to die now I made no objection to his having them as this is in California." It has been suggested that the last words mean that there was then no law to which to appeal, Utah being part of the unorganized territory of California. Letter from Chauncey Swan to Mary Swan, 2 Sept. 1849, "Letters of a Forty-Niner," *Iowa Journal of History*, 47 (1949): 70. Other forty-niners, however, appealed to Mormon courts. It is more likely that Swan really believed the man meant to kill him, perhaps out on the trail. Mention should also be made of an emigrant who indicated hearing rumors or stories of violence caused by concurrent ownership. "[T]here is very few emigrants or Partnership companys but what Quarrels among themselves, some of them divideing teams making 2 carts of 1 wagon — some even fighting and stab[b]ing &c" (T. C. Lewis, Notes).

Starving the Elephant

9 | THE VALUE OF PROPERTY

Correct conclusions should not be based on incomplete evidence. Were we to attribute overland conduct to a legal behavior instilled at home and carried onto the trail, we would grasp but half the story. What must not be overlooked is that while emigrants could bring with them the law of the east, they could not bring the conditions of eastern life.

Much has been made of the social background of those who traversed the overland trail. It explains, we have thought, the respect emigrants showed for person, property, and legality. That same background, however, could have contributed to a heightened sense of homesickness, a feeling of isolation detaching individuals from reality, and (due to a radically different physical environment) a discouragement tending toward pathological depression. All these factors would have produced behavior patterns the opposite of those conjectured for persons of social backgrounds based on family, community, and church. It is therefore necessary to spend a few pages considering just how perilous was the trip, and how conducive the conditions of survival may have been to making travelers forget their upbringing and satisfy their needs with force.

Coming from the very apex of eastern civilization, a New Hampshire forty-niner was shocked to learn that the overland trail might be more dangerous than he had feared on leaving home. "Almost every traveler that we meet," he noted, "who has ever been west of the Rocky Mountains, gives it as his opinion that there is not grass enough in the region of the country to sustain one-half of the stock that is now on the California trail; and they are of opinion that the present immigration cannot reach California this season."[1] Less than three weeks later, a party of

---

[1] Entry for 10 June 1849, Webster, *Gold Seekers* p. 44.

Virginians heard a similar prediction from experienced mountain fur trappers encountered on the trail. "This [news] has thrown a gloom over all of us," one Virginian wrote, "as we have not now more provisions than will last us through, providing we have nothing to stop us."[2]

Gloom was a recurring theme. "A gloomy time," a thirty-year-old Illinoisan wrote while halting on the Sweetwater with his sick companions; "had some sad thoughts of home for a day or two past — of wife and children that I perhaps may never see again. God be merciful."[3] Exactly a month afterward, an Ohio man about to depart from Salt Lake City was even more depressed.

> This morning I feel down-in-the-mouth, for I feel just as if I were leaving home; in fact much more, for already I have been disappointed badly in the roads and in the sorrows and trials of the trip, and knowing that the worst of the journey is yet to be completed. I almost wish I never had been born. But we hitched up and started on, casting a wishful look behind, where all seems to be happiness, peace and plenty, but ahead all is discouragement, toil, hunger and death.[4]

If homesickness was the source of depression — a nostalgia for the "happiness, peace and plenty" of the past — it was compounded by a sociality confined by a reality of isolation, a fear of never returning, and a sense of being trapped in self-created folly. "I was verry home sick when I was at Saint Louis," an emigrant wrote just six miles beyond Saint Joseph, "and I still feel as though I had Done the foolishest thing in Life to start   But what can I do   I have no money and I am ashamed to come Back."[5]

To equate the emigrant's homelonging with that of today's college student or traveler abroad will not do. It was more similar

---

[2]Entry for 28 June 1849, Hoffman, "Diary," p. 65.

[3]Entry for 30 June 1850, Henry Sterling Bloom, "Diary: 1850" (ts., California Historical Society, San Francisco).

[4]Entry for 30 July 1850, Coy, *Great Trek*, p. 168.

[5]Letter of 9 May 1850, Peacock, *Letters*, p. 11.

to that of the military draftee, not so much a matter of being away from home, as being among the unfamiliar and fearful of what the next day might bring.

What was to be feared was the routine as well as the unfamiliar. Otherwise minor annoyances, encountered often enough, can become physical hardships. On the great plains and in the deserts of the Rocky Mountains, overlanders could not even take fire for granted. As early as 13 May, finding no wood on the prairie, each member of a company "took one & a half hard biscuit for supper — and went to bed."[6] Sage brush and buffalo dung were servicable substitutes, though one burned too quickly[7] and the other, in such scanty supply it often had to be husbanded,[8] was generally good fuel for cooking but might not generate enough heat for a farrier or blacksmith.[9]

These and similar points need not be checked off. One side of the same coin should not be emphasized at the expense of the other. The pressure to abandon taught legal ways probably came less from emigrants being separated from the comforts of home, than from subjection to the discomforts of a life for which few were prepared. The everyday problem of contending with the dust of wagon travel, might have been of less consequence had it not made eyes sore[10] and tempers irritable. We have seen the dependence travelers had on their animals. Consider what that dependence meant when every night there was danger of stampedes which could disperse the herd or cause injury to man and beast.[11] Worse was to learn that enthusiasm could not compensate for inexperience, and ineptness was destroying horses and oxen. A New Hampshire company was no farther than Fort Kearny before its members discovered that packing was a

---

[6]Entry for 13 May 1852, Dalton, Diary, p. 5; similarly, entry for 10 June 1852, Anable, Second Journal.

[7]Entry for 22 June 1863, Yager, "Diary," Part 2, pp. 20-21.

[8]Leeper, *Argonauts*, p. 18.

[9]Lavender, *Westward*, p. 226.

[10]Entries for 28 May and 9 June 1849, J. H. Johnson, Journey.

[11]See, e.g., entry for 23 May 1850, Grindell, Sketch Book.

delicate matter, requiring a skill obtained by practice. "The backs and shoulders of many of our mules," one man lamented, "have become very sore and [are] in a serious condition, many of them having lost large patches of skin, and the prospect, at present, seems to be that few of them will survive to reach California the present season."[12] "[T]he trouble with stock," an 1854 traveler observed, "is enough to try the pachance of Jobe."[13]

Little from their past experience had prepared emigrants for survival on the overland trail. Just to persevere, most had to surmount that past. The task was somewhat eased when the perils of the present caused men to abandon some niceties of their upbringing. "The River was full of dead cattle, horses, and mules — and we were compelled to use the water," one emigrant wrote of the Humboldt.[14] "It requires some little practice to relish a beverage in which putrescent flesh has been for months steeping," another observed. "But here we have no choice."[15] Less than a month later, ceasing to wonder at human adaptability, he concluded that outward appearances might well presage permanent alterations of character.

> "A man may get used to anything," is an old saying, the truth of which is pretty clearly demonstrated on this journey. Traveling in constant clouds of dust, dirty faces, hands, and clothes, become less and less offensive, so that as we draw towards the termination of the journey, we see for a general rule, a dirty rabble. Men have stomachs that are far from being squeamish. I have seen a man eating his lunch, and gravely sitting upon the carcass of a dead horse, and we frequently take our meals amidst the effluvia of a hundred putrescent carcasses. Water is drank with a good relish, into which we know that scores of dead animals have been thrown, or have fallen. I saw three men eating a snake the other day, that one of them had dressed and cooked, not because they were in

---

[12]Entry for 18 June 1849, Webster, *Gold Seekers*, p. 48.

[13]"Letter from John S. L. Taylor to Rachel Taylor, 24 July 1855" (ms., photocopy, Washington State Library, Olympia).

[14]Evans, Letter.

[15]Entry for 9 Sept. 1850, Langworthy, *Scenery*, p. 109.

want of food, but as a rarity, or perhaps, rather by way of bravo, to show others that nothing would turn their stomachs.[16]

If the conditions of overland life caused many emigrants to abandon formerly cherished standards of physical propriety, we may wonder why they did not do the same with social, legal, and behavioral standards. Unfortunately the answer must be less precise than we seek, for once again we may be attempting to measure the immeasureable. "The hardships of the overland route to California are beyond conception," a forty-niner warned. "Care and suspense, pained anxiety, fear of losing animals and leaving one to foot it and pack his 'duds' on his back, begging provisions, fear of being left in the mountains to starve and freeze to death, and a thousand other things which no one thinks of until on the way, are things of which I may write and you may read, but they are nothing to the *reality*."[17]

II *The Penalties of Travel*

We may grant that physical pressures were immeasurable, yet we must attempt to measure them. It is not difficult to imagine that individuals far from home, thrown into an environment for which they were ill prepared, forced to adhere to unending physical drudgery, could forget the rules of propriety, abandon the taught norms of social behavior, and, in a fit of depression or temper, turn with violence upon their companions. The possibility raises questions about homicide, battery, or similar acts of aggression which are beyond the concern of this book. Our attention is confined to legal behaviorism as manifested by attitudes toward rights in property.[1] For that more limited

---

[16]Ibid., entry for 5 Oct. 1850, pp. 129-30.

[17] Letter from J. L. Stephens to the *Marietta* (Ohio) *Intelligencer*, 6 Sept. 1849, quoted in T. D. Clark, "Appendix," p. 160.

[1]The question of homicide and related "crime" on the overland trail has not yet been investigated. The study will have to include not only offenses as defined in American law but also offenses against the group or company peculiar to overland travel. For

inquiry, we may measure the immeasurable by considering the extent of forces tending to alter conduct by obliterating habits of taught legal standards. On the overland trail there were three main forces working against the past: the presence of sickness, the fear of death, and the threat of starvation.

Sickness was an ever-constant companion on the westward journey, seldom more so than during 1849 and 1850, the first two summers of the overland gold rush.[2] During those years, emigrants had a sense of being surrounded by cholera — at the place of rendezvous along the Missouri River[3] and in Texas,[4] as well as out on the trail as far west as today's Idaho and Nevada.[5] Other common ailments were diarrhea, dysentery, scurvy, and the mysterious "mountain fever."[6]

Some companies were forced to turn back due to sickness;[7] among others there could be as many as two sick men in each wagon.[8] A few trains were traveling hospitals, no sooner did one man die than another became ill,[9] occasionally leaving barely

---

preliminary considerations see "Prosecuting the Elephant;" David J. Langum, "Pioneer Justice on the Overland Trails," *Western Historical Quarterly*, 5 (1975): 421-39.

[2]For studies of medicine on the overland trail see George W. Groh, *Gold Fever; Being a True Account, Both Horrifying and Hilarious, of the Art of Healing (So-Called) during the California Gold Rush* (New York: William Morrow & Co., 1966); Read, "Diseases."

[3]Entry for 26 June 1849, William North Steuben, "Journals" (ms., C-F 183, Bancroft Library).

[4]Entry for 9 June 1849, Audubon, "Overland," p. 113.

[5]Entry for 15 July 1850, Gilmore, Overland Journey, p. 14; entry for 29 July 1852, Coupler, Crossing the Plains, p. 17; entry for 31 July 1852, Wigle, Copy, p. 14. For a physician's account of cholera on the trail see entries for 21-22 May and 7-8 June 1850, Maynard, Pocket Diary.

[6]For a physician's description of "mountain fever" see entry for 7 June 1850, Parker, Notes; entry for 25 June 1849, Nixon, Journal. Smallpox and "tipus fever," though much less common than the diseases named above, also caused deaths. See, e.g., entry for 15 May 1849, J. H. Johnson, Journey.

[7]Entry for 9 June 1850, Bennett, *Overland Journey*, p. 16; entry for 6 June 1852, Kahler, Leaves from the Diary, p. 26.

[8]Entry for 13 June 1850, Thomasson, Diary.

[9]Entries for 11 and 16 June 1850, Pomroy, Diary, pp. 20, 27.

enough able-bodied members to muster a burial detail.[10] There are even second-hand accounts of sick being abandoned by their companions, left alone to die.[11]

If disease was bad, death was worse. It was so frequent on the overland trail, that life surely seemed cheaper than it had back east, and when life is less esteemed, respect for property rights must be affected.

"During the first 170 miles of our journey, we must have averaged 4 new made graves daily," a forty-niner wrote.[12] Another counted fifty-seven graves at one campground.[13] A conservative estimate of deaths for the decades during which the trail was traveled reckons ten burials for each mile.[14] 1852 was not a year that historians recall as being memorable for illness, yet diaries and letters make it clear that the emigrants of 1852 thought they were surrounded by the threat of disease and of dying.[15] One company left Ash Hollow that year with seventeen members. Fourteen were dead by the time the survivors reached Fort Laramie.[16] "Sickness and death in the states is hard but it is

[10]"Of the entire company that started for California, at one time numbering ninety-eight, only four were able to help me perform the last rites for poor Coombs" (entry for 22 March 1849, Audubon, "Overland," p. 107).

[11]Entry during July 1850, "Across the Plains in 1850: Journal and Letters of Jerome Dutton," *Annals of Iowa*, 3rd ser., 9 (1910): 469.

[12]Letter from D. Jagger, 5 June 1849, *Western Reserve Chronicle* (Warren, Ohio), 11 July 1849, p. 2, col. 5.

[13]Mattes, *Platte River Road*, p. 88.

[14]Ibid., p. 82.

[15]Entries for 9-12 May 1852, Crane, Journal; entries for 2-5 June 1852, Chadwick, Diary; entry for 3 June 1852, Kitchell, Diaries, p. 16; entries for 5-6 and 12 June 1852, Jay Stillman, "Recollections of a Trip across the Plains in 1852" (ts., Washington State Historical Society, Tacoma), p. 5; entry for 14 June 1852, Cornell, Description, p. 19; entry for 30 June 1852, Moreland, Diary; entry for 28 July 1852, Bailey, Trip, p. 18; entry for 2 Aug. 1852, A. Richardson, Diary of 1852; entry for 7 Aug. 1852, Wigle, Copy, p. 13; Moore, Journal of Travails; Parsons, Reminiscences, pp. 2-3; Andrew Vanbuskirk, "Diary" (ts., 881 [William Vanbuskirk Papers], Oregon Historical Society), p. 4, Kahler, Leaves from the Diary; Eaton, *Overland*, pp. 42-43, 55, 138-40; Mattes, *Platte River Road*, pp. 304-10.

[16]Eaton, *Overland*, p. 103. For detailed recordings of grave counts in 1852 see Turnbull, "Travels," p. 177; Hampton, Diary(ts.), pp. 2-5; W. Johnston, Diary. See also letter from Silas Miller to his brother, 24 Nov. 1852 in Wayman, *Diary*, p. 34n18; entry for 9 June 1852, Moreland, Diary.

nothing to be compared with it on the plains," Lydia Rudd observed shortly after three members of her train died.[17]

There is no need to pursue statistics. For those on the overland trail, the historical reality mattered less than the immediate impression. Thinking they were surrounded by sickness and death, emigrants not only sensed danger, they reacted to it. The dominant urge was to rush forward at all costs. Even those whose companies remained healthy heard enough tales to spur them on. If the desire to reach California as quickly as possible, either to dig gold or to avoid the mountain snows, was not incentive enough, the instinct for self-preservation surely was. In such situations, according to academic theories of behavior, abstract rights to property would enjoy a low priority.

There is yet a stronger point that can be made. To live daily with sickness and death, to hear of it from all sides, and to witness its effects on neighboring trains, even if not within one's own camp, removed the average emigrant that much further from the familiar world of family, community, and law. The more harsh the environment, the more alien the physical universe, the more desperate the circumstances, the more difficult it was to adhere to, or even recall, the legal and social behavior of a world left far behind.

III   *The Tragic Errors of Forty-Nine*

To round out what may be an unprovable hypothesis — the separation and alienation of emigrants from the taught legal behavior of the east — attention must be focused on the threat of starvation. It was a peril emigrants feared more than they did Indians, spurring them on as much as the knowledge that snow soon would block the mountain passes.

The degree to which overland travelers faced starvation varied from emigration to emigration. During early years shortages of both animals and foodstuffs could be acute. By 1853, as we saw in

----

[17]Entry for 23 June 1852, Rudd, Notes. For comments that year by physicians treating illness see Dalton, Diary, pp. 3-13; entry for 30 June 1852, Wayman, *Diary*, p. 60.

the third chapter, conditions were altered, for John Smith was able to replenish his larder on a fairly consistent basis.

Individuals as well as emigrations differed. Some overland travelers never faced hunger; others were on famine rations for weeks on end. It is to these persons, during the worst of times, we must turn. The story is not told by averages, but extremes: those few times when hunger, among a large number of the people, became so acute that we could expect even law-minded men to enforce the law of survival by violating the law of private property. There were two such occasions during the history of the overland trail. The first was on Lassen's cutoff during 1849, the second occurred during the latter half of the entire 1850 emigration.

There were, to be sure, other times when starvation either threatened or actually happened, but they did not involve exceptional numbers of emigrants. Indeed, one reason for the occurence of shortages in particular places, such as Hastings cutoff across the salt flats of Utah, was that they were sparsely traveled. With fewer travelers, there was less opportunity to buy or to borrow.

A similar example is the southern trail across Texas and along the Gila River in 1849. Cholera struck early and large companies disintegrated before going one-fourth the way. The route was unknown, distances misjudged,[1] the desert unanticipated,[2] and way stations, at which provisions could be obtained, poorly stocked and far between.[3]

---

[1] One party took fifty-five days just getting from San Antonio to El Paso. "Their provisions gave out before they reached El Paso; so that four spoonfuls of 'cold flower' were the daily ration allowed each man" (Bieber, *Southern Trails*, p. 198).

[2] "We had a fahrenheit thermometer with us which we frequently hung up on the cottonwood trees near the stream [Gila] when in camp, and it would show as high as 150 degrees in the shade. We were obliged to travel at night by the light of the stars and moon, as we were unable to live in the hot sun" (Robert Eliot, "Overland to California in 1849" [ts., copied from the *Essex County Republican*, Port Henry, New York, 16 March 1899, State Historical Society of Wisconsin, Madison], p. 9).

[3] For suffering on the southern trail see generally, Cardinell, "Adventures;" Hayes, Diary.

A third example is Death Valley. Having started late, or traveled slowly, a party of forty-niners found themselves in Salt Lake City, where they should have remained for the winter. Too impatient for caution, yet wishing to avoid the snows of the Sierras, they headed southwest, into an unexplored region where experienced fur trappers led by Jedediah Smith had almost perished twenty-three years earlier. They thought they would be safe, for Mormons encouraged them to leave,[4] and they were able to hire Mormon guides.[5] But becoming ever more impatient, trusting luck rather than experience,[6] and hoping to find a mountain pass that did not exist,[7] groups of individuals broke away from their original companies. Desperate with hunger,[8] small parties groped blindly, crisscrossing one another's paths,[9] seeking an escape from the desert as they buried companions; and steadily moved further beyond recollection of their former lives.[10]

The blunder of 1849 causing the greatest suffering, because committed by the largest number of people, was not Death Valley. It was the less famous but better documented Lassen's cutoff. Emigrants entering California by Lassen's cutoff thought they were taking a shortcut.[11] Totally misinformed, they soon learned that far from being a shortcut, Lassen's was not even a cutoff. Rather than eliminating miles, it was a longer route, taking forty-niners over some of the most treacherous terrain in the American west, to a place they did not want to go.

---

[4]Leonard Babcock, "Recollections of Overland Journey, 1849, and Experiences in California, etc." (ms., C-D 789:1, Bancroft Library); letter from DeWitt Day in Lorch, "Gold Rush," p. 363.

[5]Coy, *Great Trek*, pp. 267, 271; Server, "Ill-Fated Wagon Train," p. 29.

[6]"Prologue and Commentary," in Nusbaumer, *Journal*, ed. George Koenig, pp. 1-2.

[7]Read, "Women and Children," p. 13; Read and Gaines, "Introduction," p. 1229.

[8]Entry for 29 Oct. 1849, Hoover, Diary; entry for 29 Oct. 1849, Hoover, Revised Journal.

[9]Read and Gaines, "Introduction," p. 1229.

[10]Senter, *Crossing*, pp. 15-16.

[11]Entry for 25 Aug. 1849, Burbank, Diary and Journal, p. 91.

Following the trail of Jesse Applegate's southern road to Oregon, Lassen's cutoff separated from the main overland route at the northernmost point of the great bend of the Humboldt River, supposedly headed directly to Sutter's Fort. Instead, it swung a wide loop across Nevada's Black Rock Desert, wandering from alkaline spring to alkaline spring, crossing the Sierras where no previous trail had been cut, ending at Lassen's ranch, which, although in the Sacramento valley, was nowhere near Sutter's Fort.[12] No other part of the trail that year was more destructive of wagons, draft animals, and emigrants.

Shortages began appearing on Lassen's cutoff even before travelers left the Humboldt.[13] They grew acute as deserts turned into mountains with no end of the trail in sight. Once in the mountains, moreover, physical difficulties were aggravated by the fact that Lassen's cutoff was one of the few places along the trail where Indians were troublesome. By appropriating horses and mules, Indians deprived emigrants not only of transportation, but of the means of carrying provisions.[14]

"The amount of suffering," a forty-niner from Michigan wrote of Lassen's cutoff, "was almost incalculable. No one except those who saw or experienced it, can have any idea of its extent . . . I saw men sitting or lying by the road side, sick with fevers or crippled by scurvy, begging of the passers by, to lend them some assistance; but no one could do it. The winter was so near, that it was sure death to tarry, and the teams were all giving out, so that the thought of hauling them in wagons was absurd. Nothing could be done, consequently they were left to a slow lingering death in the wilderness."[15]

---

[12]Lassen's ranch was near today's Vina, California.

[13]Entry for 2 Aug. 1849, Mann, Portion; entry for 16 Aug. 1849, Gray, *Off at Sunrise*, p. 81; entry for 18 Aug. 1849, I. Hale, "Diary," p. 111.

[14]Entry for 3 Oct. 1849, Bruff, *Journals*, p. 203; entry for 30 Aug. 1849, Delano, *Across the Plains*, p. 92.

[15]James D. Lyon, quoted in Read and Gaines, "Introduction," pp. 611n172, 1010n27. See also entry for 17 Sept. 1849, Castleman, Diary.

The prospect of starvation hung over most who left records of Lassen's cutoff.[16] "Provisions out, & none can be had any way," is a typical diary entry.[17] Indians made hunting dangerous, and though some meat was obtained that way,[18] most came from worn-down animals killed for the purpose[19] or "from the carcasses of cattle that had died from exhaustion."[20] What very few provisions were for sale were costly.[21]

The number perishing on Lassen's cutoff for want of food will never be known. Perhaps as many more survived only because they were met by government relief parties.[22] "Hundreds are coming in daily from all over the mountains, sick, and almost starved," a physician wrote while witnessing the emigration stagger into Lassen's ranch. "At every place where the road came near water were camps of overland men, all sick and sometimes so feeble as to be dependent upon passersby for water. Few were well and the further we advanced the worse matters became."[23]

IV *The Year of Starvation*

Tales of hardship may reveal the strength of the human spirit and something of the will to survive, but unless we can gauge the stress hardships exerted upon individuals, they indicate little about social and legal behaviorism. No emigrant spoke directly to the point. Most thought of difficulties on the overland trail in terms of physical challenge and physical triumph, not as a testing of their adherence to standards of conduct. "As I look back upon

---

[16]Entries for 20-22 Aug. 1849, Farnham, "From Ohio," pp. 419-20; entry for 4 Sept. 1849, Benson, Forty Niner, p. 60; entry for 21 Oct. 1849, Castleman, Diary.

[17]Entry for 1 Oct. 1849, Caldwell, "Notes," p. 1266.

[18]Entry for 24 Sept. 1849, Lott, Copy, p. 10.

[19]Entry for 3 Oct. 1849, Stuart, *Roving Life*, 1:72.

[20]Entry for 18 Aug. 1849, McCall, *Wayside Notes*, p. 70.

[21]Entry for 15 Sept. 1849, Sedgley, *Overland to California*, p. 59; entry for 22 Sept. 1849, Foster, Journal, pp. 81-82.

[22]*Scharmann's Overland Journey*, pp. 42-43; Goldsmith, *Overland*, p. 84; entry for 1 Oct. 1849, Batchelder, Journal, pp. 138-39.

[23]Stillman, "Around the Horn," pp. 167-68.

this great crusade, this rush for Gold," Henry Page, a forty-niner from Illinois, wrote his wife, "I am lost in wonder, that so few left their bones to be a monument of this great march — Though the cholera stalked in our rear and cut off some, yet I suppose that a larger proportion escaped death than in any other instance upon record, where so large a number of men, passed over such an extent of country, depending as they were alone, upon their own resources for food — A march of 2000 miles through a wilderness was never so successfully prosecuted — and if large numbers again take the overland route, I look for much suffering and distress."[1]

Page's prediction proved as accurate as his recollections. Bad as Lassen's cutoff may have been for those forty-niners taking it, the hardships experienced by the entire 1850 emigration to California were worse.[2]

A number of adverse conditions, some caused by nature, others of human creation, combined to made 1850 the most perilous in the history of the overland trail. The first difficulty was posed by an acute shortage of grass and grain[3]; a famine so well publicized that a forty-niner, writing from Sacramento, warned his brother not to come to California that year, because "there is not a sufficient quantity of grass to feed those animals."[4] The problem was dryness, lasting from the Mississippi River[5] to the Great Basin, where grass was in limited supply even during the wettest seasons.[6] Keeping in mind the wild thunderstorms that terrified overland emigrants most other years, we learn something of

---

[1]Letter from Henry Page to Mary Page, 3 April 1850, Page, *Wagons*, p. 257.

[2]Entries for 4 and 11 May 1850, Abbey, *A Trip*, pp. 114, 116.

[3]Entry for 29 April 1850, Blood, Diary, p. 1.

[4]Letter from Thomas Bedford to A.M. Bedford, 26 May 1850 (ms. 2610, folder 2, State Historical Society of Missouri, Columbia).

[5]The shortage began worrying some emigrants as early as eastern Iowa (entry for 8 April 1850, McKinstry, *Diary*, p. 75).

[6]Entries 16 April and 12 July 1850, Payne, Account, pp. 4, 71. Emigrants complained of the lack of grass almost everywhere along the trail. At the Big Blue: entry for 20 April 1850, Millington, Journal, p. 12; entry for 12 May 1850, J. N. Jones, Journal, p. 8; entry for 18 May 1850, Read, Journal. From the Missouri to Fort Kearny: entries from 12 to 24 May 1850,

the uniqueness of 1850 by the fact one party was not delayed by rain until reaching the northeast corner of today's Nevada.[7]

Overland travel followed a relentless dynamics. Scarcity of grass forced anxious emigrants to gamble with their stock. Avoiding one catastrophe, they risked a second. If they started too soon, they chanced starving their animals. If delayed, they drove the stock at a forbidding pace to avoid Sierra snows.[8] Diaries of 1850 indicate that most waited for at least the first sign of grass.[9] Those who started earlier either had to turn back,[10] or carry feed for the animals,[11] increasing the weight hauled and

---

Rhodes, "Journal," pp. 62-63. Along the North Platte; letter of 19 May 1850, Dulany, Papers; entries for 13 to 16 June 1850, McCanne, Diary. At Fort Laramie: Marshall, Letter; letter of 25 May 1850, Z. S. Tuttle, Letters; "Letter from Aaron Broughton to Linda Broughton, 9 June 1850," (ts., "Fort Laramie Journals," vol. 2, Fort Laramie National Historic Site, Fort Laramie, Wyoming; letter from Milo Andras to O. Hyde, 19 July 1850, *Frontier Guardian*, 2 Oct. 1850, p. 3, col. 1. Beyond Fort Laramie: entry for 10 June 1850, Shepherd, *Journal*, p. 12. Between the North Platte and the Sweetwater: entry for 21 June 1850, A. Brown, "Journal," p. 22; entry for 4 July 1850, J. Wood, *Journal*, p. 42; entry for 6 July 1850, Dowell, Journal, p. 26; letter to the *Guardian* from Orson Hyde, 30 July 1850, *Frontier Guardian*, 2 Oct. 1850, p. 2 col. 1. On the Sweetwater: entry for 6 June 1850, Parker, Notes; entry for 19 June 1850, W. Hanna, Journal, p. 3; entry for 29 June 1850, Pomroy, Diary, pp. 30-31; entry for 10 June 1850, Keck, Journal; entry for 10 July 1850, Starr, Tour of the West. Near Fort Hall: entry for 28 July 1850, McKinstry, *Diary*, p. 219.

[7]Entry for 26 July 1850, Gilmore, Overland Journey, p. 17.

[8]Entries for 29 April and 12 May 1850, Payne, Account, pp. 11, 22. See also entry for 8 May 1850, C. W. Smith, Journal; Mattes, *Platte River Road*, p. 52; William S. Greever, *The Bonanza West: The Story of the Western Mining rushes, 1848-1900* (Norman: University of Oklahoma Press, 1963), p. 14.

[9]At St. Joseph: letter from Joseph Price to Elizabeth Price, 28 April 1850, J. Price, "Letters," p. 244; entry for 5 May 1850, Gilmore, Overland Journey, p. 6. At Kanesville: letter of 23 April 1850, Z. S. Tuttle, Letters.

[10]Entry for 10 May 1850, J. N. Jones, Journal, pp. 6-7; entries for 10 and 14 May 1850, L. Sawyer, *Across the Plains*, pp. 24, 27; entry for 11 May 1850, Lane, Diary; entry for 12 May 1850, W. S. McBride, Diary; entry for 15 May 1850, Read, Journal; entry of 21 May 1850, Griffith, Diary, p. 36.

[11]Letter of 18 April 1850, Brouster, Letters; entry for 26 April 1850, McGlasken, Journal, p. 2; entry for 29 April 1850, Parker, Notes; letter of 1 May 1850, Dulany, Papers; *Frontier Guardian*, 1 May 1850, p. 2, col. 4; entry for 5 May 1850, Keck, Journal; entry for 5 May 1850, Albert Zieber, "Diary" (ms., Oregon Collection, University of Oregon), p. 12; entry for 9 May 1850, Stimson, Overland, p. 35; entry for 11 May 1850, Clapp, *Journal*, p. 16; entry for 13 May 1850, Loomis, *Journal*, p. 13; entry for 16 May 1850, W. S. McBride,

weakening the very livestock the feed was intended to save.[12]

Colonel William W. Loring had commanded the march of the mounted riflemen to Oregon in 1849. In his report of the expedition, Loring advised emigrants to start at the earliest possible date, recommending they leave on 1 April, carrying "twenty days of forage." This feed should last until the Platte, he thought, then grass would be found "in sufficient quantities."[13] Nature failed to cooperate in 1850. Although at least one of the two thousand and more wagons to depart that year reached the Sweetwater still hauling some feed for the animals,[14] few parties got anywhere near that distance before the grain was exhausted.

There is no action more prescient of the tragedy to come on the 1850 overland trail than that of those emigrants not far beyond Missouri, "obliged to give their provisions to their animals to keep them alive."[15] Some overland travelers that year took extra flour just for that purpose,[16] but most jeopardized their own food supply to sustain the cattle. Even that risk did not pay for emigrants who saw their animals "running down rapidly," a condition one owner blamed on "eating too much corn without hay or grass."[17]

The shortage of grass was far more serious than is commonly supposed, as it contributed a number of conditions to the 1850 emigration which, when combined, produced disaster. It meant, for example, that many emigrants left the Missouri without

---

Diary; entry for 21 May 1850, C. W. Smith, Journal; letter from J. M. McEwen to wife, 30 May 1850, "McEwen [Family] Papers" (ms., Missouri Historical Society, St. Louis).

[12]One wagon carried eight hundred pounds of bread for the horses, two hundred pounds for the emigrants (letter of 20 May 1850, Peacock, *Letters*, p. 12).

[13]Loring, "Report," p. 342.

[14]Entry for 25 May 1850, Stimson, Overland, p. 40.

[15]Carr, letter. A Mormon coming east reported that the first emigrant company encountered had fed their animals grain "and when that was exhausted they had fed [them] their flour (letter from Robert Campbell to the Editors, 7 July 1850, *Frontier Guardian*, 24 July 1850, p. 1, col. 6).

[16]"I shall carry flour   hard bread & chop[p]ed wheat for feed equal in nourishment to 130 bushels of oats that with grass I think will sustain my horses (letter from Samuel Huston to Nathan Huston, 2 May 1850 [ts., State Historical Society of Iowa, Iowa City]).

[17]Entries for 1 and 4 May 1850, Stimson, Overland, pp. 32-33.

sufficient funds, having spent their money buying feed, some even wandering from frontier town to frontier town looking for grain.[18]

Even when grass appeared on the plains it was not as abundant during 1850 as other years, and many emigrants seeking an adequate amount were compelled to push their animals from place to place in search of forage, often stopping due to exhaustion at sites where there was water but no grass or grass but no water.[19] "[W]e are," one man wrote of his animals near Devil's Gate, "obliged for the present to make short drives and give them time to fill themselves."[20] Not only did emigrants progress more slowly, but the cattle were being driven further, at more frequent intervals, and exhaustion was added to starvation.[21]

The animals of 1850 began dying sooner than was usual on the overland trail,[22] which meant that a relatively high percentage of the emigration that year packed or walked the last several hundred miles. As early as the Sweetwater River, one traveler estimated, "[t]he greater   part of the horse and mule companies were packing on account of the food being so poor."[23]

The emigrants were not only in trouble but, more important to our thesis, they knew they were. "Last year," one man observed when only as far as Court House Rock, "all along [the] Platte, grass could be mown & stock fattened, & the same was again expected; whereas — stock, since striking Platte['s] main N[orth] and S[outh] forks have rapidly become poor, an excessive drought prevailing. I anticipate much suffering, as here is the

---

[18]*Weekly Missouri Statesman*, 24 May 1850, reprinted in *California Emigrant Letters*, p. 95; Ferguson, *Gold Fields*, p. 10.

[19]Entries for 7 and 20 June 1850, Wolcott, Journal.

[20]Entry for 25 May 1850, Stimson, Overland, p. 40.

[21]Just five days after crossing the Missouri River, one emigrant passed a company of ox teams and noted that "some of them, are in a state of starvation (entry for 29 April 1850, Turner, Diary).

[22]On the first twelve days of the trip, one man counted seventeen dead horses and mules, "that have sunk under the fatigue of [the] journey" (entry for 17 May 1850, Gilmore, Overland Journey, p. 3). See also Keller, *Trip*, pp. 6-20.

[23]Entry for 30 June 1850, Chalmers, "Journal," p. 44.

place our stock was to fatten & prepare themselves for crossing the arid, barren districts 't other side [of the] mountains."[24] "Some of us," a physician from Indiana confided to his journal, "are no doubt doomed never to reach California and others perhaps may never get home to their friends and families."[25] The date of this entry was so early it must be noted. It was the 15th of May. Little wonder that even before reaching the continental divide, emigrants began "to wear *sterner* faces, there is no longer the hilarity that there was, pressing onward regardless of sacrifice or consequences seems to be the order."[26]

The story of physical sufferings in 1850 could go on and on. The dryness of the season did more than retard the grass. It made travel "extremely uncomfortable on account of the dust."[27] Days seemed "hot enough to roast potatoes in the sun."[28] There is no need to go on, however, for it was not just the shortage of forage that made 1850 the year of overland travail. The main cause was not physical but man made: the average emigrant that year left the Missouri River without sufficient provisions.[29]

Those going overland in 1850 knew of the vast destruction of property the year before. Forty-niners had written letters home, many of which were published in newspapers,[30] telling of the burden of property on the overland trail.[31] The emigrants of 1850,

---

[24]Entry for 10 June 1850, Wolcott, Journal.

[25]Entry for 15 May 1850, W. S. McBride, Diary.

[26]Ibid., entry for 12 June 1850.

[27]Entry for 14 May 1850, Gilmore, Overland Journey, p. 2.

[28]Letter of 20 May 1850, Plummer, letter, p. 3.

[29]How much sickness there was in 1850 is not clear. Some emigrants thought there was very little (letter of 9 June 1850, J. H. McBride, Letters; entry for 11 August 1850, Gilmore, Overland Journey, p. 20). A physician, however, reported much illness (letter of 21 June 1850, Ayres, Letters).

[30]"Letter from H. Swearinger to D. Swearinger, 14 June 1849" (ms., photocopy, "Western Travel Envelope," Missouri Historical Society, St. Louis); entry for 12 May 1849, Audubon, "Overland," p. 110.

[31]See, e.g., Bidlach, *Letters*, pp. 21, 38-39; Lorch, "Gold Rush," p. 313n12; *California Emigrant Letters*, pp. 88-94; Unruh, The Plains Across, p. 217. For an even earlier published warning see letter of 29 June 1847, Ingersoll, *Overland in 1847*, p. 25.

an eastward-bound Mormon noted at the North Platte ferry, "had learned wisdom by the things their friends last year had suffered, and come on in quite a different style."[32] Few, in 1850, "started with provisions sufficient to last them across the plains" and "no train took too much."[33] For some unexplained reason, many emigrants that year thought the trip shorter than it was, and "provided themselves only for 60 or 70 days."[34] With progress delayed due to the search for grass, hunger became that much more prevalent on the trail.[35]

A second error was also caused by the experiences of 1849. The emigrants of 1850 thought they could travel lightly and, when finding no grass, that they could afford to feed their provisions to the animals, expecting to purchase what they needed at the forts, trading posts, or Salt Lake City, or to live on the gleanings from the road as many forty-niners had done.[36] There was however, little food abandoned that year, and the forts had nothing to sell.[37] Quite a few, therefore, were forced to go to Salt Lake City, where forty-niners had found abundant supplies.[38] As the Mormons had

---

[32]Letter from Robert Campbell to the Editors, 7 July 1850, *Frontier Guardian*, 24 July 1850, p. 2, col. 1.

[33]Letter from Arthur St. Clair to the Editor, 26 October 1850, *Clinton Republican*, Wilmington, Ohio, 10 Jan. 1851, p. 1, col. 7; Abbott, *Recollections*, pp. 59-60.

[34]Letter of 15 Sept. 1852, Kuhliwein, Letters, p. 21. See also letter from S.H.N. Patterson, 29 July 1850, *California Emigrant Letters*, p. 115.

[35]Letter of 26 June 1850, J. Price, "Letters," p. 253; Delano, *Life*, pp. 236-37; Stimson, Overland, p. 8; Keller, *Trip*, pp. 7-8; Lorch, "Gold Rush," p. 314n12; Webb, *Trail*, p. 138.

[36]Forty-niners: entry for 31 May 1849, Stitzel, Diary, p. 94; entry for 19 July 1849, Batchelder, Journal, p. 50; "We are saving our stores and living on gleanings from the road, and even add to our stock of some things" (entry for 23 July 1849, Stuart, *Roving Life*, 1:40).

[37]Entry for 1 May 1850, Blood, Diary, p. 2; entry for 11 June 1850, "Overland to the Gold Fields of California in 1850: The Journal of Calvin Taylor," ed. Burton J. Williams, *Nebraska History*, 50 (1969): 136; Carr, Letter. But see entry for 23 May 1850, Parker, Notes. There were also shortages at Council Bluffs (*Frontier Guardian*, 1 May 1850, p. 2, col. 2; entry for 21 April 1850, Keck, Journal).

[38]Entry for 2 July 1850, Chalmers, "Journal," p. 44; Carr, Letter; letter from R. Luther Myrick to Thomas Myrick, 30 Dec. 1849, Myrick, *Letters*, p. 7.

much less for sale in 1850, prices were very high.[39] Some emigrants obtained food only by helping with the harvest, or because they had items, such as dried fruit, to exchange.[40]

The route was longer and few provisions were available; those two facts alone did not make 1850 worse for some who went via Salt Lake City. Add to them a very serious error. Advised that California was about twenty days away, many reached the Humboldt River, three weeks after leaving the Mormon settlements, out of food, with the most difficult part of the trail still ahead.[41]

Every year was bad along the Humboldt — alkaline water bloating the cattle, only willows for fuel, and the sparse grass often covered with salt. The Humboldt of 1850 posed an additional hazard. Vast quantities of snow melted that summer, and the western rivers were swollen.[42] The Humboldt overflowed its banks, narrowing the bottom land and inundating much of what little grass existed. To feed their stock, emigrants swam or waded the sometimes turbulent stream,[43] and one man said that as many people were drowned that summer as died from hunger.[44] His estimate may have been an exaggeration. Hunger, not drowning, dominated travel down the Humboldt in 1850, and it was hunger that made the year unique.

As far back as Chimney Rock in western Nebraska, a man noted that "there has been more suffering on this trip than one can

[39]Entry for 29 June 1850, Abbey, *A Trip*, p. 140; entry for 3 July 1850, Griffith, Diary, p. 65; entries for 12 and 27 July 1850, Starr, Tour of the West; Summers, Letter. But see letter of 13 July 1850, J. H. McBride, Letters.

[40]A. Brown, "Journal," p. 24; entry for 22 July 1850, Moorman, *Journal*, p. 51.

[41]Entry for 15 Aug. 1850, McKinstry, *Diary*, p. 258; entry for 5 Aug. 1850, Chalmers, "Journal," p. 51; Webb, *Trail*, p. 150.

[42]Letter of 13 July 1850, J. H. McBride, Letters.

[43]Entry for 28 June 1850, Lewis Kilbourn, "Overland Journey" (ms., 1508, Oregon Historical Society, Portland); entry for 15 July 1850, Read, Journal; entries for 29 July to 3 Aug. 1850, Griffith, Diary, pp. 78-79; entry for 3 Aug. 1850, W. Hanna, Journal, p. 5; entry for 13 Aug. 1850, Newcomb, Journal; entry for 23 Aug. 1850, Dowell, Journal, pp. 41-42; entry for 20 Sept. 1850, Langworthy, *Scenery*, p. 118; Delano, *Across the Plains*, p. 104.

[44]"Letter from William A. Carter to His Wife, 11 August 1850" (ts., 542, State Historical Society of Missouri, Columbia).

well imagine, and how it is to end God only knows."[45] As he was to learn, it ended on the salty Humboldt River and the bone-dry Forty-Mile Desert, with thousands of crawling stomachs, thousands of desperate men.[46]

v *The Humboldt*

More than one emigration had its starving time; that of 1850 was different in severity, not in kind. There are many accounts of what life was like that summer. A few excerpts from almost any diary would outline the story. Following are seven from that of Solomon Gorgas, a journal in the Huntington Library's collections, selected because it is typical as well as unpublished.

The wagon in which Gorgas traveled was better managed than most. By the early date of 13 July it had been on the Humboldt only eleven days and already close to the Meadows, the halting place where hay was mowed and preparations made for crossing the Forty-Mile Desert.

13 July 1850: "We are nearly out of provision[s] and it is probable that we shall have to be ten or twelve days out yet. What shall become of us God only knows. Yesterday we bought a half side of bacon and four quarts of corn meal & paid Ten dollars in gold for it. — I had to beg very hard for it at that."

14 July 1850: "This has been one of the most painful days to me that I have travelled since I left home. The distress which I have witnessed of those who travel near us & the immense distruction of property is truly sickening — we have passed some thirty or forty dead & dying horses and mules — many wagons abandoned & clothing & all that is useful & almost indispensable to poor wretched man cast by the wayside in distress & in order to avoid famine and starvation.... [S]ucceeded in getting a little food, enough we think to take us to the great grass Point where we take grass for the desert."

---

[45]Carr, Letter.

[46]Entry for 16 July 1850, Shepherd *Journal*, p. 23; entry for 23 July 1850, Kilgore, Journal, p. 49.

15 July 1850 (at the Meadows): "Hundreds are pleading for flour or any kind of provisions but mostly in vain."

19 July 1850 (at Ragtown on the Carson River): "[T]he Whole emigration is famished . . . no body has anything to spare & what is going to become of us God only knows."

20 July 1850 (on the Carson a mule gives out and the wagon has to be abandoned): "It is difficult for one who is not placed in our situation to imagine the distress which such a sudden change of fortune produces in the mind after clinging to all that is valuable & labouring to the utmost extent of our physical person for 83 long & tedious days, thus to be forced to throw away everything and escape for our lives."

21 July 1850: "Oh! the toils and servitudes of this rout[e]! they are great indeed & doubly great when want & privation are added."

Continuing on foot, Gorgas and his party arrived in Hangtown five days later. One of the first to complete the overland journey that year, he watched the remainder of the emigration pour across the mountains. "It is," he wrote his wife from California, "a common sight every hour through the day, & has been for the last two weeks past, to see women & children — whole families — coming in on poor starved oxen, who are tottering for want of strength   packed with the scanty supply of clothing & entirely out of provision, many of them almost dead with hunger & broke down by the excessive toils of the endless journey."[1]

Worse times lay behind. Going through South Pass the day after Gorgas reached the Humboldt River Lucian Wolcott marked the change transforming 1850 into the year of walkers on the overland trail. "A large proportion of emigration," he wrote, "is now packing on mules & horses & not a few on their backs."[2] Ahead at the Bear River, conditions were the same. "We see already upon the road," C. W. Smith noted, "numerous stragglers,

---

[1]Letter of 9 Sept. 1850, Gorgas, Letter.
[2]Entry for 3 July 1850, Wolcott, Journal.

men having lost their team and provisions, and those who started unprepared."[3]

Gorgas reached the Humboldt on the second of July. It was a date by which only the strongest teams and best organized wagons could have traveled so far, companies that we would guess planned well and carried everything they needed. Yet already there were shortages.[4] Two days later, on 4 July, an American mess threw away "some damaged pilot bread that was entirely unfit for anyone to eat." A German who was out of provisions "gathered it up & eat it with a relish." One of the Americans was shocked. "I gave him some fried bacon & boiled rice & he made a dinner." They met the German again the next day. "[H]e said he had had nothing since but the mouldy bread & not enough of that. We gave him some water of which he drank more than a quart & rode on."[5]

All along the Humboldt, begging was "constant."[6] Eight days down the river, a man estimated receiving at least twenty applications for food a day,[7] but with "a vast number of teams now on the road and near all out of provisions there is none to be had."[8]

The conditions of overland starvation were such that the weaker a company the more perilous was the situation. "When good grass is reached," James A. Payne wrote on 18 July, "those that have plenty of provisions, can lay by a day or so and rest their animals, but not so with us; it was all the time push or starve."[9]

[3] Entry for 23 June 1850, C. W. Smith, Journal.

[4] Entry for 2 July 1850, Gorgas, Diary. In fact, an emigrant who crossed the Forty-Mile Desert on the remarkably early date of 4 July "saw several emigrants out of provisions on the Humboldt" (letter of 20 July 1850, Brouster, Letters).

[5] Entry for 5 July 1850, Parker, Notes.

[6] Entry for 11 July 1850, C. W. Smith, Journal. See also entry for 23 July 1850, Wallenkamp, Diary; entry for 12 Aug. 1850, Frink, *Journal*, p. 92; entry for 11 Sept. 1850, C. Jones, Diary. Writing on 12 Sept., a correspondent of the *Sacramento Transcript*, who was at the Meadows, estimated that 15,000 people "are now destitute of all kinds of provisions" *(California Emigrant Letters*, p. 115).

[7] Entry for 18 Aug. 1850, McKinstry, *Diary*, p. 264.

[8] Entry for 13 July 1850, Grindell, Sketch Book.

[9] Entry for 18 July 1850, Payne, Account, p. 76.

The sense of desperation may be gleaned by considering Payne's predicament the next day. One of his party's pack animals fell into a slough "going clear under water." The men pulled the animal out after which they

> got at our little sack of bread, which was entirely soaked; it had been hard bread but was now quite soft. We stretched out a rubber blanket that I had and spread the mess upon it, and all sat around as intent as ever you saw a set of men, picking the pieces apart, as they were all stuck in a mat. Here were six men around this little dab of dough, picking up every little crumb, and separating them so that they could dry, rolling the little bits between finger and thumb, making a sort of pill, and placing them separate so that they could dry.... I don't think we lost an ounce of our bread.[10]

Some travelers along the Humboldt during the starving year of 1850 survived on fish, frogs, and berries,[11] but most either puchased or begged. For many, the chief source of food was draft animals, shot by their owners, who distributed or sold the meat to the needy.[12] A point to be made later is that the "owner" made all decisions. A point made now is that while prices were high, higher sums were offered. Ten days down the Humboldt, a man would have given "$10 for 5 lbs of flour, and could not get it."[13] We know two dollars a pound was unusual, so many

---

[10]Ibid., entry for 19 July 1850, p. 77. Even water-soaked flour could be precious. "We had about 6 spoons of flour left, I sifted some water thru my shirt and this soup was all we had to eat that evening [25 July 1850]" (Scheller, Autobiography, p. 4).

[11]Fish: entry for 1 Sept. 1850, Bennett, *Overland Journey*, p. 41. Frogs: entry for 9 Aug. 1850, Chalmers, "Journal," p. 51; entry for 2 Sept. 1850, McKinstry, *Diary*, p. 287. Berries: Haight, Trip, p. 28.

[12]Entry for 25 July 1850, W. Hanna, Journal, p. 5; entry for 29 July 1850, Rhodes, "Journal," p. 70; entry for 11 Aug. 1850, Chalmers, "Journal," p. 52; entry for 12 Aug. 1850, Gilmore, Overland Journey, p. 21; entries for 20 and 27 Aug. 1850, Dowell, Journal, pp. 41, 43; entry for 27 Aug. 1850, McKinstry, *Diary*, p. 273; entry for 5 Sept. 1850, Bennett, *Overland Journey*, p. 42; letter of 7 Sept. 1850, Albert G. Annibal, "Correspondence" (ts., Eastern Washington State Historical Society, Spokane); entry for 11 Sept. 1850, C. Jones, Diary.

[13]Entry for 17 July 1850, C. W. Smith, Journal. See also Eberstadt, "Introduction," p. 76n117.

emigrants were amazed when seeing it paid.[14] One termed the amount "extremely high."[15] A few starving men were reported to say they "would pay any price"[16] for food, but even "any price" was too low when vendors had nothing to sell.

Starvation to the degree known on the overland trail during 1850 has a vital, overlooked significance for historians seeking to measure law-mindedness. Respect for personal rights to property meets its ultimate test when food can neither be purchased nor begged. In 1850 that test occurred along the Humboldt when, as

First Desert Stretch on Leaving the Humboldt River

numerous diaries and letters tell, emigrants surrounded by live animals they did not own, "were eating the carcasses of dead

---

[14]Entry for 5 July 1850, Keck, Journal; entry for 31 Aug. 1850, McKinstry, *Diary*, p. 286; letter of 26 Aug. 1850, Gill, *Letters*, p. 20. See also entry for 10 Aug. 1850, Stauder, Memorandum, p. 36; entry for 27 Aug. 1850, McKinstry, *Diary*, p. 274.

[15]Entry for 6 Aug. 1850, Paschel, Diary, p. 50.

[16]Entry for 21 Aug. 1850, McKinstry, *Diary*, p. 269.

cattle!"[17] If unable to obtain "putrefied flesh,"[18] they tried to satisfy their hunger with the feed that dead horses no longer needed,[19] and when that was not available, their bones. Imagine the anxiety of one man reduced to the last extremity. He and his companions were only three days down the Humboldt, knowing they were far from where they could obtain relief by procuring supplies.

> Our provisions are nearly gone and we have at least three weeks travel to go before we get to where there is plenty of food, but we must trust to providence. We came across the remains of an ox that the packers had killed and divided what they could cut off. We found the bones here and made soup of them, thickened with a little flour, which made two or three good meals.[20]

VI   *A Representative Case*

John Wood, from Greenfield, Ohio, was one who crossed the overland trail from Saint Joseph, Missouri, to California, during the dreadful year of 1850. His story took on an added edge when he became one of the unlucky emigrants who went via Salt Lake City, found little to buy, and continued on, not by the more-traveled route north of Salt Lake, but directly west across the terrible salt flats of the Utah desert. This route was known as Hastings cutoff, and on it occurred the needless deaths of 1850, duplicating those in Death Valley and on Lassen's cutoff in 1849. They were needless because no one should have gone that way. It was far safer, though longer, to go north of the lake and rejoin the

---

[17]Evans, Letter, See also Delano, *Life*, p. 239; entry for 26 Aug. 1850, A. Brown, "Journal," p. 27; entry for 30 July 1850, Wallenkamp, Diary, p. 9; entry for 31 July 1850, Ingalls, *Journal*, p. 39; letter of 14 Nov. 1852, Kuhliwein, Letters, p. 24; Eberstadt, "Introduction," p. 86. For rumor that dead animals were being eaten see entry for 13 July 1850, Parker, Notes.

[18]Letter to the *Sacramento Transcript*, 15 Sept. 1850, *California Emigrant Letters*, p. 116.

[19]"This morning we bought some bran and some shorts from a man who was hauling it along to feed his horse, but we appropriated it to another use... which we relished as being good" (Coy, *Great Trek*, pp. 178-79.)

[20]Entry for 8 Aug. 1850, Chalmers, "Journal," p. 51.

main California road near the City of Rocks. Unfortunately, Wood and his companions either did not know this fact, or gambled on the shortcut. Still, they were not wholly unlucky. Although they lost their wagon, they survived, reaching the Humboldt River with a cart and several oxen.

To place the hardships of 1850 in the perspective of an individual, we should follow John Wood as he traveled down the Humboldt. He arrived on the river on the 22nd of August.[1]

24 August 1850: "I have gone ahead, in order to overtake as many wagons as possible and buy provisions.... I suppose that I have asked to buy of more than one hundred men this forenoon, but with no success. I find it very hard to arouse the sympathies of the people; money, a man's best earthly friend, is no inducement for men to part with bread, on this trip."

25 August 1850: "This morning we eat the last pound of beef; we have now nothing left but coffee. We bought thirty-five pounds of beef this evening, at 10 cents per pound, and feasted on coffee and roast beef.... To-day a young man fell in with us, who told me ... he could get but very little by begging and he lived chiefly upon frogs and wild roseberries, which are tolerably plenty in some places along this road."

26 August 1850: "Our cattle are now getting so poor that it takes two to make a shadow. I think they will never weather the storm.... Beef and coffee for supper."

27 August 1850: "To-day I saw another man begging for bread, but could get none; he had no money; however, he could get none anyhow, for one-half the emigrants are literally starving, as we are; have nothing but their cattle and probably some tea or coffee; some cannot live on it, and lie down and die, apparently with pleasure; in fact, some have told me they wished they were dead and out of trouble; while others, under the same circumstances, would laugh at the calamity, which shows the difference in men. I also came across some wild roseberries and eat a good mess, which turned my thoughts on bread; but that is not hard to do these days."

---

[1]The following quotations are from J. Wood, *Journal*, pp. 84-91.

242

28 August 1850: "Now came my suffering time, with many others, in the same situation, but we traveled on for several miles and sat down to rest in the sand which tired us so. Oh, what would I give for one more drink; it seems to me that I could drink my own blood. I now think I can never reach the river, if I have to walk. After we had rested a short time, we started on and soon a man came riding along and I asked him how much he would charge me to let me ride to the river, to which he replied "what is right," so I told him he should have it and mounted the pony, and not having been on a horse's back for several months, it made me feel good all over. I rode to the river, which was about five miles, and now found that I was more hungry and tired than thirsty, but we had nothing to eat and nothing could be got here, notwithstanding there are a great many encamped here. We offered them any amount for something to eat, but no, they said they were starving themselves. Here there is no grass at all; nothing but willows, and they are browsed perfectly bare, so our cattle had to fast until morning, as well as ourselves."

29 August 1850: "[W]e are afraid if we kill a steer this morning, we will never be able to get across the desert, so we concluded to go ahead until we find grass for our stock and then kill one. [W]e started, and had not gone far until we came across some hungry men skinning an old ox, which had been left on the road to perish, by some emigrant. They took what they wanted and we then helped ourselves to as much as we could carry, and rolled on some distance and stopped on the river and went to roasting beef, but here we found short grass for our cattle.... The beef we got this morning is very bad and to-day being so very warm, the flies blowed it all over, and some of the mess being out of the article, we must kill something. After we had been in camp a short time, some of the boys saw the willows shake across the river and soon discovered it to be a steer, left on account of being lame; the word now was, kill him and take his hind quarters, heart and liver, so a number of the boys swam over and cut his throat."

30 August 1850: "We went twenty miles to-day and stopped on the river, tired and hungry, hopeless and way-worn."

31 August 1850: "Yesterday, after we encamped for the night, some of the messes being destitute of meat, they killed some old cows, which had been left to perish, and took their hearts and livers, and this morning finding we would not have enough to do us across the desert, we took about forty pounds out of the hind quarter of one of the said old cows, which we hauled in our little cart, which is now, and has been for a long time, used as company stock. We traveled about fourteen miles and reached the beginning of the Humboldt Sink, which we have heard so much talk about, and encamped for the day, as there is some grass here and our cattle are perishing for it, and here is almost a city of wagons, all encamped, resting their cattle; and oh, how many care worn faces I see here, and I must acknowledge that I add one more to the number. All are preparing and dreading to cross, by far, the worst desert we have met with yet. They, perhaps, would not mind it, and neither would I, if we had plenty to eat; but here are hundreds already lamenting their anticipated death, and suffering on the burning plain."

Wood was mistaken. He was not at the Humboldt Sink, but at Humboldt Meadows, where emigrants made hay for the Forty-Mile Desert. It was not until 2 September that Wood and his companions, gathering strength to cross the desert, rested at the Sink, that barren stretch where nature provided the penultimate challenge to the overland traveler and the poison waters of the Humboldt disappeared into the sands of Nevada. There Wood found "a man from Missouri, who had a large train of wagons loaded with hams and fruit, which he sold at 65 cents a pound; and we, having a little money left, spent the last cent we had for about two-thirds of a ham and three pounds of fruit."[2]

There is no need to follow John Wood across the Forty-Mile Desert. The story of that section of the overland trail has been told many times. Every year it was the dreaded part of California travel, made more tragic in 1850 by the weakened condition of so many emigrants and the death of so much of their livestock.[3]

---

[2]Ibid., entry for 2 Sept. 1850, p. 92.

There were two roads across the Forty-Mile Desert, one to the Truckee River, for those heading toward Sacramento, the other to the Carson, for those going to the gold mines around Placerville or to the south. Both routes were strewn with the bodies of mules, horses, and oxen, covered with the skeletons of wagons and carts, and, in 1850, dotted with the graves of human beings.[4] Beyond lay the cool waters of the rivers, the first trees to give shade from the burning sun for several hundred miles, and the barrier of the Sierra Nevada, where more animals would perish, more wagons would be abandoned, and more emigrants would die.

We may ignore the desert and mountains. They do not change the picture. John Wood's account of eight days along the Humboldt tells enough of the hardships of 1850. What is more significant, he tells us something of how those hardships affected emigrants' attitudes and emigrants' perceptions toward property, and the rights of ownership. It is important, therefore, that we understand what he has told us.

Choice of words is especially significant when we seek to evaluate attitudes toward abstractions, and Wood's words reveal a good deal. On the first day, we are told, he "asked to buy [food] of more than one hundred men... with no success." It was, he then reflected, "very hard to arouse the sympathies of the people." When using the word "sympathies," John Wood was not speaking of begging or charity. He meant persuading others to sell to him property he wished to purchase. Money was his "inducement" to arouse those "sympathies," and money, a "man's

---

[3]How weak men became that year due to lack of food was demonstrated some miles beyond where the Sierras began. An emigrant, alone and on foot, came to a place where he had to climb. "He was so weak he could not climb, so he wandered around trying to find a place where he could get over; in his travels he found five dead men, and several others that were, like himself, looking for a place to climb... all weak from want of food" (entry for 2 Sept. 1850, Frink, *Journal*, p. 116).

[4]One man counted nine hundred sixty-five graves marked along the entire trail that year, "and computes 5000 as the number of persons that must have perished during the past season." Also, "He counted of dead mules, 1061; dead horses, 4960; and dead oxen and cows, 3750" (*The Ohio Statesman*, 2 Dec. 1850, quoted in Eberstadt, "Introduction," p. 91n137).

best earthly friend" failed Wood because, along the Humboldt River that August of 1850, money was "no inducement for men to part with bread."

The attitude of a second man, unspoken but unambiguous, reveals almost as much. It was manifested on 28 August, the day Wood feared he lacked strength to make the river on foot. Seeing an emigrant come along on horseback, the question Wood asked was "how much he would charge me to let me ride to the river." The attitude to be noted is not that the horse rider was generous — not demanding all Wood could pay, but readily proposing to accept "what is right." Rather, the attitude to be noted is the willingness, more typical of the overland trail, to bail the animal. The man asked for no security. He assumed Wood, surely a stranger to him, shared his notions concerning personal rights in property. The horse was his. As its "owner," he expected to find it waiting for him when he reached the river.

Next day Wood's role was reversed. He was "owner" and that fact, ownership, posed a dilemma for him and his partners. After at least twenty-four hours without a meal, all were hungry. They had food, a live animal, but "we are afraid if we kill a steer this morning, we will never be able to get across the desert." It was a cruel choice: to restore some of their physical strength by eating now, or better ensure their survival later by preserving their already meager resources for traversing the desert.

The dilemma is understandable. Less clear is the puzzling reference to property occurring in the entry for 31 August. The party with which Wood traveled had picked up meat "which we hauled in our little cart, which is now, and has been for a long time, used as company stock." What is meant by "company stock" will never be known, partly because it is unclear with whom Wood was associated. Possibly he and his original companions from Ohio had been joined by stragglers with whom they were sharing the cart. For our purposes, the meaning is irrelevant. What is striking is the notation, not its sense. In the midst of all his suffering, Wood took the trouble to say something about the ownership of property. As a concept, ownership still mattered even in the worst of times.

It may be that Wood, when he chose the words "company stock," was saying that only the use of the property, not its "ownership" had changed. Even so, he described that use by words of ownership. The pain of starvation, and threat of death, had not altered the pattern of thinking through which this man had learned to describe the world.

Another ambiguous reference to property rights, one whose precise meaning would be worth knowing, occurred in the entry for 29 August. After lamenting that beef recently acquired was "very bad," Wood noted that "some of the mess being out of the article, we must kill something." The revealing words are "some of the mess." Wood did not say the mess was out of meat, but only some of its members. He obviously was commenting on personal ownership. The question left unanswered is, how that ownership was created. If, as Wood himself stated, everyone in the mess "helped" themselves to the meat they had found, it is possible each man took for himself. If not, that is, if taken as company property, it subsequently had been divided into personalty.

Although the origin of the personalty is unclear, the consequences are not. Either those "out of the article" did not take as much as the others, or had eaten the shares they took. They did not own or have a claim on the remaining meat and, to provide them with food, it might be necessary "to kill something," even though that "something" was mess property, belonging in part to those who "owned" as yet uneaten meat.[5]

We could wish that Wood had commented on this situation. It may be one of the most extreme instances of property ownership determining behavior on the overland trail. That very morning, even though they had not eaten for a day or more, these same men

---

[5]Two days later Wood said something that seems to make a similar statement concerning property. "[S]ome of the messes being destitute of meat, they killed some old cows, ... we took about forty pounds out of the hind quarter of one." Most likely, however, he was referring to other messes than his own, to those belonging to neighboring companies. Wood and his mess, therefore, were helping themselves to a hind quarter left behind, not to an animal they had owned in common (entry for 31 Aug. 1850, J. Wood, *Journal*, pp. 90-91).

were "afraid" to convert a draft animal into meat. It might be needed crossing the desert. Now, with some of the party without personally-owned food, attitudes changed. "[W]e must kill something," Wood said, even though there were individual members of the group who possessed, and apparently owned, beef.

Had Wood commented, we might know whether he and his companions gave the matter much thought or, like other emigrants we have encountered, simply took personal ownership for granted. With killing an animal such serious business, we may guess that alternatives were weighed. An obvious one was to share the meat on hand. Perhaps there was not enough, but Wood did not say so, instead stating that they might be forced to sacrifice an animal they wanted to keep alive. Considering his words, the existing circumstances, and what we have learned from other emigrants, the best explanation is that, once shortages had developed, food was no longer common property within either the traveling company or the concurrent-property-owning mess. Those eating less were entitled to hoard what they preserved. The rule was not to redistribute food already personal. One reason probably was that, when the next ox was killed, it too would be partible and become personalty. The owners of the existing meat would have lost private property had they, to spare the ox, shared what they had on hand.

There is a second lesson from John Wood's quotations, supporting what we previously learned about the separation of personal and concurrent property within companies. When at the Humboldt Sink, he wrote, "we . . . spent the last cent we had for about two-thirds of a ham and three pounds of fruit." The pronoun "we" is to be taken literally. The mess spent its "last cent," not Wood. Next day, while on the Forty-Mile Desert, he paid one dollar and a half to buy his one remaining personally-owned oxen a gallon and a half of water,[6] and later contracted with the proprietor of a wagon to have his clothes hauled to the

----

[6]Ibid., entry for 3 Sept. 1850, p. 94.

mines for five dollars.[7] It would appear, therefore, that the mess purchased the ham as mess property. If we can judge by what was said previously, the ham was divided into severalty before being cooked, each member receiving an equal share.

In a sense, Wood and his companions were fortunate. Unlike John Smith, who replenished his property while traveling up the Oregon trail, they arrived at their destination with little more than their clothes and blankets. But they did save their lives, getting to California in what was, for 1850 emigrants, relatively good condition. One reason they did so is that, while sometimes desperate, they never were starving. Passing down the Humboldt with the high tide of emigration, they always had the good luck to find stray cattle. These animals they appropriated to their own use and converted into food. Wood did not have to subsist on offals or the maggot-covered flesh of dead horses. Though he and his companions had, as Wood said, a "suffering time," they were always able to obtain food, either by killing an ox that they "owned" or by converting to their exclusive "possession" cattle abandoned and no longer claimed as personal "property" by former owners.

As John Wood does not comment upon the right of appropriation, we cannot know if he acted upon legal principles when taking up strays. But just about every emigrant who has left us personal thoughts justified acquisition, not in terms of physical possession or need, but of legal right. The final questions we must ask of our evidence, therefore, are what privileges mere physical "possession" conferred upon overland emigrants, and how they defined the concept they termed "ownership" and the abstraction they called "property."

---

[7]Ibid., entry for 5 Sept. 1850, pp. 98-99.

10 | THE IRRELEVANCE OF POSSESSION

The question we are asking is what the men and women going to Oregon and California during the 1840s and 1850s understood by "ownership" and what they meant by "property." That we must dig deeply for the answer is because our evidence is indirect. As none of our informants considered the question, none has left us an answer. More understood than articulated, law was for them less a command than a rule of conduct, a guide not only to property use, but to political organization, moral conduct, and judicial behavior.[1]

Typical of overland emigrants who understood but did not articulate "law" was Henry Wallenkamp. He was from the town of Washington, Missouri, and crossed the continent to California in 1850. By the time he and his mess reached Nevada's Forty-Mile Desert, their draft animals were jaded. Nine miles short of the Carson River the mules could no longer draw the wagon. While Wallenkamp remained behind to guard their property, his companions unhitched the animals and drove them ahead to where they could feed, drink and recruit. "Paid 25 cents for 1 pint of water; then $2.00 for 1 gal[lon]," Wallenkamp wrote of the time he waited for the others to return. "Along here 10 miles from the desert some men have stationed themselves, carry water to emigrants at $1.00 per gal. and steal and pick up every loose animal around and about — also part of our mules."[2]

Wallenkamp's meaning is not as clear as we would wish. Whether he lost some of the mules he was guarding is a question that cannot be answered. More interesting is what he meant by the term "pick up." Were the desert traders buying animals from emigrants or appropriating abandoned property? Wallenkamp

---

[1]"Governance of the Elephant"; "Tied to the Elephant"; "Prosecuting the Elephant."
[2]Entry for 3 Aug. 1850, Wallenkamp, Diary, p. 10.

said "steal and pick-up," apparently contrasting "steal" with "pick up." The traders it would seem were stealing some animals, picking up others. The distinction may have been made by an emigrant writing under rather trying circumstances and could have been loosely applied. Still, we must not overlook the fact that it was a distinction of law. Unless everything that was "picked up" was paid for, Wallenkamp was saying that the conversion of property in one category by the traders was stealing, the conversion of property in a different category was not.[3]

The most dramatic instances of overland emigrants distinguishing between property owned and property stolen occurred when men, not claiming to be owners or not acting on authority from the owners, seized from others possession of goods known or believed to be stolen. Twenty-two-year-old Harlow Thompson from Illinois was still in eastern Nebraska during 1859 when some of his horses disappeared. Thinking them stolen, he went in search back down the trail and encountered an elderly man doing the same. The older emigrant described in detail the animals he had lost and rode on. At a stage station Thompson found the man's property and, despite protests of the manager, took the animals into his possession. Thompson suspected the manager had stolen his own horses but, not seeing evidence of them, appropriated no substitutes as reparations. He did, however, seize the old man's and the legal theory upon which he acted must have been that possession gave the possessor no claim on

---

[3]Other emigrants made the same distinction. As we shall see in the next chapter, food, wagons, and animals abandoned by their owners could be taken up by anyone wishing to claim them. The fact to be noticed when the evidence is examined is that between rival claimants need did not establish right. Rather, right was based on concepts which, when unraveled, should help to clarify notions of ownership shared by nineteenth-century Americans. Under certain circumstances, for example, the test could be a prior claim. It was this that persuaded one emigrant he did not have a claim to an abandoned animal he had sought to possess in southeastern Idaho. "Found a steer where we camped," he wrote. "Abel & I went out to examine it & one of Clarke's men came up & claimed it because he saw it way back" (entry for 3 July 1859, Crandall, Diary).

property he had stolen. Thompson was going in the direction of the owner, he could return them, so he took the horses.[4] Suspicion, on the other hand, was not enough to justify seizing other property in legal setoff.[5]

Remarkably, emigrants not only thought the act of recapture privileged without expressed authorization from the "owner," they even exercised it when the property was possessed by Indians. One man indicated no surprise when informed by a total stranger that his missing horse had been recovered. "He said he saw an Indian have [sic] him, and knowing him to be an American horse, he told the Indian that he had stolen him: upon which the Indian gave him up."[6]

If the emigrant owner was not amazed to retrieve his horse that way, we should be. Consider what we are being told: so highly were property rights regarded that cross-cultural barriers and physical dangers took second place. Finding themselves in a somewhat similar situation, two other emigrants even risked starting an Indian war for the sake of someone else's claim to ownership. They were in the vicinity of the Bear River when they saw an Indian riding a horse they recognized "as belonging to some of their acquaintances that that [sic] was on a head they seized the horse & Indian & was forcing them along when the Indian . . . put the whip to his horse & they in full pursuit." The horse threw the Indian.

> The men in pursuit one armed with a double Barreled gun the other with a pair of holster Pistols but neither of the Pistols was charged so the man that had them threw one of them at the Indian but the Indian picked it up & defended himself with it until he reached the

---

[4]Thompson said he returned the animals when meeting the old owner at Bear River. If this fact is true he kept possession for a long time for the Bear was crossed either in today's Idaho or today's Utah. (Thompson, Across, pp. 23-28, 39).

[5]A young girl, however, recorded how her brother, when searching for a missing mare, learned it had been stolen, recovered it from the thieves, and took — she says "stole" —one of theirs. "Tom met us this evening with the horses, our own and another, which he stole from the horse thieves" (entry for 7 July 1852, Egbert, Record).

[6]J. Hale, *California*, pp. 14-15.

> water where he plunged in . . . the man fired both bar[r]els of his
> gun at him   it was looked upon at the time [as] it was a very rash
> action in them [to] take the horse away & besides that they
> attacked his person & it was supposed killed him.[7]

The action was more than rash, it was perilous, placing the
entire emigration in danger had the man died. If any Indian law
would have been known to emigrants it was that international
homicide led to war. Unless the two emigrants were psychopathic
Indian haters or reckless braggarts, there is only one reasonable
explanation for their conduct: they not only believed they had a
right to act, they felt a sense of duty to recapture stolen property.
We shall return to this incident later.

It is astonishing to note the extent to which emigrants responded
to that sense of duty and jeopardized life and limb to uphold a
legal abstraction. Along Nevada's Humboldt River a sizeable
group, with sufficient time for reflection and conscious of the
danger, prepared "for a fight with the [I]ndians" rather than
surrender property belonging to men who were, to them, total
strangers.

> Some emigrants, a night or two before, had lost 2 horses; the
> description of which they sent back to a train behind them. The
> indians brought these horses to the train having the discription of
> them — the horses being branded. The indians claimed 2 shirts and
> a bed quilt, for bringing them; which the white man paid.
> Afterwards, a white man, who acted in the capacity of an
> interpreter, came with a company of indians, and demanded the
> horses. And after the emigrants refused to give up the horses, the
> indians mad[e] some threats, and left. We camped on the west side
> of the creek — Clark's train camped with [us], the evening, for the
> first time: and we agree[d] to travel together. Thacher and Sharp
> camp with us, this evening. The train that have the stray horses
> camped on the east side of the creek, opposite us. Keep a double
> guard to night.[8]

---

[7]Entry for 6 July 1850, Gundlach, Minutes.
[8]Entry for 30 July 1853, J. Miller, Journal, p. 56.

The story must be reiterated. It is more than a tale of danger, it is a revelation concerning nineteenth-century American attitudes toward ownership. The owner of the two horses sent word of his loss back down the trail to other emigrants. A rearward company accepted custody of the strays, paying either a ransom or a reward to some Indians bringing them in. When a second group of Indians demanded the animals, the possessing company refused to surrender them despite the threat of attack. Even more impressive, at least two other companies[9] — the writer's and "Clark's train" — prepared for trouble. As far as can be determined from this account, no one argued that the Indians be given the horses. Had some emigrants done so, the evidence would be even more convincing, as it would indicate that in the face of opposition the majority was determined to uphold ownership right. Some of these men did not know the owner,[10] yet were drawn into a situation where they might have had to defend with force his claim to two horses. So strong was the concept of ownership among these people that a majority[11] was not only willing to do so, they probably thought there was no alternative.

Two facts stand out in all extant accounts of retrieving lost or stolen property on the overland trail. First, possession was not the test of title. When emigrants decided if an individual had a right to property they based their judgment on a legal abstraction they called "ownership," not on the physical reality of possession. Second, when stolen goods were taken up, the person taking them acted as trustee for the "owner."

We might think that when the owner was not available or might never be seen again, emigrants would hesitate. Surprisingly, absence of the title holder generally was not significant. Just as Thompson seized the old man's animals not knowing if he would

---

[9]It is not clear whether "Thacher and Sharp" were two companies or two individuals.

[10]It is evident that the writer did not, and likely that members of his company did not either. The company taking custody of the horses may have.

[11]At least a majority of the company with the animals. The writer's and Clark's trains may or may not have been consulted.

ever meet the owner again, other emigrants acted on the belief that goods should be seized from a wrongful possessor, and did so even if it meant converting property to their own use. An explanation given by one emigrant of 1852 was that thieves "had no right" to possession. "We met a man who was driving several cows," she wrote in her journal. "[T]he men in the other waggon recognized 4 of them, belonging to a man from their country, with whom they had intended to travel. They asked the men where was the owner of the cows? and why was he driving them back? he said first that he was the owner, & that he had bought them; but as he could not tell where the man was, nor describe him, they concluded he had no right to them; & final[l]y he said to them four he had found, & they took them away from him; & as one of them gave milk, we were enable[d] to live quite well."[12]

Although we might emphasize the subsequent employment and express skepticism, it is obvious that these emigrants stressed the wrongful possession. Legal principles respecting rights to ownership not only justified, they motivated conduct. Those seizing stolen property made haste to return it as soon as the owner was overtaken or his identity ascertained. If they learned that the man whom they thought had stolen the property in fact owned it, he was entitled to get it back. The two emigrants who shot the Indian at Bear River, "took the horse on to the man that had owned him but when they reached him he informed [them] that he had traded the horse to the Indian   so 2 days after they sent the horse back to his owner wh[o] I have since heard has recovered."[13]

We can be even more positive. The "owner" not only had rights acknowledged by other emigrants, he could demand possession

---

[12]Entry for 16 May 1852, Frizzell, *Journal*, p. 15; Eaton, *Overland*, pp. 44-45.

[13]Entry for 6 July 1850, Gundlach, Minutes. On occasion the fact that the property being returned had multiple owners caused complications. Thus the stranger taking the horse from the Indian (see p. 253 above) had difficulty determining title, for the horse was owned concurrently: "He also stated that Steele claimed him; but he had been advised not to deliver him to Steele, until he heard from me. I told him that one quarter of the horse belonged to me. I requested him to keep the horse, until Steele and I could have a settlement" (J. Hale, *California*, p. 14).

from those finding or taking up his stray animals. A forty-niner company from Lynn, Massachusetts, was eating dinner when several loose oxen strolled into sight. "[S]ome of the Co[mpany] saw them first," a member wrote, "& run for dear life after them   arrived first & claimed all but one   he was so poor the wolves would not eat him" On the basis of possession, therefore, the men seizing the oxen claimed title good against those not so swift — indeed, against all the world except, as events showed, the "owners." Next day a party from Michigan overtook the Lynn company, recognized the oxen, "claimed them & drove them off."[14] Three years later, in the same stretch of western Nebraska, a small traveling group encountered an old black cow returning to the Missouri. "Some of the boys thought the journey too long and too lonesome for a single traveler, and after much coaxing induced the old thing to turn back. But no sooner had we camped than her alleged owner made his appearance, and recognizing her old and familiar form claimed his child's pet; a sad blow to some of the boys who hungered for milk in their coffee."[15]

Generally those taking up animals did not expect to obtain title. The purpose of assuming possession was to accommodate the "owner" and protect the property. A judge from Indiana "came across 31 head [of] stray cattle, (worth $1000 or less) and drove them along 3 hours with great difficulty when I met the owner who *thanked* me took them and went off."[16] A young man from St. Louis lost his horse "with all my worldly wealth upon his back" while crossing Nevada's Forty-Mile Desert. At the Truckee River "I regained my horse   some kind person had taken him in charge."[17]

Innocent or nontortious possession seems never to have been confused with "ownership." Neither forceful recapture from a wrongful holder under dangerous circumstances nor extended periods of time converted mere possession into undisputed

---

[14]Entry for 25 June 1849, Churchill, Journal, p. 32.

[15]Eaton, *Overland*, p. 108.

[16]Entry for 21 May 1852, Crane, Journal.

[17]Entry for 21 Sept. 1850, Stine, Letters.

ownership. Emigrants recovered animals two days, five days, fourteen days, and nineteen days after they had been lost.[18] Even French Canadian traders and others not members of the emigration could claim what they "owned" and it would be surrendered. Indeed, some diaries make it appear that all one had to do was claim and the animals were handed over.[19]

All types of goods, not just animals, could be reclaimed if lost. No finders-keepers rule existed on the overland trail. "I found a good, green Spanish blanket," an emigrant gloated on 30 June 1856. "I found the owner of the blanket I found the other day, and gave it [to] him," he wrote three days later.[20] Conversely, the owner of the blanket, had he known where to look, would not have hesitated to ask its return. On Goose Creek in today's northeast Nevada, a forty-niner helped himself to blankets another emigrant told him had been abandoned. "After dark a gentleman called for them saying he had hauled his wagon off and neglected to take his bedding. Of course I gave them up."[21] Just beyond Ash Hollow, a second forty-niner discovered his India-rubber rainwear missing. "I knew," he wrote, "they were safe yesterday afternoon & was confident a train which passed yesterday evening after we camped must have picked them up. So saddling one of our ponies I started in pursuit & after a hard ride of six miles overtook it, & on inquiring I found that one man belonging to the train had picked up goods of the description I gave & with some difficulty I found him & recovered my valuable articles."[22]

There is an ancillary point not to be overlooked. Our evidence reveals more than what legal consequences nineteenth-century

---

[18]Entry for 23 Aug. 1849, Gray, Passage; entry for 6 Aug. 1849, Love, Diary; entry for 21 Sept. 1849, Brainard, Journal.

[19]"[T]ook up 21 head of oxen and brought them on to this place. When we arrived here they were all claimed by some French traders located at this point" (entry for 30 July 1849, R. G. Miller, Journal, p. 13).

[20]Entries for 30 June and 2 July 1856, J. R. Brown, *Across the Plains*, p.48.

[21]Entry for 7 Sept. 1849, Stuart, *Roving Life*, 1: 60.

[22]Entry for 26 June 1849, Perkins, *Gold Rush Diary*, pp 45-46.

Americans associated with possesssion. It also tells us that people on the overland trail expected that their lost or strayed property would be returned. Lawyers took the expectation for granted. A New York attorney who was destined to be chief justice of California wrote in his diary: "Charles returned with the horse to the old camp to seek his revolver & bowie knife which he accidentally left at that place." No other comment is made.[23] A forty-niner missed three horses and concluded they "are given up as lost unless some train catches them & brings them on." The next day "[t]he lost horses were picked up by a train behind & recovered."[24] In fact, if animals were not found the presumption could be that they had been stolen.[25] After looking several hours for four missing horses, a Wisconsin man "took a horse and went back till I was satisfied by meeting hundreds that he was not on the road back but was stolen but how I could not tell."[26]

We might think this suspicion so prevalent that emigrants would be reluctant to take up stray animals for their owners. Being thought a thief could lead to trouble. When the Wisconsin man recovered his horse he believed that "had it not been for our Capt[ain] the men [who had the horse in their possession] would have been whipped to all intents and purposes."[27] A forty-niner went looking for missing oxen in "a train that pass[ed] us at noon." Had he not found a woman in possession, a companion thought, "[I] expect they would have got a good Cursing."[28]

---

[23]Entry for 22 July 1849, Searls, Diary (ms.).

[24]Entries for 19 and 20 May 1849, J. W. Wood, Diaries.

[25]Although, not always. "[F]ound our stray horses this evening. Reevely's cousin found them in possession of some emigrant[s]. [P]resume they followed them" (entry for 25 June 1850, Stauder, Memorandum).

[26]Entry for 18 May 1852, Fox, Memorandum, p. 8. The word "stolen" was somewhat loosely defined on the overland trail. A man from Illinois, for example, wrote: "Had one of our oxen stolen last night by an emigrant. We rode on and overtook them and got him five miles from camp." No further explanation is offered. See entry for 25 May 1852, "The Diary of John Joseph Callison: Oregon Trail—1852" (ts., Western Americana Collection, Beinecke Library), p. 6.

[27]Entry for 19 May 1852, Fox, Memorandum, p. 9.

[28]Entry for 28 July 1849, Hackney, "Journal," p. 177.

Another forty-niner notified everyone he knew, including a family named Baker, of how he had found and taken possession of stray horses in the Black Hills. Later, near Fort Boise, Baker informed McClure, the boss of the train in which the man was traveling, that the horses might be stolen. The man's reaction tells us much concerning attitudes among overland emigrants. "I told him," he wrote of Baker, "that his Son had asked me where I got the Horses, & that I told him the whole Story, as I had Mr. McClure, & those in his Train, & there is where you got all the information that you have, & upon that you brand me with Horse Stealing. I am Sorry on account of the Boy that is with you, But you have been in my camp long enough, & dark as it is you must leave & he did."[29]

It would appear, therefore, to have been a serious matter if one were caught with property belonging to a stranger, yet emigrants were unconcerned. Stray animals as well as other items of value were routinely taken up. It could be argued that those publicizing their findings by posting notice of what they had taken, or going in search of the owner, were protecting themselves from a charge of theft.[30] That speculation may be true, but the better explanation seems to be they wanted to return the property to its owners. Possession worried them as little as it established right.

The irrelevance of possession as the criterion for right is most convincingly outlined by those emigrants who took up property believing they were acquiring title. Two forty-niners in a Wisconsin company "found a very fine horse which seemed to have been deserted in consequence of a very bad wound in the breast." They kept the horse only two days when it "was called for this evening by the owner having strayed away."[31] A Mormon train in today's Nebraska came across thirty-seven head of cattle

---

[29]Entry for 29 Aug., 1853, Owen, My Trip, p. 30.

[30]Notice: entry for 2 June 1849, J. W. Wood, Diaries. Search: "A time or two parties came to our train from before us inquiring if we had lost any of ours, and would to the next train or two if not too far ahead, they having picked up some strays" (Burroughs, Reminiscences, p. 47).

[31]Letter of 5 June 1849, Fairchild, Letters, p. 26.

"evidently lost by some emigrants ahead of us; the most of them were work-cattle." The time was late July, and as they were far behind the gold-rush emigration, it was reasonable to assume the owners were hundreds of miles ahead and long since had abandoned their property. Next day the company divided the cattle among themselves. A week later "the owners came for the cattle we had found. They belonged to Captain Owens' Company of gold-diggers, from New York and Wisconsin; they lost them during a severe storm, which lasted two days and one night."[32]

Even emigrants who tried to conceal possession of taken-up property conformed to the prevalent legal behavior. They knew they had to surrender possession should they be detected and the owner assert his right. An interesting illustration was recorded by Helen Carpenter traveling in a train of three wagons. She and her husband had one wagon, her father and mother the second, and a man named Dobbins the third. They were at the rear of the 1857 emigration and had been attacked by Indians just before passing the City of Rocks. Despite their small numbers, they had fallen behind at Dobbins' urging. He had talked the other two wagons into traveling slowly by contending that their draft animals were too jaded to be pushed. Once the cattle recruited, Dobbins argued, they could catch up. Even after the attack he wanted to remain behind and might have done so had not Mrs. Carpenter's family driven on, leaving him alone. Mrs. Carpenter had been puzzled by Dobbins' behavior, for she thought him a coward. It was not until he overtook the emigration and rejoined the others that she learned what Dobbins had been doing. "Since we caught up with the trains, seven head of the cattle that Dobbins picked up on the way has [*sic*] been claimed, and taken," she wrote. "At last we know why he wanted to lag behind. His greed is still greater than his cowardice, which we thought could not be excelled."[33]

---

[32]Entries for 27-28 July and 4 Aug. 1849, M. M. Morgan, *Trip*, pp. 3-4.
[33]Entry for 4 Sept. 1857, Carpenter, Trip, p. 99.

We need not be surprised that Dobbins returned the cattle. Superior numbers guaranteed that he would. It is his prior behavior that is more revealing. His sense of legal obligation was not typical of overland travelers,[34] but his knowledge of the law was. Dobbins wanted the animals, and to keep them accepted a risk that for him was out of character. His greed overcame his cowardice because he knew that (even though the cattle would have belonged to the Indians had he not taken them up) "ownership" had priority over mere possession.

There was one minor qualification to an owner's right of return; he might have to pay to retrieve his property. It was not always the rule. Some who offered to pay were refused.[35] In the overwhelming majority of cases payment is not mentioned. When it is, the writer generally does not indicate who initiated the notion: whether the finder demanded money or the owner voluntarily offered a reward.[36] Yet we do encounter a few owners saying they "had to pay" the finder for his "trouble,"[37] or complaining of the "very steep price."[38]

It is possible some emigrants thought that the finder's efforts created a demand-right against the owner on the finder's behalf.

---

[34]There were cases of attempted theft and concealment. Some emigrants, for example, found a missing mule "in the possession of a fellow who was very much disposed to act the rascal — refusing to let them see it after they had described it. They talked pretty plainly to him and took possession of the mule, which they [sic] had evidently stolen" (entry for 18 Aug. 1850, Moorman, *Journal*, p. 69). "By this time I discovered that emigrants' true character was here [Fort Laramie] developed; all moral restraint thrown off, they become reckless in regard to truth and honesty, and totally selfish. I had a coat stolen from me by one of this company, which I found on his back, after overtaking him near the South Pass of the Rocky Mountains" (J. Hale, *California*, p. 15).

[35]For example, entry for 7 June 1853, H. Stewart, Diary, p. 9.

[36]Typical is the following: "[C]ome across our cattle today a company has brought them along   they found them at the Bluffs we Paid $7 1/2 for them" (entry for 29 May 1852, Hosley, Journal).

[37]Entry for 23 Sept. 1849, Gray, Passage.

[38]Entry for 25 June [c. 1850], William W. Gilbert, "Diary" (ts., "Fort Laramie Journals," vol. 3, Fort Laramie Historic Site, Fort Laramie, Wyoming), p. 6. See also 21 May 1849, Wilkins, *An Artist*, p. 34.

Surely James Pritchard had some such notion in mind when he proposed one of the first arbitration settlements in Nebraska's legal history.

> While here McNeely found . . . two Oxen that had been left in the hurry to start this morning. They belong to different men . . . About 4 P M we met the Owners of the cattle returning for them. We had tied them to the hind part of our wagons. I Supposed that the catching and bringing the cattle along was entirely a matter of accomodation in McNeely to the Owners, and when the Gentleman [*sic*] road up and claimed the cattle I told them, to loos[e] them, and take them. They said that they would see the man who caught the steers first & Sati[s]fy him for his trouble. They road on and met McNeely who charged them $5 apiec[e] for his trouble. They said that was too much. They gave McNeely $5,50 cts and he claimed the $10. The gentlemen came to me as Commandant of the train, to Know whether they could get their cattle. I told them that they could — and that they should have them. Some sharp words ensued when I proposed to leave it to 5 disinterested men which was agreed to. And they decided instantly that the Gentlemen had paid McNeely enough, whereupon the cattle were given up and the Owners took them off.[39]

It is evident that no custom of the road had emerged. The owners and McNeely both thought he was entitled to something for "his trouble." Whether McNeely's claim can fairly be characterized as a sort of overland lien estopping the owner's right of return until paid, is not clear. McNeely may well have believed so as he seems to have been inclined not to surrender the cattle unless paid his price. Pritchard, the captain of the train, thought otherwise. Nothing was owed, he reasoned, basing his legal theory on the dual foundation of overland conditions and overland custom. "It is," Pritchard explained, "a well Known fact that every Emegrants stock is liable to go a Stray, as they have no other pastureage than the wide, and unbounded domain, which is

---

[39]Entry for 22 May 1849, Pritchard, *Diary*, pp. 67-68.

equally free and accessable to all — And the common practice amongst the Emegrants is to catch for and assist each other to protect their stock without the hope of fee or reward."[40]

A reading of overland diaries and letters makes it reasonably certain that most emigrants agreed with Pritchard. Possession of property, even possession plus "trouble" invested in that property, did not affect another person's right of ownership. Yet if a finder and preserver such as McNeely demanded payment he was usually paid, even if he was an Indian[41] — unless, of course, the owner suspected that the finder was a thief who had taken the animal and held it for ransom.[42] To the extent that the payment was rationalized, it seems to have been for services rendered, not for settling a claim upon the property clouding the title of ownership.

---

[40]Ibid., p. 68

[41]Indians often were hired to track stray animals. If not, and if they took up a stray horse or ox, they were always expected to return it when confronted. They usually did not demand payment. One who did was a Pima who had the horse of an emigrant from Missouri on the Gila River route. He wanted $2.00, the Missourian had $1.50, so the Pima and his chief accompanied the emigrant back to camp for the money. See entry for 19 Oct. 1849, Powell, Diary. p. 143.

[42]Also on the Gila trail, a New Yorker reported some emigrants promising four Mexicans three dollars if they found some missing horses. The Mexicans "were gone but a few moments when in they came with horses, no doubt having them hid, when the boys told them to go to hell" (entry for 27 Dec. 1849. Eccleston, *Overland*. p. 246).

Rights to the Elephant

11 | THE CONCEPT OF OWNERSHIP

Emigrants crossing America's overland trail can be compared to passengers on an ocean liner. Confined within narrow social and physical boundaries, they quickly adjusted to a routine daily schedule — a set pattern of activities creating a world in itself far removed from the rhythm of life they had known and to which they would return. But because overland emigrants were a transitory population, in temporary association, passing from place to place, almost daily encountering a different set of neighbors, that pattern or rhythm of society lacked the permanence necessary to develop a code of binding customs. There is, therefore, one generality about overland legal behavior that is inescapable — rules shaping conduct on the trail had their roots in laws remembered from the youths of emigrants.

Although the evidence may be disputed, our materials seem to indicate only one rule universally acknowledged as customary law by emigrants. Unfortunately, we cannot be certain it was indigenous to the overland trail; historians must give attention to the topic of property law on the western frontier before we can discount the possibility that it arose from social practice back in the sparse settlements of Missouri and Iowa, if not farther east.[1] That rule was the law of abandonment: a custom by which ownership passed from a person relinquishing possession to a person taking possession for the purpose of converting the property to his own exclusive enjoyment.

The law of abandonment was summarized by John Edwin Banks, a forty-niner entering California by the Donner Pass. He

---

[1] An intriguing hint of the folk law that may have developed on the frontier is suggested by an emigrant passing through western Missouri in 1849. His party had lost cattle. A local resident offered to sell them four oxen, "for which he asked 100$ and the priviledge of the lost ones if he should find them" (entry for 21 May 1849, Wilkins, *An Artist*, p. 34).

was traveling with a company from Athens, Ohio, that had picked up two oxen on the Nevada desert. "[F]inding no claimant, we brought them on and worked them." Banks and his companions had not gotten far up the eastern slopes of the Sierras, however, before a Missouri company claimed the animals and accused the Ohioans of theft. "One cannot be too much on his guard," Banks complained. "I am sorry we ever had a connection with the oxen, but I may here add it has been generally understood whatever property left, oxen or otherwise, ceased to be claimed by their former owner."[2]

The legal theory, as Banks said, was that abandoned property "ceased to be claimed by their former owner." It was "the customs of the plains," William Smedley observed, "a deserted wagon being counted public property, and anyone being privileged to appropriate a wheel, a tongue, a bolt, or whatever will serve his purpose better than his own."[3] The legal concept was appropriation. It was not only, as a historian says, that "any property left behind was no longer claimed by the owner,"[4] but also it was property, as one emigrant explained, that "we appropriated to our own use"[5] — or, more loosely, "Falling heir to a number of little things belonging to the part of the mess that had gone ahead, we loaded up."[6]

Emigrants appropriated to their own use and converted to their exclusive ownership almost every type of property abandoned. They not only took up wagons[7] but such wagon accessories

---

[2]Entry for 9 Sept. 1849, Banks, "Diary," p. 83.

[3]Entry for 9 Aug. 1862, Smedley, *Across the Plains*, p. 43.

[4]Unruh, The Plains Across, p. 220.

[5]Entry for 28 July 1853, J. Miller, *Journal*, p. 55; entry for 8 June 1849, Gray, *Off at Sunrise*, p. 32.

[6]Entry for 1 Aug. 1849, Hixson, Diary.

[7]There are too many examples to be listed. Provided here is a sampling showing the range of this customary rule in both time and geography. On the Sweetwater River: entry for 28 July 1849, Hall, Diary, p. 8. On the Rio Grande in New Mexico: entry for 16 July 1849, Fouts, Diary. On the North Platte: entry for 31 May 1850, C. W. Smith, Journal. Along the Humboldt: entry for 23 July 1850, Loomis, *Journal*, p. 98. On the Carson River:

as tongues,[8] axle trees,[9] and wheels.[10] Other wagon parts were claimed as well,[11] as were draft animals,[12] provisions,[13] utensils,[14] and even books.[15] There was no custom restricting use to the original purpose or function of the item appropriated. In treeless areas, wagons were taken not only for transportation but for fuel,[16] and during periods of shortage abandoned draft animals

---

entry for 24 July 1849, Keck, Journal. Near California's Feather River: entry for 4 Sept. 1851, Welsh, Diaries. At the Nevada-Idaho line: entry for 29 June 1852, W. Johnston, Diary, p. 8. On the Oregon trail: Ellmaker, Autobiography, p. 10; entry for 13 June 1859, Wilkinson, Journal. On the Gila River trail: entry for 3 Dec. 1849, Eccleston, *Overland*, p. 221.

[8]Entry for 5 June 1849, Dr. T., Journal.

[9]Entry for 21 June 1849, Benson, Forty Niner, p. 23; entry for 1 July 1853, Cowden, Diary, p. 14; entry for 24 May 1840, Josselyn, Journal.

[10]Entry for 15 June 1849, Farnham, Gold Rush, p. 9; entry for 26 June 1849, Lott, Copy, p. 4.

[11]Entry for 3 June 1849, I. Hale, "Diary," p. 71; *Scharmann's Overland Journey*, pp. 14-15; entry for 24 June 1849, Farnham, Gold Rush, p. 12; entry for 24 July 1849, Josselyn, Journal.

[12]Entry for 5 Nov. 1865, E. M. Lewis, Route (discussed in "Sharing the Elephant," pp. 208-09).

[13]Entry for 8 June 1849, Gray, *Off at Sunrise*, p. 32; entry for 17 July 1849, Bruff, *Journals*, pp. 46-47; entry for 1 July 1849, Perkins, *Gold Rush Diary*, p. 49; entry for 28 Aug. 1849, Benson, Forty Niner, pp. 56-57; *Recollections of John McWilliams, His Youth, Experiences in California and the Civil War* (Princeton: Princeton University Press, n.d., p. 62. One forty-niner who was not traveling with a wagon but packing, wrote that he could find anything he needed, even in the Wyoming wilderness beyond Fort Laramie. "[W]e do not portend[sic] to carry provisions with us but when meal times came we selected such as we wanted" (Richard Ness, "Overland Diary to California" [ms., Western Americana Collection S-709, Beinecke Library]).

[14]Entry for 12 June 1850, W. S. McBride, Diary. One man, finding "a deserted camp," "brought away a tent and a half bushel of corn meal. When companions heard the news, they went and got some things they needed" (entry for 6 July 1859, Wilkinson, Journal, p. 92).

[15]"Facilities for the acquisition of knowledge, are becoming ample among these barren deserts [Humboldt]. Lying by the wayside, are a great variety of books. . . . From this extended library I frequently draw a volume, read and return it" (entry for 21 Sept. 1850, Langworthy, *Scenery*, p. 119).

[16]Entry for 12 May 1850, Turner, Diary; entry for 7 June 1850, Bourne, Diary; entry for 9 June 1850, McGlasken, Journal; entries for 16 July and 2 Sept. 1851, Welsh, Diaries. Bacon abandoned by others was also appropriated for fuel (see entry for 27 May 1849, Farnham,

were converted into food.[17]

Emigrants needed no legal theory to distinguish appropriation from stealing. Had they been asked, however, most would have relied upon the doctrines of intention or good use. Convertible goods, a woman reasoned, "have been left for any one that might want them."[18] To burn abandoned wagons, a forty-niner asserted, "is the best use we can make of them."[19] These explanations were, of course, practical justifications. A more legally accurate theory was offered by a Scots-born Illinoisan who crossed in 1850. "Near our camp," he wrote, "stood a good waggon that had been left by sone [sic] one unable to haul it farther. We without any hesitation demolished it and made a blazing fire which enlivened the camp. Instances are now becoming very common of waggons being left and as it is well understood, they will be left to rot. No hesitation is made in using them in the manner we have done."[20] Expressed in legal terminology, the right to convert abandoned wagons into fuel was based on observed custom established by frequent usage.[21]

Gold Rush, p. 4). One emigrant converted "a very handsome and new *Gothic bookcase*" into firewood (see entry for 22 July 1849, Bruff, *Journals*, p. 51).

[17]Entries for 9, 11, and 13 Oct. 1849, Bruff, *Journals*, pp. 212, 215, 219; entry for 13 Aug. 1850, Udell, *Incidents*, p. 29; entry for 9 June 1853, Woodworth, Diary, pp. 12-13; "Esther Brakeman Lyman Letter, 1853" (ts., 8079, California Historical Society); entry for 8 July 1855, Bardin, Diary, p. 13. There did not always have to be a shortage. As early as the crossing of the South Platte, when food lay scattered at every camp site, "[a] stray steer, in good condition, was driven into our camp, butchered and distributed. His meat was a luxury, and no owner ever appeared to demand compensation" (entry for 18 June 1849, Reid, Diary. p. 24).

[18]Entry for 10 June 1850, Frink, *Journal*, p. 50.

[19]Entry for 6 July 1849, Farnham, Gold Rush, p. 14.

[20]Entry for 15 June 1850, McGlasken, Journal, p. 18.

[21]Need was not a factor creating right. When, however, property was abandoned, need was sometimes stated as justification for appropriating it. On the Nevada desert section of Lassen's cutoff, a party "halted for the night and as we found an old deserted waggon we took possession of it for fire wood there being no wood here but a few scattered sage bush" (entry for 6 Sept. 1849, Castleman, Diary). "We passed today a wagon that had been abandoned with apparently everything in it, — provisions, camp equipment, and all . . . ready to be hitched to by any one wanting an outfit of the kind" (entry for 5 Aug. 1849, Benson, Forty Niner, p. 48).

No matter the theory, the rule was uniform. Ownership passed from the person abandoning to the person taking. An incident that occurred on Lassen's cutoff during 1849 may help to illustrate the legal concepts guiding emigrant behavior toward abandoned property. It involved Ananias Pond, left by his company with one companion to guard a wagon they could take no farther but did not wish to abandon. Trying to put together a team that might haul the wagon, Pond walked a long distance searching for oxen abandoned as jaded and now recruited. After dark he found several which, at some risk from bears and Indians, he got back to his camp. Next morning Pond was still resting in the wagon when

> my partner went out . . . to water & Drive to feed the Oxen. He soon returned Stateing that a Mr. Heustis was driving all the Oxen I had described as haveing found   And was goeing to yoke up and go on with them   But that Mr H Stated that he was then with his family, Team given out, Provis[ions] gone also, & he wished to do the fair thing & finally wished to se[e] me. Accordingly I went to his Waggon where he had the Oxen collected. I would not be positive that more than one of mine were with them   this was one that was with a Muly ox of his the day before but he could not be found this morning. So in the end I let him have my Ox Claim, for $2.00 Cash & am entitled to the Muly if I can find him.[22]

Close attention should be paid to what Pond said as well as how he said it. He calls the oxen "mine" but speaks of selling "my Ox Claim" not of selling "my" ox. If we can read anything into his words, he was implying that by taking up the stray animal he had established a "claim," giving him some rights, though not quite ownership good against the world.

We do not know what Heustis said and it may not matter. His legal behavior is more revealing than Pond's words. Apparently during the night the animals had wandered. Heustis collected several, some of which might have come from the bunch taken up by Pond the evening before. Pond was certain of only one.

Again we must not be in haste to draw the wrong conclusion.

---

[22]Entry for 2 Oct. 1849, Pond, Journal.

The evidence does not tell us that with a family and the need to move immediately, Heustis had an equitable claim to the animals that Pond acknowledged by settling for a reasonable sum. What we are told is that Pond had a legal "claim" Heustis felt had to be quieted even though it rested on little more than temporary possession. A lawyer might say that Pond's ownership was no better than Heustis'. That lawyer would be stating good law, not only for the eastern states but for the overland trail. On the trail, however, there was a difference of emphasis, for the question there was less whether Pond's "claim" was better than Heustis', than whether it was as good. Heustis had possession and intended retaining it. By asking Pond to settle, he was not recognizing adverse ownership, he was acknowledging the claim of prior appropriation. From that perspective, "ownership" to what had been abandoned property was less an absolute than a gradation based on circumstances.

II *The Mystic Core of Ownership*

Prior appropriation was not the entire rule. Heustis purchased Pond's claim not only with money but by transferring rights to the muly ox that strayed away. As Pond says, the ox was his "if I can find him." Surely he did not limit that claim to finding the animal, a stray. If some other emigrant had already taken it up as abandoned, Pond would cite the transfer and assert ownership. The property had not been abandoned and prior appropriation should not prevail.

While we must rely on Pond's account and sorely miss Heustis' own words, there can be little doubt Heustis believed he had the say about who got the missing muly ox. There were other emigrants who thought ownership vested them with similar privileges. Most who abandoned property gave little thought to its future use. Sometimes they would stack it in neat piles "beside the road for all that need it,"[1] placing no specific restrictions on

---

[1] Entry for 16 July 1849, Staples, "Diary," p. 135. See also entry for 3 June 1849, Delano, *Life,* p. 63.

"need" except the general hope that the goods would "be of some service to those who might come after us."[2] A few were more precise, apparently believing they had the right to say how their abandoned property was used. "Dont' tear me to pieces, but take me along," was written on the side of a wagon left on the trail.[3] Another had "a card" attached, "This wagon and plunder is left for the use of the emigrants: Please dont destroy this wagon, for it might be of great service to some poor Emigrant like ourselves."[4] Perhaps the request was honored, for it was dated a month before the day it was noticed. Just two months earlier another forty-niner found a sign on an abandoned wagon along the Sweetwater. " 'To emigrant wanting wagon, take it, but do not destroy if not taken.' This is a man after my own heart."[5]

The last comment implies that the wishes of "owners" were respected, but we may wonder to what degree.[6] If absentee ownership was a viable legal concept, why did emigrants, forced temporarily to leave property they did not intend to abandon, feel it necessary to post guards?

---

[2]Entry for 21 Aug. 1849, Batchelder, Journal, p. 87.

[3]Mary Fetters Hite Sanford, "A Trip across the Plains: March 28-October 27, 1853" (ts., California State Library), p. 9.

[4]Entry for 3 Sept. 1840, Bruff, *Journals*, p. 162. "Saw ... one old cow by the road with a paper pinned on her head, it stated that she had been left to die, but if anyone choose, they might have her, but requested that they not abuse her as she had been one of the best cows" (entry for 28 May 1852, Frizzell, *Journal*, p. 20).

[5]Entry for 3 July 1849, Benson, Forty Niner, p. 29. Some notes may have been intended to inform people that the property was abandoned and could, with good conscience, be taken up. A Wisconsin company "passed one cow with a libel [label] on her [that] any one wants her can have her" (entry for 26 May 1852, Turnbull, "Travels," p. 165; Mattes, *Platte River Road*, p. 52).

[6]The most interesting specimen of legal behaviorism in this regard occurred when an Iowa company, near Chimney Rock in western Nebraska, found "a nice new wagon ... with the request written upon it, that it might not be burned." The man taking it respected the request, and "made firewood of his old one" (Haight, Trip, p. 9). Most owners abandoning property may have felt that they had nothing to say about its disposition once taken up. That same year in central Wyoming another emigrant wrote: "Left our heavy wagon, for the good of other comers, who will probably burn it" (entry for 18 June 1850, Ingalls, *Journal*, p. 26).

The need to relinquish temporary custody of property, while still intending to recover possession, occurred most frequently on the Forty-Mile Desert. A hundred or more miles of Humboldt River water proved too much for many animals. Bloated and sick, thousands collapsed, dying where they lay; others, losing their strength, were unable to draw wagons. To save what they could, emigrants unhitched, drove the cattle to water, and, after they recruited, returned for the wagons and the men left to guard them. It tells us much about legalism on the overland trail to discover the practice explained in terms of law. "One of us has to remain constantly at the Waggon," a forty-niner wrote. "If we did not it would be considered as abandoned by the owners & therefore considered as lawfull Prize to any who might need it or any of its contents."[7] Presumably, it was believed that a posted notice reserving ownership would not be sufficient. In one case, two boys from Iowa, ages eleven and thirteen, were left three weeks guarding a wagon and its contents.[8] Of course, if no one was available to stay behind, an owner planning to return for the property might state his claim in writing and hope it would be respected.[9]

A puzzling question, unanswered by direct evidence, is whether emigrants thought it stealing for someone to take up property left without a guard but with ownership rights reserved. Our best evidence comes from attitudes expressed about the numerous

[7]Entry for 29 Sept. 1849, Pond, Journal (Pond was on Lassen's cutoff, not the Forty-Mile Desert).

[8]Henry O. Ferguson, "A Trip to California" (ts., California Historical Society, San Francisco), p. 10.

[9]On the Gila route, a forty-niner put up a notice in both English and Spanish. "It was addressed to all parties who might cross the desert, and stated that in consequence of the loss of nearly all his animals he had been compelled to leave three of his wagons — two there, and one nine miles back — but that he intended to return and hoped they would not be mutilated" (Bieber, *Southern Trails*, pp. 230-31). Another notice that year read: "This wagon I le[a]ve in care of Capt Bruff, I intend to make a Return trip for it" (entry for 15 Nov. 1849, Bruff, *Journals*, p. 639). "[A] horse we passed today had a notice tied to his tail requesting emigrants to 'let this horse alone as he is left for a friend coming on behind'" (entry for 7 Aug. 1849, Mann, Portion, p. 16).

caches located almost the length of the trail, containing all sorts of property, even "Several Law Libraries."[10] Two emigrants used the word "rifled" when noting that caches had been dug up and their treasure removed.[11] It is, however, unclear what "rifled" is supposed to connote. It may mean to steal unlawfully, but one of the two men using the terms reported open caches without making a moral or legal judgment,[12] while the other himself appropriated or "rifled" a cache of liquor.[13]

Whatever we make of this evidence, it must not be concluded that overland custom forbade owners from retaking property they had left behind. Certainly those who temporarily relinquished possession without "abandoning" (in the sense of leaving the property to be taken up and converted by others) felt they had the right to reassert ownership even if they had to employ force.[14] Three forty-niners while on the Forty-Mile Desert decided to pack. They left their wagon and pushed ahead to water with their animals. Although maintaining no guard and

---

[10]Entry for 5 Oct. 1849, Doyle, Journal.

[11]Entry for 15 Nov. 1849, Bruff, *Journals*, p. 640; entry for 4 Sept. 1851, Welsh, Diaries.

[12]"This was a cache, no doubt, formed to resemble a grave, which some cute chaps had opened & emptied" (entry for 20 July 1849, Bruff, *Journals*, p. 48). "Had sent a mormon wagon out for it, but found, on reaching it, that some knowing one had abstracted $200 worth, and left a note to that effect" (Ibid., entry for 3 Aug. 1849, p. 68).

[13]"Co[mpany] find 4 b[arre]ls [of] whiskey and one cask of brandy buried by the road side a little way from camp. [E]very one fills his water cask with brandy or whiskey all the brandy 30 gals [was] taken. Several drinkers in the Co. but can't agree whether the liquor is whiskey or alcohol, to the surprise of many no one drinks any to speak of" (entry for 28 Aug. 1851, Welsh, Diaries).

[14][O]ne of our companions had a few miles back been compelled to leave a horse, which from mistaken feelings of sympathy for the poor animal, he had neglected to kill. While sitting there [on the Forty-Mile Desert], a company of packers came along the road, when, although it was so dark that I could not distinguish one animal from another, our friend caught up his rifle, cocked and presented it towards one of them, exclaiming in an angry tone, "Get off that horse, you g-d d-n-d scoundrel, or I'll shoot him down under you." The fellow slid off the horse instantly, when our friend gave him one of the "dog-onit-est" blowings up, as the Missourians say, that one fellow ever got for riding the poor animal after he had given out. It was our friend's horse . . . The fellow sloped without saying a word in his defence. Entry for 5 Aug. 1850, Ingalls, *Journal*, p. 41.

posting no notice of reservation, they thought they had the right to return and claim what, to all apparent intents and purposes, had been abandoned. "[T]hare ware," one recorded, "a train of packers come to the waggon & burnt up my trunk coocked what they wished and brought off the most of the provision[s] they thought the waggon had been abandoned but when they come to hear that I gave the waggon to a man that would draw my provision[s] to the river so we could pack the rest of the way to california they gave the most of it up again which we divided with them."[15]

III *The Abstraction of Ownership*

There may be an inclination to make little of this evidence, to say it only repeats what already we have seen: that people on the overland trail distinguished the reality of possession from the abstraction of ownership. After all, what more does it show than that some packers on the Forty-Mile Desert, having possession of an abandoned outfit apparently claimed by no one, readily "gave the most of it up again" when confronted by the owners? That is the wrong lesson to be drawn from this set of facts. What should be asked is why possessors surrendered any (not to mention "most") of what they possessed. The answer apparently lies in the strength of that legal abstraction — the abstraction of "ownership." The abstraction of ownership was so strong on the overland trail that not only could a finder lose title to things taken up and claimed, but a good-faith purchaser for value, from a person in possession, could lose the property if it were claimed by a prior possessor who had lost it or from whom it had been stolen.

The rule also was universal. Emigrants suspecting that something offered for sale had been stolen would not buy it.[1] They might not know the law of the east, but they knew what could

---

[15]Entry for 15 July 1849, Cosad, Journal. For another example of an unguarded wagon later repossessed see entry for 1 Sept. 1849, Jagger, Journal.

[1]See e.g., entry for 5 Nov. 1849, Eccleston, *Overland*, p. 200.

happen on the overland trail: should the owner of the property appear, they might be the losers. The right of return was not qualified by the fact the possessor was a purchaser in good faith. "EMIGRANTS. — Look out for stolen horses!" Salt Lake City's *Deseret News* warned, "an Indian stole a horse and gun from our city, sold them to an emigrant. The stolen property has since been overhauled and restored, and the Indian punished, but who pays the emigrant?"[2]

This warning may not provide the best example, because, if there was any exception to the rule, it occurred when the vendor was Indian. Anyone purchasing a horse from an Indian ran the risk of having the animal claimed by its "owner." It is, however, possible that an innocent purchaser from an Indian had a counter claim. A case that might have taught us much if it had not been so briefly reported occurred in 1849. One or more Sioux "stole a horse and sold it for a bag of flour and a plug of tabacco, but the owner soon found and redeemed him"[3] The term "redeemed" is more vague than we would wish. It may mean the "owner" seized the animal or it may mean he gave something in exchange for possession. In most of the known cases, the owner paid. "Yesterday about noon," a typical account explains, "our little brown horse Barney came along with a pack on his back in the custody of a packer. He stated that he had bought him from an Indian which was probably true as we [had] met two Indians soon after we left the place where we had lost him. He had given as he stated 3 or 4 dollars worth of provisions & ammunition for him. So Booth gave him about 2 quarts of rice, & took the horse back."[4] Near the Sink of Humboldt, another emigrant exchanged his watch with some Indians for a yoke of oxen. A few hours later he learned that the animals had been stolen. "The rightful owners established their claim and after a compromise the oxen were

---

[2]Quoted in *Frontier Guardian*, 18 Sept. 1850, p. 2., col. 5.
[3]Entry for 5 June 1849, I. Hale, "Diary," p. 72.
[4]Entry for 30 June 1850, Parker, Notes.

joint property. The watch being the profit of the middleman."[5]

We must not make too much of the notion of compromise or of Indian title. Indian ownership of abandoned emigrant property was recognized;[6] problems occurred when the property had not been abandoned. The good-faith purchaser seems to have acquired some claims against the "rightful owner," but due to the brevity of extant accounts the nature of these claims is not clear enough to reveal a legal theory. Most likely they were nothing more than rights to argue for some recompense. After all, the purchaser had bought the animal from the Indians, cared for it, and kept it on the trail where the owner could redeem it.

The fact remains, however, that there was an owner: a person not in possession who had a superior claim and felt he had a right to assert that claim, even assert it with force if resisted.[7] The concept is best illustrated by considering the case of an Indian, undoubtedly a Sioux, who was an innocent purchaser. He was found in possession of an army horse and "could not be made to understand why it should be taken from him, as he had come honestly by it." After first seizing the animal, the officer in charge decided to return it. A man present believed the step was taken because "there was no probability the Indian had himself stolen the horse but obtained it from some deserter, that the regimental

---

[5]Catherine Margaret Haun, "A Woman's Trip across the Plains in 1849" (ms., HM 538, Huntington Library), pp. 23-24.

[6]Even small, impoverished nations such as the Pima. See, e.g., entry for 12 Dec. 1849, Eccleston, *Overland*, pp. 229-30.

[7]California traders conducting business on the western end of the Forty-Mile Desert (generally at Ragtown on Carson River) purchased worn-out stock, asking no questions about ownership. They also were believed to steal cattle from exhausted emigrants. When an "owner" found his animals in their possession they would sometimes refuse to surrender them and occasionally the issue of right was settled by force. "One company lost all their oxen but found three of them in possession of a trader, branded. He would not give them up — they took them forcibly . . . the rest of their stock they never found" (entry for 31 Aug. 1850, McKinstry, *Diary*, p. 286). Three years later, also near Ragtown, "a man sold some stock that they had picked [up] to the traders, the owners of the stock came [and] took them, the traders went ahead and over took the men brought them back tied them and w[h]iped them like dogs" (entry for 26 Aug. 1853, Zilhart, *Diary*, p. 17).

mark was unknown to them, and that prairie law as well as equity in such cases allowed the Indian to retain the animal."[8]

That explanation is nonsense. The army returned the horse to avoid trouble with the Sioux, not because of prairie law.[9] When Americans were found with military property they had to surrender possession, no matter how innocent had been their purchase.

A company of forty-niners at Fort Laramie were rearranging their gear and lightening the weight carried by their animals when "an officer of the Fort, stalked into camp and informed us that one of our mules was under the brand of the United States, and he would take it as the property of the same. On repairing to our mules, he selected the finest mule in the gang and pointed to what had escaped our attention, the mark — U.S. The Quartermaster decided the mule belonged to the United States, therefore we must give it up, which we did very reluctantly."[10]

It is words — and attitudes revealed by words — that contain the clues we seek. The forty-niners whose mule was repossessed by the army at Fort Laramie claimed it had been "bought of the Government at Santa Fe last winter and brought in this spring to Independence, where we purchased her." They were outraged

---

[8]Entry for 11 June 1849, Cross, "Journal," pp. 84-85; entry for 11 June 1849, Gibbs, "Diary," p. 313.

[9]The officer ordering the horse returned noted that when it was seized, the Sioux had "moved off quite incensed at the wrong they conceived had been done one of their party." Although he took into account the fact the "Indian had obtained him in good faith," the animal the officer noted was "stolen property," and the motivating reason for releasing it was pacification. "[D]uring the night they would have given us much trouble to secure our horses having it in their power to have annoyed us considerably without the least fear of being punished" (entry for 11 June 1849, Cross, "Journal," pp. 84-85).

[10]Entry for 29 June 1849, J. E. Brown, *Memoirs*, p. 13; J. E. Brown, "Gold Seeker," p. 140. Too much emphasis should not be placed on the fact that there was a "U.S." brand. It was evidence, true enough, but did not make the case special. Saying they "had witnesses that they had purchased them, although they were not branded U.S.," Army officers took mules from other forty-niners. See entry for 16 July 1849, Eccleston, *Overland*, p. 68. Occasionally, the military may have had another purpose in mind. "The officers of the fort [Laramie] tried to frighten us away from the good feed by pretending we had some U.S. mules in our train" (entry for 8 July 1849, Stuart, *Roving Life*, 1:36).

by "this high handed piece of villainy," as one of them termed it. "The protection afforded to emigrants by the chain of Military Posts is only another name for robbery." Expressed more moderately, they believed the animal theirs not merely as innocent purchasers, but because the army, having sold it, was no longer owner.[11]

The army's attitude tells us much. The quartermaster did not accuse the emigrants of stealing the mule; they were acknowledged innocent purchasers.[12] Yet as "owner" he had the right of seizure.

Of course we may suspect that had they had sufficient strength, the forty-niners would have resisted. More relevant to our argument, had the army proven that the mule was never sold (that the person from whom it was purchased at Independence was not the "owner") the emigrants would have given up possession without using harsh words like "villainy" and "robbery."

Well over a month later and hundreds of miles farther west in the Snake nation, another company of forty-niners was encamped on a small creek. "[H]ere," one of them reported, "we had a gentleman by the name of Goodfellow to come and clame a government horse which one of our men had found on green river   he would not give the horse up so we all informed mr. Goodfellow that he could not get [the] horse as he had no more right to him than we had."[13]

It is evident that like the quartermaster at Fort Laramie, Goodfellow was making his claim on the basis of a brand. The company apparently admitted the ownership — the writer calls it "a government horse" — but doubted Goodfellow's authority to repossess it.

---

[11]Entry for 29 June 1849, J. E. Brown, *Memoirs*, p. 13; J. E. Brown, "Gold Seeker," p. 140.

[12]This fact is surmised by the reception the commanding officer gave to their request that the mule be returned. He returned it. "He is a Gentleman in every sense of the word." See entry for 29 June 1849, J. E. Brown, *Memoirs*, p. 14; J. E. Brown, "Gold Seeker," p. 141.

[13]Entry for 6 Aug. 1849, Castleman, Diary.

Seventeen days later the company was traveling along the Humboldt River. Foster, the man who had taken up the horse, and Churchill, the company's captain, were alone, drinking at a stream, when Goodfellow arrived with two companions. He

> ordered Foster to give up the horse which he said he would not do Goodfellow then ordered one of them which he called Wadkins to take the horse W. dismounted and proseded [*sic*] a few paces towards the horse when Foster told him to keep his hand off the horse or he would shoot him at this Goodfellow & Jeffers which was the others name both drew revolvers and said that they would [word missing] him but Foster held on to the horse and said he would shoot the first man that tuched the horse and as Churchill never carried arms he gathered a stone and told Foster not to give up the horse so they gave up this prospect which would have cost them some tro[u]ble if they had undertaken to take it through.[14]

The facts are as clear as we could wish. Foster was prepared to use deadly force to retain possession of a horse he had taken up, against a man he believed had no legal claim to repossess. Churchill, who was not armed and seemingly running a grave risk, supported him. It was the next event that sums up both the concept of ownership as it was understood by overland emigrants and the legal behavior they followed when confronted by legitimate claims to ownership. "Churchill told them that they should show their authority before we would give up the horse which they said the[y] could do when the[y] came to Dr. White who was a short distance [ahead]." Next morning, Foster, Churchill, and others in their company "drove on at a brisk gate untill noon when we came up with the Pioneer train we went and seen Dr. White he showed us his order from Col. McIntosh to take up government stock an[d] deliver them to governor Smith of Cal. so we gave up the horse to White." Thus, men prepared to risk their lives to retain possession against a person who could not prove ownership, readily surrendered the same property to one convincing them he represented the "owner."

---

[14]Ibid., entry for 23 Aug. 1849.

Of course the brand made identification easy, but its importance is not that it persuaded Foster he had to surrender the horse. What is significant is that Goodfellow would not have made the claim if there had been no brand. There were, however, occasions when the demand was made without such positive identification. Then, while law still determined attitudes, numbers and relative strength determined conduct.

Near the end of Lassen's cutoff of the overland trail, Charles Gray was searching for the horse of a sick friend. We have met him before — the New York City man who had not had much experience with animals. After dark he came across a party that had taken up a stray horse. "I described him generally," Gray wrote, "colour, size, mane, tail, &c & *they all concluded he was mine*, but could not determine till morning." With the light of dawn they were able to inspect the animal more closely.

> I saw the horse & knew him instantly. I however had somewhat err[e]d in 2 particulars. I told them I believ'd he *was shod all round & was not branded*, whereas his hind feet were not shod & there was a brand on his hind leg. This brand was almost obliterated, looking exactly like a vein, & not one man in 50 would ever have known he was branded at all. So upon this the man who found him doubted my right to him & insinuated so. I told him however that although I had fail[e]d in an *exact* description of the horse yet the general description I had given of him last night was (as I said before) such as agreed with him exactly & that I could prove it by 20 men.[15]

The compromise was that the man in possession promised to bring the animal into the California settlement where Gray's friend, the horse's owner, and Gray's other witnesses were expected to be. When the man arrived and was satisfied Gray had been correct, the owner "*gave* him $5 in gold & a bottle of brandy worth $4 more *here* & with which he was well satisfied." Gray, on the other hand, "gave him a kind of '*blowing up*' for acting in the

---

[15]Entries for 4-5 Oct. 1849, Gray, *Off at Sunrise*, pp. 120-21.

manner he had; in which however he was somewhat justified, to tell the truth."[16]

Gray's "blowing up" arose from annoyance at not getting the horse to ride, not from the legal behavior of the other man. As Gray admits, the man was "somewhat justified." Gray's own identification had been faulty. He had not established a right to the animal. When the owner did, the horse was surrendered.

iv *A Representative Case*

Our lesson is not one of legal understanding alone. That overland emigrants shared common notions about ownership is impressive. That they respected ownership is even more noteworthy. But what can too easily be missed is the lesson about legal behaviorism. Those notions and that respect produced a pattern of conduct guiding social exchange on the overland trail. Owners who sought lost stock expected it to be returned once ownership was established. Emigrants taking up stray animals knew they might have to surrender possession unless the animals had been abandoned or the owners not found.

If our historians and fiction writers have not deliberately misled us about conflict resolution on the American frontier, then they have been misled by the evidence. They have read violence into events that were not violent and one reason may be that they have been misinterpreting the facts. Not understanding the legal behaviorism that determined conduct, they have assumed that when confrontations did not terminate in shooting or stabbing, the reason was retreat by one side, not shared notions governing legal behavior.

A case representative of law and behavior on the overland trail provides our final example. While long, it is worth our attention. The fact it almost led to the use of force makes it untypical of overland resolutions. That force was not employed, however, makes it typical. Moreover, the disagreement was not only about

---

[16]Ibid., entry for 8 Oct. 1849, p. 126.

ownership but the meaning of "ownership," also a rare occurrence. The possessors claimed that, as they had taken up the stray and "doctered him" they had a "right to him." That the two sides confronted one another and did not fight should be marked by historians. Fiction writers would have had them drawing guns. In real life, legal behavior dictated that when the possessors saw that their definition of "ownership" was not persuasive and that the claiming party was insisting on his rights, they surrendered possession and acknowledged ownership.

The event occurred at the Little Sandy in western Wyoming. The reporter, Cyrus C. Loreland, belonged to a company of drovers taking cattle from Missouri to California.

> Here we met with a train that had one of our stears that we had lost a few days ago. One of the boys went to get him but they refused to give him up then 4 of our men went armed with guns and revolvers determined if we could not get him one way we would another. The boys went up and asked the Captain if he had got a stray stear in his train. C. no I reckon not. Boys. yest you have & there he is that is my stear & I am going to have him C. you cant have the stear & I for bid you going in my cattle. Boys. Is that stear yours. C. No. Boys. Then what is your reasons for still holding on to him. C. We found him up the road give out   we took him up doctered him & there fore we have aright to him.

Regrettably, events are being reported secondhand and the words of the possessor of the cattle may not be recorded accurately. He admitted the animal was not his property but then made a legal argument that apparently sought to prove right to possession if not to ownership. Less puzzling is the legal behaviorism of the "boys." They may have gone to the confrontation "armed with guns and revolvers determined if we could not get him one way we would another," but their conduct belies these words. Instead of meeting the possessor's legal argument with an argument of force, they countered with an argument of fact and an argument of law. "The stear was not give out," the "boys" are said to have contended. "Suppose you should loose all your cattle and we should find them and work them a few days and you should come after them and I should say that you should not have them; you ask me my reasons & I tell you I have found them and have been working them several days & there fore I am agoing to keep them." Faced with a rhetorical question much like during the Socratic phase of a first-year class in property law, the possessor responded much as a first-year law student, for, we are told, he "makes no reply."

The legal discussion had ended and what happened next is subject to conflicting interpretations. It is possible that the possessor tested his will and found he lacked the resolution to support his legal theory with force. Conversely it can be plausibly contended that the outcome turned on "ownership." The possessor of the steer had strength on his side, thirteen men against four. He flaunted that advantage to see how strongly the owners believed they were in the right. When they showed a determination to stand firm, he yielded to their definition of ownership, surely knowing it was the one most emigrants would have supported.

> Boys. Are you going to drive the stear out from your cattle. C says nothing. Boys (makes a start to drive out the stear) If you dont drive him out I shall (they get the stear nearly out [).] C cries for his men (12 in number) head that stear and turn him back   this was done several times   one of the boys was riding up to head the stear and turn him out again when C who was riding clost to him raised a stick which he held in his hand appearantly for the purpose of striking B. At the same moment B placed his hand on his revolver which he had by his side. C. cries out hold on I am prepared as well as you. B. back away then as soon as you please. C. come now lets reason the case. B. well I am a reasonable man but the stear is mine and I am going to have it. . . . C well hold on I will drive the stear out   B well that is all that I want   Thus ended this row.

A final exchange took place, a minor event, but one that helps to tell our tale. "After C. had give up the stear and our boys started off with him then C wanted to make up with our boys and part as good friend[s] but they were too much of the rascal to make friends with so our boys left them without saying any more."[1]

---

[1]Entry for 13 July 1850, Loveland, Diary, pp. 28-29.

The "boys" were passing judgment on "C's" legal behavior; they were saying that his arguments of law had not been sincere. He possessed their property and attempted to deprive them of what they owned by bluffing a show of force. He was unworthy of their friendship for he had acted differently than his fellow emigrants.

If, to a degree, we must guess at what the "boys" intended, it is an educated guess. While some emigrants might have at least shaken hands, most would also have condemned C's legal behavior. Not all who traveled the overland trail got to see the elephant. But had they come across the animal we may be confident how they would have behaved. Had they thought it a stray or one that could be returned to its owner, they might have taken it up. They would not have claimed title unless they knew the elephant had been abandoned and had no "owner."

12 | THE CONCEPT OF PROPERTY

The theories of nineteenth-century American socialists were seldom inspired by native institutions. Those who contended that people, if free to make choices, would replace private property with a more equal sharing of resources, received their ideas from Europe.[1] Notions such as that of Edward Bellamy that "[p]roperty will not, in the long run, be respected which is without some reasonable basis in industry or desert," were never tested by empirical American data.[2] They might have been, for during the settlement of the west there were opportunities for Americans to alter their perceptions of exclusive possession and adopt more collectivistic methods of ownership. They did not do so on a permanent basis, rarely if ever temporarily — not even when faced with emergencies such as imminent starvation or extreme inequality of distribution when a few owned what many desperately needed.

Surely, had socialists wished to measure the strength of property traditions among nineteenth-century Americans, they could not have done better than to examine legal behavior on the overland trail. As we have seen, the ingredients for empirical study are all there and to repeat them seems almost superfluous: a well-documented event, in which large numbers of persons participated, and vast amounts of property were taken along, often under very difficult circumstances that often accentuated the theoretical unfairness of wealth. If there is a deficiency in the

---

[1]"Introduction," to *Constitution and Records of the Claim Association of Johnson County, Iowa*, ed. Benjamin F. Shambaugh (Iowa City: State Historical Society of Iowa, 1894), p. x; Richard T. Ely, *Recent American Socialism* (Baltimore: Johns Hopkins Univ., 1885), pp. 231-304.

[2]Speech of 1889 quoted in Arthur E. Morgan, *Edward Bellamy* (New York: Columbia Univ. Press, 1944), p. 257.

285

evidence to which critics of private property might object, it is that travelers on the overland trail may not represent an exact cross section of the population. There is, however, a balancing consideration too easily overlooked: far removed from their familiar legal environment, these people were often under great pressure to reformulate their legal values and alter their legal behavior. Indeed, it may even be asserted that more than other Americans, they had the opportunity — perhaps even the motivation — to abandon conventional attitudes toward property. Temporarily at least, they might have formulated new definitions of ownership, given new emphasis to political equality, and devised new schemes of distribution.

The data must not be misunderstood. Overland emigrants did not set out on the trail to the Pacific with social experiment in mind. If we agree that it has been demonstrated that they appreciated distinctions between various methods of owning property and were guided by the way they understood rights in property, then it must also be acknowledged that they did not question the social usefulness of personal and exclusive possession. As previous chapters have sought to explain, a man's condition was determined by private resources, not according to any frontier ideal of equality. One historian has gone so far as to assert that "[o]n the emigrant trail the principal distinction was one of property, and a man's social status was judged by the size and quality of his outfit."[3] It is not necessary to agree with so sweeping a generality to acknowledge that property ownership not only contributed to an emigrant's comfort and safety, but also conferred privileges we usually do not associate with the fabled social democracy of the westward movement.

One example should illustrate the potential influence that, thanks to shared concepts about the privilege of ownership, possession of property could confer upon a single individual. Due to annoyance from dust, the favored position in any train was up front. The customary practice was rotation: the wagon that went

---

[3]Mattes, *Platte River Road*, p. 66.

first one day went last the next.[4] It was an ironclad law in most companies, one we would expect to be universal considering what is sometimes said of frontier equality in nineteenth-century America. There was an exception, however, for some companies gave preference to property rather than to individuals. "Our rule was," an emigrant explained, "as many wagons as a man had, so many days he drove at the head of the train, then dropped to the back end." What she meant was that he dropped back to the most advanced position held by one of his wagons. It was a hired teamster that choked on dust at the "back end." [5]

Even in companies where formal democracy was the constitutional norm, property on the overland trail could have its privileges. P. H. Elsworth was a Missourian who in 1852 sold passage for California to about seventy-five persons for one hundred dollars each. With the money he purchased wagons, horses, and provisions. Once the trip began the company elected a captain other than Elsworth. His duties are not specified, but even if he was not empowered to take command — the usual meaning of "captain" — at the very least he spoke for those who voted "unanimously" for him and thought his office important enough to elect a successor when the first occupant died. Yet when crucial decisions were made, Elsworth made them. In today's western Nebraska, driving over a stretch bare of grass, a man dying of cholera "begged for the sake of God to stop." It was Elsworth, not the elected captain, who ruled that they must push on until forage was found. Later he alone decided they would go by way of Salt Lake rather than Fort Hall, a controversial decision about which many companies argued and which generally was determined by majority vote.[6]

It must not be concluded that Elsworth got his way because the

---

[4]Ibid., p. 54.

[5]Lydia Milner Waters, "Account of a Trip" (ts., extracts, "Fort Laramie Journals," vol. 5, Fort Laramie Historic Site, Fort Laramie, Wyoming), p. 3.

[6]Entries for 29 April, 1 and 22 May, 21 June, and 24 July 1852, Verdenal, Journal, pp. 3, 8, 17, 26-27.

teamsters worked for him. The passengers, it might be argued, had to go where the wagons went and the drivers of those wagons obeyed their employer. That explanation is more plausible than likely because it does not jibe with economic realities on the overland trail. Hired hands were contractees, true enough, but they were not dependent on those hiring them. Rather, their employers were more likely to be dependent upon them. Teamsters usually signed on for passage and a fair share of the provisions.[7] If they did not like the route selected or the pace of travel, they could easily leave and hire themselves to another train.[8]

The better explanation is that Elsworth had his way because he was the owner. The decision where his wagons and horses were to go was his decision and his alone. To the extent that property rights dominated over other considerations such as human compassion for a dying man or majority rule, the Elsworth case was typical of legal conditions on the overland trail.[9]

---

[7]For example, James A. Payne made an agreement with a wagon owner to be taken from St. Louis to Sacramento. "He was to furnish me with an animal to ride, bridle and saddle, provisions and all kinds of other necessary equipments for a trip of this kind, and to go through with as little delay as possible." In return, Payne and four other hired men "were to cook, stand guard and do all that was necessary in regard to the horses and mules, such as greasing, hitching up, etc." (entry for 15 April 1850, Payne, Account, p. 2). Terms could, of course, be more detailed. That same year, for example, a Missourian "advertised for 12 mechanics to go to California, via Oregon and work and give me one half the net proceeds for 12 months after our arrival in the country. I got my number" (Harvey, To California, p. 28).

[8]Teamsters felt free even to leave family groups, not only on the California but on the less crowded Oregon trail. Thus a young man who drove a family wagon wrote just beyond Bear River: "This morning...thare was three of the boys that got it in them to leave the train & myself was one of the three this ra[i]sed quite an excitement amoung the croud some of them tried to persuade us to stay by coxen others by sw[e]aring but all far nothing.... we went our own way despite all the train they don[e] all they knew with tears in thare eyes but just like Boys we went our way" (entry for 10 Aug. 1852, J. N. Lewis, Book, pp. 94-95).

[9]Similarly, along the Humboldt, the passengers of the Pioneer Line wanted to divide "the train." Each plan voted by the majority was reported to the proprietor who "exercised the veto and announced that he would be the boss, and that hunger would yet bring the passengers to reason" (entry for 21 Aug. 1849, Reid, Diary, p. 53).

II *The Absoluteness of Property Rights*

The most striking aspect of attitudes toward property on the overland trail was not the respect shown to property rights by the average emigrants. It was rather, the absolute nature in which those rights were regarded. If the perceptions of nineteenth-century Americans are accurately mirrored in the attitudes of overland travelers, it is evident they would put remarkably few restrictions on personal ownership. An emigrant with title to property could do with it whatever whim and fancy dictated.

We may gauge the overland emphasis on absolute property rights by turning once again to the matter of abandoned property. In an area of acute shortages, far from markets where stock could be replenished, it might be expected that a rule would be formulated   or, if not a rule, surely an argument   restricting owners from destroying abandoned property and conferring title to it on those in need.

There was no such rule, and one reason there was none was that the doctrine of exclusive ownership was so absolute that a counter custom had little chance of emerging. Due to the strength of that doctrine, gross antisocial behavior was not only legally acceptable, it was not even questioned. "Destruction," a newspaper correspondent reported from the Green River, "seems to have been the prevailing emotion of everybody who had to leave anything on the trip. Wagons have been wantonly sacrificed without occasion by hundred, being fired for the apparent purpose of preventing them from being serviceable to anybody else."[1] We have already seen that such conduct was not the norm, but it was prevalent enough for some emigrants to say "pure cussedness" was the only reason some wagons were burned. "Because they cannot sell them — they seem to be determined that they shall be of no use to any one else."[2] There is no reason to

---

[1] *Daily Missouri Republican*, 25 Oct. 1849, quoted in Hannon, "Introduction and Notes," p. 128.

[2] Entry for 18 June 1849, Benson, Forty Niner, p. 22. See also Stephens, *Jayhawker*, p. 12.

ask if the author's facts were correct. It is his condemnation of behavior that commands attention. He condemned its morality without questioning its legality. Emigrants complaining of such conduct used words like "selfishness," not unlawfulness.[3]

Attitudes are as revealing as phraseology. "In this the selfish nature of man was plainly exhibited," Alonzo Delano wrote of 1849. "In many instances the property thus left was rendered useless. We afterwards found sugar on which turpentine had been poured, flour in which salt and dirt had been thrown, and wagons broken to pieces, or partially burned, clothes torn to pieces, so that they could not be worn, and a wanton waste made of valuable property, simply because the owners could not use it themselves, and were determined that nobody else should."[4] It must be emphasized that these thoughts were not entered into a private diary to be tucked away and forgotten. Delano was writing for publication and it is fair to assume that he selected his words with some care. Yet even he raises questions of morality, not legality. In extant journals and letters, the act of destruction is frequently deplored, the right to destroy is never doubted.

As previously pointed out, there was no doctrine of communal sharing on the overland trail, no demand right created by one emigrant's desperation on another emigrant's surplus. When provisions were granted as gifts or sold rather than destroyed, the receiver wrote of generosity, not of just expectations.[5] Going down Nevada's Humboldt River during 1850, the year of abject want, an Ohio physician was delighted to purchase food from a passing company. "I bought some beans of them at about 12 1/2 cents a pound when they were offered 50 for them the day

---

[3]Entry for 31 July 1849, Chamberlain, Diary. "Wantonly": entry for 16 June 1849, Kirkpatrick, Journal, p. 15. "A verry bad practice": Marshall, Letter. See also entry for 17 July 1853, Murray, Journal, p. 80.

[4]Entry for 3 June 1849, Delano, *Life*, p. 63. See also entry for 17 July 1849, Bruff, *Journals*, p. 47.

[5]Entry for 3 June 1849, Delano, *Life*, p. 63; entry for 17 Aug. 1846, Bryant, *Journal*, pp. 186-87; Manlove, Trip, p. 6; letter from J. L. Stephens to the Marietta (Ohio) *Intelligencer*, 6 Sept. 1849, T. D. Clark, "Appendix," p. 161; entry for 10 Jan. 1850, Hayes, Diary, p. 169.

before. I record this as a rare example of generosity on the plains."[6] The fact that sellers were abandoning their wagons to pack and no longer could carry this food was not a factor placing obligations on them or vesting rights in the buyer. The owner and the law of supply and demand, not folk law, decided how goods were disposed.

Using evidence from the overland trail as a reflection of nineteenth-century American legal mores in general, there is a special question to be asked. It is, to what extent property rights were regarded as absolute. Some conclusions will be furnished in the final chapter. For the moment we will seek preliminary answers by examining data from the most extreme overland examples: items that were bestowed by nature, not created by labor. For emigrants crossing the continental divide to the Pacific, these items were water, grass, and game.

On the overland trail, even under the most trying conditions, water possessed was water "owned." Crossing stretches of desert, those who had the foresight to carry water with them enjoyed exclusive rights to that water and its distribution. Those who were not prepared, had no utensils for transporting water, or no money for purchasing either utensils or water, suffered from the lack.[7]

Grass could also be made an exclusive possession by prior appropriation. A company first at a grazing plot might preempt the place until the animals were satisfied and it moved on. Those who cut hay owned a commercial item that could be bartered or sold. Shortages did not create demand rights with which people in need could obtain either a fair share of what was available or a

---

[6]Entry for 5 July 1850, Parker, Notes.

[7]Taking examples from the Texas-Gila trail only, see entries for 29 May and 21-22 June 1849, Cox, "Diary," pp. 44, 50, 128; entry for 10 Aug. 1849, Eccleston, *Overland*, pp. 93-94. Later, when leaving Tucson, Eccleston was told he faced a long desert without water. "This altered our arrangements," he wrote, "& we set to work to fill everything with water that we had. Our mess were rather better prepared than the others, having 3 casks & two India Rubber bags, holding together about 80 gals." (ibid, entry for 13 Nov. 1849, p. 204). For the sale of "gourds" in that vicinity see Foreman, *Marcy*, p. 302.

claim on any surplus. Shortages increased the value of what had been harvested and therefore its price. Take the Forty-Mile Desert during 1850. At Humboldt Meadows a man "bought some hay tied up in small bundles, for which he paid twenty cents each."[8] On the other side of the desert — at Ragtown on the Carson — "They cut hay and haul it up from the sink of Carsons River and sell it from 25 to fifty cts. per bundle, about as large round as a man's arm. It would take $5 to feed a hungry ox."[9] From the river to the Sierras one man found that "feed" was "plenty" but expensive "at one dollar and fifty cents per pound."[10] Even in the mountains grass was being sold "at the rate of three hundred Dls a ton."[11]

Social practice did not determine law. Legal theory reflected the taught traditions of yesteryear, not daily experience on the overland trail. If all mentions of begging for water or food were added up and compared, cases of sharing would probably outnumber cases of avarice, yet custom and judgment consistently accorded to an "owner" the right to hoard and to refuse. Even persons craving water possessed by someone else treated it as the exclusive property of the possessor. Two men on Lassen's cutoff in 1849 stopped for the night at a place without water. "We camped," one of them wrote, "near two wagons, one from Missouri and one from Wisconsin. We asked the old Missourian for water to drink and he refused us. The man from Wisconson heard him and gave us water to drink and for coffee both night and morning. (They both had the same amount of water)."[12]

We cannot be certain, but the writer's reference to the two men having the same amount of water was probably a moral judgment, not a legal comment. If the line is thin there is no need

---

[8]Entry for 9 Aug. 1850, Frink, *Journal*, p. 87.

[9]Entry for 31 Aug. 1850, McKinstry, "Diary," p. 286. See also entry for 20 Aug. 1850, Newcomb, Journal.

[10]Summers, Letter.

[11]Entry for 3 Aug. 1850, Kilgore, Journal, p. 57.

[12]Entry for 8 Sept. 1849, Benson, Forty Niner, pp. 62-63.

to belabor the point. The significant fact is not the writer's annoyance or even the social conscience of the Wisconsian, but that the men in need asked the Missourian to share and he felt he had a right to refuse. The decision as to whether he had enough to spare was his to make. If there is an unusual feature to this account it is that those needing the water apparently asked for it, they did not offer to buy it.

Of course, they could have been out of funds, but even when that was the case, emigrants usually offered to barter. Four months later, for example, two Germans were still trapped in Death Valley. One wrote: "Hadapp and I had such an overpowering thirst we even tried to drink the salt water. It was here I tried to exchange my coat and two shirts for a drink of water. We had overtaken two wagons where there was plenty of water, but we failed to obtain any. The man who refused to give us water was forced to abandon an ox on account of sickness. We shot him and caught his blood in a vessel and drank it down, only regretting that there was not more of it to quench our thirst. This only made us more thirsty."[13]

If we are surprised that these Germans offered to purchase from a man with "plenty of water," we should reflect that the extent of that surprise is a measure of how far propagandists for governmental beneficence have removed us from the legal mentality of the nineteenth-century. Today the word "right" is easily applied to solve difficulties they thought of as private, and now people can persuade themselves they are "entitled" to what once they would have said they did "not own."

We are entitled to make judgments, but they should not be anachronistic. All across the Great American Basin men sold water on the various branches of the overland trail. During the tragic migration of 1850, the practice began as early as Hastings cutoff. A week beyond Salt Lake City an emigrant wrote that "now we begin to pass a great many dead and dying cattle, and see men suffering extremely for water, but here some men have

[13]Entry for 8 Jan. 1850, Nusbaumer, *Journal*, p. 48.

hauled out water to relieve the emigrants, which they sell at $1 a gallon."[14] Later, another emigrant "heard of great prices being given for water on this salt plain and much suffering for the want of it." One man he met reported paying "two doll[ar]s for a quart of water on the Salt desert."[15] Another spoke of ten dollars, twenty dollars, up to five hundred dollars being offered for a single drink.[16] Some, "who had got through safe, returned and sold water at a dollar a quart."[17] Twenty-five miles before Relief Springs, a company from the Cherokee nation "came to where some Emegrants had waggons loaded with water which they had brought from the spring to sell to folks, as they came up   they sold it for one dollar per gallon."[18] At least one such wagon, perhaps more, "had been sent by subscription to relieve the distressed."[19] Most, however, were private enterprise, seeking personal profit in an area where some would say there was no law.[20]

The conversion of potable water into exclusive, personal property continued along the Humboldt River,[21] and obtained the status of a major commercial enterprise on the Forty-Mile Desert. During that difficult year of 1850, water was sold on the Forty-Mile Desert as early as the last week of July. The price was

---

[14]Entry for 6 Aug. 1850, J. Wood, "Diary," p. 172; entry for 6 Aug. 1850, J. Wood, *Journal*, p. 66.

[15]Entries for 14 and 21 Aug. 1850, McKinstry, *Diary*, pp. 257, 268.

[16]Unruh, The Plains Across, p. 215.

[17]Entry for 25 Aug. 1850, Bennett, *Overland Journey*, p. 39.

[18]Entry for 10 Aug. 1850, J. L. Brown, "Cherokee Journal," p. 202.

[19]Entries for 30-31 July 1850, Moorman, *Journal*, pp. 56-57. Also that year, there was thirst on the part of the trail that went around the northern end of Salt Lake. "Good water would have commanded any price on the route to-day; but it was not obtainable for either love or money" (entry for 29 July 1850, A. Brown, "Journal," p. 24).

[20]Thirteen years later there would still be water mongers on the Hastings cutoff. See entry for 3 July 1863, Abby E. Fulkerth, "Diary of the Overland Journey of William L. Fulkerth and Wife from Iowa to California in 1863" (ms., photostat, Bancroft Library), p. 49.

[21]Entry for 12 July 1850, Kilgore, Journal, p. 44.

"2 bits for a quart of water."[22] Less than two weeks later, another emigrant paid the same for a pint.[23] "Along here," he wrote when about nine miles from Carson River, "some men have stationed themselves, [and] carry water to emigrants at $1.00 per gal." Even so, he "Saw emigrants nearly perishing, frothing at the mouth for want of water."[24]

Prices varied that year, and varied from day to day, not just between the Carson River route and the Truckee River route. While several diaries mention one dollar a gallon,[25] others reported the same amount of water selling for seventy-five cents,[26] and, for some unexplained reason, one emigrant purchased at "6 shillings per gallon."[27] The quality varied even more. "[V]ary Bad water heare," one emigrant wrote of the Forty-Mile Desert,[28] while another found that "it was warm and a pint cup full which they sold for 12 1/2¢   did no good at all."[29] But a woman who purchased a gallon for a dollar was satisfied. "After the nauseous stuff of the Humboldt 'sink,'" she wrote, "this spring water was more than an ordinary luxury."[30]

Taste, of course, did not give value to water on the Forty-Mile Desert. Nor should scarcity be thought the major consideration. The true source of value came from the exclusive rights enjoyed by those "owning" the water and the fact those rights were acknowledged. We must avoid oversimplification. Possession alone may not explain the "propertyness" conferring rights to

---

[22]Entry for 25 July 1850, Grindell, Sketch Book.

[23]Entry for 3 Aug. 1850, Wallenkamp, Diary, p. 10. A third man that year paid the same price for a glass of water (Haight, Trip, p. 31).

[24]Entries for 3-4 Aug. 1850, Wallenkamp, Diary, p. 10.

[25]Entry for 2 Aug. 1850, Abbey, *A Trip*, p. 154; entry for 10 Aug. 1850, Gundlach, Minutes; entry for 27 Aug. 1850, Moorman, *Journal*, p. 75; Haight, Trip, p. 31.

[26]Entry for 11 Aug. 1850, McCanne, Diary; entry for 30 Aug. 1850, McKinstry, *Diary*, p. 285.

[27]Entry for 19 Aug. 1850, Chalmers, "Journal," p. 53.

[28]Entry for 11 Aug. 1850, McCanne, Diary.

[29]Entry for 30 Aug. 1850, McKinstry, *Diary*, p. 285.

[30]Entry for 16 Aug. 1850, Frink, *Journal*, p. 98.

water. If emigrants theorized at all, which is doubtful, labor probably played a role. The water had to be hauled onto the desert either from the Truckee or Carson rivers.[31] The "owner" did more than merely possess the water. More decisively, that particular water would not have been available had that person not brought it onto the desert.

In later years, wells were dug in the desert, the private property of those who dug them. By 1852, emigrants "found traders all through the desert with water and hay to sell."[32]

> [T]heir is a water & liquor station every 2 & 4 miles between him [a trader from Wisconsin] & the end of the desert or Carson River   only 7 miles at the last of it without any one stationed without you meet the teams on the road & they will sell you from the 20 miles on   if you want a good deal from 75 50 cts to 25 the lowest & 2 Bits pr drink or all kinds of Liquors   it is better for a man to buy than to load down his Horses   carry only enough to serve himself & stocks the first 20 Miles.[33]

That this last was good advice is demonstrated by the diary of a man who had passed over the same route eight days before. "[D]rove all day and all night," he wrote, "seeing hundreds of dead animals."[34]

By 1859 these informal enterprises had become regular business

---

[31] Thus that year an emigrant wrote that "a man with a large pair of mules had two casks of water out some 5 miles on the desert to sell to the weary traviler at 10 cts. per glass" ("The Gold Rush Diary of Martin Wise Miller, Wayne County, Indiana, 1850" [ts., Iowa State Historical Department, Division of Historical Museum & Archives, des Moines], p. 7).

[32] Entry for 9 Aug. 1852, Graham, Journal, p. 18. See also entry for 12 July 1852, Keen, Diary, p. 61; entry for 2 Aug. 1852, Mrs. F. H. Sawyer, Notes from a Journal, p. 26; (commenting on 10 Aug. 1852) "Letter from Ernst W. Jaehnig to His Parents, 16 February 1855," printed as "A Trip to California in A.D. 1852," in the West Bend News, West Bend, Wisconsin, 7, 14, and 21 March 1929 (Wisconsin German Collection Box 4, State Historical Society of Wisconsin, Madison); entry for 11 Sept. 1852, Hosley, Journal; Cole, Early Days, p. 106; Unruh, The Plains Across, p. 402.

[33] Entry for 27 July 1852, Turnbull, "Travels," p. 206.

[34] Entry for 19 July 1852, W. Johnston, Diary, p. 11.

establishments.[35] One, located half way across the Forty-Mile Desert on the Carson River route, had a mail station attached.[36] The price was still high considering the amount of money most emigrants carried,[37] and the product was far worse than water previously hauled out from the rivers — so bad at times that the cattle "refused it"[38] — but no matter the price or quality, it was the vendible property of the seller and the buyer "had to pay."[39]

III *The Absoluteness of Personal Rights*

Labor was a factor contributing to the creation of rights in other types of property besides water. Game killed on the trail generally belonged to the hunter shooting it. He could dispose of it as he pleased, keeping a share,[1] selling it,[2] or giving permission to others to take what they wanted.[3] It is also likely that assistance in running down the animal[4] or helping in some way to obtain the

---

[35]Perhaps even as early as 1856. See J. R. Brown, *Across the Plains*, p. 99.

[36]Entry for 4 Aug. 1859, Crandall, Diary.

[37]"I paid ten dollars for ten gallons of water" (entry for 3 Aug. 1859, Casler, *Journal*, p. 33); "... we had to pay one dollar for each of the oxen's water" (Kunkel, Memoirs, p. 5); "... stock can be watered at one shilling a head" (entry for 26 Sept. 1859, Harriet Booth Griswold, "Diary [of 1859 Overland Journey]" [ms., California Historical Society, San Francisco]).

[38]Entry for 7 Aug. 1859, Wilkinson, Journal, p. 109.

[39]Kunkel, Memoirs, p. 5.

[1]Entry for 19 May 1853, Welsh, Diaries.

[2]Entry for [2]7 Sept. 1849, Pond, Journal; entry for 1 Aug. 1850, "Travels Continued of J. A. Keck" (ms., File K234, Iowa State Historical Department, Divison of Historical Museum & Archives, Des Moines).

[3]Entry for 4 Oct. 1849, Lord, Journal; entry for 12 June 1850, McKinstry, Diary, p. 39B.

[4]"All join indiscriminately in the chase & when one is killed all take a slice" (entry for 1 June 1849, J. A. Johnson, Note Book). See also entry for 17 June 1852, Frizzell, *Journal*, p. 25. The rule was also followed by some of the Indians who, along with forty-niners, chased and killed a buffalo. "[W]hen I Came up two Indians was Carving him up — giving out pieces to the Several Claimants (reserved to themselves the two first Choice), which soon devoured the animal" (entry for 8 June 1849, Burbank, Diary and Journal, p. 32).

carcass created for second and third persons demand rights on the animal.[5]

Specially manufactured products were another species of property on the overland trail. Most notable were craft for ferrying goods across the numerous rivers. A few companies brought boats with them — either made for the trip and hauled in a wagon, or a wagon that was caulked. These boats were company property, exclusive against the world. No matter how desperately others might need them they were employed only as their owners directed.[6]

Even public utility did not create public rights. Evidence further on will show that ferries and bridges as well as boats could be privately owned. A point to be made now is that among the privileges of private ownership was the right of destruction. At the last crossing of the North Platte, a Missouri company consisting of seventeen wagons

> had made some boats of their own and were crossing about 4 miles below the mormon crossing   we [an Ohio company] tried to get the use of their boats to cross in.   they said they made them for their own use and calculated to distroy them as soon as they got over so as to prevent others from crowding them so hard from behind   they said they made theirs and if we wanted to get over we might do the same.   we offered them fifty Dollars for the use of it.   but to no use so we turned out our teams & conmenced making one of our own.[7]

---

[5]"Today Stevenson shot an antelope & brought into camp at night 1/2 of it having given the other 1/2 to the man that helped him to carry it." (entry for 29 May 1849, J. A. Johnson, Note Book). The claim could also be created by contract. "[A] man who had shot an antelope . . . offered us half if we would carry it to the river . . . which we did" (entry for 11 July 1852, Anable, Journal, pp. 23-24).

[6]E.g., entry for 18 June 1859, Chillson, Diary; Read and Gaines, "Introduction," p. 493n185. A Texas company had "a wagon fitted up specially for this expedition, the bed or boddy of the wagon was built in the shape of a scow boat — both ends turned up and constructed so as to be water tight. Oars were carried on the sides and when we reached a River too deep to ford — Our Boat was placed in the water and everything ferried to the opposite shore" (Cox, "Reminiscences," p. 131).

[7]Entry for 11 June 1849, Tinker, "Journal," p. 77.

Shortly after getting to work, the Ohio company heard cries from the Missouri company. Two Missourians were drowning and the Ohioans rescued them. Grateful, the Missourians "offered us the use of their boats & men to help us over," which the Ohio company accepted. Before the crossing was completed a Pennsylvania company arrived and asked to use the boats. "[B]ecause we would not give the boats up to them they thretened to take them away from us by force." The Missourians aiding the Ohio company sent news to their main party about three miles in advance. "[T]hey ammediately stop[p]ed their train & armed seventy men to the teeth and marched them to the ferry to protect us and see that the boats were distroyed."[8]

On first reading, this story may reveal two attitudes about property exclusiveness on the overland trail. Read more deeply it may not. The Missouri and Ohio emigrants had the same theory of law: they thought the rafts exclusive private property. The Missouri company "made" its boats and, as the Missourians told the Ohioans, those boats were property to be disposed of as the owner saw fit even if the motives were selfish and conflicted with the needs of others. If the Ohio company "wanted to get over [it] might do the same." The actions of the Ohioans show that they shared these concepts. They started to manufacture their own boat when the owner of the first refused to sell.

The evidence of the Missourians and the Ohioans may be belied by conduct of the Pennsylvanians. If we consider only what is said, it would appear that the Pennsylvania company denied the Missouri company's claim to absolute enjoyment. Perhaps it did; perhaps the Pennsylvanians theorized that an owner planning to destroy useful property forfeited exclusive rights, that those in need could appropriate what they needed. Of course it is also possible that the Pennsylvania company was unconcerned with rights. It could have intended invoking a law of strength, backing down when confronted by superior numbers.

---

[8]Ibid., entries for 11-12 June 1849, pp. 77-78.

There is, however, another explanation, and that explanation washes. The Pennsylvanians may have misunderstood the title transferred by the Missouri company to the Ohio company. They may have believed that the Ohioans had not received exclusive ownership, that the boat was a type of quasi-public property peculiar to the overland trail: boats held by their possessors with a restrictive covenant running in favor of subsequent potential users prepared to meet the terms set by the original builder.

The legal theory was as much one of a public trust as of private property. Eight days after the Pennsylvanians retreated, on 20 June 1849, a second Missouri company arrived at the crossing of the North Platte. They assisted "the 'Rough & Ready' company, from whom we were to get the boat in which they crossed by paying them $20 the sum which they paid."[9] "One raft sells at twenty dollars," an emigrant coming two days later explained; "each person is pledged to sell at the same price."[10] This pledge explains why another emigrant, one year later, would term such a boat "a public concern."[11]

By the 25th of June, 1849, there were "a number of boats of this kind" crossing the North Platte and selling "for thirty to forty dollars each."[12] The public covenant on the property and its price were known to emigrants because those inquiring learned of them and there were many inquiring — large throngs and long waiting lines. One company reported its boat was "promised twenty-four hours ahead," another had to wait three days.[13]

The legal right enjoyed by those waiting to ferry was simply explained: "After a company has crossed, it sells the boat to another company." What was created was a contractual as well as

[9]Entry for 20 June 1849, McLeod, Note Books.

[10]Entry for 22 June 1849, Banks, "Diary," p. 24.

[11]Entry for 20 June 1849, Gilmore, Overland Journey, p. 9.

[12]Entry for 25 June 1849, Benson, Forty Niner, p. 24. See also entry for 25 June 1849, McCall, *Wayside Notes*, p. 43.

[13]Entry for 22 June 1849, Banks, "Diary," p. 24; entry for 20 June 1850, Gilmore, Overland Journey, p. 9.

a personal-property right. "The other company is to have it for the same price when we're through and thus passes to the next company."[14] The right, therefore, was not only to obtain title but at a price certain.[15] "[T]he last man sells it to the next one back, so they all get their pay till it comes to the last train who will be the loser of" the money.[16]

We will never know, but it is possible that the Pennsylvanians who attempted to seize the boat on the North Platte from the Ohio company thought they were enforcing a property right. Had they offered to pay a specific sum we could be more certain. At least one company, using force to seize this type of property, justified its actions by relying on the "public concern" granted by the running covenant.

> At the [Elkhorn] river there was a ferry boat that had been built by an emigrant, who after he had taken his train across the river, sold the boat to the next train for two dollars and fifty cents, expecting each train to do the same. The man who had charge of the boat when we came there wanted to sell it for thirty dollars, but our people took the boat, paying him two dollars and fifty cents for it, and after our train had gone over we sold it to the next train for the same price.[17]

It would not do to think only of ferries, boats, and rivers. Emigrants who took the trouble to hack out a straighter, shorter, or better road could convert their labor into a property interest by collecting tolls.[18] So could the owners of wagons who had space to haul extra freight. Just as proprietors of boats claimed

---

[14]Entry for 25 June 1849, Benson, Forty Niner, p. 24; entry for 23 June 1849, Farnham, Gold Rush, p. 12.

[15]"It had been built by some of the first emigrants, sold to others and then again sold to others with no diminution of the original price, till it came into our hands. We paid $40 for it, and when done with it, sold it immediately for the same" (entry for 23 June 1849, Dundass, *Journal*, p. 30).

[16]Entry for 24 June 1862, Jane A. Gould, "Her Journal: Oregon-California Trail, 1862" (mimeograph, Iowa State Historical Department, Division of Historical Museum & Archives, Des Moines), p. 27.

[17]J. G. Fish, Crossing, pp. 1-2.

[18]Entries for 15 to 29 July 1852, Egbert, Record.

exclusive use and the privilege of earning income,[19] and those wishing to use those boats expected to have to pay,[20] so possessors of wagons could do the same and emigrants seeking passage knew and accepted the fact they would have to pay. They traveled at the sufferance of the property owner. Desperate as their plight may have been, overland travelers asserted on more fortunate property owners no demand rights based on equity, necessity, or communistic principles. If they wished to save their goods as well as themselves, they paid for their passage either with cash,[21] labor,[22] or by the rental[23] or transfer[24] of their property.

This material is not new; we have seen similar attitudes before. The one new point now being stressed is exclusiveness accorded property ownership on the overland trail. The owner had more than an acknowledged right to possession, he was absolute master. We shall see in the last chapter that, as a result of exclusiveness, ownership of property often conferred privileges we usually do not associate with frontier America. For the moment there is one final example to be considered which, because it is familiar, may serve to illustrate the kind of analysis

---

[19]"We also hired our boats to emigrants [at Green River] today at $5 per team for crossing" (entry for 4 July 1849, Hoffman, "Diary," pp. 66-67).

[20]Entry for 3 June 1851, Zieber, Diary, p. 53. Two men pushing wheelbarrows from the Missouri River to California were asked how they crossed streams. They replied "that if they could not wade them conveniently they would wait for a train, and hire a wagon to carry them over" (entry for 1 June 1852, Keen, Diary, p. 31).

[21]Entry for 23 May 1849, Nixon, Journal; entry for 8 July 1850, Pomroy, Diary; Caldwell, "Notes," p. 1269.

[22]A physician, forced to leave his wagons, arranged to have part of his "loading" hauled, he, in return, to "take charge of the property" (entry for 5 Sept. 1849, McLane, "Leaves," 2:1269-70).

[23]Entry for 23 July 1849, Decker, Diaries, p. 127.

[24]Three men abandoning their wagon on the Platte offered a fourth emigrant "4 Steers [and] 2 yoke of cattle to hall their Grubb & luggage to Portland, Oregon. I consented and we all got threw" (Harvey, To California, p. 41). "Gave Jack (my mule) & waggon to Mr. Russle to car[r]y our baggage &c to the diggins"(entry for 17 Sept. 1849, Lotts, Copy, p. 9). One emigrant who shot two prairie hens gave them to a man with a team "to get my baggage halled" a few miles (entry for 21 April 1850, Lewelling, Excerpts, p. 2).

needed to understand nineteenth-century legal concepts but which historians have neglected to apply.

It is furnished by E. A. Spooner, a forty-niner from Adrian, Michigan, who, in one respect, may be considered typical of the emigrants who crossed the continent by the overland trail: he took for granted an owner's right to the exclusive and undisturbed enjoyment of private property. "Met a company of two wagons of Californians on their return home today," he noted in his diary. "They were Missourians. One of the teams had run away & broken the Capt[ain] of the Co[mpany]'s thigh, who being chief proprietor of the concern, obliged all to return."[25]

Similar tales have been used by historians to illustrate such aspects of pioneer life as physical peril, fortitude, or misadventure. Overlooked is the striking lesson taught about law and attitudes concerning the moral force of law. The returning Missourians must have been keenly disappointed. They were far out on the trail, somewhere beyond Fort Kearny, and it seems that even if one or two went back in one wagon with the injured man, the others could have gone on with the second wagon. We may well wish we had their thoughts. Without them we must speculate, but if we can rely on evidence from other emigrants, the Missourians' explanation most likely would have been that the wounded man owned the property and when he decided to take both wagons back they all had to return.

There is, however, no need to guess at Spooner's reaction. Perhaps without reflection, he used the word "obliged," indicating that he saw nothing unusual about a property holder dictating the lives of others even in an area where supposedly there was no "law." He was not alone. Others — we may safely say most — shared his legal attitudes.[26] That the second wagon could be

---

[25]Entry for 28 May 1849, Spooner, Diary.

[26]Here follows all that another forty-niner wrote about such an incident. He offered no comment — perhaps saw nothing about which to comment. "During the afternoon, we met nine men returning with five wagons, the owner of the train having been run over,

monopolized by its owner for his exclusive enjoyment called for no comment. The legal folkways and social values learned east of the Missouri were carried and respected west of the river. Those who went to see the elephant might argue about its appearance, they did not dispute its ownership.

crushing his thigh badly" (entry for 6 June 1849, Joseph Sedgley, "Overland to California" [ts. extracts, Fort Laramie Historic Site, Fort Laramie, Wyoming], p. 21). Similarly see entry for 6 May 1853, Knight, Journal, pp. 7-8.

13 | THE HABIT OF PROPERTY

"Uniformity" may be an appropriate word, "universality" another, for summing up overland emigrants' thinking about ownership and property. They "universally" defined the two words "uniformly." For these men and women of the mid-nineteenth century, "ownership" meant the right to possession. Thinking did not run in circles. Possession did not confer ownership. There were only two exceptions to that rule. One occurred when the item possessed had been abandoned by the previous owner and taken up by the possessor as his personal property. The second involved a product of nature, such as water, grass, or game. The exclusive possession of these commodities bestowed title upon the possessor. Possession per se had only two other discernible property attributes. It may have conferred the right to a finder's fee against the owner, and gave priority against third parties wishing to possess.

The term "property" cannot be so simply defined as "ownership" because, as understood on the overland trail, the abstraction of "property" was less a conceptual entity than a collection of rights. The primary right associated with "property" was the right to an exclusive and undisturbed enjoyment. The right to enjoyment was so exclusive that it would not be understood by thinking of it only as a right barring others from sharing derived benefits from items owned as property. The privilege of barring others from beneficial enjoyment encompasses such specific rights as to refuse to share items owned, the right to hoard an excess of items owned, and the right to destroy items owned even if those items were in short supply, if others could not obtain those items, or if fellow emigrants were in dire need of those items.

There is a second question aside from definitions relating to uniformity and universality. It concerns application. To what extent did overland emigrants uniformly apply and universally follow their taught, shared notions of "ownership" and "property"? For answers we must revert to the material of four chapters ago — the hardships of Lassen's cutoff and of the 1850 emigration. Our evidence concerns emigrants acting under pressures, stress, and needs that might have caused them to abandon or ignore momentarily principles of ownership and property.

Attention first should be given to persons outside the dominant group. On the overland trail there were several categories of individuals or occupations not part of the emigrations. Among the most prominent categories were soldiers, guides, trappers, and Mormons. Only three, however, were concerned with property ownership to the extent they deserve special consideration. They are independent traders, ferry operators, and Indians.

We have seen the extent of business on the overland trail, the goods traders had for sale and the prices charged.[1] We have not, however, identified these individuals. Some were Americans, of course, fur trappers mostly, though a few seem to have come out from the frontier regions for the season.[2] Others were people with whom — except for being white men — the average emigrant did not relate. The majority were French from Canada,[3] a fact noted by a remarkable number of diarists,[4] one of whom described the trail between Scotts Bluff and Fort Laramie as a country where "French traders are as thick as hasty Pud[d]ing."[5]

---

[1]See chapter four above.

[2]Especially near the western end of the California trail.

[3]Although at least one was from France, not Canada. See Mattes, *Platte River Road*, pp. 307-08.

[4]See, e.g., entry for 10 June 1849, W. G. Johnston, *Overland*, p. 93; entry for 18 June 1849, Dr. T., Journal; entry for 7 Aug. 1849, Bruff, *Journals*, pp. 76, 78; entry for 26 May 1850, Thomasson, Diary; entry for 29 May 1850, W. S. McBride, Diary; entry for 5 June 1850, Payne, Account, p. 38; entry for 14 June 1850, Parker, Notes; John B. Hill, *A Story of the Plains in 1850* (ts., California Historical Society, San Francisco), p. 12; entry for 15 June 1852, Keen, Diary, p. 41; Eaton, *Overland*, p. 181; entries for 28-29 June 1853, Cowden, Diary; entry for 1 June 1854, Sutton, Diary, p. 9; entry for 7 Aug. 1857, Carpenter, Trip, p. 68; entry for 12 June 1859, Wilkinson, Across the Plains.

[5]Entry for 11 June 1852, Anon., Diary.

Another contingent of outsiders among traders was made up of Mormons.[6] Although most were Americans, the average emigrants may have thought Mormons more alien than many foreign born. "They are," a Missourian wrote, "regarded as being worse than Indians."[7] Surely they were more disliked, mistrusted, and, especially by people from Missouri and Illinois, more feared.

Even when traders came from backgrounds similar to those emigrants, life among the mountains had so altered habits and lifestyles that easterners found them a breed apart. As people reacted differently to a given personality, there is no point in speaking of individuals. In one month, for example, Jim Bridger was described as "a frank, open-hearted mountaineer," and "the greatest liar I ever saw."[8] The 1846 emigration reports Captain Richard Grant of the Hudson's Bay Company's Fort Hall accommodating and generous. Two years later an emigrant complained that Grant was "not that charitable gentleman that we expected to see, but a boasting, burlesquing, unfeeling man."[9] What can be said is that collectively the traders were viewed as a class apart.[10]

Emigrants readily identified one factor making independent traders different: living as they did, they were "not much better than the Indians."[11] "[T]hese men," a forty-niner noted of Bridger and his partner, "have habits like Indians, long hair, skin clothing, quick perception & active motions."[12] While Bridger, and the

---

[6] Entry for 17 June 1849, Hixson, Diary; entry for 21 July 1849, Armstrong, "Diary," p. 46 (and Banks, "Diary," p. 47); entry for 11 Aug. 1853, Cowden, Diary.

[7] Entry for 21 July 1854, Ebey, Second Diary, p. 187.

[8] Entry for 1 Oct. 1849, M. M. Morgan, *Trip*, p. 12; letter of Oct. 1849, Senter, *Crossing*. See also entry for 13 July 1849, Jewett, Journal, p. 19; letter from James Frazier Reed to James Keyes, 31 July 1846, in *Overland in 1846*, pp. 279-80.

[9] D. L. Morgan, "Introduction and Notes," p. 98; entry for 28 Aug. 1848, Geer, "Diary," p. 163.

[10] Francis Parkman, who disliked the emigrants going to Oregon in 1846, wrote that "they are very suspicious and mistrustful, and seem to think the traders their natural enemies" (D. L. Morgan, "Introduction and Notes," p. 108).

[11] Letter of Oct. 1849, Senter, *Crossing*.

[12] Entry for 15 June 1849, Decker, *Diaries*, p. 98.

traders at Fort Laramie and Fort Hall, resided in wooden buildings,[13] others lived in what many emigrants misnamed "wigwams,"[14] with Indian women that for some reason were usually referred to as "squaws."[15] "The traders," a female emigrant observed, "are mostly Frenchmen who usually marry Squaws & they therefore agree very well with the Indians."[16] In fact, a trader might have several wives,[17] a bad enough state of affairs, made worse by fanciful stories emigrants told one another, such as that women were purchased "from their fathers, a young squaw being valued at a good horse,"[18] or that "the traders treat their wives badly, making them tan the skins of animals, & then leaving them as caprice dictates."[19]

If living styles were not sufficient to set traders apart, business habits would have clinched the matter. Emigrants thought traders spent most of their time gambling and "dont value gold any more than you do so much grain;"[20] that they did no useful

---

[13]"This old house [Fort Hall] is now filled up with low dirty French, that have squa[w] wifes   any quantity of Indians and half breeds" (entry for 6 July 1851, Hadley, Journal).

[14]Entry for 9 June 1849, Tolles, Diary, p. 25; entry for 14 June 1854, Sutton, Diary, p. 11. Actually, traders' dwellings were more similar to the lodges of Plains Indians — "skins sewed together and stretched over poles about fifteen feet in height, a small opening being left at the top for the escape of smoke" (entry for 10 June 1849, W. G. Johnston, *Overland*, p. 94).

[15]Entry for 15 June 1849, Cosad, Journal; entry for 6 July 1849, Austin, Diary; entry for 13 July 1849, Jewett, Journal, p. 19; entry for 23 July 1849, Burbank, Diary and Journal, p. 63; entry for 7 Aug. 1849, Bruff, *Journals*, pp. 76, 78; entry for 5 June 1850, Payne, Account, p. 39; entry for 25 June 1851, Buckingham, Diary, p. 65; entry for 15 June 1852, Mrs. F. H. Sawyer, Notes from a Journal, p. 12; entry for 19 July 1853, McClure, Journey, p. 100; entry for 22 June 1854, Goodell, Crossing the Plains, p. 11; *Autobiography of Lorenzo Waugh* (Oakland, Calif.: Pacific Press, 1883), p. 191.

[16]Entry for 20 July 1860, M. C. Fish, Daily Journal, p. 51.

[17]One had "half a dozen Squaws for wives some of them being tolerable good looking" (entry for 8 July 1860, M. C. Fish, Daily Journal, p. 46).

[18]Entry for 29 June 1849, *Geiger-Bryarly Journal*, p. 127.

[19]Entry for 27 June 1851, Buckingham, Diary, p. 67.

[20]Entry for 13 July 1853, Belshaw, Journey, p. 13. See also entry for 7 Aug. 1849, Bruff, *Journals*, p. 76; Eaton, *Overland*, p. 181.

work but were "vagrants who come out here and take up with a squaw for safety and brush a mud hole to make money to buy whiskey and tobacco;"[21] that to monopolize overland business they spread among Indians false reports about the danger of cholera and smallpox;[22] and that they were responsible for Indian "depredations."[23]

Besides being socially and economically outsiders, traders were thought "Sharpers"[24] and "Skinners,"[25] making as much as one hundred dollars a day.[26] A commonly used adjective for overland prices was "exorbitant."[27] As early as 1847 a traveler to California termed traders "almost destitute of honesty or human feelings," and Brigham Young compared them to "the wreckers on the sea-board, [who] lie in wait to prey upon the misfortunes, carelessness, and ignorance of the traveler — having no eye to pity, and, unless at the utmost rates of extortion, no dispostion to save."[28]

Emigrants were not economically naive. They knew prices rose with both scarcity and demand, and when a trader needed an article they possessed, were as willing as he to sell high.[29] Yet

[21]Entry for 19 July 1853, McClure, Journey, p. 100. But see entry for 29 June 1849, *Geiger-Bryarly Journal*, p. 125.

[22]Entry for 17 June 1849, Dr. T., Journal.

[23]Entry for 11 June 1854, Ebey, Diary, p. 89; entry for 28 July 1862, Smedley, *Across the Plains*, p. 35.

[24]Entry for 19 June 1849, Burbank, Diary and Journal, p. 41.

[25]Entry for 14 June 1854, Ebey, Diary, p. 101.

[26]Entry for 24 June 1849, Decker, *Diaries*, p. 106. See above p. 109n2 above; entry for 27 June 1850, Loomis, *Journal*, p. 62; letter of 17 July 1853, "Oregon Bound, 1853: Letters of S. H. Taylor to the *Watertown* [Wisconsin] *Chronicle*," Oregon Historical Quarterly, 22 (1921): 138.

[27]Entry for 2 Sept. 1845, Palmer, *Journal*, p. 99; entry for 25 July 1849, Wilkins, *An Artist*, p. 57; Mattes, *Platte River Road*, p. 308.

[28]Unruh, The Plains Across, pp. 366, 424.

[29]Entry for 18 June 1853, Owen, My Trip, p. 14.

when purchasing, they gave the impression prices were set less by economics than by sin.[30]

Few overland travelers gave traders credit for being out on the trail, for the short selling season, or for the risks involved in an isolated, unprotected enterprise. When comparisons were made, they were invariably to prices at home.[31] "Everything you buy," an educated forty-niner wrote of Fort Laramie while it was still a private trading post, "cost four times as much as it is worth and every thing you sell brings perhaps one tenth its value."[32]

Yet emigrants paid. They may have groused, and thought of alternatives,[33] but they paid. The testing time was surely 1850, when thousands of starving men crossed the Forty-Mile Desert and arrived at Ragtown on the Carson River, where traders from California had set up shop. John Wood, whom we followed down the Humboldt in Chapter 9, heard of Ragtown while at the Meadows. "We understand," he wrote, "we can get anything that we want in abundance for the money. This would be great news to the thousands if they had plenty of money."[34] Wood was surrounded by desperate men. He expected they would pay or continue to go hungry.

Those who in 1850 lived to stagger across the Forty-Mile Desert

---

[30]"Oh! how many professors [of religion], even including many of the clergy, are implicated in this, and yet in the sight of God, it is even more aggravating than stealing" (entry for 18 April 1853, Allyn, "Journal," p. 376).

[31]Entry for 6 Aug. 1849, I. Hale, "Diary," p. 101; entry for 27 June 1852, Anable, Second Journal.

[32]Entry for 3 June 1849, Dr. T., Journal. In fact, prices may have been low compared to what they would become. Flour that sold for fifty cents to one dollar fifty cents at the height of the emigration, sold at Fort Laramie for eleven or twelve dollars by the third week of August. See letter of 24 Aug. 1849, Senter, *Crossing.*

[33]Along the Sweetwater an emigrant's horse's shoes became loose. "[W]e came one day to a man sitting by the roadside with a half-bushel measure full of horse nails to sell at the modest price of a "bit" or twelve and one-half cents apiece. No amount of remonstrance or argument about taking advantage of one's necessity could bring down the price; so I paid him ten dollars in gold for eighty nails. I really wanted to be alone with that man for awhile, I loved him so" (Cole, *Early Days*, p. 65).

[34]Entry for 31 Aug. 1850, J. Wood, *Journal*, p. 91.

found traders whom some called "speculators,"[35] running establishments such as one described as "a perfect skinning post for emigrants,"[36] where prices were "extremely high," "enormous," "extravagant,"[37] or "exorbitent . . . , all to strap the poor starving emmigrant."[38] It did not matter that "few have the money to pay the price of provisions,"[39] horses, oxen, and wagons would do as well. "I have," a physician from Pennsylvania wrote, "seen a good but thin horse given for six pounds of flour."[40] Another man, also on the Carson, "saw a good mule exchanged for twelve pounds of flour! and a horse for seven pounds of the same article!"[41] "Many a fine outfit," an eighteen-year-old youth from Wisconsin observed, "has been sold by hungry men for a few pounds of flour and bacon. These know how to sympathize with Esau in the sale of his birthright."[42]

We may gather a sense of how difficult was the choice for emigrants, by considering a tale told by the same Wisconsin youth. California traders had set up shop in a small tent somewhere in the eastern Sierras, most likely Beckwourth's Valley. There were, it is important to note, only two traders present. They were outnumbered by emigrants, though by how much is not stated.

---

[35]Letter of 26 Aug. 1850, Gill, *Letters*, p. 20.

[36]Entry for 10 Aug. 1850, Abbey, *A Trip*, p. 156.

[37]Entry for 6 Aug. 1850, Paschel, Diary, p. 50; entry for 14 July 1850, Parker, Notes; entry for 12 Sept. 1850, Bennett, *Overland Journey*, p. 43.

[38]Entry for 30 July 1850, Christy, *Road*. Watching the astonishing quantities of supplies pour out of the mountains, early arrivals predicted that the law of supply and demand would soon tumble prices. See entry for 11 Aug. 1850, Gundlach, Minutes; entry for 6 Sept. 1850, McKinstry, *Diary*, p. 291. It is, however, doubtful if supply ever caught up with demand. See prices quoted in entry for 19 Aug. 1850, Chalmers, "Journal," p. 53; entry for 6 Oct. 1850, Langworthy, *Scenery*, p. 130.

[39]Entry for 14 Sept. 1850, Steele, *Across the Plains*, p. 208.

[40]Letter of 23 July 1850, Plummer, Letter.

[41]Entry for 28 Aug. 1850, A. Brown, "Journal," p. 28.

[42]Entry for 14 Sept. 1850, Steele, *Across the Plains*, p. 208.

We tented near them, and this evening three men offered to trade them a large mule for flour. Knowing that its owners were destitute of both money and provisions, the traders took advantage of their necessity and offered them six pounds of flour for the mule.

"No," said one, "we can't agree to that; six pounds would not last us half way to the mines, and when the mule and flour are gone we will starve. Certainly you can let us have enough flour to last us in, say twenty-five pounds and the mule is yours."

"Can't do it," said the trader decidedly.

"Well," came the reply, "we can't agree to your terms; we'll eat the mule first."

Turning away from the tent, they went a few rods down the creek and built a fire. Soon one was observed coming back.

"Now I reckon they've come to their appetites," said one of the traders to his companion.

The man came up and tried to bargain with them again.

"Six pounds or nothing," was the reply, making ready to weigh the flour.

Tired and starving, yet with dignified independence he walked back to his companions and after a short consultation the mule was shot.[43]

II *The Testing Ground of Ferries*

The facts tell the story. Those two traders in Beckwourth's Valley owned the flour and if they would not give more than six pounds for a mule, it was their privilege. The property rights of the meanest trader on the overland trail were respected. The tale would have been the same had they been wealthy speculators. Legal behavior was uniform. Overland emigrants did not discriminate between big business and small. And there were both on the trail: the small enterprises of isolated traders and the larger investments in ferries at the North Platte and Green rivers.

No overland property was more valuable than that belonging to ferrymen. The lesson taught by this species of property covers more than size or wealth. We have already seen that emigrants

---

[43]Ibid., pp. 209-10.

owning boats or caulked wagons held them as securely as any other personal property. Persons wishing to enjoy them had to purchase, rent, or pay to be ferried across a stream.[1] Appearing on the Kansas River as early as 1845,[2] ferries spread across the trail as far south as the Bear River and as far north as Fort Boise, generally owned and operated by men from outside the emigration: mountaineers, Indians, and especially Mormons.

Emigrants were sorely tested to respect the exclusiveness of rights to commercial ferry property. We know their minds by their complaints: that tolls were "enormous"[3] and "[t]he owners Coin money"[4] — that "[t]hese ferrymen were making fortunes,"[5] "pocketing their 100$ per diem,"[6] even taking in "one hundred Dollars before Breekfast."[7] One ferryman in 1852 supposedly told an emigrant that he made "from 15 to 18 hundred dollars" a day,[8] an unbelievable sum at that time. There was even a man who estimated that the Mormon ferry across the North Platte would gross $250,000 in the six weeks of its operation.[9]

---

[1]Purchase: entry for 2 July 1849, Lott, Copy, p. 4; entry for 24 June 1849, Violette, Day Book, p. 8; entry for 21 June 1849, Hackney, "Journal," p. 51. Rent: entry for 10 June 1850, L. Sawyer, *Across the Plains*, p. 51. Pay to be ferried: entry for 31 Aug. 1852, Yeargain, Diary, pp. 17-18; Coy, *Great Trek*, p. 255.

[2]Entry for 12 May 1845, Palmer, *Journal*, p. 38; entry for 20 May 1846, George McKinstry, "Diary," in *Overland in 1846*, ed. Dale L. Morgan, p. 204.

[3]Entry for 16 June 1852, Cooke, *Crossing the Plains*, p. 33.

[4]Entry for 29 June 1854, Ebey, Diary, p. 132.

[5]Entry for 12 June 1850, Payne, Account, p. 44. Similarly, entries for 27 June and 6 July 1852, Anable, Journal, pp. 20, 22.

[6]Entry for 20 June 1850, Wolcott, Journal.

[7]Entry for 4 July 1850, Kilgore, Journal, p. 40.

[8]Entry for 19 June 1852, John Clark, "The California Guide" (ms., Western Americana Collection, Beinecke Library); Unruh, The Plains Across, p. 407; Eaton, *Overland*, p. 154.

[9]Letter of 23 June 1850, J. H. McBride, Letters. Five days later a second emigrant wrote: "This ferry is one of the greatest fortunes I have seen for a long time   the supposition is that the ferry will clear some two hundred thousan[d] dollars in about two or three months" (letter of 28 June 1850, Jefferson Bridgford, "Letters" [ms. photocopy, California Historical Society, San Francisco]). The profits of this ferry were also described as "an endless fortune" (entry for 2 July 1850, J. Wood, *Journal*, p. 39), and "a little fortune" (entry for 6 June 1849, Berrien, "Diary," p. 313). These figures are far too high, although

Tolls might have been less astonishing had emigrants not compared them with those paid at home. Some were as low as fifty cents, but the average was around six dollars a wagon. One man described two dollars as "a great prise [sic]," and another called eight dollars "the way to wring hard-earned money from the starving poor."[10] Just thinking about the tolls "casts rather a blue streak over our prospects," an emigrant of 1854 wrote.[11] Another emigrant wanted the federal government to take over the ferries.

> [I]t would be a little something in Uncle Sams pocket, & remove an obstruction, I might have said destruction, because property, & even lives are lost, by trying to swim their teams across for as small as the sum may seem, many have not got it, for they have probably laid out all their money for their outfit, . . . but let the case be as it may, no one let him have ever so much money, likes to have it extorted from him.[12]

When charged sixteen dollars for ferriage at Green River a doctor wrote of "Robbers,"[13] and some emigrants "swore hard,"[14] yet tolls were paid, even by emigrants lacking cash. One wagon with an abundance of food, finding "only coin would pay our way over a formidable stream," sold flour and bacon to other emigrants, and boarded a lone horseman for a week at twenty

---

one of the ferrymen did report proceeds for seven weeks work in 1849, including blacksmithing, to be $6,465.00 (Unruh, The Plains Across, p. 369). It should be noted that at the time the fabulous profits for 1850 were being guessed at, a nearby rival ferry was said to have been sold for only seventy-five dollars (entry for 21 June 1850, Stauder, Memorandum, p. 18). The important point, however, is that many emigrants thought such amounts of money were being made. At that time, as a forty-niner said, to make from fifty to one hundred dollars a day, was "almost equal to gold digging!!!" (entry for 4 July 1849, Wilkins, An Artist, p. 52).

[10]Entry for 12 July 1850, Belshaw, Journey, p. 13; entry for 22 Aug. 1853, Longworth, Diary, p. 43.

[11]Unruh, The Plains Across, p. 423.

[12]Entry for 18 June 1852, Frizzell, Journal, p. 26.

[13]Unruh, The Plains Across, p. 409.

[14]Entry for 31 Dec. 1849, Hayes, Diary, p. 144.

dollars to raise cash for the Green River ferry.[15] Others shoed horses or sold property such as their riding animals for ferriage money.[16]

If we ask why emigrants paid, we are told they had no choice. "This is very high toll," one wrote of a charge of five dollars a wagon, "but the water being swift and deep, you are compelled to fork over."[17] This explanation may appear to be an argument of physical necessity, but we may wonder if it was. Unlike the traders selling provisions to passing emigrants, ferrymen were generally vastly outnumbered. "[F]rom the noise & bustle, one would fancy himself to be on the Levee at St. Louis," a forty-niner wrote of the crowd gathered at the Green River ferry.[18] Between 50 and 400 wagons, occasionally more, could be waiting to be ferried across a stream.[19] With little else to do but sit and grumble, emigrants might have compared legal theories, concluded that Mormons at the North Platte or Frenchmen at the Green River were profiteering at their expense, and taken collective action to protect their interest.[20] Thus when diarists said they had no choice

---

[15]Lavinia Honeyman Porter, *By Ox Team to California: A Narrative of Crossing the Plains in 1860* (Oakland, Calif.: Oakland Enquirer Publishing Co., 1910), pp. 87-88.

[16]Unruh, The Plains Across, p. 413; see also entry for 9 July 1853, Pengra, Diary, p. 37.

[17]"Letter from T. J. Ables to Father and Mother, 12 October 1857" (ts., HM 16763, Huntington Library). Another emigrant, however, at the same river and asked to pay a toll of five dollars, wrote: "[F]ew indeed grudged the money when they can have [the] opportunity of passing this dreadful stream thus safely and expeditiously" (letter of 23 June 1850, J. H. McBride, Letters).

[18]Entry for 14 July 1849, Burbank, Diary and Journal, p. 63.

[19]Entry for 6 June 1849, Berrien, "Diary," p. 313; entry for 9 June 1849, John Boggs, "Diary, 1849" (ms. photocopy, C-F 124, Bancroft Library); entry for 10 June 1849, Pease, Diary to Oregon, p. 12; entry for 2 July 1849, Burbank, Diary and Journal, p. 51; entry for 17 July 1849, Austin, Diary; entry for 14 June 1850, Griffith, Diary, p. 51; entry for 18 May 1853, Murray, Journal, p. 36; entry for 27 May 1853, Williams, Journal, p. 24.

[20]The point must be stressed that the emigrants did know the ferries were owned by Mormons, French, or other outsiders. See, e.g., entry for 8 July 1849, Jewett, Journal, p. 18; entry for 23 July 1849, Reid, Diary, p. 43; entry for 29 May 1850, McGlasken, Journal; entry for 25 June 1851, Hadley, Journal; entry for 25 June 1851, Buckingham, Overland Diary, p. 16; entry for 18 July 1852, Anable, Journal, p. 26; entry for 2 July 1853, Luark, Later Diary, p. 35; entry for 25 July 1853, Murray, Journal, p. 85; entry for 15 July 1854, Ebey, Diary, p. 173.

but to pay, they were referring not to necessity dictated by physical strength, but a necessity compelled by the average emigrant's respect for property rights.

It is revealing that in the very few known accounts of violence, emigrants may have acted on legal principles that they believed justified refusal to pay toll. This explanation is certainly true for those cases about which we have sufficient first-hand evidence to evaluate motivation. In two, the ferryman is said to have reneged on an oral contract; attempting to raise the fare after part of a company crossed the river, and was forced by threats or superior numbers to adhere to the original agreement.[21] Other situations concerned men in possession of ferries or bridges which emigrants understood they had not built.

Unconsciously implementing the doctrine that mere possession without labor or purchase did not confer "ownership," and that the possessor "had fallen on" a "plan to extract a little money from the weary wayfarer," emigrants might refuse to pay.[22] "This evening," a Missourian wrote after crossing the Bear River, "we passed a 'Toll Bridge' over a small branch kept by a Mormon chap who wished us to 'fork over' 25 c[ent]s per waggon for the privilege of crossing — but as we knew the bridge to have been built by emigrants and that the young gent had no right to it we drove over without paying *anything*."[23] By saying the Mormon "had no right" to the bridge, the writer was stating a conclusion of law, not only denying that the Mormon "owned" the property, but justifying its free use by others. Similarly, emigrants concluded that a ferry was not owned by three "land pirates in possession" who demanded toll. A Presbyterian minister reporting the incident did not object when his company, "[t]ook possession of the raft, and made considerable addition to it, and passed over

---

[21]Eaton, *Overland*, pp. 189-90. Similarly, see entry for 23 July 1849, Wilkins, *An Artist*, p. 57.

[22]Luark, Later Diary, p. 47.

[23]Entry for 21 July 1854, Ebey, Second Diary, pp. 186-87.

the teams, and made up a purse of $10, and gave it to the man who claimed the raft, and told him to be off."[24]

It might be thought that emigrants, aware of popular notions about human behavior, were telling different stories among themselves. Yet with one possible exception[25] hearsay tales were much the same as those reported by eyewitnesses.[26] According to one, the ferryman, attempting to capitalize on rising waters, increased a toll already covenanted. The emigrants objected, a fight is said to have resulted, and four men killed.[27] In the only other account found, the ferry at Green River in 1852 is said to have cost eighteen dollars, a sum so outrageous that emigrants seized the boat, appointed a committe to keep tally, and paid the owner four dollars a wagon.[28] Unfortunately, our informant, William Thompson, wrote his memoirs sixty years after the event. No contemporary diary mentions this seizure or such high prices. One report of crossing the same day as Thompson says that the toll was seventeen dollars and fifty cents, but does not indicate how many wagons were ferried at that price. As the writer had paid a bill of forty-eight dollars and fifty cents at the North Platte ferry, it is likely he was tabulating a collective cost,

----

[24]Entries for 17 and 18 May 1849, Foster, Journal, pp. 15-16. Similarly, an unclear account seems to say that emigrants refused to pay toll at some Sierra bridges because the bridges had been built by the government. See entry for 12 Sept. 1852, C. L. Richardson, Journal, p. 179.

[25]It is said that in 1859 at the Maryville ferry in Nebraska, within the line of frontier settlement, "Under the influence of whiskey and angered by the toll, some [of those joining the Pike's Peak gold rush] attempted to seize the boat. Several men were killed in the ensuing gunfight" (Mattes, *Platte River Road*, p. 149). Occasionally there may have been incidents of men using threats or force to obtain priority of service. See Unruh, The Plains Across, p. 367.

[26]There is one eyewitness account of a pistol drawn by an emigrant quarreling with a ferryman, but apparently nothing more occurred. See entry for 17 May 1852, John G. Glenn, "Journal" (ms., 284, Oregon Historical Society, Portland).

[27]Entry for 31 May 1852, Crane, Journal; entry for 29 May 1852, Moreland, Diary. Crane was one hundred eighty miles beyond the place where this incident is said to have taken place when told the story. Moreland also was not present.

[28]Entry for 4 July 1852, William Thompson, "Reminiscences of a Pioneer" (ts., "Fort Laramie Journals," vol. 4, Fort Laramie Historic Site, Fort Laramie, Wyoming), p. 2.

317

not for one wagon only.[29] Another factor casting doubt on the reliability of Thompson's memory is that before he arrived at Green River a rival ferry had been started, forcing what had been a monopoly to lower tolls from eight to five dollars per wagon.[30] Ten days after Thompson left, there were still two ferries operating.[31] In any event, assuming Thompson's details are correct, the important factor is not that emigrants objected to profiteering, but that they did not punish it. While seizing the boat, they still paid the ferryman. The price Thompson says they set, four dollars, was more than any had paid back east but certainly less than many tolls on the overland trail.[32] Probably it was what they thought fair.

These few exceptions, if exceptions they can be called, help to prove the rule that prices set by ferrymen on the overland trail were honored. No doctrines of fairness, equity, or necessity justified greater numbers imposing more moderate tolls. But the ferryman's exclusive right to enjoy the fruits of his property as he saw fit was not absolute. As demonstrated by that rival ferry

---

[29]Entries for 24 June and 4 July 1852, "Copy of Diary, as Kept by William B. Baker, 1852" (ts., California State Library, Sacramento), pp. 4, 6.

[30]Entry for 26 June 1852, Andrews, Journal.

[31]Entry for 14 July 1852, Conyers, "Diary," p. 464.

[32]It is difficult to arrive at precise tolls, not only because emigrants generally mention totals paid and do not itemize, but also because rival ferries may account for different prices. Consider the Green River ferries the year Thompson crossed the overland trail. One man paid six dollars to have a wagon ferried (entry for 30 June 1852, Graham, Journal, p. 13). That same day, another traveler paid three dollars for the same service (entry for 30 June 1852, Kitchell, Diaries, p. 32). Other prices charged at Green River that year follow. Three dollars a wagon: entry for 15 July 1852, Hampton, Diary (ts.); entry for 31 July 1852, J. N. Lewis, Book, p. 86. Four dollars: entry for 22 July 1852, Kahler, Leaves from the Diary, p. 42. "From $5 to $7 per Waggon": entry for 24 June 1852, Turnbull, "Travels," p. 181. Six dollars per wagon: entry for 7 July 1852, Egbert, Record, p. 32; entry for 9 July 1852, Dalton, Diary, p. 21. Seven dollars a wagon: entry for 14 June 1852, Rose, Diary; entry for 14 June 1852, W. Johnston, Diary, p. 6; entry for 22 June 1852, Humphrey, Journal. One man was charged eight dollars (entry for 9 June 1852, Keen, Diary, p. 38). The only hint of violence that year, contained in any contemporary diary, occurs in that kept by the emigrant who recorded what is the highest toll mentioned that clearly was charged for ferrying only one wagon. "Paid $9.50 to be ferried and nearly quarelled in the bargain or after it" (entry for 18 June 1852, Fox, Memorandum, pp. 20-21).

started at Green River in 1852, an owner could not claim a monopoly.

Persons who built ferries, it is clear, had exclusive rights to their property and to its earnings, including the right to set the rate of those earnings. But emigrants' notion of exclusive ownership was not so broad as to bar from the immediate vicinity other franchises or other methods of passage. If a ferryman's tolls were too high, there was no legal reason travelers could not ford in the area of his enterprise.[33] If he did not want them to open a ford, his one recourse was to lower his prices.[34] By the same principle, anyone was free to build a raft[35] or start a competing ferry, and when profits were high, emigrants often did.

Competition forced tolls down at the Green River ferry in 1849 as well as 1852.[36] During 1850 when the ferryman, using a wagon box for a boat, was charging twenty dollars, someone found the abandoned ferry from the year before and went into business at ten dollars per crossing.[37] Even the famous Mormon ferry on the North Platte was forced to lower the "exorbitant charge" of five dollars a wagon[38] to , it is said, fifty cents, when some California emigrants stopped long enough to build and operate a rival enterprise.[39] Although the Mormon government chartered monop-

---

[33]Entries for 5 and 9 June 1850, "The Memoirs of Lemuel Clarke McKeeby,"*California Historical Society Quarterly*, 3 (1924): 51-52; entry for 26 July 1853, Murray, Journal, p. 86; entry for 22 July 1854, Ebey, Diary, p. 192.

[34]Unruh, The Plains Across, p. 371. By the same token, when usually fordable places were flooded, emigrants "chose" to pay toll. See entry for 11 June 1852, C. L. Richardson, Journal, p. 57.

[35]Entries for 10 and 11 June 1849, Pease, Diary to Oregon, pp. 12-13.

[36]Though the reduction from five to three dollars was not large enough to satisfy one emigrant, "[W]e paid, with the conviction that while competition is the life of trade, it does not always make bills within the bounds of reason" (entry for 10 July 1849, Dundass, Journal, p. 35). There were then three competing ferries at Green River. See entry for 14 July 1849, Burbank, Diary and Journal, p. 62.

[37]Entry for 12 June 1850, Parker, Notes. Similarly, a month later at Green River, emigrants went into association with some mountain men to spur competition. See entry for 19 July 1850, Steele, *Across the Plains*, pp. 111-12.

[38]Entry for 8 July 1849, McLeod, Note Books.

[39]Entry for 15 July 1849, Staples, "Diary," p. 136.

olies within its territory,[40] competition continued at the North Platte,[41] beyond Brigham Young's jurisdiction, until 1852 when one company bought "the rest out."[42] Purchase seems to have been the only way of eliminating competitors. When a bridge was constructed over the North Platte, the bridge company, an emigrant was told, "bought & destroyed all the Boats to prevent competition."[43]

III *Property Rights of Indians*

Our evidence must be understood in its correct legal and historical perspective. Emigrants constructing and patronizing rival ferry operations did not believe they were depriving the owner of the first ferry of property rights. Most lawyers would have agreed. They would have said that legal principles conferring exclusive rights to property owned were not compromised, were not even abridged.

Should the rule upon which overland travelers acted be reduced to a legal maxim, it would be that priority of operation did not confer monopoly privileges upon the owner of a common carrier or public utility. That doctrine was in harmony with contemporary American constitutional theory. Only recently, Jacksonian judges had defeated efforts by lawyers of the Hamiltonian school to establish the rule that the granting of a franchise by the state vested the owner with exclusive property rights to all potential business rising within the purview of the charter. What the decision meant was that legislatures were free to incorporate competing ferries, bridges, or turnpikes, and grantees of these charters did not have to compensate the proprietors of the prior ferry, bridge, or turnpike. To deprive another of potential profits by competition was not an illegal

---

[40]Unruh, The Plains Across, p. 419.

[41]Entry for 30 June 1850, Starr, Tour of West.

[42]Entry for 10 June 1852, Coupler, Crossing the Plains.

[43]Entry for 29 June 1854, Ebey, Second Diary, p. 132.

taking of property unless the first franchise owner, in unambiguous, definitive terms, had been vested with exclusive, monopolistic rights.[1] Emigrants when they permitted competition were, in fact respecting property "rights" — the right of a boat owner to solicit business or the right of an individual to transform trees he had felled into a ferry.

There was one condition of ferry ownership concerning which, due to the conduct of some emigrants, it might be argued that property rights were not respected. When we analyze the evidence, however, it may be one of those exceptions that help to delineate the general rule. It occurred when Indians claimed to own a ferry or a bridge, and demanded toll either as individual owners or as agents for their nations.

There are, in fact, two rules that are delineated. One is the rule that ownership conferred absolute rights to enjoyment, the other that labor was a test of ownership. Whenever we encounter emigrants refusing to pay toll at Indian-operated ferries and bridges, and explaining why, the reason given is either a belief that Indians could not have constructed the facility, or that Indian governmental institutions were not sophisticated enough for the tribe to be "owner" by right as well as "owner" by possession.

Prejudice may be one explanation, ignorance another, of why so many overland travelers decided that Indian proprietors of ferries and bridges were unfairly capitalizing on the work of others. "Here is a good bridge built by some emigrants," an entry typical of the type reads, "but the Indians have taken possession of it and demand toll."[2] When Pawnees made that demand in 1852, a party out of Kanesville refused to pay. "The immigrants," one member explained, "had made a bridge across a deep creek and the Indians wanted us to pay toll to cross, but we were too many for them, so they had to stand back and we crossed and

---

[1]The Proprietors of the Charles River Bridge v. The Proprietors of the Warren Bridge and others, 26 *U.S.* 420 (1837).

[2]Entry for 23 May 1852, Egbert, Record, p. 16. See also entry for 2 May 1853, Washburn, Journal, p. 8.

went on."[3] Next year, another group from Kanesville reached Wolf Creek where, a diarist wrote, there was "a bridge which had been washed away recently; but rebuilt by the emigrants who were just crossing. But when I drove on the bridge an Indian stepped in front of the team and demanded 50 c[en]ts. I reached for my old gun in the wagon and motioned the Indian off the bridge which he was not slow to obey, but muttered another threat as he did so."[4] In these accounts there are two common factors. One was the use or threat of violence, the other the assertion that Indians had taken possession of property constructed by another person and for which they had not paid.

We need not be convinced that we know the true motivation these emigrants had for ignoring the Indian toll collector to be impressed that in both cases an implied excuse had to do with the concept of ownership. A third man stated the idea in more colorful language. "At about noon," he wrote, "we crost a deep narrow creek, that some company ahead of us had bridged for their own convenience. After the company left, some noble red men took possession of the bridge and demanded toll of other trains that came along. Not having a heavy purse now we concluded to let them charge it and we would settle with them when we came back, hoping we may have more money then than now."[5]

While the evidence is not inconsistent, it is imprecise, and definitive legal doctrines are elusive. We cannot be certain, but it does seem that emigrants deciding to "charge it" were not denying the existence of Indian "ownership" so much as treating it as less absolute than rights in property enjoyed by non-Indians. This possibility is suggested by emigrants who negotiated tolls lower than first demanded by the Indians and referred to the bargaining as making "a treaty,"[6] or attributed payments to

---

[3]Parsons, Reminiscenses, p. 1.

[4]Luark, Later Diary, p. 2. See also entry for 30 April 1853, Luark, Diary, p. 16.

[5]Entry for 21 May 1853, Cowden, Diary, pp. 4-5.

[6]Mary Jane Long, *A True Story: Crossing the Plains in the Year of 1852 with Ox Teams* (McMinnville, Ore.: 1915), p. 2.

"[a]cting on the peace principle."[7] What these words imply is that some emigrants who paid did not acknowledge the Indians' right to collect, only their power.

One impression provided by the evidence is that if the toll was exorbitant, and the Indian operator would not be "reasonable," emigrants refusing to pay had clearer consciences than had the bridge or ferry been American, Canadian, or even Mormon owned. Indians, like other franchise owners, sometimes set impossible fees. At a bridge they possessed, rightly or wrongly believed by overland travelers to have been emigrant-built and abandoned after first used, the Pawnees demanded a toll of "one steer from each team." Only after the Pawnees refused their offer to pay with other goods did the emigrants force their way across.[8]

It must be emphasized, however, that in most situations emigrants did not threaten Indian proprietors. They did not resort to arguments about unjust prices nullifying rights of the "owner."[9] They paid.[10] They did so even though calling the price "extravagant"[11] and when they were numerically superior.[12]

---

[7] Entry for 20 May 1853, Williams, Journal, p. 21.

[8] Entry for 26 May 1852, Conyers, "Diary," p. 436.

[9] A recent historian has argued that 1852 emigrants crossing Wolf Creek in what is today Doniphan County, Kansas, and who paid one dollar per wagon, were "grossly overcharged by the Kickapoo Indians who maintained the toll bridge" (Eaton, *Overland*, p. 37). That price, as well as fifty cents, twenty-five cents, and "six bits" a wagon, was, however paid. See entry for 7 May 1852, Lydia A. Rudd, Notes by the Wayside En Route to Oregon (ms., HM 27519, Huntington Library); entry for 11 May 1852, Frizzell, *Journal*, p. 13; entry for 12 May 1852, McQueen, Diary; entry for 24 May 1852, Hosley, Journal; entry for 20 May 1852, William P. Hampton, "Diary of 1852" (ms., California State Library); Cole, *Early Days*, pp. 19-20.

[10] At Wolf Creek: entry for 26 April 1850, Abbey, *A Trip*, p. 111; entry for 26 April 1850, A. Brown, "Journal," p. 18. At the Kansas River: entry for 18 May 1846, Bryant, *Journal*, p. 29; entry for 28 May 1849, Sedgley, *Overland to California*, p. 18; entry for 28 May 1849, Churchill, Journal, p. 18. At Papea Creek: entry for 1 June 1852, "Diary of Rev. John McAllister, a Pioneer of 1852," *Transactions of the Fiftieth Annual Reunion of the Oregon Pioneer Association* (Portland, Ore.: Chausse-Prudhomme Co., 1925), p. 474; entry for 7 May 1853, Knight, "Diary," p. 40. Beyond the Grande Ronde River (an Indian toll road "for which they charge toll $1 per wagon"): entry for 11 Aug. 1851, Robe, Diary, p. 63.

[11] At Portneuf River: entry for 19 July 1852, E.B.M. Hanna, Journal, p. 77.

[12] Generally, the Indian toll collector, alone or aided by only one or two others, was far outnumbered. One exception, when the sight of armed Indians persuaded forty-niners to

When most emigrants thought the toll "exorbitant," they acted precisely as when confronted by "exorbitant" tolls at white-owned enterprises. They either forded the river,[13] constructed temporary facilities permitting them to avoid payment, or asserted a counter property right — a right surprisingly acquiesced in by the Indian proprietors of the bridge or ferry.[14] They built competing facilities. At a time when the Indian charge at Wolf Creek was said to be five dollars a wagon, "[t]here were four such bridges constructed in two days."[15]

It also may be that some emigrants, taking for granted the existence and validity of Indian property rights, nevertheless looked more closely at Indian claims to property than at comparable claims by non-Indians. Such a possibility is hinted in the diaries of two emigrants reporting that their companies had paid Indian tolls to drive over bridges, one noting that the bridge had been "made" by the Indians,[16] the other that the bridge was kept "in repair by the Indians."[17] More consciously explicit were those who did not question the right of Indians to own ferries or bridges, even ferries or bridges built and abandoned by Americans, yet doubted if United States law allowed them to collect tolls. When we find these emigrants, despite their questions, paying toll to the Indians we are told a great deal. When we discover they did so because of labor rendered by the Indians, we are told even more. "In our travel we find many improvements made by the Indians," one explained on a day he crossed three Indian-constructed toll bridges. "They, I presume, would have no legal

---

stop arguing and pay the toll, was recounted in a memoir written many years after the event (Caples, Overland Journey, p. 1).

[13]Entry for 19 July 1852, E.B.M. Hanna, Journal, p. 77.

[14]Aside from the Indian ferrymen, there was the nation itself to be considered. There is one report of white ferrymen paying "the Pawnees 350 dollars for the right of ferrying" (entry for 24 May 1853, Murray, Journal, p. 41).

[15]Entry for 10 May 1852, T. E. Potter, The Autiobiography of Theodore Edger Potter, (Concord, N.H.: The Rumford Press, 1913), p. 31.

[16]Entry for 15 May 1852, Kahler, Leaves from the Diary, p. 16.

[17]Entry for 20 May 1853, Williams, Journal.

right to charge, but they were made across bad places and the charge was so small that all paid them."[18]

What the writer meant when he presumed Indians had "no legal right to charge" tolls is not clear. We may be certain he was referring to United States law, but specifically to what "legal right" cannot be answered. It is unlikely that it refers to some vague notion that the intercourse act[19] — the federal statute governing American relations with the Indian nations — required interracial businesses to be licensed. Perhaps it reflected the general attitude of nineteenth-century America that the Indian country was not "owned" by the nations residing there, but was part of the public domain and, as such, belonged to every citizen. When some Indians whose tribe is not identified demanded a toll, a forty-niner would later recall, her party "resolved that the demand was unreasonable! That the country we were traveling over belonged to the United States, and that these red men had no right to stop us."[20] The words of Addison Crane are even more revealing, for he was both a lawyer and a judge. At Wolf Creek he paid a one dollar toll to some member of the Sac and Fox nation. Later that same day he paid Iowas fifty cents to cross a second bridge. "The Indians at both bridges," he noted, "produced papers signed by the Indian Agent requesting the payment of toll rather as a matter of policy to conciliate the Indians, than as a right in them to demand it."[21]

That Judge Crane's law was incorrect does not concern us. It is his belief we must consider. That he, an educated lawyer, thought Indians had no "right" legally to charge toll, helps explain the attitude and therefore the conduct of many of his fellow overland travelers. For the one claim to property ownership uniformly disparaged by emigrants, and sometimes even resisted, was the demand by Indian nations that fees be paid either as toll for

---

[18]Entry for 11 May 1850, Payne, *Account*, p. 20.

[19]*United States Statutes at Large* (1834), 4:729.

[20]Royce, *Frontier Lady*, p. 13.

[21]Entry for 7 May 1852, Crane, *Journal*.

passing through their territory or as compensation for the use of wood, grass, and water found on their land.

Indians, particularly during the first years of the 1850s, frequently attempted to levy such charges. The Kickapoos once had agents at the Missouri collecting ten cents from each wagon entering their territory.[22] A fifty-cent toll assessed at a Sac and Fox bridge was not only for crossing, but included a tax "for the use of wood, grass and water,"[23] or for the "privilege of traveling through our country."[24] Although a party of Sioux "demanded some gifts" in 1849,[25] the next year others asked not for goods or money but that emigrants sign a petition to Congress seeking "remuneration for the rite of way through their Territory."[26] All Indian nations, a superintendent of Indian affairs stated, believed "that the whites have no right to be in their country without their consent,"[27] a legal doctrine the opposite of that expressed by emigrants leaving us their thoughts on the question.

Again the point must be emphasized that many, perhaps a majority of the companies paid. They may not have given precisely what the Indians demanded, but after bargaining did give something. They paid "to buy our way through,"[28] "for the grass that the cattle eat,"[29] and in consideration that nothing be stolen.[30] On the same day that Samuel James's party had a "difficulty with the Pawnees" and "let them have two cows and

---

[22]Letter from "Old Boone" to the *Weekly* (Missouri) *Statesman*, 7 June 1850, printed in *California Emigrant Letters*, p. 98.

[23]Entry for 5 May 1852, Andrews, Journal.

[24]Wigle, Copy, p. 8

[25]Entry for 8 June 1849, Burbank, Diary and Journal, p. 32.

[26]Entry for 20 May 1850, Kilgore, Journal, p. 23.

[27]Thomas Harvey, superintendent of Indian affairs at Saint Louis, quoted in Unruh, The Plains Across, p. 242.

[28]White, "Letter," p. 10.

[29]Entry for 24 May 1850, "Journal of John T. Williams, 1850," *Indiana Magazine of History*, 32 (1936): 397.

[30]Entry for 23 May 1846, Bryant, *Journal*, p. 38.

some flour,"[31] the captain of Harriet Buckingham's company promised a calf to a band of Omahas.[32] "[I]t is wise to do so," she explained, "as they will stampede the cattle some dark night if not well treated."[33]

It is evident that Buckingham did not think her company's payment to the Omahas satisfied a "legal" claim. Other emigrants were more specific, calling Indian demands for passage money or for grass, wood, and water, "blackmail"[34] or, as Buckingham did, "tribute."[35] Interestingly, Judge Crane also used the word "tribute."[36] If a lawyer did not think that possession of territory by Indians gave them title to levy tolls for transit, it is not surprising so many laity among the emigrations thought the same. "[We] paid no attention nor respect to them," one man wrote,[37] summing up the attitudes as well as the actions of many fellow emigrants.[38]

It was in these situations alone that physical strength determined property rights on the overland trail. Emigrants believing that Indian demands for compensation had no more legal validity than naked force, resisted — if strong enough.[39] Weak parties, as

---

[31]Entry for 5 May 1851, James, Diary, p. 3.

[32]Entry for 5 May 1851, Buckingham, Diary, p. 7.

[33]Ibid., entry for 6 May 1851, p. 13.

[34]Entry for 17 May 1849, Breyfogle, Diary (ms.).

[35]Entry for 6 May 1851, Buckingham, Diary, p. 13; entry for 20 May 1849, Pattison, Diary, p. 4.

[36]Entry for 27 May 1852, Crane, Journal. When an unidentified Indian stopped a wagon train, and trouble was avoided by the intercession of a Pawnee "chief," the "chief" was paid what one emigrant termed "a small tribute" (entry for 13 May 1852, Cooke, *Crossing the Plains*, p. 23).

[37]Entry for 9 June 1851, Zieber, Diary, p. 56.

[38]*Edmund Booth (1810-1905) Forty Niner: The Life Story of a Deaf Pioneer, Including Portions of His Autobiographical Notes and Gold Rush Diary, and Selections from Family Letters and Reminiscences* (Stockton, Calif.: San Joaquin Pioneer and Historical Society, 1953), p. 7. See also entry for 10 May 1853, G. N. Taylor, Diary, p. 5.

[39]Graphically demonstrated by a party that refused to pay a few Kaws but three days later paid "tribute" to other members of the same tribe. See entries for 18 and 21 May 1845, Snyder, "Diary," pp. 225, 226.

one man put it, might treat the demand "as equal to a command, and accordingly shelled out."[40] Or, as another explained, "[t]he emigrants paid the toll rather than incur the displeasure of the Indians."[41] Something could be made of the fact that the last writer was a Protestant minister. If his words mean anything, he too saw Indian demands resting on physical force, not property right.

Emigrants theorized less about why they were privileged to reject Indian demands for passage and estovers, than why Indians had no right to demand them. As toll collecting was not a traditional Indian enterprise, it could be dismissed as "a skeem of speculation got up by the Indian agent."[42] American law also provided an excuse, for one did not have to know law to reason that toll taking for passage over the public domain was illegal.[43] We have noted that nineteenth-century Americans considered the Indian country part of the public domain, and thought they had a stronger claim to it than did the Indians.[44] Even a United States Army officer said that the idea of compensating Indians for the use of wood "was of itself too absurd to think of for a moment."[45] And a homeopath, writing to a Protestant newspaper named *The Western Christian,* termed the demand "a gross imposition. The timber used is worth nothing at all to the Indians, being mostly dry wood."[46]

---

[40]Entry for 9 June 1849, Howell, Crossing the Plains.

[41]Wigle, Copy, p. 8.

[42]Entry for 2 May 1852, *Diary of Jay Green: Covering the Period May 1, 1852, to July 27, 1852, during the Crossing of the Plains and Mountains in a Journey from Duncan's Ferry, Missouri, to Hangtown, (Placerville) California* (Stockton, Calif.: San Joaquin Pioneer and Historical Society, 1955), p. 7. See also Eaton, *Overland,* p. 37.

[43]Caples, Overland Journey, p. 2; "A Sketch of the Life of W[illiam] F. Holcomb, 1888" (ms., C-D 5205, Bancroft Library), pp. 10-11; entry for 26 May 1852, Conyers, "Diary," p. 436; Eaton, *Overland,* pp. 78-80.

[44]Carl C. Rister, *Land Hunger: David L. Payne and the Oklahoma Boomers* (Norman: Univ. of Oklahoma Press, 1942), pp. 21, 36-38, 50, 71-74, 93-95.

[45]Entry for 22 May 1849, Cross, "Journal," p. 41.

[46]Letter from Israel Lord to *The Western Christian,* 27 May 1849, Lord, Journal.

Prejudice favoring Indians could lead today's historians to condemn overland attitudes, without realizing that emigrants were thinking in a crosscultural context of deeper than usual dimension. The reality may be both more and less objectionable than appears at first glance.

A point previously made needs little more than repeating: emigrants knew and acted on the belief that, with the exception of stolen property, individual Indians owned what they possessed. If they wanted to own an Indian's horse, emigrants sought to buy it.[47] If they wished to use an Indian raft, they bargained with the owners to rent it.[48] We have already seen that there were numerous Indian traders along the trail, selling anything from products such as salmon and vegetables to their expertise as woodsmen,[49] implying that they expected overland emigrants to understand and act on their notions of personal ownership. The concept of property was not likely to cause difficulty; the question of what objects could be "owned," however, was less clear.

When an emigrant removed items from an Indian grave or a medical student cut open an Indian corpse, overland travelers said property rights were violated.[50] They also thought the word "steal" accurate when writing that an Indian's horse or other item of personal ownership had been taken by an emigrant. But what verb describes the appropriation of wood on an open plain?

---

[47]Entry for 1 July 1849, Wilkins, *An Artist*, p. 50; entry for 12 Aug. 1849, Austin, Diary.

[48]Entry for 25 Aug. 1849, Pease, Diary to Oregon, p. 36; Dawson, *Narrative*, p. 68.

[49]In addition to sources cited earlier see: entry for 2 Aug. 1849, Reid, Diary, p. 47; entry for 30 Aug. 1851, Zieber, Diary, p. 78; entry for 6 Sept. 1851, Robert Harvey Renshaw, "Journal" (ts., 418, Oregon Historical Society, Portland), p. 26; entry for 4 Aug. 1852, Wigle, Copy, p. 15; entry for 10 Sept. 1852, Moore, Journal of Travails; entry for 4 Sept. 1853, Murray, Journal, p. 13; entry for 31 July 1851, Robe, Diary, p. 10.

[50]Entry for 9 Aug. 1845, James Field, Jr., "Crossing the Plains" (ts., 520, Oregon Historical Society, Portland), p. 34; entry for 30 May 1849, Berrien, "Diary," p. 309; entry for 6 June 1849, Delano, *Across the Plains*, p. 25; entry for 20 May 1859, "Diary of J. W. Powell while Crossing the Plains from Marenzo, Iowa, to Placerville, California, with Ox Teams in 1859" (ms., California Historical Society, San Francisco), p. 9.

Aside from the issue of whether Indians could charge tolls for use of timber, water, and grass, there is the question of whether such items, before taken into possession by an emigrant, were "property."

Understanding that they were entering treeless stretches of from 18 to 200 miles, and perhaps even of 275 miles,[51] emigrants loaded firewood onto their wagons.[52] By later years the treks without timber became longer, a fact of which some travelers were aware. "From where we first camped," an 1863 emigrant noted just after leaving the North Platte, "there is not a solitary willow switch on it any wher[e], though I was told that in forty nine the whole way was thick with willow trees, the emigration since that time having clean[ed] them out."[53] It would not have occurred to the writer that he might have used the word "stolen," rather than "cleaned out" — that early emigrants, when stripping an area of lumber, were "stealing" the property of nomad tribes or hunting bands dependent on that wood for fuel or weapons. Nor would the word "stolen" have been understood by an emigrant who, also in the valley of the North Platte eleven years earlier, wrote: "Some distance back of camp on a bluff stood a lone cedar that our train cut down and halled to camp which served us for wood."[54]

The Indian perspective demands a crosscultural application of law that may be beyond our comprehension. A perspective absurd to the nineteenth-century emigrant remains absurd to us.

---

[51]Eighteen miles: entry for 16 May 1849, Pease, Diary to Oregon, p. 4. One hundred seventy-five miles: entry for 29 May 1853, Knight, Journal, p. 15. Two hundred miles: entry for 7 June 1862, Hamilton Scott, "A Trip across the Plains" (ts., 596, Oregon Historical Society, Portland); entry for 24 June 1862, Clough, Diary, p. 120; entry for 24 May 1864, Loughary, Brief Journal, p. 7. Two hundred seventy-five miles: entry for 9 June 1849, Burbank, Diary and Journal, p. 33.

[52]For example: entry for 25 May 1846, Bryant, *Journal*, p. 42; entry for 15 June 1849, Wilkins, *An Artist*, p. 44; entries for 22-23 May and 1 June 1853, Murray, Journal, pp. 39-40, 47.

[53]Entry for 22 June 1863, Yager, "Diary," Part 2, p. 20.

[54]Entry for 29 May 1852, Thorniley, Diary.

Historians, even those believing they write sympathetically from the Indian point of view and intending to make judgments only in the light of Indian values, tend to apply our law to Indian actions and therefore use our words to judge those actions. The point is not that a historian would say "conspiracy" where an Indian might say "war," "massacre" where an Indian might say "battle," or "kidnap" where an Indian might say "take prisoner." The point is that these terms would not occur to a historian.

Consider again the word "steal." Traveling up the North Platte in 1852, an emigrant discovered that "the emigration has driven them [Elk] and Buffalo back from the river." He also recorded passing "a small Indian village." Next day he noted that "some of our party went on a hunting expedition but found no game."[55] The writer knew that elk and buffalo were scarce, blamed the emigration for driving away the game, and realized that Indians, who might depend on these animals for food lived in this area. Moreover, his own party was not short of food. Yet, when some members of that party went hunting, he made no comment and probably recognized no moral or legal issue. Potential moral or legal questions that might have been raised could have been answered by the maxim that animals of the forest were not objects of property ownership prior to being captured or killed. That rule was certainly true — in American law.

The argument is not that nineteenth-century overland emigrants and twentieth-century historians saw the facts but missed the meaning. They knew what was going on and some even condemned "[t]he needless and wanton slaughter" of the buffalo.[56] What they missed was the legal perspective, for there was more to be criticized about killing game than that food was not needed or meat was left to rot on the plains. To apply the law of one culture to an entirely different legal culture is to sow the seeds of misrepresentation.

---

[55]Entries for 1 and 2 July 1852, Anable, Second Journal.

[56]Entry for 23 May 1864, Loughary, Brief Journal, p. 7. Similarly, entries for 8 and 13 June 1849, Foster, Journal, pp. 30, 35.

It may be obvious to say that legal terms or legal maxims must be applied with caution to crosscultural patterns. More easily overlooked is the likelihood that without compensating for a crosscultural fact situation, law words and even non-law vocabulary are not only ambiguous, but can be wrong. An excellent illustration drawn from the history of the overland trail comes from diaries and letters commenting upon interracial strife on the Humboldt River. The most economically-backward Indians encountered on the overland trail lived there. They had not mastered agriculture, could not domesticate horses, and lacked the materials for making effective hunting weapons. Besides, their country was a harsh, barren desert, capable of sustaining little life. As a result, the Indians of the Humboldt lived off small game, berries, and roots. For them, the months that successive emigrations traveled down the river were harvest times. They not only ate dead cattle, and ran off live ones, but crippled horses, mules, and oxen with arrows in the night, forcing emigrants to abandon the animals, leaving behind what was for Humboldt River natives a feast of incredible proportions.

We need not quarrel with emigrants who said that Indians, appropriating horses and cattle for food or converting them to other uses, "stole" those animals.[57] The question is whether the word has meaning when applied to only one side of the crosscultural equation. What of the non-Indian or emigrant side? While Indians of the Humboldt ran off emigrant cattle, emigrants were catching fish in the river, killing frogs along banks, and picking berries from the bushes. We have already noted that during the great famine of 1850, some travelers survived on frogs and berries.[58] Even during better years, many picked berries,[59]

---

[57]See, e.g., entry for 15 Aug. 1853, G. N. Taylor, Diary, p. 20; entry for 26 May 1854, Elizabeth Austin, "Diary of Elizabeth Austin (Mrs. Capt. Henry Roeder) Crossing the Plains — 1854" (ts., University of Washington), p. 2; entry for 23 July 1862, Clough, Diary, p. 139.

[58]See chapter nine. Even men not complaining of starvation helped themselves to currants and other wild food. On the eighth day down the Humboldt, "we found plenty of

not out of necessity, but to vary their diet or to satisfy a craving for berry pie.[60] From one perspective they were reaping the free fruits of nature, from another they were taking what starving Indians depended on for survival.

Criticism need not be limited to emigrants and historians.[61] Lawyers were also estopped by cultural predilections from asking questions that we might think should have occurred to them. Benjamin Franklin Dowell was one such lawyer. A traveler on the California trail during the frightful sufferings of 1850, he was a graduate of the University of Virginia and had practiced in Memphis, Tennessee. In the area between the Green and Bear rivers, Dowell met a party of Snake Indians. "Some of them," he observed, "have very fine American horses which the[y] either stole from the emigrants or swap[p]ed with them."[62] Later, on the Humboldt, he did not use the same word — "stole" — when reporting food his party appropriated from nature. "Fish and small game [are] plentiful," he noted on the second day down the river. "One of the boys killed two wild geese and several rabbits."[63] By the fourth day Dowell was rejoicing at his good fortune. "The general health of our company is much better than it has been since we arrived on the Platte," he wrote. "The fresh fish and wild game doubtless has been of great service in restoring us to better health."[64] In fact, Dowell continued to shoot game the length of the Humboldt without once considering the

---

highbush cranberries, we picked them and found them delicious" (entry for 28 July 1850, W. Hanna, Journal, p. 5). For frogs see entry for 18 Aug. 1850, Moorman, *Journal,* p. 69.

[59]One woman picked berries from the Sweetwater River to the Sierras. See entries for 25 June and 18 Sept. 1852, C. L. Richardson, Journal, pp. 82, 186.

[60]Entry for 29 June 1851, Hadley, Journal; entry for 25 July 1852, Kahler, Leaves from the Diary, p. 44.

[61]It may be even more common for historians than emigrants to use the word "steal" to describe the appropriation of American-owned horses by Indians along the Humboldt. See, e.g., Potter, "Introduction," p. 176n22.

[62]Entry for 25 July 1850, Dowell, Journal, p. 32.

[63]Ibid., entry for 16 Aug. 1850, p. 40.

[64]Ibid., entry for 18 Aug. 1850, p. 40.

legal implications. "We saw several blacktail rabbits," he wrote on the fourteenth day. "I killed the second one I ever saw."[65]

Hunting was difficult, even dangerous, along the Humboldt, and Dowell's tale is not typical. Yet hunting occurred,[66] and no emigrant reporting it — or berry picking, or fishing — ever raised questions concerning property ownership. The fact is not surprising. If the thought did not occur to a lawyer, it would not have occurred to other nineteenth-century Americans. Indeed, it would be an innovative historian, more law-minded than most, who associated hunting, berry picking, or fishing with conversion of property. Yet what if an Indian did? What if an Indian said that the emigrants, not in need, who appropriated berries and frogs along the Humboldt were "stealing" from natives known by those emigrants to be always in want; or even that Indians in need, who helped themselves to what appeared to be a surplus of animals possessed by emigrants, were not "stealing"?

These are questions that cannot now be answered. They must be deferred to another book, one dealing with interracial law on the overland trail. All that can now be said is that when we employ the word "steal" to describe the conversion of an emigrant's horse by an Indian but not to hunting or fishing by emigrants, our meaning may be clear, but only because the law we apply is our law, the law of a single culture in a multicultural legal world.

---

[65]Ibid., entry for 28 Aug. 1850, p. 43.

[66]And could produce "a good supply of game" (entry for 8 Sept. 1849, Austin, Diary). Fishing, too, could be bountiful. One party, on the north fork of Bear River, tied together two wagon covers and caught "about 200 lbs of fish" (entry for 25 July 1852, Moore, Journal of Travails).

Respecting the Elephant

14 | THE BEHAVIORISM OF PROPERTY

The evidence is clear and so are the conclusions that flow from that evidence. Definitions of property law were understood by nineteenth-century Americans on the overland trail, personal rights to property were respected, and respect for property provided those nineteenth-century Americans with a norm for social behavior.

The behaviorism instilled by property poses questions of social values that historians tend to resist. It is easier to accept the other extreme, expressed in the flippant cynicism of Marxist formulae. Yet, when measured against facts, not assumptions, these become questionable. How much substance is there, for example, in the assertion that "the ideology of the ruling oligarchy" of eighteenth-century Britain, placed "a supreme value upon property" which found "its visible and material embodiment above all in the ideology and practice of the law?"[1] Or in the argument that rules of property were imposed upon the people of nineteenth-century America by an elitist legal profession serving the greed of a corporate managerial class?[2] The evidence we have seen from the overland trail demonstrates that the sanctification of property was accepted by a far wider social spectrum than merely the wealthy and their lawyers. To know and respect rights to personal ownership, nineteenth-century Americans needed guidance of neither trained bar nor legislature.

Our preconceptions have been challenged and we know the challenger must be wrong — surely that is the first reaction on

---

[1]Douglas Hay, et al., *Albion's Fatal Tree: Crime and Society in Eighteenth-Century England* (New York: Pantheon 1975), p. 13.

[2]See J. P. Reid, "A Plot Too Doctrinaire," *Texas Law Review*, 55 (1977): 1307; Stephen B. Presser, "Revising the Conservative Tradition: Toward a New American Legal History," *New York University Law Review*, 52 (1977): 700.

reading the theory of a forty-niner from Bath, New York, "that men beyond the reach of the civil and statute law are more sensitive to the rights of others, and so more disposed to regard them."[3] The initial tendency is to reject such naivete out of hand, but in this case to do so is to reject the evidence.

Resolved, the bylaws of an overland company from Iowa provided, "that we will render mutual assistance to each member of the organization in case of sickness or other misfortune, and that we will respect the feelings and property of all . . . ."[4] The resolve to respect property may not impress us, but the degree to which the resolve became the norm for behavior should.

The degree of respect was our theme when we sought to measure the extent of suffering on the overland trail, especially during the starving times of Lassen's cutoff and the 1850 emigration. The lesson drawn from the evidence was that no matter the reality — whether they exaggerated the peril or not —emigrants believed they were in danger of starvation. Their state of mind was surely aggravated by memory of the Donner tragedy, made more acute for those who passed by and saw what one emigrant termed the "Cannibal Cabins"[5] and others called "Cannibal Camp."[6] The "pile of bone which lay bleaching around,"[7] was "truly an appalling sight,"[8] causing forty-niners to reflect on their own precarious plight. "[A]s we looked upon our scanty supply of provisions with no prospect of recruiting it, we could not help feeling that we were in a horrible situation."[9]

---

[3]Entry for 9 Oct. 1849, McCall, *Pick and Pan*, p. 19.

[4]"By-Laws and Regulations of the Dubuque Emigrating Company," 29 April 1852, in Cooke, *Crossing the Plains*, p. 19.

[5]Entry for 29 Aug. 1849, Mann, Portion, p. 22.

[6]Entry for 3 Sept. 1849, Kirkpatrick, Journal, p. 31.

[7]Entry for 21 Aug. 1849, Jagger, Journal.

[8]Entry for 21 Aug. 1849, Hoffman, "Diary," p. 73.

[9]Entry for 29 Aug. 1849, Mann, Portion, p. 22. See also entry for 9 Aug. 1849, Buffum, Diary; entry for 20 Aug. 1849, "A Portion of the Diary of John A. Markle, Written in 1849 while Enroute over the Emigrant Trail to Calilfornia" (ts., California State Library), p. 14; entry for 22 Aug. 1849, Love, Diary; entry for 3 Sept. 1849, Hackney, "Journal," p. 189; entry for 12 Sept. 1849, Banks, "Diary," pp. 84-85.

Diaries are filled with expressions of concern that bad as were conditions on the overland trail, they would soon be worse: that shortages will become widespread ("I am fearful that destitution will stare many an emigrant in the face before he gets to California");[10] that those behind will undergo even harder times ("The distress & sufferings in the rear, must be very great, at this time");[11] that the sufferers coming up will surely experience desperation ("It must be drea[r]y to them to look forward on the future when provisions will be more scarce among the trains");[12] and that some will fall by the wayside ("Thousands must suffer and many starve").[13] Yet the only criticism or comment about the behavior of these desperate men is that sufferings had made them profane.[14]

Whether concerned with food for humans[15] or grass for animals,[16] comments took a similar turn. The concern was for the survival of others, not worry about the safety of their own property. Byron N. McKinstry was typical of the overwhelming majority. "Some people are getting rather short of grubb," he noted while traveling Hudspeth's cutoff. "What will these do before they get through?"[17] Sixteen days later McKinstry answered his own question. "These must eat horses and carrion I am afraid," he wrote of men "without money" to buy food.[18] Jared Fox said much the same about emigrants able to feed themselves,

---

[10]Entry for 27 July 1850, Newcomb, Journal.

[11]Entry for 4 Nov. 1849, Bruff, *Journals*, p. 258.

[12]Entry for 14 July 1849, Farnham, "From Ohio," p. 404-05.

[13]Entry for 14 Sept. 1849, Steuben, Journal. See also entry for 9 June 1849, Dr. T., Journal.

[14]Entry for 16 Aug. 1850, Udell, *Incidents*, p. 29; entry for 15 July 1850, Parker, Notes.

[15]See, e.g., entry for 22 Sept. 1849, Foster, Journal, pp. 81-82.

[16]See, e.g., entry for 6 July 1849, Benson, Forty Niner, p. 30; entry for 22 July 1849, Joshua D. Breyfogle, "Diary" (ts., Dartmouth College); entry for 28 July 1849, *Geiger-Bryarly Journal*, p. 170; letter from R. Luther Myrick, 7 Nov. 1849, Myrick, *Letters*, p. 2; entry for 7 May 1850, L. Sawyer, *Across the Plains*, p. 19; letter of 27 June 1850, J. H. McBride, Letters.

[17]Entry for 2 Aug. 1850, McKinstry, *Diary*, p. 233.

[18]Ibid., entry for 18 Aug. 1850, p. 264.

but not their animals. "Grass is scarce," he reported on 16 June, "Teams must die and then the people. I pity the thousands behind."[19] A month later matters seemed just as bad. "What can they do but die when they come in the hot weather where we leave nothing," Fox asked. "Thousands of cattle and horses must die and consequently hundreds of men women and children — perhaps more than hundreds, maybe thousands."[20]

Almost always, the worry was that others would suffer, not that suffering would cause its victims to commit acts of violence. Rarely do we encounter emigrants saying that because the property of others had been lost, destroyed, or exhausted, their own property might be stolen.

Exceptions were so few they may be detailed in a single paragraph. These included some men who felt they had to guard their property[21] and a lawyer on the Humboldt who, during the famine year of 1850, thought provisions so scarce that "[u]nless we get through soon we may expect to see several fights."[22] Traveling down the Humboldt a month earlier, a physician from Ohio heard a fellow emigrant say he would steal before starving and wrote in his diary, "I fear robbery more now than any other danger."[23] Also on the Humboldt that year, a third man wrote: "We have had daily applications for flour, bacon, etc., and in fact they have been so pressing in their demands, that we deem it necessary to keep a strict guard over our wagons at night."[24]

It is revealing that these quotations all come from the worst of times — 1850 along the Humboldt. Yet even for that terrible year they are far from representative of emigrant attitudes. More typical was Lorenzo Sawyer. "As I drove our famishing animals before me," he recalled of his eleventh day on the Humboldt,

---

[19]Entry for 16 June 1852, Fox, Memorandum, p. 20.

[20]Ibid., entry for 15 July 1852, p. 31.

[21]All of whom are discussed prominently to prove overland violence in Unruh, The Plains Across, pp. 183-84, 213, 280.

[22]Entry for 28 Aug. 1850, Dowell, Journal, p. 43.

[23]Entry for 5 July 1850, Parker, Notes.

[24]Entry for 25 Aug. 1850, Bennett, *Overland Journey*, p. 39.

"my thoughts were employed in calculating the amount of provisions I could carry upon my back, and how long they would be likely to last me, as I had come to the conclusion that we should soon be compelled to adopt this alternative."[25]

The last word, "alternative," is the key. What alternatives to starvation were occurring to desperate people? They are not the alternatives we have been taught to expect. "I never saw such hungry men," Lemuel Clarke McKeeby wrote while going down the Humboldt in 1850. "[M]any talk seriously of killing their horses and eating them and running the risk of getting through on foot."[26] E. S. Ingalls thought that alternative drastic, but not because of the risks in packing. "I have noticed several dead horses, mules and oxen, by the road side, that had their hams cut out to eat by the starving wretches along the road; for my own part I will eat the lizzards which infest the sage bushes, before I eat the stock that died from the alkali."[27]

For neither McKeeby nor Ingalls was the "alternative" to steal. Nor was it for a physician who was at Lassen's ranch when the forty-niners, "sick, destitute, and almost starved," came in from Lassen's cutoff. "They met here with harpies to prey upon them," he wrote, "and they were often compelled to sell their teams for food enough to last them to Sacramento City."[28] Similarly, when a company of men lost their horses on the Snake River, Michael F. Luark could see no alternative "except by disbanding in which event they may individually be taken in by other companies & so escape Death by starvation or at the hands of the Indians."[29]

The expectation that property rights would be respected was as unmistakable as it was universally expressed. Even emigrants at the beginning of the trip, when noting that some men were leaving the frontier with little or no goods, did not express fear. They do not seem to have realized that men without food could

[25]Entry for 6 July 1850, L. Sawyer, *Across the Plains*, pp. 84-85.

[26]Entry for 15 July 1850, quoted in Webb, *Trail*, p. 162.

[27]Entry for 31 July 1850, Ingalls, *Journal*, p. 39.

[28]Stillman, "Around the Horn," p. 167.

[29]Entry for 18 July 1853, Luark, Later Diary, p. 45.

become a menace on the overland trail.[30] On the whole, they proved correct. Violence and self help were not the norm of behavior for those who were suffering. Instead of employing force to take food from those possessing it or to compel those with a surplus to share what they had, hungry emigrants begged not just for provisions but begged to be allowed to purchase what they needed.[31] Large sums of money were offered for water[32] as well as for food, even between men traveling in the same company.[33] There is no indication that those who refused to sell feared retaliation, even though some seeking to purchase were as persistent as they were desperate.[34] Observing a seven-man party sell all their horses, a homeopath from Wisconsin thought "they had no choice — to sell or starve — as begging was out of the question as long as they had a team."[35] For him there were only two alternatives, to buy or beg. "Those having no money," a forty-niner explained, "cannot buy nor beg, but must go without."[36]

Attitudes of have-nots did not differ from those of haves. Those facing starvation had the same thoughts as those with food: they had to buy, beg, or go without. Stranded late on Lassen's cutoff with nearly the entire emigration out of provisions, a forty-niner saw no alternative but to "purchase what we can, and on short rations spin it out."[37] "This morning," a man wrote on the Humboldt route the next year, "several of us started out amongst the many wagons to buy some flour and bacon, but none could we get, at any price, all being very scarce themselves; so after

---

[30]See, e.g., entry for 21 May 1852, Hickman, *Overland Journey*, p. 6.

[31]Entry for 28 Sept. 1849, Gray, Passage.

[32]Entry for 16 July 1850, Clapp, *Journal*, p. 40; entry for 30 Aug. 1850, McKinstry, Diary, p. 122; entry for 29 July 1850, A. Brown, "Journal," p. 24; (8 Nov. 1849) Server, "Ill-Fated Wagon Train," p. 36; (1849) Cardinell, "Adventures," pp. 60-61.

[33]Entry for 23 May 1850, Parker, Notes.

[34]Entry for 23 Aug. 1849, Castleman, Diary; entry for 31 Aug. 1849, Mann, Portion, p. 23; Manlove, Trip, p. 7.

[35]Entry for 13 Aug. 1850, Shepherd, *Journal*, p. 38.

[36]Entry for 15 Sept. 1849, Sedgley, *Overland to California*, p. 59. See also entries for 19 and 23 July 1850, Kilgore, Journal, pp. 46-47, 49.

[37]Entry for 3 Oct. 1849, Bruff, *Journals*, p. 203.

breakfast we started on our way, inquiring of every man we passed, who had a team, if he could let us have some provisions at any price, but we could get none."[38] The writer was John Wood, the emigrant whom we met in Chapter 9 when we followed him down the Humboldt during the starvation of 1850. Later, when crossing the Forty-Mile Desert, Wood sought shelter from the blazing sun beneath the wagon. After resting,

> I crawled from under the wagon, and found myself so tired, hungry and weak, that it seemed to me I could not go; and, after looking around amongst the many that were seated around the wagon, I found some men eating boiled oats. I told them they were better off than I, for I had nothing. They then offered me a share, which I gladly accepted, and gave them some money to buy water with, for they could get none without.[39]

Again, the same conclusion: without money you went without. The universality of this dilemma was demonstrated two days later when an American Indian wrote in his journal, "No flour to be had for love or money."[40]

When the emigrants did manage to purchase they often had to pay high prices — $1.50 for a soup bone[41] and "15 dolers for a pail of flower"[42] to give just two examples from along the Humboldt in 1850. Of course all prices were not high,[43] just as all offers were not accepted,[44] and some sellers were troubled by the rates they were charging;[45] yet there seems little doubt that the prevailing opinion was that many vendors were profiteering at the expense

---

[38]Entry for 21 Aug. 1850, J. Wood, *Journal*, p. 79.

[39]Ibid., entry for 3 Sept. 1850, pp. 95-96.

[40]Entry for 5 Sept. 1850, J. L. Brown, "Cherokee Journal," p. 207.

[41]Entry for 13 July 1850, Parker, Notes.

[42]Entry for 11 July 1850, Grindell, Sketch Book.

[43]Entry for 30 July 1850, Wheeler, Diary.

[44]Entry for 17 July 1850, C. W. Smith, Journal; entry for 20 Oct. 1849, Bruff, *Journals*, p. 332.

[45]Entry for 28 Sept. 1852, Cornell, Description, p. 72; entry for 2 Aug. 1849, Hixson, Diary.

of unfortunate men.[46] Prices were described as "exhorbitant"[47] and "enormous,"[48] and while some said that they were "mighty pleased to get it for that,"[49] others were outraged[50] or simply astonished. The Ohio homeopath who crossed the overland trail in 1850 was just two days down the Humboldt when he wrote:

> Some are now, and have been, for many days, entirely out of provisions; and the price asked by those who have, or think they have an overplus, is really astonishing — one dollar per pound for flour, and others are even asking two dollars; bacon sixty cents, and everything else in proportion; but the fact is, there is a general scarcity. We saw some men who are packing through on horses or mules, let animals and all their clothing go for as little food as possible, take them through on foot. This, of itself, is sufficient to show the state of things that exist.[51]

Passing as he was through a mass of starving people, the homeopath intended to comment on how desperate was the situation. From the perspective of law and order, it does not seem desperate at all. Indeed, it is no exaggeration to say that the emigrants who traveled America's overland trail gave little thought to solving their problems by violence or theft. We have seen that some ate the flesh of dead oxen or beef with maggots while surrounded by healthy animals they could have shot. Those who suffered losses early in the trip and were able to go back, did so. The disappointment and embarrassment for some must have been extremely bitter, but hundreds returned. They did not use weapons to force their way through. While a few of those who were destitute may have employed tricks to obtain food, most begged, and those who were "too proud to beg" got along as best

---

[46]Entry for 13 Oct. 1849, Bruff, *Journals*, p. 219.

[47]Entry for 28 Sept. 1849, Gray, Passage; entry for 30 July 1849, J. A. Johnson, Note Book.

[48]Entry for 14 July 1850, Parker, Notes; entry for 1 Sept. 1849, Perkins, *Gold Rush Diary*, p. 115.

[49]Entry for 24 Aug. 1850, Wheeler, Diary.

[50]Entry for 20 July 1850, Gorgas, Diary.

[51]Entry for 16 July 1850, Shepherd, *Journal*, pp. 23-24.

they could or employed someone to beg for them. If they could not beg, they borrowed and when they could not borrow they depended on their credit.[52]

We may close this survey by turning again to the words of John Wood. He was at Ragtown, on the Carson River, when finally forced to part with the last of his animals.

> Flour sells at $1,25 per pound, corn meal 1,00 per pound, wheat bread 1,50 per pound, pies do; molasses $4,00 per gallon, liquor 50 cents per dram, &c &c. All kinds of roguery is going on here; men here are doing nothing else but steal horses, cattle and mules. The traders here are all from the gold mines; located here to rob the suffering emigrants. When we looked around us this morning and saw provisions in abundance, our hearts were cheered once more, but we had none, neither had we any money, so we immediately killed one of our steers and sold a part of it for 20 cents per pound and bought some flour. Now we had but one steer left, which we sold for $22,50, and divided the money amongst us. Now it was every man for himself, and our little band was disorganized.[53]

Wood's words reveal as much as his actions. He tells us that the traders at Ragtown were there "to rob the suffering emigrants" and were stealing cattle. Yet he and his fellow overland travelers did not resort to force to keep possession of the animals they had struggled so hard to bring across the desert. Instead, they parted with their last steer to buy flour, permitting the traders to "steal" from them.

There were two alternatives to selling your last animal: you could eat less or not at all. Just a few days before Wood was "forced" to sacrifice his steers, another party had discovered that a meal at Ragtown would cost more than ten dollars. "We thought this a little too digging," one wrote, "and put up with a little soup and bread."[54] Back on the Humboldt that same year, a man

---

[52]For citations and quotations supporting this paragraph see John P. Reid, "Paying for the Elephant: Property Rights and Civil Order on the Overland Trail," *Huntington Library Quarterly*, 41 (1977): 50-51.

[53]Entry for 4 Sept. 1850, J. Wood, *Journal*, pp. 97-98.

[54]Entry for 27 Aug. 1850, Moorman, *Journal*, p. 76.

attempted to purchase food for his sick companion. "A tall, raw-boned Shylock, in the form of a white woman, offered to sell one pound of flour for two dollars; he refused to pay, and chose hunger rather than to be robbed when they were starving."[55]

II Deviations from the Norm

Human beings were on the overland trail. That fact has not been overlooked. There were incidents of violence, though generally not involving property.[1] Cases of stealing occurred and, more frequently, cases of suspected robbery.[2] Unfortunately, thieves seldom are identified.[3] Those that are include every category of individual on the overland trail — fellow emigrants,[4] even members of the same company,[5] professional abactors,[6] traders, and, most often, Indians[7] and Mormons.[8]

Of course there were men resolved to use force if they found themselves in certain situations.[9] A party of eight Germans hurried down the Humboldt, intent on overtaking wagons ahead.

[55]Thissell, *Crossing the Plains*, p. 117.

[1]Exceptions are a mountaineer who struck an emigrant for refusing to sell food to starving men and an emigrant who fired a pistol at a partner who stole his horse. See entry for 7 Aug. 1850, Ingalls, *Journal*, pp. 42-43; entry for 17 Aug. 1852, Anable, Journal, p. 32.

[2]Entry for 4 Oct. 1849, Austin, Diary; entry for 21 July 1850, Dowell, Journal, pp. 30-31; entry for 29 July 1850, Christy, *Road*.

[3]Entry for 30 May 1850, Griffith, Diary, p. 44; entry for 1 July 1850, Clapp, *Journal*, p. 35; entries for 17 and 21 July 1850, Gundlach, Minutes; entry for 9 July 1851, James, Diary, p. 10; entry for 5 Aug. 1851, Luark, Diary, p . 53.

[4]Entry for 15 July 1850, Clapp, *Journal*, p. 39; entry for 15 July 1850, Murray, Journal, p. 79; entry for 31 July 1850, Dowell, Journal, p. 31.

[5]Entry for 27 Aug. 1850, Starr, Tour of West; entry for 13 Aug. 1864, Louisa Moeller Rahm, "Copy of Diary" (ts., Washington State Historical Society, Tacoma), p. 8.

[6]Entry for 24 May 1849, Burbank, Diary and Journal, p. 21; entry for 14 May 1852, C. L. Richardson, Journal, p. 28; entry for 31 May 1853, Handsaker, Journal, p. 7.

[7]Entry for 15 May 1853, Murray, Journal, p. 31.

[8]Marcus McMillan, "Reminiscences" (ms., University of Washington).

[9]Which did not have to involve starvation or jaded animals. When a minority of one company urged returning due to lack of grass in 1850, a member resolved, "I shall take a team and provisions enough to take me safely through or I am not my mother's son" (entry for 12 June 1850, Asa Call, "Diary" [ts., State Historical Society of Iowa, Iowa City]).

"If so," one wrote, "they will have to give us some food. If they do not, we will take it by force."[10]

A few emigrants openly spoke of robbery, a fact significant enough — perhaps *unusual* enough — to be noted by diarists.[11] "The oldest man in the mess," an Ohio physician traveling down the Humboldt in 1850 reported of a wagon camped near his, "is a pious old yankee, but he said he would buy as long as he could buy & then beg as long as he could beg, after that he would rob before he would starve."[12]

John Wood said much the same. "I have," he wrote while also on the Humboldt, "offered men two dollars a pound for flour and bacon, but no, they wouldn't take ten, they would see a man die first, and then they wouldn't. Well, I know one thing, very certain, we have some steers that will be chewed very fine, before we starve to death, and then some body's 'else' will have to die if we get hungry."[13]

We might surmise that all emigrants were making such statements, and maybe they were. Even if we could prove that they were, it would not do to make too much of the fact. Consider just what the "pious old yankee" said. Recalling the context in which he spoke it may be argued he was being moderate. It is one thing to claim that the law of survival gives you the right to steal, another that it gives the right to kill. Accepting the existence of "rampant lawlessness" on the American frontier, we might expect that many men would say that the threat of starvation morally (perhaps even legally) justified the use of violence to obtain provisions — at least from those who had a surplus.[14] Instead, the

---

[10]*The Overland Journey of Joseph Francl*, ed. Rose Rosický, introduction by Richard Brautigan (San Francisco: W. P. Wreden, 1968), p. 46.

[11]On the Humboldt in 1850, "I saw six men eat their last bite   one said the world owed him a living and he meant to have it   that he would not kill his horse after bringing him this far" (letter of 20 July 1850, Brouster, Letters).

[12]Entry for 5 July 1850, Parker, Notes.

[13]Entry for 24 Aug. 1850, J. Wood, *Journal*, p. 84.

[14]That was the attitude of one man with a surplus who was asked to sell even on the Forty-Mile Desert where a company "threatened rather hard, said that they should take

assertion that robbery — not homicide — may take precedence over the rights of property is so unusual, that one could read hundreds of overland diaries before finding assertions anywhere as bold as those of "the pious old yankee" or John Wood.

Only one report has been discovered of emigrants threatening to kill for property. As the potential victim came from outside the emigration, it may be another exception proving the rule. Two forty-niners on the southern trail had their horses taken by Indians near the Gila River. A member of their train with "4 or 5 spare animals" refused to sell any of them and there was no one else from whom to purchase. Most significantly, they apparently gave no thought to stealing from the man, instead deciding "to way lay the approaches to camp and to dismount the first Indians that came along to the extent of [an] animal each, even if it cost Indian life."[15] The plan was not executed, but the thought was there.

We know nothing more of the incident, only the account, as told by a third party, and it would be unwise to analyze it. Better to turn to those events in which force was actually employed, to the extent that a threat was made, to obtain property.[16] There are only four, of which three are worth considering as they are first-hand accounts, written by the perpetrator of the violence.[17]

---

provisions any how. One man said by God I won't starve. I should not have blamed them to have taken things by force from our wagon at least, for we might have spared something and bought again, as they say that there is plenty when we get across the desert" (entry for 30 Aug. 1850, McKinstry, *Diary*, p. 283).

[15]Harris, Account, p. 112.

[16]Threats may also have altered property ownership in an incident occurring in the Humboldt. "A company of packers encamped near us, and made a demand for provisions. On being told our own supplies were short, they said they knew better, that they were 'entirely out, and by God they must have some!' The matter was arranged by selling them a young heifer, which they were not long in butchering" (entry for 28 Aug. 1850, Bennett, *Overland Journey*, p. 40).

[17]The fourth is quite similar to one of these incidents. A Mormon had twenty-five head of fat cattle. "The starving emigrants offered him two hundred dollars for one ox. The Shylock refused to sell at any price . . . . [N]ext morning twenty-five starving men, with rifles in hand, walked into his little herd and killed the best ox they could find. (The author ate a piece of it). Then the Shylock offered to take one hundred dollars for the ox, but it was too late. He had played the wrong card" (Thissell, *Crossing the Plains*, p. 114).

In 1850, a physician from Missouri named William Allen was captain of an Oregon-bound train numbering about sixty wagons. For reasons that do not bear on property and law, the company became trapped in the Cascade Mountains and, before the harsh weather relented, lost between six and seven hundred head of cattle. Only a single bull remained for food when the snows began melting and

> A Frenchman came along with some Indians driving some very fat cattle, taking them from upon the Columbia, to Oregon City. I offered to purchase. He asked us as much as $200. for a beef. I told him we had not the money to pay — we were there   he could see our situation — everything was lost but ourselves and clothes —we had sent to the valley for assistance, but when we would get it we could not tell — all this talk got not beef. I talked to my men like this: "Gentlemen, God only knows when we will get out of these mountains. We may all perish; the snow falls here to the depth of two or three hundred feet; all egress or ingress may be cut off. In that event these cattle may save our lives. If you are willing to let perhaps the last chance slip of getting something to keep ourselves and children from perishing, you can do so, I am not. My advice is 'Boys to your guns. Surround that bunch of cattle; shoot down some of them; guard the balance until we see further.'" In one hour from that time my family had plenty of fat beef. The Frenchman "vanmoosed the ranche."[18]

Gilbert L. Cole was crossing the Forty-Mile Desert in 1852 when he came face to face with a situation that balanced his sense of desperation against his respect for the rights of a property owner.

> For the want of vegetables or acid of some kind, I had been troubled for a week or so with an attack of scurvy in my mouth, the gums being swollen because of the alkali dust. This not only caused me pain and misery, but created a strong and constant desire for something sour. While riding past an ox team I noticed a jug in front end of the wagon. Upon inquiry of the driver, I found the jug contained vinegar. I offered him a silver dollar for a cupful, but he

---

[18]W. R. Allen, Letter.

> refused to part with any of it, saying that he might need it himself before he got through. He was afoot on the off side of the wagon, where the jug was setting. I was sort of crazy mad and drawing my revolver, I rode around the rear of the wagon, thinking I would kill the fellow and take his jug of vinegar. But when he began to run for his life around the front yoke of cattle I came to my senses and hastened away from his outfit.[19]

The third quotation comes from Lassen's cutoff during 1849 and, with the exception of that of Allen, is probably the only first-person account that we have describing a taking of property that a lawyer might define as larceny. Oliver Goldsmith was packing with four companions. They were on foot and very hungry.

> One day we met an old man, driving a yoke of oxen with a heavy wagon load of provisions. We proposed buying some and he told us his price was two dollars a pound for everything we could eat. We remonstrated at such robbery, telling him he had more provisions than his team could possibly carry to the journey's end and that he would be sure to lose what he had. He said provisions were worth that in California. We told him he could never get there, that he would probably be snowed under trying to cross the Sierras, as it was so late. Then we offered him twenty-five cents a pound for provisions enough to last us (five men) two days, telling him we had had nothing to eat for twenty-four hours. He stuck to his price — two dollars a pound. After a consultation we decided we must make the most of the chance, as there was no knowing when we would have another opportunity of getting anything, so we marched up to him and said there were five of us to his one, and that we intended to take what we needed at our own price, twenty-five cents a pound, which we did. The old fellow looked a bit dazed, but merely remarked, "I guess you're all right."[20]

Too little should not be read from these accounts. The relatively restrained conduct of lawbreakers tells more than that unnecessary violence may not have been the norm on America's

---

[19]Cole, *Early Days*, p. 109.
[20]Goldsmith, *Overland*, pp. 68-69.

nineteenth-century frontier. Of course, the fact that both Cole and Goldsmith avoided excessive force (Cole drawing back when "I came to my senses") deserves emphasis. So too do the facts that all three men were willing to pay for provisions, that they offered to purchase before resorting to self help, and that Goldsmith and his companions paid one eighth the asking price or what they insisted was fair.

These facts tell something about how property rights were respected and private force legitimized on the overland trail, and even more besides. As significant as the actions of the lawbreakers were the expectations manifested by Allen and the victims of these acts of violence. Allen's words are unmistakable. His speech is premised on the assumption that, despite their desperate straits and overwhelming superiority in numbers, his men would hesitate to seize the beef of the Frenchman, that they had to be persuaded to do what was necessary to save their families. The same reckonings should explain why the Frenchman set an impossible price on cattle he did not want to sell. He failed to anticipate the violence it ignited. His arrogance and lack of caution may indicate he had no fear his property would be taken. Certainly we can draw that conclusion from the conduct of the other two victims. Both the owner of the vinegar jug on the Forty-Mile Desert and the old man with the wagon on Lassen's cutoff acted as they might have had they been in an eastern city surrounded by police protection. Indeed, if appearances can take the place of words, they thought that there was no need for police on the frontier. Look at their conduct and the expectations upon which that conduct was based. The two men owned property, they each received a reasonable offer for that property, yet each, asserting rights as an owner, rejected what was offered. Most revealing of all is the inference drawn from their conduct: they expected their adversaries to understand, acknowledge, and respect both their property rights and their right to dispose of their property as they saw fit, including the right to reject a reasonable offer from men who felt their survival might depend upon obtaining that property for themselves. The owners were taken by surprise when Cole and Goldsmith concluded that the situation was too desperate for normal behavior.

That Cole backed down, put away his gun, and rode off without the vinegar tells much about law-mindedness in nine-teenth-century America. That the man Cole might have killed did not anticipate violence reveals even more. He and the old man with the wagon were both on the American frontier, apparently unaware of the rampant lawlessness sometimes said to have characterized it. We may express surprise, even disbelief, but the implications of their conduct cannot be denied: they believed that respect for rights of personal ownership in property was a strong enough social or legal value on the overland trail to overcome panic, desperation, and the craving for survival.

III *Respect for Property Rights*

Our task once more is to measure that respect for property. Small incidents may hold more lessons than is sometimes thought. On Lassen's cutoff in 1849 two pairs of men were left behind by the onrushing tide. One pair, waiting for the means to bring in their wagons, saw some passing emigrants leave ailing oxen behind. Behaviorism that puts survival above abstractions would dictate that the men requisition discarded property for their own use. They did not do so until satisfied the animals were truly abandoned. "My Companion has asked several if we could have them if we get them to Grass & water. They all Readily gave answer in the affirmative."[1] A month and a half later the second brace was facing starvation when a third man arrived driving three oxen found in the mountains. He said he was keeping two and gave them the third — which "we might kill and eat." The men desperately needed food but doubts that the animal belonged to the granter produced a surprising legalism. Thinking "it might not be his," they "desired him to shoot [it] himself, which he done."[2] They then took the meat and ate it. Like the first

[1]Entry for 30 Sept. 1849, Pond, Journal.
[2]Entry for 19 Nov. 1849, Bruff, *Journals*, p. 645.

pair that sought permission before appropriating abandoned animals, they craved the property but were unwilling to accept it merely because they were in great need. The other man might kill it, they would not. The act of conversion was his, it was not theirs.

We might think the rights of property in these two cases so nebulous that desperate men would not hesitate to take what they needed. The individuals involved thought them clear and significant enough to command respect.

There is an important point yet to be noted about that respect. Evidence has been presented showing the extent to which emigrants understood the contemporary law of property. What has not been discussed is the fact that they generally were willing to accord an owner more control over his property than he would have enjoyed at common law. It is amazing how absolute they thought property rights were. A case in point was a man who started across the continent with several wagons. One he drove himself, the remainder he lent to other emigrants "with this understanding, that the teams and wagons were to be turned over to him as his property when they arrived at their destination." One wagon was taken by a family. The father became sick, the children were unable to walk, and the mother drove. The "owner," fearful the draft animals could not haul so much weight, decided to protect his property. Repossessing the wagon, he put out the family — man, woman, and children were left on the Oregon trail beyond Fort Boise.[3] By their comments it appears that other emigrants thought his conduct morally objectionable. But they did nothing except provide the family with alternative transportation, indicating they apparently thought it not legally wrong and therefore had to be tolerated.

Depending on the condition of the wagon, lawyers would have contended that the bailee had a contractual right to the wagon until reaching the place of delivery in Oregon, or at least an equitable right to its use until arriving at a place of safety. In the legal hierarchy of overland emigrants, personal ownership was so

[3]Entry for 23 Aug. 1852, Conyers, "Diary." See also entries for 3-4 Aug. 1849. J.A. Johnson, Note Book.

exclusive it nullified contract or equity principles that at common law modify property rights. That one man or company had more than necessary for survival while others were starving did not mean that the surplus belonged to the needy, not even if they were members of the same wagon train and traveling together. By the time the tiny emigration of 1841 reached the Humboldt, it had become a starvation march, rarely killing game, and forced to slaughter "an ox every two or three days."[4] The captain of the company, a man named Bartleson, wished to move faster than most of the party, "[b]ut his dependence was on the oxen for beef — for it was now all we had to live upon" and he could not travel faster than the owners.[5] When one of his mules broke a leg, "Bartleson agreed that we might kill him and eat him," also making the others "promise to pay him when we reached California."[6] Having sold on credit, Bartleson bought on credit. "Boys," he proposed one afternoon to the owners of the oxen, "our animals are much better than yours, and we always get out of meat before any of the rest of you. Let us have the most of the meat this time, and we will pay you back the next ox we kill."[7] Once Bartleson had possession of extra meat, he and his "mess" abandoned the company, riding off to the safety of California on their stronger mules.[8]

The key concept in the overland emigrants' definition of property was exclusive. Two men, one with a bad leg, might lose their horses and have to walk. They might propose to a companion that as "he had 4 or 5 spare animals to buy one each of him." Should he refuse they continued on foot.[9] If a group of men were starving they might have no recourse except to kill a horse,

---

[4]Entry for 18 Sept. 1841, Bidwell, *Journey*, p. 29; G. R. Stewart, *Trail*, p. 27.

[5]Entry for 5 Oct. 1841, Bidwell, *Journey*, p. 32.

[6]Dawson, *Narrative*, p. 24.

[7]Bidwell, *Echoes*, pp. 54-55.

[8]Entry for 7 Oct. 1841, Bidwell, *Journey*, p. 32.

[9]Harris, Account, p. 112.

but the owner, not the majority, made the decision. No custom of the trail or general expectation nullified the exclusiveness of personal rights.[10]

In 1849 many emigrants abandoned their wagons and took to packing, in the expectation they would be able to purchase provisions from the wagons.[11] This fact was well known along the trail, but made no difference. Even if every emigrant knew these expectations, they did not change the law of ownership: packers had no claim on wagon owners. In fact, some wagon owners thought the opposite, exercising exclusive property rights to the point of refusing to "sell to a *packer*, because as they said, packers could travel faster than they could."[12]

The point has been made before that even the most trying circumstances, such as the 1850 emigration along the Humboldt, did not alter property rights one iota: those starving had no equitable claims on the well supplied. There is much evidence from the perspective of property owners supporting this rule.[13] From the perspective of the victim there may be less, but it is more apodictic when we consider testimony such as that furnished by J. Goldsborough Bruff, a forty-niner left behind on Lassen's cutoff. When surplus food came into sight he did not think he had a right to convert it merely because he was hungry and the owner did not need it for survival. During October an Irishman drove by "with an ox-wagon, to the rear of which was attached a large hen-coop, full of *chickens* and *roosters*. And Pat swore by the '*howly mother of Moses*,' that he'd starve before he'd kill one of

---

[10]Ferguson, *Gold Fields*, pp. 66-67.

[11]Entry for 12 July 1849, Cross, "Journal," p. 133; entries for 13 and 20 Sept. 1849, Batchelder, Journal, pp. 76-77, 121; entry for 28 Aug. 1849, Mann, Portion, p. 22.

[12]Letter from J. L. Stephens to the *Marietta* (Ohio) *Intelligencer*, 6 Sept. 1849, T. D. Clark, "Appendix," p. 161.

[13]Entry for 6 July 1850, L. Sawyer, *Across the Plains*, pp. 85-86; entry for 7 July 1850, Clapp, *Journal*, p. 37; entries for 31 July and 5 Aug. 1850, Ingalls, *Journal*, pp. 39, 40; entry for 4 Sept. 1850, Bennett, *Overland Journey*, p. 42; letter from R. Luther Myrick to Thomas Myrick, 30 Dec. 1849, Myrick, *Letters*, p. 9.

'em: intending to make a grand speculation in California on them." Bruff was generous. "Success Pat!" he wrote in his journal.[14]

Two months later, when matters were desperate, a pair of oxen wandered up to Bruff's camp. They were, he knew, the property of a man named Roberts, also trapped in the mountains. The oxen were starving and useless for much except food, but past experience had taught Bruff that it would be futile to ask Roberts, a possessive man, if he would sell one. "[B]ut really," he observed, "I think the meat of their oxen would be better appropriated for our benefit, than left, as it will be, for the benefit of grizzlers and wolves. — Who will assuredly nab them to-night." Bruff had a gun but did not use it. "Roberts oxen are gone," he noted the next day, "doubtless devoured by this time."[15]

Respect for property did not mean respect for avaricious owners. It was rights, not persons, that were respected. Insistence on property rights could cause ill feeling and make one a social leper. It would not, however, make him a "criminal" in the sense that he had violated the rules of the trail. During one of the more perilous moments on the Death Valley route of 1849, a man named Hall either had the foresight or the luck to possess "plenty" of water but would not share it with any of his companions. "He even refused to give a lady some," one member of the party wrote. "He gave it to his oxen. Thereby plainly showing that He would rather see a man without water than his oxen."[15] The next day there was "Considerable ill feeling in camp owing to Mr. Hall on yesterday refusing to give a lady some water (which was very scarce during the travel over the 34 mile streach on which we were 36 hours without water) . . . . Mr. Hall was very much sensured by all in the train and left him no friends."[17]

---

[14]Entry for 13 Oct. 1849, Bruff, *Journals*, p. 218.

[15]Ibid., entries for 13-14 Dec. 1849, pp. 660-61.

[16]Entry for 9 Oct. 1849, Hoover, Diary.

[17]Entry for 9 Oct. 1849, Hoover, Revised Journal.

Hall may have been without friends but his exclusive possession of water was not disturbed, just as it had not been the day before. The thirsty people traveling with Hall surely outnumbered him and during a thirty-six hour ordeal must have been sorely tempted to seize the water, especially when he fed it to his oxen. They did not however, and the only plausible explanation is that the water was his property to dispose of as he saw fit.

It is important to emphasize the category of the property Hall "owned": it was nothing but ordinary water. That under the exacting circumstances of Death Valley, water could be individually owned and the owner's rights to water respected is as striking a fact as any skeptical socialist could demand. There can be no better evidence of exclusive possession. If, even with those conditions, water could be personally owned and denied to others, anything could be.

IV   A Representative Case

Perhaps it is not surprising that of the hundreds who have left accounts of the overland trail, only Oliver Goldsmith on Lassen's cutoff, Dr. Allen in the Cascade Mountains of the Oregon Territory, and a few emigrants who passed through Mexico admit that they appropriated property without the consent of the owner. Many others mention being desperately hungry. Indeed, they were certain that death awaited them beyond the next bend of the Humboldt River, but they do not admit that they stole to stay alive or that they thought of larceny as an alternative. One might suggest that had they been guilty of robbery they would have been ashamed to have mentioned the fact, even though they could have justified it. Perhaps so, but the fact that they were ashamed would have told us almost as much about attitudes toward property rights as does the fact that average overland emigrants beyond the restraint of organized law enforcement did not covet, they did not rob, they respected property.

We may be certain that robbery was not the norm on the overland trail, not by the word of middle-class, educated diary writers saying that they, themselves, honored their fellow citizens' possession of property personally owned. We may rather be certain when we realize that they do not say that others used violence to obtain property. They were not apprehensive of being robbed, and followed a behaviorism characterized by the assumption that people would buy, they would not take, and that if the owner did not wish to sell, the decision would be respected.

It is attitudes and behavior even more than words that reveal to us the conditions of what today is called "law and order" on the overland trail and later in the mining camps of California. It is well to read between the lines. Writers do not always mean what they say. James A. Payne, a forty-eight-year old Virginian who crossed the plains in 1850, was appalled at the amount of property being jettisoned at the crossing of the North Platte. "Not only wagons are thrown away," he wrote that night, "but guns, axes, bedclothes and sometimes mens clothings. When men begin to see starvation staring them in the face, property has no value."[1]

Payne was wrong. Property, even in the face of starvation, continued to have a value because it continued to be respected, as his own progress toward California was to prove. Payne's party was one of the first to run short of supplies — as early as Sublette's cutoff — and for a much longer time than most of his fellow travelers, Payne knew the fear of starvation and the anxiety of finding sufficient provisions. It was he, it should be recalled, who sat by the banks of the Humboldt squeezing water from his soggy bread, husbanding each crumb, and boasting that nothing but the taste had been lost. Yet desperate as Payne may have been when he writes of obtaining food, he refers only to the opportunity of buying, of purchasing what he and his companions need, not of resentment against those who possess more or hostility toward those who might be harboring a surplus. As much as the unexpected gift, the chance to buy gives him the feeling of release, the occasion for rejoicing.

---

[1]Entry for 12 June 1850, Payne, Account, p. 45.

7 July 1850 (near the junction of Sublette's cutoff and the Fort Hall road): "[W]e bought today, 18 pounds of flour and a man gave us a peck of beans, which is quite a treat. We are singing today."[2]

23 July 1850 (11th day on the Humboldt): "Fortune smiled upon us today and we found a man who sold us nine pounds of beef and we had beef soup for dinner but we are badly off for bread, having nothing in that line but a little dust, which did pretty well to pour in our soup; we have to eat it with a spoon anyhow."

26 July 1850 (at Humboldt Meadows): "Just after leaving camp we fell in with a clever fellow, and he sold us 20 pounds of flour for $20.00, and we guessed at the weight; but when it comes to starving money has no value."

31 July 1850 (on Carson River): "Our condition is a critical one. Our animals are all broken down and scarcely able to crawl along; provisions all gone; no money of consequences; 300 miles of desolate country yet to pass, and in that the snow mountains; it is almost enough to craze a fellow."

2 August 1850 (after crossing Carson Desert): "We ate our last meal yesterday for dinner, but today we bought three pounds of bacon for $3.75 and two pounds of sugar for $1.50. [S]o we shall have something to eat."

4 August 1850 (entering California): "He [a man met on the trail who had been in California for one year] showed me a ham that he bought yesterday, paying $37.50 for it. We have got so that very little answers our purpose and there is but little money amongst us."

7 August 1850 (in the Sierra Nevada): "This morning I fell in with a hunter who had killed a deer and he gave us half of it and I met a trader who sold me two pounds of potatoes for a dollar. We

---

[2]Payne's attitude is more typical than not. Emigrants out of supplies did not feel they were "owed" by others. Instead, they were grateful for gifts. Hungry on Lassen's cutoff, a forty-niner was given by a stranger "a half dozen crackers and some dry bread for which I offered to pay, but he would accept nothing. May he be recompensed with plenty of gold dust" (entry for 5 Sept. 1849, Benson, Forty Niner, p. 60).

had a stew-pot and made a dinner of venison and potatoes I shall never forget. I am sure it was the best dinner I ever had in my life. We have been living for the last three months on fat bacon and bread that had been hard tack, but we had packed it on our mules in sacks until there was not a piece bigger than your thumb nail, and a couple of weeks ago we had got that soaked in the river, and then had to eat the rest with a spoon as long as it lasted. We yet had a little tea but no sugar. You can imagine what a treat this was."

We need little imagination to know it was a treat. Payne had been worried about starvation at least since crossing today's Idaho. He had squeezed the alkali water of the Humboldt from his only supply of bread, begged his way across the desert, and willingly — indeed gratefully — paid prices that a year earlier would have astonished him. After reaching the safety of the diggings, Payne reflected on the experience: "We had undergone all kinds of hardships and danger, nearly starving at times, loosing our wagon 500 miles from our journeys end, and many times not two days provisions ahead and at the time we could see no possible way to get any unless we ate a mule."[3]

They "could see no possible way" of obtaining food unless they ate one of their pack animals. These words reveal the prevalent attitudes of emigrants who crossed the continent on the overland trail during 1849 and 1850 and determined the conditions of law and order in early California. Stealing and violence were not "possible" alternatives to starvation. Other emigrants wrote similar words, for that was the way the vast majority thought: the alternative to starvation was to purchase from property owners willing to sell.

Crossing the Forty-Mile Desert a year before Payne, two men lost an ox needed to pull their wagon. "[W]e thought ourselves fortunate in getting another in his place," one of them wrote, even though "we paid a fair price."[4] On the southern section of the overland route during 1849, at the Gila River beyond Tucson, an

---

[3]Payne, Account, p. 97.

[4]Entry for 6 Sept. 1849, Dundass, *Journal*, p. 51.

emigrant took what he called the "last" expedient. "Having been a little improvident on the road, I had not a dollar left on reaching this place — and having to recuperate our stock of provisions a little, I was forced to the last expedient — that of selling a part of my outfit — a Pistol Blanket and Shirt was all that I sacrificed."[5] A month later on Lassen's cutoff, the northernmost section of the route to California, hundreds of starving stragglers were asking the same questions: "The great enquiry, here, by the Emmigrant is *'how far is it to Lassen's?' 'Has Lassen flour to sell?' 'What does he charge?' (or ax) for it?'* &c."[6]

In their words we see their attitudes reflected. There was no "possible" alternative to purchasing what they needed. When they were able to buy, even at high prices, they were "fortunate." The "last expedient" was not stealing, it was the sale of their property to get funds that would persuade someone to sell them food. And as they neared the end of the trail, they did not ask if there was food ahead. They asked whether there was food for sale at prices they could afford.

v *Conclusion*

On the lawless nineteenth-century American frontier, we are told, "laws were . . . made on the spot in response to the needs of the settlers."[1] Legal historians have been hard pressed to find such laws. It is only in the area of property and property rights that changes are discernible, and these are limited. Except for definitions of possession and rules governing exclusive control of minerals, water, and open range, the law of the east was the law of the west. The concept of private property remained largely inviolable, even when conditions were trying and people desperate.

If there was any part of the western frontier where we might not expect to find eastern law, it should be the overland trail, the place where there was no legal machinery and individuals told

[5]Cox, "Diary," pp. 145-46.
[6]Entry for 23 Oct. 1849, Bruff, *Journals*, p. 238.
[1]Gough, "British Columbia," p. 280.

themselves, "there is no law." Yet there was not only law, it was a law hardly distinguishable from the law emigrants thought they were leaving behind.

In a superficial study of the nineteenth-century bar, Perry Miller concluded that the American legal mentality is a triumph of mind over heart.[2] True, Miller was engaged in the historian's sport of sneering at lawyers, yet what he said should not be dismissed out of hand. The dichotomy of mind against heart is useful shorthand, reminding us that for law to be law it must be more than equity. Had Miller looked at evidence from the overland trail, he might have been less flippant. So far as property is concerned, if the actions and attitudes of emigrants prove anything, it is that the legal mind of the nineteenth-century American bar had more heart than the legal mind of America's nineteenth-century laity. The supposedly heartless mind of law was more evident on the overland trail than in any eastern courtroom. Losses fell upon "owners" who incurred them. If draft animals failed, even families had to pack,[3] and if they strayed, were killed, or stolen, the owners were to be "pitied,"[4] not accorded rights or shares to oxen and mules possessed by other emigrants. Those suffering the loss knew they had to hire passage[5] or "work our way through, or work for our board untill we get through."[6]

Of course such people were not left behind if they lacked money, or being women, children, or infirm could not work their way. But when young men donated their wagons to families[7] or

---

[2]Perry Miller, *The Life of the Mind in America* (New York: Harcourt, Brace & World, 1965).

[3]Even in the earliest, smallest, and most perilous of emigrations. See entry for 12 Sept. 1841, Bidwell, *Journey*, p. 27.

[4]Entry for 1 June 1849, Hackney, "Journal," pp. 136-37.

[5]"[T]he thought of our teams being gone struck terror in some of our minds. Then several talked of giving five hundred dollars for some one to take them on" (J. N. Jones, Journal, p. 12).

[6]Entry for 12 Aug. 1862, Clough,, Diary, p. 153.

[7]Entry for 31 Aug. 1849, A. Delano, *Across the Plains*, p. 92, and see also p. 103; *Overland in 1849: From Missouri to California by the Platte River and the Salt Lake Trail; an*

emigrants took up collections to aid the needy,[8] they were not motivated by legal obligation but by a sense of duty to "our fellow men [which] forbade us leave them in a destitute condition."[9]

We may grant that in most cases, the heart was dominant on the overland trail, without agreeing with Miller that the triumph of heart rescues law from crass professionalism. When describing actions of the heart, overland emigrants betrayed a legal mind that would have done justice to any eastern lawyer. People in need were said to depend "on the charity of those who have means,"[10] or "upon the charities of those who have provisions for food to sustain life."[11] Ownership remained the salient concept, and it was for the "owners" to decide who received relief and who was refused. "There is a considerable amount of suffering on the road," an 1850 emigrant wrote when about halfway down the Humboldt River. "In most cases we have given a little but our own supplies are running short and hereafter we have determined to extend relief only in extreme cases of suffering."[12]

When speaking of "charity" in the context of property, ownership, gift, and acceptance, emigrants were doing more than borrowing the terms of law. They were, in fact, discussing law. A pattern of behavior based on mutual expectations concerning duties and rights may as accurately be labeled "legal" behavior as may behavior dictated by fear of police enforcement. What their words and conduct tell us is that for nineteenth-century Americans the definition of binding "law," vesting rights and imposing obligations, was not limited to a command or set of commands from the "sovereign" backed by threats or by force.

Account from the Letters of G. C. Pearson, ed. Jessie H. Goodman (Los Angeles: 1961), p. 42.

[8]Entry for 13 July 1859, Wilkinson, Journal.

[9]Entry for 13 Aug. 1850, Starr, Tour of West.

[10]Entry for 14 July 1849, Farnham, Gold Rush, p. 16.

[11]Entry for 13 Aug. 1850, A. Brown, "Journal," p. 26.

[12]Entry for 1 Sept. 1850, Bennett, *Overland Journey*, p. 41.

Nor was "law" some abstraction discovered or justified by appealing to "natural" or universal rules of ideal deportment. Law was the taught, learned, accepted customs of a people.

Loose concepts must not be used too loosely. The "custom" guiding emigrants on the overland trail must not be confused with the classic custom of primitive jurisprudence. It was not the law of the folk — of kinship or blood vengeance —existing in societies before government can command adherence to legislated standards. Rather it was the expression of an agrestic, community-centered world we have lost, a custom bottomed on the sovereign's law, learned by living in a coercive state, and instilled into the marrow of social behavior.

Avoiding one mistake must not mislead us to another. To dismiss the custom of the folk does not mean we should think of the custom of the trail. By using the word "custom" in a nonlegal sense, a forty-niner warned us not to ask why overland emigrants did not spin a more sui generis course. "Everything," she explained, "was at first weird and strange in those days, but custom made us regard the most unnatural events as usual."[13]

The problem was not that the overland emigrants were constantly on the move, but where they were moving and how. We may admit that like merchant seamen they were a floating population, separated from social roots and apprehensive of facing some of nature's most fearful perils. But even a mariner who changed ships at every port could anticipate encountering familiar customary behavior aboard each vessel and shared with the men among whom he was in contact a common profession. The overland emigrant was trudging a path he might never walk again, for which he had no preparation, and was in the company of people with whom he shared little except language, nationality, some common background, and law. They met, associated, broke up, and passed on down the trail, never to meet again.

---

[13]Luzena Stanley Wilson, *'49er: Memories Recalled Years Later for Her Daughter Correnah Wilson Wright* (Mills College, Calif.: The Eucalyptus Press, 1937), p. 5.

These were not conditions permitting action to become habit, habit to become usage, usage to become custom, and custom to become law.

The emigrants did not have the time to let the new evolve from the old. They could not be guided by the custom of the trail for there was no trail custom. They had little choice but to do what they in fact did do. They turned to the law of the eastern states, the law they thought they had left on the banks of the Missouri River but which they had, in truth, carried with them across the plains, over the mountains, and onto the desert.

When the Boston-Newton Company was about to leave Massachusetts and head west for the gold fields of the Sierras, Edward Everett gave its members some advice. "Take the Bible in one hand," he said, "and your New England civilization in the other and make your mark on that country."[14]

Everett assumed that out on an untamed frontier beyond the restraining influence of church and family life, the young men of Massachusetts would establish a stable society should they adhere to the moral principles of their Christian faith. To a remarkable extent they did. New England civilization was replanted in more arid soil. Yet it may well be wondered if the morality they and their fellow emigrants carried with them was only the morality taught by organized religion. There was also the morality instilled in them by the standards of legal conduct they had observed in the communities of their youth.

Few emigrants traveling the overland trail to the Pacific coast could have explained the meaning of "words of purchase" or fee simple absolute, yet all understood and a vast majority respected the legal principles vesting in the individual exclusive enjoyment of property lawfully possessed. The overland travelers of 1849 and 1850 had been taught the lesson of the Good Samaritan and knew of Jesus' injunction to love their neighbors as they loved themselves. They might have interpreted the tenets of their faith to mean that no one should be allowed to hoard a surplus of

---

[14]Hannon, "Introduction and Notes," p. xv.

provisions unless paid a high price to part voluntarily with what was not needed for survival. Instead, they respected the rights of property owners much as if still back east in the midst of plenty. By respect for their neighbor and their neighbor's property they were, more often than not, adhering to a morality of law.

One Emigrant's Personal Property Priorities. *"Get up at sunrise. Set my watch, fix* my *pants eat* MY *breakfast. Look at* MY *steers and drive in* MY *Bull 'Perry'* . . .

Acknowledgments

Researching a book on the overland trail entails many overland journeys, each accumulating a set of overland debts. For hospitality enjoyed while on the road, a sincere word of appreciation is due to Mr. and Mrs. Robert J. Beckmann, of Lake Forest, Illinois, Professor and Mrs. Robert Popper, of the School of Law, University of Missouri-Kansas City, Dr. and Mrs. William D. Walsh, of Woodside and Atherton, California, and Professor Gerald Gunther and Dean J. Keith Mann, of Stanford Law School. Invaluable, professional, and courteous assistance was rendered by librarians, too numerous to mention, extending along the overland trail from Archibald Hanna on the Atlantic to Mary Wright on the Pacific. The formulation and presentation of concept owes an immeasurable debt to Winifred Freese of *The Huntington Library Quarterly*, Priscilla Knuth of the *Oregon Historical Quarterly*, William E. Nelson of *The American Journal of Legal History*, and the student editors of *The Hastings Law Journal, UMKC Law Review, Brigham Young University Law Review, Creighton Law Review, University of Puget Sound Law Review*, and *Hastings Constitutional Law Quarterly*. Special thanks are due to Professor Sandra Myres for sharing her elephants, to Martha Webb for bearing the burden, to Betty Leigh Merrell for her guidance, and to Carol Pearson and Robert Bouchard for "C & S." The last two are responsible for any errors. It was Gerhard O. W. Mueller who called to my attention the important contribution made to overland historiography by Franklin Pierce. Finally mention must be made of Ray Allen Billington and the Honorable Martin Ridge. Their contribution was not substantive but adjective, symbolic yet no less real. Any historian, starting from New Hampshire and traveling mile after weary mile across the overland trail, who arrives in California and encounters those two polymaths strolling in their gardens, knows, at last, that he has seen the elephant.

JOHN PHILLIP REID

Copyright Acknowledgment

The author is grateful to the following libraries for permission to quote from the works listed below.

The Bancroft Library, University of California, Berkeley: "Diary of Ellen Tompkins Adams" (ms., photostat); Henry Sheldon Anable, "Journal Kept by H.S. Anable While on the "plains" in 1852" (ms., C-F 137:1); Henry Sheldon Anable, 'Journal' [Rewritten from original Journal with additions to 1854"] (ms., C-F 137:2); Henry Austin, "1849 Diary of Henry Austin" (ms. photocopy, C-F 157); James Bardin, "A Diary of a Pioneer 1855" (ts., C-F 229); Amos Batchelder, "Journal of a Tour Across the Continent of N. American in 1849" (ms., C-B 614); Ezra Bourne, "Diary of an Overland Journey to California in 1850" (ts., C-F 142); Sandy Bradford, "Letters" (ms., 69134c); Jerry Berry Brown, "Journal of a Journey Across the Plains in 1859" (ms., 69177c); W.W. Call, "Overland Journey" (ms., C-D 5178); James H. Compton, "Diary" (ms., C-F 224); W. Scott Ebey, "Diary" (ms., P-B 217); Mary C. Fish, "Daily Journal Written During An Overland Journey to California" (ms., C-F 140); Isaac Julian Harvey, "To California in 1850" (ms., C-D 5091A); "Diary of Benj. Hayes' Journey overland from Socorro to Warner's Ranch from Oct. 31, 1849 to Jan. 14, 1850" (ms.); Charles Hentz, "Correspondence with his Mother" (ts., C-B 704); "Diary of H. Hoth [Tage Buch von H. Hoth aus Schleswig, 1854]" (ts., translation, C-F 67); Elijah Preston Howell, "Crossing the Plains" (ts., C-F 121); "Journal of George E. Jewett, 1849" (ts., C-F 20); "Journal of Charles A. Kirkpatrick 1849" (ms., C-D 207); S.A. Lane, "Diary of Trip Overland From Akron, Ohio to Sacramento" (ms. photostat); Horace Barton Pomroy, "Diary" (photostat, C-F 128); J.W. Powell, "Book to California" (ts., C-F 127); Niles Searles, "Diary" (ms.); Jacob Stitzel, "Overland Diary, March 20 - Aug. 26, 1849"

367

(ms., microfilm 66-6800); Dr. T., "Journal of his Experiences Crossing the Plains in 1849," (ms., C-B 383:1); "Journal of Albert King Thurber" (ts.); John M. Verdenal, "Journal Across the Plains 1852" (ts.); "The Letters of Epaphroditus Wells of Downers Grove, Illinois, to his Wife Emma B. Wells Written from April 1st 1849 to September 29, 1851, Concerning his Overland Journey to California and his Experiences While There" (ts., C-B 731A). Quoted by permission of The Bancroft Library.

The Beinecke Rare Book and Manuscript Library, Yale University: D.B. Andrews, "Journal of an Overland Journey From Indiana to California, March 30 to August 16, 1852" (ms., Western Americana Collection #4); "Diary of P[hilip] F. Castleman While Crossing the Plains to Calfornia Commencing from the time he left St. Joseph, Mo., With a Seeth of his trip from home which was in Larve, Co. Ky to St. Joseph, Mo." (ms., Western Americana Collection); Simon Doyle, "Journal and Letters of Simon Doyle" (ms., Western Americana Collection #144); "Note Book of John A. Johnson During his Voyage to & Residence in California" (ms., Western Americana Collection); Thomas Cotton Lewis, "Memorandum or Notes" of Thos. C. Lewis & Son (ms., Western Americana Collection #302); Alexander Love, "Diary of an Overland Journey From Leesburg, Pennsylvania . . . March 20 to August 23, 1849" (ms. Western Americana Collection #309); Letters of Leonard Mason (ms., Western Americana Collection #333); Letter from Charles G. Moxley to Emily Moxley (ms., Western Americana Collection #712); "Journal of Silas Newcomb of Madison, Wisconsin, 1 April 1850 to 31 March 1851" (ms., Western Americana Collection #359).

California Historical Society, San Francisco: Anonymous, "The Diary of an Unknown Scout Accompanying a Company of Covered Wagon Emigrants from St. Joseph, Missouri, to California, May 2, 1852" (ts.); Joseph Newton Burroughs, "Reminiscences of 1856 Overland Journey," (typescript, 1911); David Cosad, "Journal of a Trip to California by the Overland Route and Life in the Gold Diggings During 1849-1850" (ms.); "Diary Kept by J[ames] S. Cowden on his Trip 'Overland' from Iowa to Cal. in

1853 with Ox Teams and Wagons" (ms. photostat); Eliza Ann McAuley [Egbert], "Mother's Diary: The Record of a Journey Across the Plains in '52" (ts.); "Diary of William H. Hampton 1852" (ts.); "Diary of Jasper Morris Hixson May 1 - August 6, 1849" (ts.); D. Jagger, "Journal: 1846-1850" (ms.); Edward M. Lewis, "My Route from New York to the West 1865" (ms.); "Letters of John M. Muscott to Ebenezer Robbins published in the *Rome [New York] Sentinel*" (ts.); C. W. Smith, "Journal of a Trip to California Across the Continent From Weston, Mo. to Weber Creek, Cal. In the Summer of 1850" (ms.).

Society of California Pioneers, San Francisco: "Copy of the Diary of Marcellus Bixby from 1852 to 1856 Kept by Him During His Trip with His Brother Jotham Bixby, from Maine to California, and their Residence in Amador County" (ts., photocopy).

California State Library, Sacramento: "Diary of J.C. Buffum 1847-1854" (ms.); N.A. Cagivin, "Diary" (ms.); Mrs. James Caples, "Overland Journey to the Coast" (ts.); William E. Chamberlain, "Diary" (ms.); "Diary of John Clifton, A 49'er: March 17, 1849 - November 28, 1852" (ts.); Jared Fox, "Memorandum of a Trip from Dalton, Sauk County, Wisconsin to Oregon and California April 12, 1852 - Aug. 12, 1854 (copied from the original by Ruth Grimshaw Martin)" (ts.); Andrew Hall Gilmore, "Overland Journey to California March 12 - September 9, 1850; together with miscellaneous accounts, October 15, 1850 - January 1, 1853" (ts.); O.J. Hall, "Diary of Forty Niner" (ts.); Amos P. Josselyn, "Journal" (ts.); "Excerpts from the Journal of Seth Lewelling, March 23, 1850 - Sept. 10, 1852" (ts.); Micajah Littleton, "Journal of a Trip across the Plains From Independence, Missouri to California May 11, 1850 - October 11, 1850" (ts.); "Copy of Judge Charles F. Lotts [sic] Diary of his Overland Trip from Quincy, Illinois May 1 - 1849. Arrived at Long Bar, California Oct. 3 -1849" (ts.); Cyrus C. Loveland, "Diary Written While Crossing the Plains in 1850 with a Drove of Cattle" (ms.); "Diary of A[ndrew] S. McClure of the Journey Across the Plains May 7 - October 15, 1853" (ts.); Alexander B. Nixon, "Journal to the Pacific Ocean" (ms., two volumes); James A. Payne, "Saint Louis to San Francisco: Being an Account of a Journey Across the Plains in 1850, Together with My Experience in Steamboating on the California Rivers Until the Fall of 1853" (edited by his son, 1895, mimeograph copy); "Copy of the Letters and Journal of Henry Atkinson Stine on his Overland Trip to California from St. Louis to Sacramento May 4, 1850 to October 25, 1859" (ts.); John C. Thorniley, "Diary of Overland Journey in 1852" (ms.); "Diary of J[ames] S. Tolles: Trip to California, April - August 2, 1849, and Experiences in California, February - April 8, 1850" (ms.); William Zilhart, "Diary, April 1853 - October 1853" (ts.).

Chicago Historical Society, Chicago: J. McGlashan, "Journal" (ts.).

William L. Clements Library, The University of Michigan, Ann Arbor: "Amos P. Bradbury Papers" (ms.).

Dartmouth College Library, Hanover: Joshua D. Breyfogle, "Diary" (ms.).

Eastern Washington State Historical Society, Spokane: Benjamin Burgainder, "Reminiscences of Benjamin (Ben) Burgainder About 1916" (ts.); Andrew Jackson Griffith, "Hancock County, Illinois to California in 1850. The Diary of Dr. Andrew Jackson Griffith" (ts.).

Huntington Library, San Marino: Mary Stuart Bailey, "A Journal of the Trip from Ohio to Cal[ifornia] (1852)" (ms., HM 2018); Robet Beeching, "Journal of R. Beeching" (ms., HM 17430); "Journey from Indiana to Oregon - Journal of George Belshaw, March 23 to September 27, 1853" (ts., HM 16765); Helen McCowen Carpenter, "A Trip Across the Plains in Ox Wagon, 1857" (ts., HM 16994); Lorenzo Dow Chillson, "Diary" (ms., HM 4293); Addison M. Crane, "Journal of a Trip Across the Plains in 1852" (ms., HM 19333); Juliett J. Fish, "Crossing the Plains in 1862," (ts., uncatalogued facsimile); Solmon A. Gorgas, "Diary" (ms., HM 651); "Overland Letters from Solmon A. Gorgas to Mary Francis Gorgas" (ms., HM 2183); Samuel Handsaker, "Journal of an Overland Trip to Orgeon" (ts., Fac. 590); Benjamin Butler Harris, "Account of a Journey from Panolo Co., Texas, to the Gold Mines, by way of Chihuahua and Sonora Mar. 25 to

Sept. 29, 1849" (ms., HM 17477, vol. 1); Joseph H. Johnson, "Diary of a Journey to California 1849" (ms., HM 19480); Israel Shipman Pelton Lord, "Journal of 1849 [composed partly of clippings entitled, "California Correspondence" written by Dr. Lord for *The Western Christian,* Elgin, Kane County, Illinois] (ms., HM 19408); William S. McBride, "Diary" (ms., HM 16956); "Western Journal of George McCowen" (ts., HM 16756); George McCowen, "Notes of a Journey Across the Plains" (ts., HM 16756); David Swinson Maynard, "Daily Pocket Diary for 1850" (ms., HM 997); Charles R. Parke, "Notes Crossing the Plains" (ms., HM 16996); William Tell Parker, "Notes By the Way" (ms., HM 30873); Elisha Douglass Perkins, "Sketches of a Trip from Marietta Ohio to the Valley of the Sacramento in Spring & Summer of 1849" (ms., HM 1547); Ananias P. Pond, "Leger and Journal" (ms., HM 19383); Lydia A. Rudd, "Notes by the Wayside Enroute to Oregon" (ms., HM 27517); Harlon Chittenden Thompson, "Across the Continent on Foot in 1859" (ts., HM 16298); John Pratt Welsh, "Diaries" [Volume 1, Overland in 1851; Volume 2, Overland in 1853] (ms., HM 30628); Lucian McClenathan Wolcott, "Journal of an Overland Trip in 1850 and Mining Near Coloma" (photocopy, HM 26614).

State Historical Society of Iowa, Iowa City: Richard A. Keen, "Diary of a Trip to California" (ts.).

Kansas State Historical Society, Topeka: Henry Shombre, "Diary" (ms.); Letter from John F. Synder, 22 May 1850 (photostat); "Diary of E. A. Spooner 1849-1850" (microfilm).

Division of Archives and Manuscripts, Minnesota Historical Society, St. Paul: Stillman Churchill, "Journal of Incidents and Travels to California" (ts.).

Missouri Historical Society, St. Louis: Letter from Dabney T. Carr to G.C. Broadhead, 31 May 1850 (ms. copy, "Western Travel Envelope"); Correspondence from William H. Dulany to his wife Susan Dulany, William H. Dulany Papers (ms.); John H. Gundlach, Minutes of my trip to California (ms.); "Wm. Lampton's Diary, Or Trip to California in 1850" (ts., "Western Travel Papers"); "Copies of Letters written by Hunt, Quincy, s and d, etc. to

St. Louis Weekly Reveille" (ts.); G.A. Smith, "Diary" (ms., "Western Travel Papers"); Letter from James Tate to Major Daniel Nolley, 1 July 1849 (ts.); "Typed copy of the diary of John Wesley Yeargain, en route to Oregon" (ts.).

Joint Collection, University of Missouri, Western Historical Manuscript Collection - Columbia, State Historical Society of Missouri Manuscripts: "Letter from William R. Allen to his brother, 4 May 1851 (ts., #545); "Letters of Dr. Samuel Matthias Ayres to Priscilla Frances Ayres" (ts., #995, vol. xxix-760); Letter from George Washington Brouster to his Parents (ms., #1832); Letter from James W. Evans to Ellis G. Evans, 27 October 1850 (ms., #1872); Elijah Preston Howell, "Diary" (ms., #1675); John Hudgins, "California in 1849" (ts., mimeographed, #2189); Carlton Jones, "Diary" (photostat, #348); G.S. Kunkel "memoirs (ts., #463); Ashley Lea, "Letters" (ms., #354); Hugh McCanne, "Diary" (ms., #1932); "Diary of Joseph Henry Merrill of a Trip to California with His Father When he was About Eighteen Years Old [1849]" (mimeograph); Letter from Samuel Craig Plummer to his wife, 30 April 1850 (ts., #2750); John A. Stauder, "Duplicate Memorandum [sic] of Travels from Lagrange Lewis County, Missouri to California" (ts., #459); Letter from Joseph A. Summers to hs Wife, 30 October 1850 (ts., #2746); Henry Wallenkamp, "Diary of a Trip to California" (ts.).

Nebraska State Historical Society, Lincoln: John H. Benson, "Forty Niner: From St. Joseph to Sacramento" (ts.); Eliphalet Crandall, "Diary" (ms.).

The Newberry Library, Chicago: "Diary of the Overland Trail 1849 and Letters 1849-50 of Captain David Dewolf (ts.); J.A. Wilkinson, "Journal: Across the Plains in 1859" (ms.). Courtesy of the Edward E. Ayer Collection, The Newberry Library, Chicago.

Oregon Historical Society, Portland: Harriett T. Buckingham [Clarke], "Overland Diary of Harriet T. [Buckingham] Clarke -1851" (ts., 1156); Harriette Talcott Buckingham, "Diary" (ms., 1156); Aaron Clough "Diary of Overland Journey to Oregon, May 15 - December 15, 1862" (ms., microfilm); Philip Condit, "Copy [of] Diary of Philip Condit 1854" (ms., 922); William

Cornell, "Description of the route to Oregon" (ms., 290); J.C. Coupler, "Crossing the Plains from St. Joseph, Mo. to San Francisco (ts., 1508); Benjamin Franklin Dowell, "Copy of his Journal (ms., 209); William Hanna, "The Journal of Wm. Hanna 1850" (ts., 693); Samuel James, "Diary" (ts., 1508); William Kahler, "Leaves from the Diary of Mr. Kahler, from McConnellsville, Ohio to Jackson County Oregon" (ms., 1508); Robert Robe, "Diary of Rev.Robert Robe 1851" (ts., 1163); John S. Zieber, "Diary of John S. Zieber" (ts., 1508).

Oregon Collection, University of Oregon, Eugene: Augustus Ripley Burbank, "Diary and Journal of a trip to California by overland (ts., copy 2); Emelia H. Hadley, "Journal to Oregon of Travails" (ts.).

The Holt-Atherton Pacific Center for Western Studies, University of the Pacific, Stockton: [D. Lambert Fouts?], "Diary" (ms., 2 F782).

Princeton University Library, Princeton: "Journal kept by Mrs. E[lizabeth] J. Goltra during her overland journey from Missouri *via* South Pass and the Boise Crossing of Snake River to Oregon in 1853" (ts.); "Dexter P. Hosley's Journal from Saint Joseph's to California by the Overland *Route*" (ms.); Lezerne Humphrey, "Manuscript Journal 1852" (ms.); Patrick H. McLeod, "1849, Going to California" (ms.); Patrick H. McLeod, "Note Books" [unbound note books numbered "1," "2," "3," "4," and "5"] (ms.); "Letters of Erasmus N. Taylor and John W. Taylor, written to their families from Placerville" (ms.); "M.A. Violette Day Book 1849" (ts.).

Manuscripts Division, Department of Special Collections, C.H. Green Library, Stanford University: Angus McQueen, "Diary" (ts.).

Archives and Manuscripts Division, Suzzallo Library, University of Washington, Seattle: Winfield Scott Ebey, "Diary" (ms., P-B 217); Anna Maria Goodell, "Diary of Anna Maria Goodell Crossing the Plains in 1854" (ts.); Amelia Knight, Journal kept on the road from Iowa to Oregon (ms., 256); John Murray, "Journal of a Trip to California or Oregon" (ts.).

Western Pennsylvania Historical Society, Pittsburgh: "The Diary of Bernard J. Reid, Esq., Written by him during his journey Overland to California in '49" (ts.).

State Historical Society of Wisconsin, Madison: Davis Brainard, "Journal of the Walworth County Mutual Mining Company, Commencing March the 20th, 1849" (ts.); "Samuel Chadwicks Travels to California in 1852" (ms.); "Diary of John Dalton, 1852 (ts.); John Grindell, "Sketch Book of the Travails from Platteville, Wisconsin to California" (ms.); "Diaries of E. Kitchell," (ts. and microfilm); "William Turner's Diary" (ts.).

Short-Title List

ABBEY, *A Trip.* James Abbey, *California: A Trip across the Plains, in the Spring of 1850* (New Albany, Ind.: Kent & Norman, and J. R. Nunemacher, 1850), reprinted in *The Magazine of History with Notes and Queries,* extra number 183, 46 (1933): 105-63.

ABBOTT, *Recollections.* Carlisle S. Abbott, *Recollections of a California Pioneer* (New York: The Neale Publishing Co., 1917).

ADAMS, C. E. M., "Crossing the Plains." Cecelia Emily McMillen Adams, "Crossing the Plains in 1852," *Transactions of the Thirty-Second Annual Reunion of the Oregon Pioneer Association for 1904* (Portland, Ore.: Peaslee Bros., 1905). pp. 288-329.

ADAMS, E. T., Diary. "Diary of Ellen Tompkins Adams" (ms., photostat, Bancroft Library).

ALLEN, Letter. "Letter from William R. Allen to His Brother, 4 May 1851" (ts., 545, 29:760, Joint Collection, University of Missouri, Western Historical Manuscript Collection — Columbia: State Historical Society of Missouri Manuscripts).

ALLYN, "Journal." "Journal of Henry Allyn, 1853," *Transactions of the Forty-Ninth Annual Reunion of the Oregon Pioneer Association* (Portland: Chausse-Prudhomme Co., 1924),pp. 372- 435.

ANABLE, Journal. Henry Sheldon Anable, "Journal Kept by II. S. Anable while on the 'Plains' in 1852" (ms., C-F 137:1, Bancroft Library).

ANABLE, Second Journal. Henry Sheldon Anable, "Journal" [rewritten from original Journal with additions to 1854] (ms., C-F 137: 2, Bancroft Library).

ANDREWS, Journal. D. B. Andrews, "Journal of an Overland Journey from Indiana to California, March 30 to August 16, 1852" (ms., Western Americana Collection 4, Beinecke Library).

375

ANON., Diary. Anonymous, "The Diary of an Unknown Scout Accompanying a Company of Covered Wagon Emigrants from St. Joseph, Missouri, to California, May 2, 1852" (ts., California Historical Society, San Francisco).

APPLEGATE, "Cow Column." Jesse Applegate, "A Day with the Cow Column," reprinted in *The Frontier Experience*, ed. Robert V. Hine and Edwin R. Bingham (Belmont, Calif.: Wadsworth Publishing Co., 1963), pp. 98-103.

ARMSTRONG, "Diary." J. Elza Armstrong, "Diary," in *Rovers*, ed. Howard L. Scamehorn.

ATHEARN, "Log Book." "The Log Book of P. A. Athearn," *The Pacific Historian*, 2 (1958): 6-7 (no. 2), 13-16 (no. 3), 9-12 (no. 4); 3 (1959): 21-23 (no. 1), 39-42 (no. 2).

AUDUBON, "Overland." John W. Audubon, "Overland by the Mexican Border Route," in *Course of Empire*, ed. Valeska Bari, pp. 98-130.

AUSTIN, Diary. Henry Austin, "1849 Diary of Henry Austin" (ms., photocopy, C-F 157, Bancroft Library).

AYRES, Letters. "Letters of Dr. Samuel Matthias Ayres to Priscilla Frances Ayres" (ts., 995, vol. 29:760, Joint Collection, University of Missouri, Western Historical Manuscript Collection — Columbia: State Historical Society of Missouri Manuscripts).

BAILEY, Trip. Mary Stuart Bailey, "A Journal of the Trip from Ohio to Cal[ifornia] (1852)" (ms., HM 2018, Huntington Library).

BANKS, "Diary." John Edwin Banks, "Diary," in *Rovers*, ed. Howard L. Scamehorn.

BARDIN, Diary. James Bardin, "A Diary of a Pioneer, 1855" (ts., C-F 229, Bancroft Library).

BATCHELDER, Journal. Amos Batchelder, "Journal of a Tour across the Continent of N. America in 1849" (ms., C-B 614, Bancroft Library).

BEECHING, Journal. Robert Beeching, "Journal of R. Beeching" (ms., HM 17430, Huntington Library).

BELSHAW, Journey. "Journey from Indiana to Oregon — Journal of George Belshaw, March 23 to September 27, 1853" (ts., HM 16765, Huntington Library).

BENNETT, *Overland Journey*. *Overland Journey to California: Journal of James Bennett Whose Party Left New Harmony in 1850 and Crossed the Plains and Mountains until the Golden West Was Reached* (New Harmony, Ind.: New Harmony Times, 1906).

BENSON, Forty Niner. John II. Benson, "Forty Niner: From St. Joseph to Sacramento" (ts., Nebraska State Historical Society, Lincoln).

BERRIEN, "Diary." "Overland from St. Louis to the California Gold Field in 1849: The Diary of Joseph Waring Berrien," ed. Ted and Caryl Hinckley, *Indiana Magazine of History*, 56 (1960): 273-352.

BILLACH, *Letters*. Russell E. Bidlach, *Letters Home: The Story of Ann Arbor's Forty-Niners* (Ann Arbor, Mich.: Ann Arbor Publishers, 1960).

BIDWELL, *Echoes*. John Bidwell, *Echoes of the Past about California*, ed. Milo Milton Quaife, Lakeside Classics, no. 26 (Chicago: R. R. Donnelley & Sons, 1928).

BIDWELL, *Journey*. *A Journey to California, 1841 — The First Emigrant Party to California by Wagon Train. The Journal of John Bidwell*, ed. Francis P. Farquhar (Berkeley, Calif.: Friends of the Bancroft Library, 1964).

BIEBER, *Southern Trails*. *Southern Trails to California in 1849*, ed. Ralph P. Bieber (Glendale, Calif.: The Arthur H. Clark Co., 1937).

"Binding the Elephant." John P. Reid, "Binding the Elephant: Contracts and Legal Obligations on the Overland Trail," *American Journal of Legal History*, 21 (1977): 285-315.

BLOOD, Diary. James A. Blood, "Diary" (ts., abstracts, "Fort

Laramie Journals," vol. 2, Fort Laramie National Historic Site, Fort Laramie, Wyoming).

Boston-Newton. *The Boston-Newton Company Venture: From Massachusetts to California in 1849*, comp. Jessie Gould Hannon (Lincoln: University of Nebraska Press, 1969).

BOURNE, Diary. Ezra Bourne, "Diary of an Overland Journey to California in 1850" (ts., C-F 142, Bancroft Library).

BRADFORD, Letters. Sandy Bradford, "Letters" (ms., 69134c, Bancroft Library).

BRADWAY, Journal. "Journal of Dr. J. R. Bradway, Delavan, Wisconsin" (ts., State Historical Society of Wisconsin, Madison).

BRAINARD, Journal. David Brainard, "Journal of the Walworth County Mutual Mining Company, Commencing March the 20th, 1849" (ts., State Historical Society of Wisconsin, Madison).

BREYFOGLE, Diary (ms.). Joshua D. Breyfogle, "Diary" (ms., Dartmouth College Library).

BROUSTER, Letters. "Letters from George Washington Brouster to His Parents" (ms., 1832, Joint Collection, University of Missouri, Western Historical Manuscript Collection — Columbia: State Historical Society of Missouri Manuscripts).

BROWN, A., "Journal." Adam Brown, "Journal," reprinted in part in David M. Kiefer, "Over Barren Plains and Rock-Bound Montains," *Montana, The Magazine of Western History*, 22 (1972): 17-29.

BROWN, J. B., Journal. James Berry Brown, "Journal of a Journey across the Plains in 1859" (ms., 69177c, Bancroft Library).

BROWN, J. B., *Journal of a Journey*. James Berry Brown, *Journal of a Journey across the Plains in 1859* (San Francisco: Book Club of California, 1970).

BROWN, J. E., "Gold Seeker." John Evans Brown, "Memoirs of an American Gold Seeker," *Journal of American History*, 2 (1908): 129-54.

BROWN, J. E., *Memoirs*. John E. Brown, *Memoirs of a Forty-niner*, ed. Katie E. Blood (New Haven, Conn.: Associated Publishers of American Records, 1907).

BROWN, J. L., "Cherokee Journal." "The Journal of John Lowery Brown, of the Cherokee Nation, En Route to California in 1850," ed. Muriel H. Wright, *Chronicles of Oklahoma*, 12 (1934):177-213.

BROWN, J. R., *Across the Plains*. J. Robert Brown, *A Journal of a Trip across the Plains of the U.S., from Missouri to California, in the Year 1856* (Columbus: The author, 1860).

BROWNLEE, "Reminiscences." "Reminiscences of Robert Brownlee," *Publication of the Society of California Pioneers for the Year 1947* (San Francisco: 1948), pp. 11-36.

BRUFF, *Journals*. *Gold Rush: The Journals, Drawings, and Other Papers of J. Goldsborough Bruff, Captain, Washington City and California Mining Association, April 2, 1849-July 20, 1851*, ed. Georgia Willis Read and Ruth Gaines (New York: Columbia University Press, 1944).

BRYANT, *Journal*. Edwin Bryant, *What I Saw in California: Being the Journal of a Tour by the Emigrant Route and South Pass of the Rocky Mountains, across the Continent of North America, the Great Desert Basin, and through California in the Years 1846, 1847* (Santa Ana, Calif.: The Fine Arts Press, 1936).

BUCKINGHAM, Diary. Harriet Talcott Buckingham [Clarke], "Diary" (ms., 1156, Oregon Historical Society, Portland).

BUCKINGHAM, Overland Diary. "Overland Diary of Harriet T. Buckingham [Clarke], 1851" (ts., 1156, Oregon Historical Society, Portland).

BUFFUM, Diary. "Diary of J. C. Buffum, 1847-1854" (ms., California State Library).

BURBANK, Diary and Journal. Augustus Ripley Burbank, "Diary and Journal of a Trip to California by Overland" (ts., copy 2, Oregon Collection, University of Oregon).

BURROUGHS, Reminiscences. Joseph Newton Burroughs, "Reminiscences of 1856 Overland Journey" (ts., California Historical Society, San Francisco).

CAGWIN, Diary. N. A. Cagwin, Diary (ms., California State Library).

CALDWELL, "Notes." Dr. [T. G.?] Caldwell, "Notes of a Journey to California by Fort Hall Route, June to Oct[obe]r 1849," in Bruff, *Journals*, pp. 1250-69.

California Emigrant Letters. California Emigrant Letters, ed. Walker D. Wyman (New York: Bookman Associates Publishers, 1952).

CALL, Journey. W. W. Call, "Overland Journey" (ms., C-D 5178, Bancroft Library).

CAPLES, Overland Journey. Mrs. James Caples, "Overland Journey to the Coast" (ts., California State Library).

CARDINELL, "Adventures." Charles Cardinell, "Adventures on the Plains," *California Historical Society Quarterly*, 1 (1922): 57-71.

CARPENTER, Trip. Helen McCowen Carpenter, "A Trip across the Plains in an Ox Wagon, 1857" (ts., HM 16994, Huntington Library).

CARR, Letter. "Letter from Dabney T. Carr to G. C. Broadhead, 31 May 1850" (ms., copy, "Western Travel Envelope," Missouri Historical Society, St. Louis).

CASLER, *Journal*. Melyer Casler, *A Journal, Giving the Incidents of a Journey to California in the Summer of 1859, by the Overland Route* (Toledo: Commercial Steam Book and Job Office, 1863).

CASTLEMAN, Diary. "Diary of P[hilip] F. Castleman while Crossing the Plains to California Commencing from the Time He Left St. Joseph, Mo., With a Seeth of His Trip from Home Which Was in Larve Co., Ky., to St. Joseph, Mo." (ms., Western Americana Collection, Beinecke Library).

CHADWICK, Diary. "Samuel Chadwick's Travels to California in 1852" (ms., State Historical Society of Wisconsin, Madison).

CHADWICK, Travels. "Samuel Chadwick's Travels to California in

1852" (ms., State Historical Society of Wisconsin, Madison). [This handwritten account is contained in the same small journal as Chadwick, "Diary." The "Diary" is written in pencil, apparently daily as the author journeyed on the overland trail. "Travels" is written in ink and may be a revised version of the earlier notes.]

CHALMERS, "Journal." "The Journal of Robert Chalmers, April 17-September 1, 1850," ed. Charles Kelly, *Utah Historical Quarterly,* 20 (1952): 31-55.

CHAMBERLAIN, Diary. William E. Chamberlain, "Diary" (ms., California State Library).

CHILD, *Overland Route.* Andrew Child, *Overland Route to California, Description of the Route via Council Bluffs, Iowa* (Milwaukee: Daily Sentinel Steam Power Press, 1852).

CHILLSON, Diary. Lorenzo Dow Chillson, "Diary" (ms., HM 4293, Huntington Library).

CHRISTY, *Road. Thomas Christy's Road across the Plains: A Guide to the Route from Mormon Crossing, Now Omaha, Nebraska, to the City of Sacramento, California,* ed. Robert H. Becker (Denver: Fred A. Rosenstock, 1969).

CHURCHILL, Journal. Stillman Churchill, "Journal of Incidents and Travels to California" (ts., Division of Archives and Manuscripts, Minnesota Historical Society, St. Paul).

CLAPP, *Journal.* John T. Clapp, *A Journal of Travels to and from California with Full Details of the Hardships and Privations; Also a Description of the Mines, Cities, Towns* ... (Kalamazoo, Mich.: Geo. A. Fitch & Co., 1851).

CLARK, B.C., "Journey." [Bennett C. Clark], "Diary of a Journey from Missouri to California in 1849," ed. Ralph P. Bieber, *Missouri Historical Review*, 23 (1928): 3-43.

CLARK, T. D., "Appendix." "Appendix" to Perkins, *Gold Rush Diary*, ed. Thomas D. Clark, pp. 158-95.

CLIFTON, Diary. "Diary of John Clifton, a 49'er: March 17, 1849-

November 28, 1852" (ts., California State Library).

CLOUGH, Diary. Aaron Clough, "Diary of Overland Journey to Oregon, May 15-December 15, 1862" (ms., microfilm, Oregon Historical Society, Portland).

COLE, *Early Days.* Gilbert L. Cole, *In the Early Days along the Overland Trail in Nebraska Territory, in 1852* (Kansas City, Mo.: Franklin Hudson Publishing Co., [1905]).

COMPTON, Diary. James H. Compton, "Diary" (ms., C-F 224, Bancroft Library).

CONDIT, Diary. "Copy [of] Diary of Philip Condit, 1854" (ms., 922, Oregon Historical Society, Portland).

CONYERS, "Diary." "Diary of E. W. Conyers, a Pioneer of 1852," *Transactions of the Thirty-Third Annual Reunion of the Oregon Pioneer Association, June 15, 1905* (Portland: Peaslee Bros., 1906), pp. 423-512.

COOKE, *Crossing the Plains.* Lucy Rutledge Cooke, *Crossing the Plains in 1852: Narrative of a Trip from Iowa to "The Land of Gold," as Told in Letters Written during the Journey* (Modesto, Calif.: 1923).

CORNELL, Description. William Cornell, "Description of the Route to Oregon" (ms., 290, Oregon Historical Society, Portland).

COSAD, Journal. David Cosad, "Journal of a Trip to California by the Overland Route and Life in the Gold Diggings during 1849-1850" (ms., California Historical Society, San Francisco).

COUPLER, Crossing the Plains. J. C. Coupler, "Crossing the Plains from St. Joseph, Mo., to San Francisco" (ts., 1508, Oregon Historical Society, Portland).

Course of Empire. The Course of Empire, ed. Valeska Bari (New York: Coward-McCann, 1931).

COWDEN, Diary. "Diary Kept by J[ames] S. Cowden on His Trip 'Overland' from Iowa to Cal. in 1853 with Ox Teams and Wagons" (ms., photostat, Bancroft Library and California Historical Society).

cox, "Diary." "From Texas to California in 1849: Diary of C. C. Cox," ed. Mabelle Eppard Martin, *Southwestern Historical Quarterly*, 29 (1925-26): 36-50, 128-46, 201-23.

cox, "Reminiscences." "Reminiscences of C. C. Cox," *Southwestern Historical Quarterly*, 6 (1902): 113-38.

coy, *Great Trek*. Owen Cochran Coy, *The Great Trek* (Los Angeles: Powell Publishing Co., [c. 1931]).

crandall, Diary. Eliphalet Crandall, "Diary" (ms., Nebraska State Historical Society, Lincoln).

crane, Journal. Addison M. Crane, "Journal of a Trip across the Plains in 1852" (ms., HM 19333, Huntington Library).

crawford, "Journal." "Journal of Medorem Crawford: An Account of His Trip across the Plains with the Oregon Pioneers of 1842," *Sources of the History of Oregon*, vol. 1, no. 1 (Eugene: Star Job Office, 1897).

cross, "Journal." "The Journal of Major Osborne Cross," in *March of the Mounted Riflemen*, ed. Raymond W. Settle, pp. 31-272.

dalton, Diary. "Diary of John Dalton, 1852" (ts., State Historical Society of Wisconsin, Madison).

dawson, *Narrative. Narrative of Nicholas "Cheyenne" Dawson (Overland to California in '41 & '49, and Texas in '51)*, with an Introduction by Charles L. Camp (San Francisco: Grabhorn Press, 1933).

decker, *Diaries. The Diaries of Peter Decker: Overland to California in 1849 and Life in the Mines, 1850-1851*, ed. Helen S. Giffen (Georgetown, Calif.: Talisman Press, 1966).

delano, *Across the Plains*. Alonzo Delano, *Across the Plains and among the Diggings: A Reprint of the Original Edition* (New York: Wilson-Erickson, 1936).

delano, *Life*. Alonzo Delano, *Life on the Plains and among the Diggings, Being Scenes and Adventures of an Overland Journey to California: with Particular Incidents of the Route,*

Mistakes and Sufferings of the Emigrants, the Indian Tribes, the Present and the Future of the Great West (Auburn and Buffalo: Miller, Orton & Mulligan, 1854).

DEWOLF, Diary. "Diary of the Overland Trail, 1849, and Letters, 1849-50, of Captain David Dewolf" (ts., Newberry Library).

Dinwiddie Journal. Overland from Indiana to Oregon: The Dinwiddie Journal, ed. Margaret Booth, *Sources of Northwest History*, no. 2 (Missoula: State University of Montana, 1928).

"Dividing the Elephant." John P. Reid, "Dividing the Elephant: The Separation of Mess and Joint Stock Property on the Overland Trail," *Hastings Law Journal*, 28 (1976): 73-92.

DOWELL, Journal. Benjamin Franklin Dowell, "Copy of His Journal" (ms., 209, Oregon Historical Society, Portland).

DOYLE, Journals. "Journals and Letters of Simon Doyle" (ms., Western Americana Collection 144, Beinecke Library).

DULANY, Papers. "Correspondence from William H. Dulany to His Wife Susan Dulany," William H. Dulany Papers (ms., Missouri Historical Society, St. Louis).

DUNDASS, *Journal. Journal of Samuel Rutherford Dundass, Formerly Auditor of Jefferson County, Ohio, Including His Entire Route to California, as a Member of the Steubenville Company Bound for San Francisco, in the Year 1849* (Steubenville, Ohio: Conn's Job Office, 1857).

EATON, *Overland*. Herbert Eaton, *The Overland Trail to California in 1852* (New York: Putnam, 1974).

EBERSTADT, "Introduction." "Introduction and Notes," in L. Sawyer, *Across the Plains*, ed. Edward Eberstadt.

EBEY, Diary. Winfield Scott Ebey, "Diary" (ms., P-B 217, Bancroft Library).

EBEY, Second Diary. Winfield Scott Ebey, "Diary" (ms., University of Washington).

ECCLESTON, *Overland. Overland to California on the Southwestern Trail, 1849: Diary of Robert Eccleston*, ed. George P.

Hammond and Edward H. Howes (Berkeley: University of California Press, 1950).

EGBERT, Record. Eliza Ann McAuley [Egbert], "Mother's Diary: The Record of a Journey across the Plains in '52" (ts., California Historical Society, San Francisco).

ELLMAKER, Autobiography. "Autobiography of Enos Ellmaker" (ts., reproduced by Lane County Pioneer-Historical Society, 1962).

EVANS, "Letter." "Letter from James W. Evans to Ellis G. Evans, 27 October 1850," reprinted as "A Missouri Forty-Niner's Trip across the Plains," *Missouri Historical Review*, 43 (1948): 38-47 (Joint Collection, University of Missouri, Western Historical Manuscript Collection — Columbia: State Historical Society of Missouri Manuscripts).

EVANS, Letter. "Letter from James W. Evans to Ellis G. Evans, 27 October 1850" (ms., 1872, State Historical Society of Missouri, Columbia).

FAIRCHILD, *Letters. California Letters of Lucius Fairchild*, ed. Joseph Schafer (Madison: State Historical Society of Wisconsin, 1931).

FARNHAM, "From Ohio." "From Ohio to California in 1849: The Gold Rush Journal of Elijah Bryan Farnham," ed. Merrill J. Mattes and Esley J. Kirk, *Indiana Magazine of History*, 46 (1950): 297-318, 403-20.

FARNHAM, Gold Rush. Elijah Bryan Farnham, "Gold Rush of 1849" (ts., "Fort Laramie Journals," vol. 2, Fort Laramie Historic Site, Fort Laramie, Wyoming).

FERGUSON, *Gold Fields*. Charles D. Ferguson, *California Gold Fields* (Oakland, Calif.: Biobooks. 1948).

FISH, J. G., Crossing. Juliette G. Fish, "Crossing the Plains in 1862," (ts., uncatalogued Facs., Huntington Library).

FISH, M. C., Daily Journal. Mary C. Fish, "Daily Journal Written during an Overland Journey to California" (ms., C-F 140, Bancroft Library).

FOREMAN, *Marcy.* Grant Foreman, *Marcy & the Gold Seekers: The Journal of Captain R. B. Marcy, with an Account of the Gold Rush over the Southern Route* (Norman: University of Oklahoma Press, 1939).

FOSTER, Journal. Isaac Foster, "A Journal of the Route to Alta California" (ts., HM 16995, Huntington Library).

FOUTS, Diary. [D. Lambert Fouts?], "Diary" (ms., 2 F782, Holt-Atherton Pacific Center for Western Studies, University of the Pacific).

FOX, Memorandum. Jared Fox, "Memorandum of a Trip from Dalton, Sauk County, Wisconsin, to Oregon and California, April 12, 1852-Aug. 12, 1854 (copied from the original by Ruth Grimshaw Martin)" (ts., California State Library).

FRINK, *Journal.* Margaret A. Frink, *Journal of the Adventures of a Party of California Gold-Seekers under the Guidance of Mr. Ledyard Frink during a Journey across the Plains from Martinsville, Indiana, to Sacramento, California, from March 30, 1850, to September 7, 1850* (Oakland, Calif.: 1897).

FRIZZELL, *Journal. Across the Plains to California in 1852: From the Little Wabash River in Illinois to the Pacific Springs of Wyoming. Journal of Mrs. Lodisa Frizzell,* ed. Victor Hugo Paltsits (New York: New York Public Library, 1915).

Frontier Guardian. The Frontier Guardian and Iowa Sentinel, Kanesville, Iowa.

GEER, "Diary." "Diary of Mrs. Elizabeth Dixon Smith Geer," *Transactions of the 35th Annual Reunion of the Oregon Pioneer Association* (Portland, Oregon: Chausse-Prudhomme Co., 1908), pp. 153-79.

Geiger-Bryarly Journal. Trail to California; the Overland Journal of Vincent Geiger and Wakeman Bryarly, ed. David Morris Potter (New Haven: Yale Univ. Press, 1945).

GHENT, *Road.* William J. Ghent, *The Road to Oregon: A Chronicle of the Great Emigrant Trail* (London, New York: Longmans, Green and Co., 1929).

GIBBS, "Diary." "The Diary of George Gibbs," in *March of the Mounted Riflemen*, ed. Raymond W. Settle, pp. 273-327.

GIFFEN, "Notes." "Notes" to Decker, *Diaries*, ed. Helen S. Giffen.

GILL, *Letters. California Letters of William Gill Written in 1850 to His Wife, Harriet Tarleton in Kentucky*, ed. Eva Turner Clark (New York: Downs Printing Company, 1922).

GILMORE, Overland Journey. Andrew Hall Gilmore, "Overland Journey to California, March 12-September 9, 1850; Together with Miscellaneous Accounts, October 15, 1850-January 1, 1853" (ts., California State Library).

GOLDSMITH, *Overland*. Oliver Goldsmith, *Overland in Forty-Nine: The Recollections of a Wolverine Ranger after a Lapse of Forty-Seven Years* (Detroit: The author, 1896).

GOLTRA, Journal. "Journal Kept by Mrs. E[lizabeth] J. Goltra during Her Overland Journey from Missouri *via* South Pass and the Boise Crossing of Snake River to Oregon in 1853" (ts., Princeton University).

GOODELL, Crossing the Plains. "Diary of Anna Maria Goodell Crossing the Plains in 1854" (ts., University of Washington).

GORGAS, Diary. Solomon A. Gorgas, "Diary" (ms., HM 651, Huntington Library).

GORGAS, Letter. "Letter from Solomon A. Gorgas to Mary Frances Gorgas, 9 Sept. 1850" (ms., HM 2187, Huntington Library).

GOUGH, "British Columbia." Barry M. Gough, "Keeping British Columbia British: The Law-and-Order Question on a Gold Mining Frontier," *Huntington Library Quarterly*, 38 (1975): 269-80.

GOULD, "Diary." Charles Gould, "Diary," printed in *Boston-Newton Company Venture*, comp. Jessie Gould Hannon.

"Governance of the Elephant." John P. Reid, "Governance of the Elephant: Constitutional Theory on the Overland Trail," *Hastings Constitutional Law Quarterly*, 5 (1978): 421-43.

GRAHAM, Journal. "Journal Kept by Alpheus N. Graham from

Coles County, Illinois, to California in the Year 1852" (ts., positive photostat, California State Library).

GRAY, *Off at Sunrise. Off at Sunrise: The Overland Journal of Charles Glass Gray,* ed. Thomas D. Clark (San Marino, Calif.: Huntington Library, 1976).

GRAY, Passage. Charles G. Gray, "An Overland Passage from Independence, Mo., to San Francisco, Cal., in 1849" (ms., HM 16520, Huntington Library).

GREGG, "Missourians." Kate L. Gregg, "Missourians in the Gold Rush," *Missouri Historical Review,* 39 (1945): 137-54.

GRIFFITH, Diary. "Hancock County, Illinois, to California in 1850: The Diary of Dr. Andrew Jackson Griffith" (ts., Eastern Washington State Historical Society, Spokane).

GRINDELL, Sketch Book. John Grindell, "Sketch Book of the Travails from Platteville, Wisconsin, to California" (ms., State Historical Society of Wisconsin, Madison).

GUNDLACH, Minutes. John H. Gundlach, "Minutes of My Trip to California" (ms., Missouri Historical Society, St. Louis).

HACKNEY, "Journal." Joseph Hackney, "Journal," in Elizabeth Page, *Wagons,* pp. 111-193 passim.

HADLEY, Journal. Emelia H. Hadley, "Journal to Oregon of Travails" (ts., Oregon Collection, University of Oregon).

HAIGHT, Trip. Henry Haight, "Trip to California in 1850; Commenced This Book May 15, 1887" (holograph transcript, State Historical Society of Iowa, Iowa City).

HALE, I., "Diary." Israel F. Hale, "Diary of a Trip to California in 1849," *Society of California Pioneers Quarterly,* 2 (1925): 61-130.

HALE, J., *California.* John Hale, *California as It Is: Being a Description of a Tour by the Overland Route and the South Pass of the Rocky Mountains* (Rochester, N. Y.: Printed for the author by W. Heughes, 1851).

HALL, Diary. O. J. Hall, "Diary of Forty-Niner" (ts., California State Library).

HAMPTON, Diary. "Diary of William H. Hampton, 1852" (ts., California Historical Society, San Francisco).

HANDSAKER, Journal. Samuel Handsaker, "Journal of an Overland Trip to Oregon" (ts., Fac. 590, Huntington Library).

HANNA, E. B. M., "Journal." Esther Belle McMillan Hanna, "Journal," in Eleanor Allen, *Canvas Caravans* (Portland, Oregon: Binfords & Mort, 1946).

HANNA, W., Journal. William Hanna. "The Journal of Wm. Hanna, 1850" (ts., 693, Oregon Historical Society, Portland).

HANNON, "Introduction and Notes." "Introduction and Notes" to *The Boston-Newton Company Venture*, comp. Jessie Gould Hannon.

HARRIS, Account. Benjamin Butler Harris, "Account of a Journey from Panolo Co., Texas, to the Gold Mines, by way of Chihuahua and Sonora, Mar. 25 to Sep. 29, 1849" (ms., HM 17477, vol. 1, Huntington Library).

HARVEY, To California. Isaac Julian Harvey, "To California in 1850" (ms., C-D 5091A, Bancroft Library).

HAYES, Diary. "Diary of Benj. Hayes' Journey Overland from Socorro to Warner's Ranch from Oct. 31, 1849, to Jany. 14, 1850" (ms., Bancroft Library).

HENTZ, Correspondence. "Charles Hentz Correspondence with His Mother" (ts., C-B 704, Bancroft Library).

HICKMAN, *Overland Journey. An Overland Journey to California in 1852: The Journal of Richard Owen Hickman*, ed. M. Catherine White, Historical Reprints... Sources of Northwest History no. 6 (Missoula, Mont.: Missoulian, 1929).

HINES, "Diary." "Diary of Celinda E. Hines," *Transactions of the Forty-Sixth Annual Reunion of the Oregon Pioneer Association* (Portland, Ore.: Chausse-Prudhomme Co., 1921), pp. 69-125.

HIXSON, Diary. "Diary of Jasper Morris Hixson, May 1-August 6, 1849" (ts., California Historical Society, San Francisco).

HOFFMAN, "Diary." [Diary of Benjamin Hoffman in] C. H.

Ambler, "West Virginia Forty-Niners," *West Virginia History*, 3 (1941): 63-75.

HOOVER, Diary. Vincent A. Hoover, "Diary of Journey from Mobile, Ala. . . . by Way of the Oregon Trail to Salt Lake City and Southward through Utah & Nevada to Los Angeles . . . (1849)" (ms., in 3 vols., HM 27628, Huntington Library).

HOOVER, Revised Journal. Vincent A. Hoover, "Journal" (ms., HM 27628, Huntington Library).

HOSLEY, Journal. "Dexter P. Hosley's Journal from Saint Joseph's to California by the Overland Route" (ms., Princeton University Library).

HOWE, *Argonauts*. Octavius Thorndike Howe, *Argonauts of '49: History and Adventures of the Emigrant Companies from Massachusetts, 1849-1850* (Cambridge, Mass.: Harvard University Press, 1923).

HOWELL, Diary. Elijah Preston Howell, "Diary" (ms., 1675, Joint Collection, University of Missouri, Western Historical Manuscript Collection — Columbia: State Historical Society of Missouri Manuscripts).

HOWELL, Crossing the Plains. Elijah Preston Howell, "Crossing the Plains" (ts., C-F 121, Bancroft Library).

HUDGINS, California in 1849. John Hudgins, "California in 1849" (ts., mimeographed, 2189, State Historical Society of Missouri, Columbia).

HUMPHREY, Journal. Lezerne Humphrey, "Manuscript Journal, 1852" (ms., Princeton University).

INGALLS, *Journal*. E.S. Ingalls, *Journal of a Trip to California, by the Overland Route across the Plains in 1850-51* (Waukegan: Tobey & Co., 1852).

INGERSOLL, *Overland in 1847*. Chester Ingersoll, *Overland to California in 1847: Letters Written en Route to California, West from Independence, Missouri, to the Editor of the Joliet Signal*, ed. Douglas C. McMurtrie (Chicago: Black Cat Press, 1937).

390

JAGGER, Journal. D. Jagger, "Journal, 1846-1850" (ms., California Historical Society, San Francisco).

JAMES, Diary. Samuel James, "Diary" (ts., 1508, Oregon Historical Society, Portland).

JEWETT, Journal. "Journal of George E. Jewett, 1849" (ts., C-F 20, Bancroft Library).

JOHNSON, J. A., Note Book. "Note Book of John A. Johnson during His Voyage to & Residence in California" (ms., Western Americana Collection, Beinecke Library).

JOHNSON, J. H., Journey. Joseph H. Johnson, "Diary of a Journey to California, 1849" (ms., HM 19480, Huntington Library).

JOHNSTON W., Diary. "Copy of Diary of William Johnston, Huntingdon, Pa." (ts., California State Library).

JOHNSTON, W. G., *Overland*. William G. Johnston, *Overland to California* (Oakland, Calif.: Biobooks, 1948); new edition of *Experiences of a Forty-Niner* (1892).

JONES, C., Diary. Carlton Jones, "Diary" (photostat, 348, Joint Collection, University of Missouri, Western Historical Manuscipt Collection — Columbia: State Historical Society of Missouri Manuscripts).

JONES, J. N., Journal. John N. Jones, "A Journal of a Trip to California" (ts., extracts, "Fort Laramie Journals," vol. 3, Fort Laramie Historical Site, Fort Laramie, Wyoming).

JOSSELYN, Journal. Amos P. Josselyn, "Journal" (ts., California State Library).

KAHLER, Leaves from the Diary. William Kahler, "Leaves from the Diary of Mr. Kahler, from McConnellsville, Ohio, to Jackson County, Oregon" (ms., 1508, Oregon Historical Society, Portland).

KECK, Journal. Joseph A. Keck, "Journal of a Trip from Harrisburgh, Van Buren Co., Iowa, to California" (ms., File K234, Iowa State Historical Department, Division of Historical Museum and Archives, Des Moines).

KEEN, Diary. Richard A. Keen, "Diary of a Trip to California" (ts., State Historical Society of Iowa City).

KELLER, *Trip*. Geo. Keller, *A Trip across the Plains, and Life in California; Embracing a Description of the Overland Route; Its Natural Curiosities, Rivers, Lakes, Springs, Mountains, Indian Tribes*... (Massillon, Ohio: White's Press, 1851).

KILGORE, Journal. William H. Kilgore, *The Kilgore Journal of an Overland Journey to California in the Year 1850*, ed. Joyce Rockwood Muench (New York: Hastings House, 1949).

KIRKPATRICK, Journal. "Journal of Charles A. Kirkpatrick, 1849" (ms., C-D 207, Bancroft Library).

KITCHELL, Diaries. "Diaries of E. Kitchell," (ts. and microfilm, State Historical Society of Wisconsin, Madison).

KNIGHT, "Diary." "Diary of Mrs. Amelia Stewart Knight: An Oregon Pioneer of 1853," *Transactions of the Fifty-Sixth Annual Reunion of the Oregon Pioneer Association* (Portland, Ore.: F. W. Baltes, 1933), pp. 38-53.

KNIGHT, Journal. Amelia Knight, "Journal Kept on the Road from Iowa to Oregon" (ms., 256, University of Washington).

"Knowing the Elephant." John P. Reid, "Knowing the Elephant: Distinguishing Property Rights on the Overland Trail," *Creighton Law Review*, 10 (1977): 640-54.

KUHLIWEIN, Letters. "Letters from Hugo Frederick Kuhliwein to His Mother" (ts., Iowa State Historical Department, Iowa City).

KUNKEL, Memoirs. G. S. Kunkel, "Memoirs" (ts., 463, State Historical Society of Missouri, Columbia).

LAMPTON, Diary. "Wm. Lampton's Diary; or, Trip to California in 1850" (ts., "Western Travel Papers," Missouri Historical Society, St. Louis).

LANE, Diary. S. A. Lane, "Diary of Trip Overland from Akron, Ohio, to Sacramento" (ms., photostat, Bancroft Library).

LANGWORTHY, *Scenery*. Franklin Langworthy, *Scenery of the*

Plains, Mountains and Mines, ed. Paul C. Phillips (Princeton: Princeton University Press, 1932).

LAVENDER, *Westward*. David Lavender, *Westward Vision: The Story of the Overland Trail* (New York: McGraw-Hill, 1963).

LEEPER, *Argonauts*. David Rohrer Leeper, *The Argonauts of 'Forty-Nine: Some Recollections of the Plains and the Diggings* (South Bend, Ind.: J. B. Stoll & Co., 1894).

LEWELLING, Excerpts. Excerpts from the Journal of Seth Lewelling, March 23, 1850-Sept. 10, 1852" (ts., California State Library).

LEWIS, E. M., Route. Edward M. Lewis, "My Route from New York to the West, 1865" (ms., California Historical Society, San Francisco).

LEWIS, J. N., Book. John N. Lewis, "My Book" (ms., P-A 335, Bancroft Library).

LEWIS, T. C., Notes. Thomas Cotton Lewis, "Memorandum or Notes of Thos. C. Lewis & Son" (ms., Western Americana Collection 302, Beinecke Library).

LINDSEY, Journal. Tipton Lindsey, "The Plains & Deserts of North America: A Journal of a Trip to California (Overland), 1849" (ms., C-F 62, Bancroft Library).

LITTLETON, Journal. Micajah Littleton, "Journal of a Trip across the Plains from Independence, Missouri, to California, May 11, 1850-October 11, 1850" (ts., California State Library).

LONGWORTH, Diary. "The Diary of Basil N. Longworth, Oregon Pioneer" (mimeograph, transcribed by The Historical Records Survey, Division of Women's and Professional Projects, Works Progress Administration, 1938).

LOOMIS, *Journal*. Leander V. Loomis, *A Journal of the Birmingham Emigrating Company: The Record of a Trip from Birmingham, Iowa, to Sacramento, California, in 1850*, ed. Edgar M. Ledyard (Salt Lake City: Legal Printing Co., 1928).

LORCH, "Gold Rush." Fred W. Lorch, "Iowa and the California

Gold Rush of 1849," *Iowa Journal of History and Politics*, 30 (1932): 307-76.

LORD, Journal. Israel Shipman Pelton Lord, "Journal of 1849" [composed partly of clippings entitled, "California Correspondence" written by Dr. Lord for *The Western Christian*, Elgin, Kane County, Illinois] (ms., HM 19408, Huntington Library).

LORING, "Report." "Report of Colonel [William W.] Loring, October 15, 1849," in *March of the Mounted Riflemen*, ed. Raymond W. Settle, pp. 329-43.

LOTTS, Copy. "Copy of Judge Charles F. Lotts' Diary of His Overland Trip from Quincy, Illinois, May 1 — 1849. Arrived at Long Bar, California, Oct. 3 — 1849" (ts., California State Library).

LOUGHARY, Brief Journal. Mrs. W. A. Loughary, "A Brief Journal of the Travels and Incidents of an Emigrant Ox Train across the Plains and Mountains from Burlington, Iowa, on the Mississippi River, to the Willamette Valley on the Columbia and the Pacific Ocean in the Year of 1864" (ts., Oregon Collection, University of Oregon).

LOVE, Diary. Alexander Love, "Diary of an Overland Journey from Leesburg, Pennsylvania, ... March 20 to August 23, 1849" (ms., Western Americana Collection 309, Beinecke Library).

LOVELAND, Diary. Cyrus C. Loveland, "Diary Written while Crossing the Plains in 1850 with a Drove of Cattle (ms., California State Library).

LUARK, Diary. Michael F. Luark, "Diary" (ms., University of Washington).

LUARK, Later Diary. Michael F. Luark, "Diary of Overland Journey, Indiana to Olympia, Wash., 1853, Written by Him in Later Life & Based on His Original Diary" (ms., University of Washington).

MCBRIDE, J. H., Letters. "Letters from John Holden McBride to His Wife" (ms., Nebraska State Historical Society, Lincoln).

MCBRIDE, W. S., Diary. William S. McBride, "Diary" (ms., HM 16956, Huntington Library).

MCCALL, *Pick and Pan*. A. J. McCall, *Pick and Pan. Trip to the Digging's in 1849. Reminiscences of California Life by an Argonaut* (Bath, N.Y.: Steuben Courier Print., 1883).

MCCALL, *Wayside Notes*. A. J. McCall, *The Great California Trail in 1849: Wayside Notes of an Argonaut* (Bath, N.Y.: Steuben Courier Print., 1882).

MCCANNE, Diary. Hugh McCanne, "Diary" (ms., 1932, Joint Collection, University of Missouri, Western Historical Manuscript Collection — Columbia: State Historical Society of Missouri Manuscripts).

MCCLURE, Journey. "Diary of A[ndrew] S. McClure of the Journey across the Plains, May 7-October 15, 1853" (ts., California State Library).

MCCOWEN, Journal and Notes. "Western Journal of George McCowen" and "Notes of a Journey across the Plains" (ts., HM 16756, Huntington Library).

MCGLASKEN, Journal. J. McGlasken, "Journal" (ts., Chicago Historical Society, Chicago).

MCKINSTRY, Diary. "Gold Rush Diary of Byron N. McKinstry, 1850-1852" (ts., Bancroft Library).

MCKINSTRY, *Diary. The California Gold Rush: Overland Diary of Byron N. McKinstry, 1850-1852, with a Biographical Sketch and Comment on a Modern Tracing of His Overland Travel by his Grandson Bruce L. McKinstry* (Glendale, Calif.: The Arthur H. Clark Company, 1975).

MCLANE, "Leaves." Allen McLane, "Leaves from a Pencil'd Journal, Found on Road (1849)," in Bruff, *Journals*, ed. Georgia Willis Read and Ruth Gaines, pp. 1269-71.

MCLEOD, Diary. Patrick H. McLeod, "1849, Going to California" (ms., Princeton University).

MCQUEEN, Diary. Angus McQueen, "Diary" (ts., Special Collection Department, Stanford University Libraries).

MANLOVE, Trip. Mark D. Manlove, "An Overland Trip to the California Gold Fields: Personal Experiences of a Forty-Niner" (ts., California State Library).

MANN, Portion. "Portion of a Diary of H. R. Mann, 1849" (ts., California State Library).

March of the Mounted Riflemen. The March of the Mounted Riflemen: First United States Military Expedition to Travel the Full Length of the Oregon Trail from Fort Leavenworth to Fort Vancouver, May to October, 1849, ed. Raymond W. Settle (Glendale, Calif.: The Arthur H. Clark Co., 1940).

MARSHALL, Letter. "Letter from George Marshall to Wife and Children, 11 May 1850" (ms., photocopy, 1500, Oregon Historical Society, Portland).

MASON, Letters. "Letters of Leonard Mason" (ms., Western Americana Collection 333, Beinecke Library).

MATTES, *Platte River Road.* Merrill J. Mattes, *The Great Platte River Road* (Lincoln: Nebraska State Historical Society, 1969).

MAYNARD, Pocket Diary. David Swinson Maynard, "Daily Pocket Diary for 1850" (ms., HM 997, Huntington Library).

MERRILL, Diary. Julius Caesar Merrill, "Diary" (ts., 371, Joint Collection, University of Missouri, Western Historical Manuscript Collection — Columbia: State Historical Society of Missouri Manuscripts).

MILLER, J., Journal. "The Journal of Joel Miller's 'Crossing the Plains' to California in 1853" (ms., C-F 220, Bancroft Library).

MILLER, R. G., Journal. Reuben G. Miller, "Journal" (ts., Facs. 503, Huntington Library).

MILLINGTON, Journal. D. A. Millington, "Journal of a California Miner" (ms., photocopy, California State Library).

MOORE, Journal of Travails. Jonathan Limerick Moore, "Journal of Travails on the Roade to Oregon" (ms., Oregon Collection, University of Oregon).

MOORMAN, *Journal. The Journal of Madison Berryman Moorman, 1850-1851*, ed. Irene D. Paden (San Francisco: California Historical Society, 1948).

MORELAND, Diary. "Rev. Jesse Moreland's Diary, Tennessee to Oregon, 1852" (ms., 1508, Oregon Historical Society, Portland).

MORGAN, D. L., "Introduction and Notes." "Introduction and Notes" to *Overland in 1846*, ed. Dale L. Morgan, pp. 14-117, 458-71.

MORGAN, D.L., "Notes to Pritchard." "Notes" to Pritchard, *Diary*, ed. Dale L. Morgan.

MORGAN, M. M., *Trip*. Martha M. Morgan, *A Trip across the Plains in the Year 1849 with Notes of a Voyage to California, by Way of Panama* (San Francisco: Pioneer Press, 1864).

MOXLEY, Correspondence. "Letter from Charles G. Moxley to Emily Moxley" (ms., Western Americana Collection 712, Beinecke Library).

MURPHY, Across. Patrick M. Murphy, "Across the Plains in the Year 1854" (ts., California State Library).

MURRAY, Journal. John Murray, "Journal of a Trip to California or Oregon" (ts., Washington State Historical Society, Tacoma).

MUSCOTT, Letters. "Letters of John M. Muscott to Ebenezer Robbins Published in the *Rome [New York] Sentinel*" (ts., California Historical Society, San Francisco).

MYRICK, *Letters. The Gold Rush: Letters of Thomas S. Myrick from California to the Jackson, Michigan, American Citizen, 1849-1855* (Mount Pleasant, Mich.: The Cumming Press, 1971).

NEWCOMB, Journal. "Journal of Silas Newcomb of Madison, Wisconsin, 1 April 1850 to 31 March 1851" (ms., Western Americana Collection 359, Beinecke Library).

NIXON, Journal. Alexander B. Nixon, "Journal to the Pacific Ocean" (ms., 2 vols., California State Library).

NUSBAUMER, *Journal*. Louis Nusbaumer, *Valley of Salt, Memories of Wine: A Journal of Death Valley, 1849*, ed. George Koenig (Berkeley, Calif.: Friends of the Bancroft Library, 1967).

Overland in 1846. Overland in 1846: Diaries and Letters of the California-Oregon Trail, ed. Dale L. Morgan, 2 vols. (Georgetown, Calif.: Talisman Press, 1963).

OWEN, My Trip. Benjamin Franklin Owen, "My Trip across the Plains: March 31, 1853-October 28, 1853" (ts., reproduced by Lane County Pioneer-Historical Society, 1967).

PAGE, *Wagons*. Elizabeth Page, *Wagons West: A Story of the Oregon Trail* (New York: Farrar & Rinehart, Inc., 1930).

PALMER, *Journal*. Joel Palmer, *Journal of Travels over the Rocky Mountains to the Mouth of the Columbia River* (Cincinnati: J. A. & V. P. James, 1847), reprinted in *Early Western Travels, 1748-1846*, ed. Reuben Gold Thwaites (Cleveland: The A. H. Clark Co., 1904-07), 30: 29-311.

PARKE, Notes. Charles R. Parke, "Notes Crossing the Plains" (ms., HM 16996, Huntington Library).

PARKER, Notes. William Tell Parker, "Notes by the Way" (ms., HM 30873, Huntington Library).

PARSONS, Reminiscences. Mary Collins Parsons, "Untitled Reminiscences" (ts., 1508, Oregon Historical Society, Portland).

PASCHEL, Diary. "Diary of Albert G. Paschel, Overland Trip to California with Ox Team, in the Year 1850" (ts., State Historical Society of Iowa, Iowa City).

PATTISON, Diary. William Pattison, "Diary" (ms., 1072, Oregon Historical Society, Portland).

PAYNE, Account. James A. Payne, "Saint Louis to San Francisco: Being an Account of a Journey across the Plains in 1850, Together with My Experience in Steamboating on the California Rivers untill the Fall of 1853," ed. by his son, 1895 (mimeograph copy, California State Library).

PEACOCK, *Letters. The Peacock Letters, April 7, 1850, to January 4, 1852: Fourteen Letters Written by William Peacock to His*

Wife, Susan, Who Remained Behind at Chemung, Illinois, While He Journeyed to California in a Covered Wagon Train, Endured Months of Disheartening Labor in the Gold Fields, and Prepared to Return to Her, a Sadly Disillusioned Man (Stockton, Calif.: San Joaquin Pioneer & Historical Society, 1950).

PEASE, Diary to Oregon. "A Diary of a Trip from St. Joseph, Mo., to Astoria, Oregon, Made by David Egbert Pease and His Wife Hannah Pegg Pease in 1849" (ms., Oregon Historical Society, Portland).

PENGRA, Diary. "Diary of Mrs. Byron J. Pengra (Charlotte Emily Sterns) Kept by Her on a Trip across the Plains from Illinois to Oregon in 1853" (ts., reproduced by Lane County Pioneer-Historical Society, 1966).

PERKINS, *Gold Rush Diary. Gold Rush Diary, Being the Journal of Elisha Douglass Perkins on the Overland Trail in the Spring and Summer of 1849*, ed. Thomas D. Clark (Lexington: University of Kentucky Press, 1967).

PERKINS, Sketches. Elisha Douglass Perkins, "Sketches of a Trip from Marietta, Ohio, to the Valley of the Sacramento in Spring & Summer of 1849" (ms., HM 1547, Huntington Library).

PIERCE, Letters. "Letters of Forty-Niner Hiram Dwight Pierce of Troy, N.Y., to His Wife, Sarah Jane Pierce" (ts., Mormon File, microfilm 44, Huntington Library).

PLEASANTS, *Twice across*. W. J. Pleasants, *Twice across the plains, 1849 . . . 1856* (San Francisco: Press of W. N. Brunt, 1906).

PLUMMER, Letter. "Letter from Samuel Craig Plummer to His Wife, 30 April 1850" (ts., 2750, Joint Collection, University of Missouri, Western Historical Manuscript Collection—Columbia: State Historical Society of Missouri Manuscripts).

POMROY, Diary. Horace Barton Pomroy, "Diary" (photostat, C-F 128, Bancroft Library).

POND, Journal. Ananias R. Pond, "Journal" (ms., HM 19383, Huntington Library).

POTTER, "Introduction." "Introduction" to *Trail to California*, ed. David Morris Potter, pp. 1-73.

POWELL, Diary. H. M. T. Powell, "Diary of 1849-1852" (ms., Bancroft Library).

POWELL, *Santa Fé Trail*. *The Santa Fé Trail to California, 1849-1852: The Journal and Drawings of H. M. T. Powell*, ed. Douglas S. Watson (San Francisco: The Book Club of California, 1931).

PRICE, H. M., Diary. Hugh Morgan Price, "Diary of a 'Forty-Niner" (ts., Jackson County Historical Society, Independence, Missouri).

PRICE, J., "Letters." "The Road to California: Letters of Joseph Price," ed. Thomas M. Marshall, *Mississippi Valley Historical Review*, 11 (1924): 237-57.

PRITCHARD, *Diary*. *The Overland Diary of James A. Pritchard from Kentucky to California in 1849*, ed. Dale L. Morgan (Denver: F. A. Rosenstock 1959).

"Prosecuting the Elephant." John P. Reid, "Prosecuting the Elephant: Trails and Judicial Behavior on the Overland Trail," *Brigham Young University Law Review* (1977): 327-50.

PUTNAM, *Journal. The Journal of Royal Porter Putam* (Porterville, Calif.: Farm Tribune, 1961).

RAMSAY, "Diary." "Alexander Ramsay's Diary of 1849," ed. Merrill J. Mattes, *Pacific Historical Review*, 18 (1949): 437-68.

READ, "Diseases." Georgia Willis Read, "Diseases, Drugs, and Doctors on the Oregon-California Trail in the Gold-Rush Years," *Missouri Historical Review*, 38 (1944): 260-74.

READ, Journal. G. W. Read, "Journal on a Trip to California, 1850" (ms., R223, Iowa State Historical Department, Des Moines).

READ, "Women and Children." Georgia Willis Read, "Women and Children on the Oregon-California Trail in the Gold-Rush Years," *Missouri Historical Review*, 39 (1944): 1-23.

READ AND GAINES, "Introduction." "Introduction and Critical Notes," in Bruff, *Journals*, ed. Georgia Willis Read and Ruth Gaines.

READING, Diary. "Diary of P[ierson] B[arton] Reading in 1843: Journal of P. B. Reading from Missouri River at Westport Landing, May 15, 1843, to Sacramento, California, Sutter's Fort, November 9, 1843" (ts., California State Library).

REID, Diary. "The Diary of Bernard J. Reid, Esq., Written by Him during His Journey Overland to California in '49" (ts., Western Pennsylvania Historical Society, Pittsburgh).

REID, "Letter." "A California Gold Rush Letter from Bernard J. Reid," *Western Pennsylvania Historical Magazine*, 44 (1961): 217-35.

"Replenishing the Elephant." John Phillip Reid, "Replenishing the Elephant: Property and Survival on the Overland Trail," *Oregon Historical Quarterly*, 79 (1978): 65-90.

RHODES, "Journal." "Joseph Rhodes and the California Gold Rush of 1850," ed. Merrill J. Mattes, *Annals of Wyoming*, 23 (1951): 52-71, (no. 1).

RICHARDSON, A., Diary of 1852. "Diary of Alpheus Richardson Crossing the Plains in 1852" (ts., R 521 Holt-Atherton Pacific Center for Western Studies, University of the Pacific).

RICHARDSON, C. L., Journal. Caroline L. Richardson, "Journal" (ms., C-F 102, Bancroft Library).

ROBE, Diary. "Diary of Rev. Robert Robe, 1851" (ts., 1163, Oregon Historical Society, Portland).

ROBINSON, *Journey*. *The Robinson-Rosenberger Journey to the Gold Fields of California, 1849-1850: The Diary of Zirkle D. Robinson*, ed. Francis Coleman Rosenberger (Iowa City: Prairie Press, 1966).

ROSE, Diary. Rachel Rose, "Diary" (ms., California State Library).

Rovers. The Buckeye Rovers in the Gold Rush: An Edition of Two Diaries, ed. Howard L. Scamehorn (Athens: Ohio Univ. Press, 1965).

ROWE, Ho for California. "Ho for California: Personal Reminiscences of William Rowe, Sr., of an Overland Trip from Rochester, Wisconsin, to California in 1853 in Company with 'Lucky' Baldwin" (ts., HM 19027, Huntington Library).

ROYCE, *Frontier Lady*. Sarah Royce, *A Frontier Lady: Recollections of the Gold Rush and Early California* (New Haven: Yale University Press, 1932).

RUDD, Notes. Lydia A. Rudd, "Notes by the Wayside Enroute to Oregon" (ms., Hm 27519, Huntington Library).

SAWYER, MRS. F. H., Notes from a Journal."Overland to California: Notes from a Journal Kept by Mrs. Francis H. Sawyer, in a Journey across the Plains, May 9 to August 17, 1852" (ts., C-F 103 transc., Bancroft Library).

SAWYER, L., *Across the Plains*. Lorenzo Sawyer, *Way Sketches, Containing Incidents of Travel across the Plains from St. Joseph to California in 1850, with Letters Describing Life and Conditions in the Gold Region*, ed. Edward Eberstadt (New York: E. Eberstadt, 1926).

Scharmann's Overland Journey. Hermann B. Scharmann, *Scharmann's Overland Journey to California*, tr. Margaret H. Zimmermann and Erich W. Zimmerman (n.p.: 1918).

SCHELLER, Autobiography. John Jacob Scheller, "Extract from Autobiography of J. J. Scheller" (ts., California State Library).

SEARLS, Diary (ms.). Niles Searls, Diary (ms., quoted by permission of the Bancroft Library).

SEDGLEY, *Overland to California*. Joseph Sedgley, *Overland to California in 1849* (Oakland, Calif.: Butler & Bowman, 1877).

SENTER, *Crossing*. W. R. Senter, *Crossing the Continent to California Gold Fields* (1938).

SERVER, "Ill-Fated Wagon Train." James Edsall Server, "The Ill-Fated '49er Wagon Train," *Southern California Quarterly*, 42 (1960): 29-40.

"Sharing the Elephant." John P. Reid, "Sharing the Elephant: Partnership and Concurrent Property on the Overland Trail,"

University of Missouri-Kansas City Law Review, 45 (1976): 207-22.

SHAW, *Across the Plains*. Reuben C. Shaw, *Across the Plains in Forty-Nine* (Farmland, Ind.: W. C. West, 1896).

SHEPHERD, *Journal*. James S. Shepherd, *Journal of Travel across the Plains to California, and Guide to the Future Emigrant* (Racine, Wisc.: Mrs. Rebecca Shepherd, 1851; reprint, 1945).

SMEDLEY, *Across the Plains*. *William Smedley, Across the Plains in '62* (Denver, Colo.?: 1916).

SMITH, C. W., Journal. C. W. Smith, Journal of a Trip to California across the Continent from Weston, Mo., to Weber Creek, Cal., in the Summer of 1850 (ms., California Historical Society, San Francisco).

SMITH, G. A., Diary. G. A. Smith, "Diary" (ms., "Western Travel Papers," Missouri Historical Society, St. Louis).

SMITH, J., Account. Dr. John Smith, "Account" (ms., HM 2295, Huntington Library).

SNYDER, "Diary." "The Diary of Jacob R. Snyder," *Society of California Pioneers Quarterly*, 8 (1931): 224-60.

SPOONER, Diary. "Diary of E. A. Spooner, 1849-1850" (microfilm, Kansas State Historical Society, Topeka).

STAPLES, "Diary." David Staples, "Diary," reprinted in *Boston-Newton Company Venture*, comp. Jessie Gould Hannon.

STARR, Tour of West. J. R. Starr, "A Tour of the West" (ms., 2473, Oregon Historical Society, Portland).

STAUDER, Memorandum. John A. Stauder, "Duplicate Memorandom [sic] of Travels from Lagrange, Lewis County, Missouri, to California" (ts. 459, Joint Collection, University of Missouri, Western Historical Manuscript Collection — Columbia: State Historical Society of Missouri Manuscripts)

STEELE, *Across the Plains*. John Steele, *Across the Plains in 1850*, ed. Joseph Schafer (Chicago: Printed for the Caxton Club, 1930).

STEPHENS, *Jayhawker*. Lorenzo Dow Stephens, *Life Sketches of a Jayhawker of '49* (San Jose, Calif.: Nolta Brothers, 1916).

STEUBEN, Journal. "William North Steuben and His Journal, 1849-1850," ed. Harry E. Rutledge (ts., California Historical Society, San Francisco).

STEWART, G. R., *Trail*. George R. Stewart, *The California Trail: An Epic with Many Heroes* (New York: McGraw-Hill, 1962).

STEWART, H., Diary. "Diary of Helen Stewart, 1853" (ts., reproduced by Lane County Pioneer-Historical Society, 1961).

STILLMAN, "Around the Horn." Dr. J. D. B. Stillman, "Around the Horn, and Early Days in Sacramento" in *Course of Empire*, ed. Valeska Bari, pp. 154-73.

STIMSON, Overland, Fancher Stimson, "Overland Journey to California by Platte River Route and South Pass in 1850" (ms., Iowa State Historical Department, Des Moines).

STINE, Letters. "Copy of the Letters and Journal of Henry Atkinson Stine on His Overland Trip to California from St. Louis to Sacramento, May 4, 1850, to October 25, 1850" (ts., California State Library).

STITZEL, Diary. Jacob Stitzel, "Overland Diary, March 20-Aug. 26, 1849" (ms., microfilm 66-6800, Bancroft Library).

STUART, *Roving Life*. Joseph Alonzo Stuart, *My Roving Life: A Diary of Travels and Adventures by Sea and Land, during Peace and War* (Auburn, Calif.: 1895).

SUMMERS, Letter. "Letter from Joseph A. Summers to His Wife, 30 October 1850" (ts., 2746, Joint Collection, University of Missouri, Western Historical Manuscript Collection — Columbia: State Historical Society of Missouri Manuscripts).

SUTTON, Diary. Sarah Sutton, "Diary" (ts., "Fort Laramie Journals," vol. 4, Fort Laramie Historic Site, Fort Laramie, Wyoming).

T., DR., Journal. Dr. T., "Journal of His Experiences Crossing the Plains in 1849" (ms., C-B 383:1, Bancroft Library).

TATE, Letter. "Letter from James Tate to Major Daniel Nolley, 1

July 1849" (ts., Missouri Historical Society, St. Louis).

TAYLOR, E. N. AND J. W., Letters. "Letters of Erasmus N. Taylor and John W. Taylor, Written to Their Families from Placerville" (ms., Princeton University).

TAYLOR, G. N., Diary. "Diary of George N. Taylor," (ts., 1508, Oregon Historical Society, Portland).

THISSELL, Crossing the Plains. G. W. Thissell, Crossing the Plains in '49 (Oakland, Calif.: 1903).

THOMASSON, Diary. A. H. Thomasson, "Diary" (ms., California State Library).

THOMPSON, Across. Harlon Chittenden Thompson, "Across the Continent on Foot in 1859" (ts., HM 16298, Huntington Library).

THOMSON, Crossing the Plains. Origen Thomson, Crossing the Plains: Narrative of the Scenes, Incidents and Adventures Attending the Overland Journey of the Decatur and Rush County Emigrants to the 'Far-Off' Oregon, in 1852 (Greensburg, Ind.: O. Thomson Printer, 1896).

THORNILEY, Diary. John C. Thorniley, "Diary of Overland Journey in 1852" (ms., California State Library).

THURBER, Journal. "Journal of Albert King Thurber" (ts., Bancroft Library).

"Tied to the Elephant." John P. Reid, "Tied to the Elephant: Organization and Obligation on the Overland Trail," University of Puget Sound Law Review, 1 (1977): 139-59.

TINKER, "Journal." Charles Tinker, "Journal of a Trip to California in 1849,"Ohio State Archaeological and Historical Quarterly, 61 (1952): 71-84.

TOLLES, Diary. "Diary of J[ames] S. Tolles: Trip to California, April-August 2, 1849, and Experiences in California, February-April 8, 1850" (ms., California State Library).

Trail to California: Trail to California: The Overland Journal of Vincent Geiger and Wakeman Bryarly, ed. David Morris Potter (New Haven: Yale University Press, 1945).

TURNBULL, "Travels." "T. Turnbull's Travels from the United States across the Plains to California," *Proceedings of the State Historical Society of Wisconsin at Its Sixty-First Annual Meeting* (Madison: 1914), pp. 151-225.

TURNER, Diary. "William Turner's Diary" (ts., State Historical Society of Wisconsin, Madison).

TUTTLE, C., "Diary." "California Diary of Charles Tuttle,"*Wisconsin Magazine of History*, 15 (1931): 69-85, 219-33.

TUTTLE, Z. S., Letters. "Letters from Ziba Smith Tuttle to Smith Tuttle" (ts., "Fort Laramie Journals," vol. 3, Fort Laramie Historic Site, Fort Laramie, Wyoming).

UDELL, *Incidents*. John Udell, *Incidents of Travel to California, across the Great Plains: Together with the Return Trips through Central America and Jamaica; to Which are Added Sketches of the Author's Life* (Jefferson, Ohio: Printed for the author, at the Sentinel Office, 1856).

UNRUH, The Plains Across. John D. Unruh, Jr., "The Plains Across: The Overland Emigrants and the Trans-Mississippi West, 1840-1860" (unpub. Ph.D. diss., Dept. of History, University of Kansas, 1975).

VARNER, Letters. Allen Varner, "Letters" (ms., HM 39975-39986 and Fac 685, Huntington Library).

VERDENAL, Journal. John M. Verdenal, "Journal across the Plains, 1852" (ts., Bancroft Library).

VIOLETTE, Day Book. "M. A. Violette Day Book, 1849" (ts., Princeton University).

WALLENKAMP, Diary. Henry Wallenkamp, "Diary of a Trip to California" (ts., vol. 7:187, Joint Collection, University of Missouri, Western Historical Manuscript Collection—Columbia: State Historical Society of Missouri Manuscripts).

WASHBURN, Journal. "The Journal of Catherine Amanda Stansbury Washburn: Iowa to Oregon, 1853" (ts., reproduced by Lane County Pioneer-Historical Society, 1967).

406

WAYMAN, *Diary. A Doctor on the California Trail: The Diary of Dr. John Hudson Wayman from Cambridge City, Indiana, to the Gold Fields in 1852*, ed. Edgeley Woodman Todd (Denver: Old West Publ. Co., 1971).

WEBB, *Trail.* Todd Webb, *The Gold Rush Trail and the Road to Oregon* (Garden City, N.Y.: Doubleday, 1963).

WEBSTER, *Gold Seekers.* Kimball Webster, *The Gold Seekers of '49: A Personal Narrative of the Overland Trail and Adventures in California and Oregon from 1849 to 1854* (Manchester, N.H.: Standard Book Company, 1917).

WELLS, Letters. "The Letters of Epaphroditus Wells of Downers Grove, Illinois, to His Wife Emma B. Wells, Written from April 1st, 1849, to September 20, 1851, concerning His Overland Journey to California and His Experiences while There" (ts., C-B 731A, Bancroft Library).

WELSH, Diaries. John Pratt Welsh, "Diaries" [vol. 1, "Overland in 1851"; vol. 3, "Overland in 1853"] (ms., HM 30628, Huntington Library).

WHEELER, Diary. George Nelson Wheeler, "Diary" (ms., HM 16939, Huntington Library).

WHITE, "Letter." "To Oregon in 1852: Letter of Dr. Thomas White," ed. Oscar O. Winther and Gayle Thornbrough, *Indiana Historical Society Publications*, 23 (1964): 9-23.

WIGLE, Copy. Abraham J. Wigle, "Copy of Manuscript Written by the Rev. A. J. Wigle" (mimeograph, 587, Oregon Historical Society, Portland).

WILKINS, *An Artist.* James F. Wilkins, *An Artist on the Overland Trail: The 1849 Diary and Sketches of James F. Wilkins*, ed. John Francis McDermott (San Marino, Calif.: Huntington Library, 1968).

WILKINSON, Across the Plains. "Journal of J. A. Wilkinson across the Plains in 1859" (photocopy, Fac 7, Huntington Library).

WILKINSON, Journal. J. A. Wilkinson, "Journal: Across the Plains in

1859" (ms., Newberry Library).

WILLIAMS, "Diary." Mrs. Velina A. Williams, "Diary of a Trip across the Plains in 1853," *Transactions of the Forty-Seventh Annual Reunion of the Oregon Pioneer Association* (Portland, Ore: Chausse-Prudhomme Co., 1922), pp. 178-226.

WILLIAMS, Journal. Velina A. Williams, "Journal" (ms., 1508, Oregon Historical Society, Portland).

WOLCOTT, Journal. Lucian McClenathan Wolcott, "Journal of an Overland Trip in 1850 and Mining Near Coloma" (photocopy, HM 26614, Huntington Library).

WOOD, J., *Journal. Journal of John Wood, as Kept by Him while Traveling from Cincinnati to the Gold Diggings in California, in the Spring and Summer of 1850* (Columbus: Nevins & Myers, 1871).

WOOD, J.W., Diaries. Joseph Warren Wood, "Diaries of Crossing the Plains in 1849 and Life in the Diggins from 1849 to 1853" (ms., HM 318, Huntington Library).

WOODWORTH, Diary. "Diary of James Woodworth: Across the Plains to California in 1853" (ts., reproduced by Lane County Pioneer-Historical Society, 1972).

YAGER, "Diary." James Pressley Yager, "Diary of a Journey across the Plains," *Nevada Historical Society Quarterly*, 13 (1970): 5-19 (no. 1), 19-30 (no. 2), 27-48 (no. 3), 27-52 (no. 4); 14 (1971): 27-54 (no. 1), 33-54 (no. 2).

YEARGAIN, Diary. "Typed Copy of the Diary of John Wesley Yeargain, En Route to Oregon" (ts., Missouri Historical Society, St. Louis).

ZIEBER, Diary. "Diary of John S. Zieber" (ts., 1508, Oregon Historical Society, Portland).

ZILHART, Diary. William Zilhart, "Diary, April 1853-October 1853" (ts., California State Library).

INDEX

purchase or rental of, 298-302 and *nn* 15, 19; 313; privileges of ownership, 298-304; waiting lines for use of, 300; as quasi-public property, 300-01 and *n*15; proprietors of, 301-02 and *n*19, 313

Bolton, _____ , 201*n*7

Boone County Company, 192-97, 198

Booth, _____ , 70, 275

Borrowing, 83-84, 150, 205-06, 225, 343

Boston-Newton Company, 174, 363

Boyer, Jonas, 209-12

Boyle, Charles Elisha, 95(*n*30)

Bradford, Sandy, 14(*n*16), 198*n*1

Brainard, David, 38(*n*8)

Brands, 276*n*7; and identification of government horses, 276-77 and *nn* 9, 10; 278, 279

Brandy: sold on the trail, 98; price of, 106; jointly-owned, 155, 170 and *n*8; cached, 272*n*13. *See also* Liquor; Whiskey

Breyfogle, Joshua D., 327(*n*34)

Bridger, Jim, 25, 94, 95, 124, 307

Bridges: tolls charged at, 72, 316, 321-26 and *nn* 9, 10, 12; Indian-owned, 72, 321-25, 326; as private property, 298, 316, 323; on Bear River, 316; government-owned, 317*n*24; on North Platte, 320; emigrant-built, 321-22, 323, 324; competing, 324

Bridgford, Jefferson, 313*n*9

Brisbane, William, 136(*n*18)

British Columbia, and frontier law-mindedness, 3

British subjects, employed at Fort Hall, 97

Brooks, Alden, 71(*n*11)

Brooks, Quincy Adams, 130(*n*4)

Brouster, George Washington, 238*n*4, 345*n*11

Brown, Adam, 294*n*19, 311(*n*41), 361(*n*11)

Brown, Elam, 104(*n*23)

Brown, J. Robert, 166(*n*10), 203(*n*13),

258(*n*20)

Brown, James Berry, 62(*n*35), 94(*n*22), 199(*n*4)

Brown, John E., 26(*n*38), 31-32(*n*6), 135-36, 277(*n*10), 278*n*12

Brown, John Lowery, 294(*n*18), 341(*n*40)

Brownlee, Robert, 4(*n*4), 7(*n*25)

Bruff, J. Goldsborough, 49(*nn* 47, 48), 103(*n*15), 104(*n*21), 105(*nn* 26, 27), 106(*n*32), 111(*n*7), 117(*n*6), 143(*nn* 7, 8), 144*n*10, 170*n*8, 174(*n*18), 174*n*19, 175-76(*n*24), 267-68*n*16, 271(*n*4), 272*n*9, 273(*n*11), 273*n*12, 308(*n*15), 337(*n*11), 340 (*n*37), 350(*n*2), 353-54, 359(*n*6)

Bryant, Edwin, 91

Bryant's company, 101

Bryarly, Wakeman, 29-30(*n*53), 60 (*n*23), 308(*n*18)

Buckingham, Harriet Talcott, 23(*n*28), 308(*nn* 15, 19), 327

Buffalo, 20, 104, 331; chips, 18, 19-20, 219; robes, 95, 105, 113; hunting of, 119, 142, 145, 297*n*4

Buggies, as trail vehicles, 37

Burbank, Augustus Ripley, 21(*n*10), 23(*n*27), 297*n*4, 308(*n*15), 309 (*n*24), 315(*n*18), 326(*n*25)

Burchard, Dr. _____ , 205, 206*n*3

Burials, 29, 223 and *n*10

Burroughs, Joseph Newton, 25-26 (*n*36), 260*n*30

Burt, Benjamin, 13(*n*11), 20(*n*5)

Business enterprises: at established trading posts, 91-98, 113-15, 307-08; at temporary trading posts on the trail, 97, 98, 310-12; and emigrants as vendors, 98-107; and sale of services, 115-24; at ferries and bridges, 312-24

Buy-out. *See* Sell-out

Caches, rifling of, 273 and *nn* 12, 13

Cagwin, N.A., 44(*n*9), 144*n*12, 165(*n*8)

Caldwell, Dr. [T. G.?], 121(*n*31), 159(*n*4), 228(*n*17)

411

Calibaugh, Peter, 118n9
California frontier: seeing the elephant at, xii; law and order at, 4-5, 6-7; and labor shortage (1849), 17; and abandoned property, 49; and alkaline water, 64; horses from sold on the trail (1841), 91; traders from on the trail, 310-12
California trail: and male emigrants, 11, 25; compared with Oregon trail, 11, 76-77, 83, 85, 128, 288n8; and youthful emigrants, 16; grass shortage on, 217-18; traders at western end of, 306 and n2. *See also* Forty-niners; Hangtown; Humboldt River; Ragtown
Call, Asa, 344n9
Callison, John Joseph, 259n26
Calvin, _____ , 66n17
Campbell, Robert, 231n15, 234(n32)
Canada, mining camps of, contrasted with United States camps, 3
"Cannibal Cabins," 336
Captain Owens' Company, 261
Carpenter, Helen McCowen, 42(n37), 114(n19), 261
Carr, Dabney T., 235-36(n45)
Carriages, as trail vehicles, 37, 53, 56, 72, 74, 75, 87, 88
Carrion. *See* Horses, as food; Livestock, as food; Mules, as food
Carson, Kit, 91
Carson River, 245; trading posts on, 97-98; abandoned property on, 237; water hauled from to Forty-Mile Desert, 296
Carson valley, seeing the elephant at, xii
Carter, Joe, 80n6
Carts, as trail vehicles: converted from wagons, 47-48, 49, 50, 77, 129; converted into packs, 49; as company property, 242, 244, 246-47
Cash. *See* Money
Casler, Melyer, 297n37
Castleman, Philip F., 50(n50), 139(n6), 147(n2), 173(n14) 268n21, 278(n13),

279(n14)
Cattle. *See* Livestock
Cattle thieves. *See* Rustlers, cattle
Chadwick, Samuel, 28 (n46), 133(n9), 208-12
Chalmers, Robert, 232(n23), 241(n20), 295(n27)
Chamberlain, William E., 39(n14), 290(n3)
Chance: role of on the trail, 102; role of in division of concurrently-owned property, 202, 203. *See also* Luck
Chapman, _____ , 80, 81
Chase, Nathan, 6(n21)
Chickens, on Lassen's cutoff (1849), 353-54
Children. *See* Women and children
Chillson, Lorenzo Dow, 23(n23), 59(n14), 111(n9), 114(n16)
Cholera, 29, 40, 120, 122, 123, 164n7, 205, 210, 222, 225, 229, 287, 309
Christy, Thomas, 98(n44), 311(n38)
Churchill, _____ , 279
Churchill, Stillman, 186(n5), 187(n6), 188(nn 7, 8), 257(n14)
Cincinnati Mining and Trading Company, as example of joint-stock company, 177-81
City of Rocks, and intersection of California trail and Salt Lake City road, 242
Claims, prior, as test of ownership, 252n3
Clapp, John T., xii, 26(n39), 129(n1)
Clark, B. C. 16(n32)
Clark, John, 167(n2), 313(n8)
Clarke's men, 252n3
Clark's train, 254-55 and n11
Clerks, as emigrants, 17
Clifton, John, 59(n15)
Clothes washing, as a vendible service, 118n8
Clough, Aaron, 360(n6)
Coffee: carried on the trail (1853), 38, 39, 69; on the Humbolt (1849), 101, 102, 242; sale of, 102, 105

Cole, Gilbert L., 78(nn 3, 4), 113(n13), 202(n11), 310n33, 347-48, 349, 350
Coleman, M., 28-29(n51)
Columbus Ohio Industrial Association, 189
Companies: and causes of dissension, 21, 140, 162n2, 203n13, 214, 287, 344n9, 352; organization of, 27, 33, 39, 78, 137, 146, 171n10, 203n13, 287-88 and n9; membership of, 29-30, 31-32, 141-42, 145, 339; and weight carried, 39, 42, 99; traveling with other groups, 101-02; as legal term, 136-37 and n1, 139; and property relationship with mess, 137-38; and private property, 140-47; and prescriptive right to corporate property, 147-50; captains and proprietors of, 148n6, 287-88 and n9, 303-04 and n26; and concurrently-owned peoperty, 148-50, 203n13; and rotation of wagons, 286-87; and ownership of boats, 298-301; turning back of, 303 and n26, 344n9; and payment of "tribute" to Indians, 326-28; and thievery within, 344
— dissolution of, 155, 177, 189; causes of, 167-77 and nn 8, 9, 10, 16; 178, 180, 186-92, 198n1; and formation of messes, 177, 179, 188-89, 190-91; methods of, 177, 179-80, 185-91 and n2, 192, 194-97. See also Arbitration; Auction; Bargaining; Lottery; Sell-out
— joint-stock, 128, 213; physicians as members of, 119-20; types of ownership within, 129, 137, 151-52; and private property, 129, 143-44; and concurrently-owned property, 137-39, 159, 172-79 and n5; examples of, 137-39, 160-61 and n6, 177-80, 193; compared with traveling company, 138-39, 167; liabilities of, 139-40 and nn 7, 8; leadership of, 141, 148, 159-60, 191-92,; organization of, 141, 175-75, 187, 191-92,

336; and gold mining, 142, 152(n3), 171-72, 186; as paramilitary organization, 143; withdrawal from, 147, 174-77, 186, 187, 214; and contractual obligation, 160; quarrels within, 166-77 and nn 8, 9, 10; 186, 187, 198n1; and messes, 167 and n1, 187; voting in, 172-80 and n20, 186-87, 191-92, 214; and weight carried, 174, 186 and n5; and forfeiture rule, 175-76, 187; converted into traveling company, 177, 179-80, 189-91; and supply wagons, 188-89; and surplus for use in California, 193, 198; and paying passengers, 193-94; boarding members of, 207
— packing: and concurrently-owned property, 148-49; Granite State as example of, 160-61 and n6
— passenger, 287-88 and n9
— traveling, 120, 128; and private property, 128-29, 142-43, 167-69 and n3, 248; examples of, 133-34, 137, 141, 142-43, 193; contrasted with joint-stock companies, 138-39; organization of, 140, 141, 168, 180, 205; and mess property, 155, 167; disputes and divisions of, 168-69 and nn 3, 7; 170 and nn 8, 10; 189-91; converted from joint-stock companies, 177, 180, 189-91; reasons for forming, 180-81; and contracts with passengers, 209-10
Competition, effect of on ferry tolls, 318, 319 and n36; elimination of, 320; attitudes toward, 320-21
Compromise, and reassertion of ownership, 275-76, 280-81
Compton, James H., 140(n8)
Condy, _____, captain of the Badger Boys, 211
Congress and California Joint Stock Mining Company, 214
Constitutions. See Companies, organization of
Contractees: traveling with compa-

413

nies or messes, 128, 139-40, 209-10; and Boone County Company, 193-94; and dissolution of joint-stock companies, 195-97; hired hands as, 288 and nn 7, 8

Contracts: for sharing, 83-85; for hire, 118; written, 130, 131; for partnerships, 130-31, 208-09; and messes, 132-33, 158n2, 165n8, 190-91; and joint-stock companies, 141, 160, 178 and n4, 214; for hauling, 178, 196, 248-49, 274, 301, 302nn 20, 24; 351; for boarding, 207; effect of circumstances on, 208-09; for passage to California, 209-10, 302n20; termination of, 214; for claim on game, 298n5; for use of boats, 300-01 and n15; violation of and use of force, 301, 316; for driving wagons, 350; nullified by property rights, 351-52

Convicts, at the diggings, 7

Conyers, E. W., 351(n3)

Cook, Thomas, 80, 81

Cooke, Lucy Rutledge, 313(n3), 327n36

Cooks, hired hands as, 288n7

Coombs, _____ , 223n10

Cornell, William, 66n46

Cosad, David, 111(n5), 274(n15), 308(n15)

Council Bluffs: ferry tolls at (1853), 72(n16); prices of goods at (1853), 90 and n29; prices of goods and animals at (1854), 131

Coupler, J. C., 320(n42)

Courts, lack of on the trail, 10

Covenants, for public use of boats, 300-01 and n15

Cow Column, 168-69

Cowley, Richard Brown, 4(n2)

Cox, C. C., 298n6, 358-59(n5)

Coy, Owen Cochran, 218(n4), 241n19

Craig, Capt. James, 9(n34)

Crandall, Eliphalet, 252n3

Crane, Judge Addison M., 106(n33), 125, 141, 142, 164(n4), 198n1,

257(n16), 325, 327

Credit, 87; and payment for services, 123-25; and notes payable, 124-25 and n42, 208; as alternative to starvation, 343, 352

Crime: at the diggings, 6-7; on the trail, 13, 221 and n1

Cross, Maj. Osborne, 9(n35), 14(n19), 277(n8), 277n9, 328(n45)

Crosscultural patterns, and problems between Indians and emigrants, 329-34

Daily Missouri Republican, 289(n1)

Dalton, John, 58(n9), 219(n6)

Darwin, Charles Benjamin, 71(n13)

David, James, 17(n34)

Davidson, _____ , 77-87 *passim*

Davidson, George, 43(n3)

Dawson, Nicholas, 158, 352(n6)

Death: fear of and law-mindedness, 221, 222-23, 224; frequency of, 223-24 and n16; on Lassen's cutoff, 227, 228; and 1849 emigration, 229; and 1850 emigration, 242, 245n4

Death Valley, 50, 226, 293, 354-55

Debts, liability of joint-stock companies for, 140 and n7

Decker, Peter, 17(n38), 27n45, 30 (n54), 33(n21), 95(n30), 171n10, 173n16, 189(n11), 307(n12)

Deer, hunted in California (1850), 357

Degroot, H., 130-31(n5)

Delano, Alonzo, 54(n18), 164(n8), 290

Demand receipts, 124

Demand rights, 262-64 and nn 36, 41, 42; 297-98 and n4, 302

Demarest, David D., 186(n3)

De Schutes River, tolls at, 75

Deseret News, 275

De Smet, Father Pierre Jean, 116

Detrich, _____ , 205

Dewolf, David, 13(n9), 38(n11)

Diarrhea, 222

Diggings, gold, in California: and

lawlessness, 3-4, 6-7; weapons at, 5-6; and law and order, 5-6, 356; sickness at, 6; and law-mindedness, 7-8; partnerships at, 130-31, 156, 199-200

Diseases, animal. *See* "Foot Evil"; Hollow horn; Murrain

Diseases, human. *See* Cholera; Diarrhea; Dysentery; Mountain fever; Scurvy; Sickness; Smallpox; Typhus

Dissolution. *See* Companies, dissolution of; Messes, dissolution of; Partnerships, dissolution of

Dobbins, _____ , 261

Doctors. *See* Physicians

Dogs, 168 and n3

Donner party, 336

Dowell, Benjamin Franklin, 21(n14), 333, 334, 338(n22)

Downer, _____ , 124

Downer, Dr. _____ , 215n4

Downer, D. C., 5(n7)

Doyle, Simon, 48(n41), 48n42, 273 (n10)

Draft animals. *See* Livestock

Drake, Jefferson, 204

Drownings, 29, 235

Druggists, and sale of services, 119

Dubuque Emigrating Company, by-laws of, 336(n4)

Dulany, D. M., 28(n48)

Dundass, Samuel Rutherford, 189 (n12), 190(n13), 301n15, 319n36, 358(n4)

Dunlap, Katherine, 99(n6)

Dust, 67 and n50, 219, 220, 233, 286-87

Dysentery, 222

Earnings, joint, sharing of, 130-31

East, return to. *See* Turning back

Eaton, Herbert, 34(n28), 256(n12), 257(n17)

Ebey, Winfield Scott, 66n46, 307(n7), 309(nn 23, 25), 313(n4), 316(n23), 320(n43)

Eccleston, Robert, 264n12, 291n7

Egbert, Eliza Ann McAuley, 253n5, 321(n2)

Elephant, seeing the, defined, xi-xii, 304

Eliot, Robert, 225n2

Elk, 331

Elkhorn River, ferry at, 74, 301

Ellmaker, Enos, 9(n33), 89-90

Elsworth, P. H., 287-88

Emigrants, overland, "seeing the elephant" defined by, xi-xii; conduct of, 8-11; and law-mindedness, 9-11, 13-14, 19, 36, 53, 127-29, 147, 150-51, 155n19, 157, 165-66, 183-84, 202-04, 212-15 and nn 3, 4; 217, 221-22, 224, 251, 265-66, 281, 285-86, 320-21, 335, 349-50, 355-56, 360-64; social character and behavior of, 11-13, 19-30, 35, 217, 286; as cross-section of population, 11-19, 286; and families, 11, 25-26, 30, 53; inexperience of, 14-15, 41-43, 220, 221; as record keepers, 18-19, toilet habits of, 19; and abstinence, 20; and homesickness, 22, 23-24, 25, 27, 217, 218-19; and expenses of trip, 31-32 and n9, 33, 69-76; outfits of, 31-34, 56; life style of on the trail, 35, 36, 42, 49, 50, 218-19, 265, 362; and problem of oversupply, 38-50, 53; and advertisement of goods for sale, 101, 105; and medical help, 119-23; fears of, 147, 160, 165, 172, 177, 178, 180, 181, 218, 221, 232-33, 336-38, 352-55; adaptability of, 220-21; and non-emigrants on the trail, 306-09 and n10; and concern for suffering of others, 337-38, 360-61. *See also* Indians, emigrant attitudes toward; Traders, emigrant attitudes toward

Emigration of 1841, 116, 145-46, 352

Emigration of 1849: California and Oregon trails compared, 11, 76-77, 83, 85; and starvation, 224-28,

229; compared with 1850 emigration, 233-35

Emigration of 1850: and value of money, 71-72; and early starts, 230-31; and packers, 232, 237; and walkers, 232, 237-38; compared with 1849 emigration, 233-35; at Ragtown and Hangtown, 237
— hardships of: alkali poisoning, 62n32; shortages, 62n32, 229-32 and nn 21, 22; 234-35; drought, 229-30, 232-33; sickness, 233n29; length of the trail, 234-35; drownings, 235; one account of, 242-44; and respect for property rights, 243, 245-49, 306, 336, 337, 338-39, 340-44; and number of deaths, 244n4
— and starvation, 68, 112, 143, 225, 228-36, 238; livestock as food, 143, 239, 240-41, 243-44, 249, 337, 339, 342, 345n11, 358; on the Humboldt, 145-46, 157-58, 235-48 and nn 4, 6; 332, 352, 353, 357-58; causes of, 230-35; and prices of goods on the trail, 310-11; and violence, 338, 339-40, 344-45 and n14, 346n16

Equality, frontier, attitudes toward, 286-88 and n9

Evans, James W., 120(n25), 220(n14), 240-41(n17)

Everett, Edward, 363

Fairchild, Lucius, 32-33(n13), 260(n31)

Farmers, as emigrants, 15, 17

Farnham, Elijah Bryan, 59(n16), 165(n9), 170n8, 267-68n16, 268(n19), 301(n14), 337(n12), 361(n10)

Feed for livestock: cost of, 58n6, 292; carried on the trail, 230-31 and nn 12, 15, 16; human consumption of, 241 and n19; availability of (1850), 292

Ferguson, Charles D., 171n9

Ferries: tolls for, 72, 73-75, 301-02 and n19, 313-15 and nn 9, 17; 316-18 and nn 24, 25, 32; 319 and n36,

323n12; and company boats, 298-301; early, 313; sale of, 313-14n9; rival, 313-14n9, 318-19 and nn 36, 37; 324; proposed take over of by federal government, 314; alternatives to, 314, 319 and n34; waiting lines for, 315, 317n25; seizure of, 316-18 and n25; abandoned, 319, 324; as monopolies, 319-21
— exclusive ownership of, 298-302, 315n20, 316-18 and n24; by Indians, 72, 73, 321, 323-24; by French-Canadians, 315n20, 323; by Mormons, 315n20, 323; by Americans, 323
— at the Green River, 312, 315; tolls for, 302n19, 314, 317-18 and n32, 319 and n36; waiting lines for, 315; seizure of (1852), 317-18; rival ferries at, 318-19 and nn 36, 37
— at Maryville, seizure of, 317n25
— Mormon ferry, 313 and n9, 315, 319; tolls for, 317, 319; rival ferry at, 319
— at the North Platte River, 312, 313 and n9, 315

Ferrymen: respect for exclusive property rights of, 312-13, 315-21; money made by, 313 and n9; as outsiders, 313, 315 and n20; emigrant quarrels with, 316-18 and nn 25, 26; and competition, 318-21; and purchase of ferrying rights from Indians, 324n14

Finder: and demand-rights, 262-64 and nn 36, 41, 42; 305; and reassertion of ownership, 273-74

Finder's fees, 262-64 and nn 36, 41, 42; 275-76, 305

Firearms. See Weapons

Fish, 239, 332, 333, 334 and n66

Fish, Juliette G., 111(n5), 301(n17)

Fish, Mary C., 308(n16), 308n17

Fitzpatrick, Thomas, 116

Flint, Thomas, 58(n10)

Flour, 38, 39; at Fort Kearny, 92, 107; sold by emigrants to each other,

416

23, 31, 35, 37; and appropriation of abandoned property, 272, 273-74 and *n*14; mail station on (1859), 297; prices of goods on (1850), 310-11; and starvation, 341, 347-48, 349; and violence, 345*n*14

Forty-niners: and respect for property, 4-5, 76-77; and respect for law, 6-8; and women among, 26 and *n*38, 27; cost of outfits, 31-32; and problem of weight, 42; and need for guides, 117. *See also* California frontier; California trail; Diggings, gold

Foster, _____ , 164*n*7, 279, 280

Foster, Isaac, 317(*n*24)

Fouts, [D. Lambert?], 27(*n*44)

Fox, _____ , 102

Fox, Jared, xi(*n*6), 203(*n*14), 259(*nn* 26, 27), 318*n*32, 337-38

Fox, Samuel, 209-10, 212

French-Canadians: as traders, 306, 347, 349; as ferrymen, 315 and *n*20

Frink, Margaret A., 61(*n*31), 245*n*3, 268(*n*18), 292(*n*8), 295(*n*30)

Frizzell, Lodisa, 37, 98(*n*1), 99(*n*3), 256(*n*12), 271*n*4, 314(*n*12)

Frogs, 239, 332 and *n*58

Frontier Guardian, 13 (*n*12)

Frontiersmen, contrasted with emigrants, 14, 17

Fuel: buffalo chips as, 18, 19-20, 219; abandoned wagons as, 45, 267, 268 and *n*21, 271*n*6; sage brush as, 219; willows as, 235; bacon as, 267-68*n*16; bookcase as, 267-68*n*16. *See also* Wood

Fulkerth, Abby E., 294*n*20

Fuller, _____ , 208

Fur-traders: and emigrants, 91, 93; and Indians, 93, 110

Fur trappers, and Death Valley, 226

Gage, Stephen T., xii, 151(*n*1)

Gambling: at the diggings, 7; by emigrants, 17; by traders, 308

Game: as exclusive property of the hunter, 142 and *n*5, 297-98 and *nn* 4, 5; 305, 331, 333-34, 357; and emigrant dogs, 168; sale of, 297; needless slaughter of, 331; Indian dependency on, 331, 332; as food on the Humboldt, 333-34, 352. *See also* Animals, wild; Hunting; Weapons

Geer, Elizabeth Dixon Smith, 104 (*n*24), 307(*n*9)

Geiger, Vincent, 112*n*10

Gibbs, George, 277(*n*8)

Gila River route: and abandoned property, 43, 49, 272*n*9; starvation on (1849), 225 and *nn* 1, 2; 358-59; and exclusive possession of water (1849), 291*n*7

Gilbert, William W., 262(*n*38)

Giles, _____ , 167

Gill, William, 311(*n*35)

Gilmore, Andrew Hall, 23(*n*24), 232*n*22, 233(*n*27), 300(*nn* 11, 13)

Githens, _____ , 162*n*2

Gold diggings. See Diggings, gold

Gold rush era, and lawlessness, 4, 6-7

Goldsmith, Oliver, 15(*n*25), 111(*n*7), 146, 175, 213-14, 348, 349, 350

Goltra, Elizabeth J., 63(*nn* 37, 38), 64-66, 84

Goodell, Anna Maria, 22(*n*21), 308 (*n*15)

Goodfellow, _____ , 278-79

Goods: surplus for sale, 91, 98-99, 100-02; hauled to the trail by traders, 98, 306 and *n*2; prices of determined by circumstances, 98-99, 100, 102, 103-04, 106-07; advertisements for sale of, 101, 105; and refusal to sell, 101, 106, 112, 353; contracts for hauling of, 178, 196, 248-49, 301, 302 *nn* 22, 24; disposal of as absolute right of owner, 289-91

Goose Creek, 78

Gorgas, Solomon A., 24(*n*30), 93(*n*13), 200(*n*6), 236-37, 238

Gould, Charles, 174(*n*20)

418

Gould, Jane A., 301(*n*16)
Government. *See* United States government
Graham, Alpheus N., 130(*n*3), 296 (*n*32)
Grande Ronde River, 86*n*18, 323*n*10
Granite State Company, 145, 149-50, 160-61 and *nn* 6, 7; 172, 173, 174*n*20
Grant, Capt. _____ , 69*n*5
Grant, Capt. Richard, 307
Grass: as exclusive possession, 291-92; as Indian property, 326-28, 330
— shortages of: in 1849, 45, 102, 217-18; in 1853, 57, 58 and *n*6, 64, 65; on the Humboldt (1850), 112, 235, 243; in 1850, 229 and *n*6, 231 32, 238, 337-38, 344*n*9; in 1852, 287. *See also* Hay
Gray, Charles G., 77(*n*1), 92(*n*5), 95(*n*28), 104-05, 124, 152-56, 164-65, 170*n*8, 262(*n*37), 266(*n*5), 280-81, 342(*n*47)
Green, Jay, 328(*n*42)
Green River: Thomas Fork of, 29; and abandoned property, 49, 289; and alkaline water, 64; ferries at, 74 and *n*26, 79, 312, 314, 315, 317, 318-19 and *nn* 32, 36, 37; and traders on, 91, 95
Greenwood, Caleb, 117
Grindell, John, 238(*n*8), 295(*n*22), 341(*n*42)
Griswold, Harriet Booth, 297*n*37
Grocery and liquor caravans (1849), 105-06
Grocery stores, at crossing of North Platte (1859), 94
Guard duty: contracts for, 118 and *n*9, 162, 288*n*7; as obligation of company members, 168-69 and *n*7, 338; and protection of temporarily abandoned property, 269, 271-72, 273
Guidebooks, 116, 117; advice of on weight, 41-42, 54; advice of on self-sufficiency, 72
Guides, 306; types of service rendered, 116-18 and *n*7; fees of, 117-18 and *nn* 4, 7; 135
Gundlach, John H., 253-54(*n*7), 256 (*n*13)
Gun powder, 38, 50. *See also* Ammunition; Weapons
Guns. *See* Weapons

Hackney, Joseph, 48(*n*40), 259(*n*28), 360(*n*4)
Hadapp, _____ , 293
Hadley, Emelia, 308*n*13
Haight, Henry, 120(*n*23), 271*n*6
Hale, Israel, 109*n*1, 171*n*9
Hale, John, 6(*n*17), 103(*n*17), 161-62, 253(*n*6), 256*n*13, 262*n*34, 275(*n*3)
Half breeds, at Fort Hall, 308*n*13
Hall, _____ , 354-55
Hall, O. J., 32(*n*8)
Handcarts, as trail vehicles, 37; wagons converted into, 47-48, 49, 50, 77, 129. *See also* Pushcarters; Wheelbarrowers
Handouts. *See* Begging
Hangtown, 5, 237
Hanna, Esther Belle McMillan, 323*n*11, 332*n*58
Hardesty, Samuel, 193, 194, 195, 196
Harker, George Mifflin, 5(*n*8)
Harris, Benjamin Butler, 214-15*n*3, 346(*n*15), 352(*n*9)
Harvey, Isaac Julian, 13(*n*8), 202*n*12, 288*n*7, 302*n*24
Harvey, Thomas, 326(*n*27)
Hastings cutoff, 178*n*4, 225, 241; sale of water on, 293-94 and *n*20
Hauling: contrasted with packing, 79; contracts for, 178, 196, 248-49, 301, 302 *nn* 22, 24; cost of on Forty-Mile Desert (1850), 248-49
Hauling animals. *See* Livestock
Haun, Catherine Margaret, 28, 276(*n*6)
Hay: making of at Humboldt Meadows, 236, 244; barter for, 291; as exclusive possession, 291-92; hauling of to the trail, 292; price of (1850), 292. *See also* Grass

419

Hayes, Benjamin, 314(*n*14)
Hayes, Sam, 201*n*8
Hentz, Charles, 43(*n*7), 46(*n*25)
Heustis, _____ , 269-70
Hickman, Richard Owen, 198*n*1
Hinkley, _____ , 201*n*7
Hinman, Charles G., 13(*n*10)
Hired hands, 37, 56, 84, 128, 360;
    teamsters as, 33, 128, 148*n*6, 158*n*2,
    162, 287-88 and *nn* 7, 8; as con-
    tractees, 287, 288 and *nn* 7, 8; and
    guard duty, 288*n*7
Hite, _____ , 87-88 and *n*25, 89
Hite, Joseph, 82*n*9
Hixson, Jasper Morris, 44(*n*10),
    46(*n*20), 49(*n*46), 91-92(*n*4), 96-
    97(*nn* 35, 37), 99(*n*4), 109(*n*2),
    114(*n*18), 115(*n*22), 201-02(*n*9),
    266(*n*6)
Hoarding, as right of property owner,
    305
Hoffman, Benjamin, 218(*n*2), 302*n*19,
    336(*n*8)
Hollow horn, 66-67 and *n*46, 68, 86
Holt County Missouri Mining Com-
    pany, 142
Homicide, on the trail, 221 and *n*1.
    See also Violence.
Hoover, Vincent A., 164*n*7, 354(*nn*
    16, 17)
Horses, 15-16, 88, 129, 288*n*7; as draft
    animals, 37; feed for carried, 40;
    dead on the trail, 46-47, 232*n*22,
    236, 245*n*4, 339; purchased by trap-
    pers, 47; poisoning of, 78, 145; sold
    by traders, 91-92, 93, 94, 95, 105,
    113-114; and Indians, 93, 94, 110,
    152, 153, 227, 253, 254-55, 275-76;
    sold by emigrants to each other,
    100; theft of, 110, 153, 252-55 and
    *n*5, 260, 276-77 and *n*9, 344*n*1; bar-
    ter of, 113-14, 342; belonging to
    U.S. government, 139, 276-79 and
    nn 9, 10; as food, 143, 249, 332, 337,
    339, 345*n*11, 352-53; borrowing of,
    144 and *nn* 10, 11, 12; privately-
    owned, 144-46 and *n*15, 152-54,

254-55, 272*n*9; company-owned,
    145; mess-owned, 145*n*15; bail-
    ment of, 243, 246; appropriation
    of, 275, 278-81; sold to raise cash,
    315, 340
— commonly-owned: prescriptive
    rights to, 148-50; division of upon
    dissolution, 204
— price of: on the Humboldt (1850),
    100*n*8; on the trail, 132, 152; at Fort
    Bridger (1849), 153; charged by
    Indians, 275; and refusal to sell,
    346. *See also* Livestock; Mules;
    Ponies; Riding animals
Hosley, Dexter P., 124(*n*43), 262*n*36
Howell, Elijah Preston, 327-28(*n*40)
Hudgins, John, 117*n*4
Hudson's Bay Company, at Fort Hall,
    96, 307
Hudspeth's cutoff, food shortages at
    (1850), 337
Humboldt Meadows: traders at, 97;
    recruitment at, 236, 244; price of
    hay at (1850), 292; price of flour at
    (1850), 357
Humboldt River, 26, 358; and aban-
    doned property, 49; traders on,
    97; and scarcity of grass, 112, 235,
    243; prices for food at (1850), 112,
    239-40, 341-42, 343-44, 345; dead
    livestock in, 220; flooding of (1850),
    235; perils of, 235-41 and *nn* 4, 6;
    245-49; early arrivals on (1850),
    238 and *n*4; begging on, 238, 338;
    and emigration of 1850, 241-45;
    sale of water on, 294; and depra-
    dation of Indian food sources on,
    332-34 and *nn* 58, 60; starvation
    on, 338, 340-41, 344-45 and *n*11,
    346*n*16, 356-58
Humboldt Sink: traders at, 97; re-
    cruitment at, 244
Humphrey, Lezerne, 44(*n*8)
Hunting: as a vendible service, 118-
    19; spoils of as exclusive property,
    142 and *n*5, 297-98 and *nn* 4, 5; 305,
    331, 333-34, 357; on Lassen's cutoff

(1849), 228; by emigrants on Indian lands, 331, 333-34; in California (1850), 357. *See also* Game; Weapons

Huntington, John, 133

Huston, Samuel, 231*n*16

Illness. *See* Sickness

Independence, Missouri, 8, 13, 44; prices of outfits at, 32, 33

Independence Rock, and alkali water, 58

Indian agents: and request that emigrants pay Indian tolls, 325; and request for emigrant "tribute" to Indians, 328

Indians: and Canadian government, 3; and appropriation of abandoned property, 262, 264 and *n*41, 276 and *n*6; and United States military, 276-77 and *n*9; and exclusive rights to game, 297*n*4; lodges of, 308*n*14; graves of violated by emigrants, 329

— emigrant attitudes toward, 15, 21, 46, 72-73, 253-55, 306, 321-34; as traders, 69, 73, 75, 87, 93 and *n*14, 329; hostility toward, 117, 137*n*1, 224, 227, 254, 261-62, 269, 327*n*6, 328, 332-33, 339; as horse traders, 152, 256, 275-76, 329, 333; and dogs of, 168; and claims to property, 324-25; and stampeding of cattle, 327; and crosscultural problems, 329-34

— ferries and bridges of, 72, 321-26 and *nn* 9, 14; 313; built by others and taken over by, 321-22, 323, 324; methods of toll collecting, 321-23 and *nn* 9, 12; tolls charged by, 321-26 and *n*9; labor of invested in, 324-25; legal right of to collect tolls, 324-25

— negotiations with: over tolls, 72, 322-23; over compensation for crossing lands of, 326-27

— as sellers of services: swimmers of cattle, 73, 75; guides, 117; trackers

of stray animals, 264*n*41; renters of rafts, 329; woodsmen, 329

— territorial and property rights of: failure of emigrants to respect, 321-34; as seen by the emigrants, 322-23, 324-25, 327, 329-30; and United States intercourse act, 325; as seen by themselves, 325-26, 329, 330-31; and collection of "tribute" from emigrants, 325-27 and *nn* 36, 39; and legal validity of compensation demands, 326-28; and ownership of natural resources, 329-30

— as thieves, 165, 256 and *n*13, 326, 332, 344; of horses, 110, 153, 227, 253 55, 275, 276 77 and *n*9, 333 and *n*61, 334, 346; and ransoms or rewards paid to, 254-55, 326; and sale of stolen animals, 275

— and traders, 91, 94, 110, 113, 307, 309; at Fort Hall, 308*n*13; marriage to, 308 and *nn* 13, 17; 309

— tribes of: Apaches, 110; Cherokees, 118*n*7, 120*n*20, 294; Diggers, 146; Flatheads, 116; Iowas, 325; Kaws, 327*n*39; Kickapoos, 323*n*9, 326; Nez Perce, 93*n*14; Omahas, 327; Pawnees, 321-22, 323, 324*n*14, 326-27 and *n*36; Pima, 264*n*41, 276*n*6; Sac and Fox, 325, 326; Sioux, 73, 93, 275, 276-77 and *n*9, 326; Snake, 333

Ingalls, E. S., 59(*n*13), 271*n*8, 273*n*14, 339

Iron City Rangers, 172

Jagger, D., 223(*n*12), 336(*n*7)

James, Samuel, 326-27

Jeffers, _____ , 279

Jewett, George E., 308(*n*15)

Johnson, John A., 24(*n*31), 45(*n*18), 100-02, 138-39(*n*5), 150(*n*13), 297*n*4, 298*n*5, 342(*n*47)

Johnson, Joseph H., 125(*n*46)

Johnston, William, 19(*n*2), 114(*n*21), 296(*n*34)

Johnston, William G., 8(*n*29), 45(*n*17), 95(*n*26), 124(*n*41), 149(*n*7), 164*n*8,

306n14
Joint-stock organizations. *See* Companies, joint-stock
Jones, John N., 360n5
Judson, Phoebe Goodell, 20-21(n6)

Kahler, William, 324(n16)
Kanesville: as an outfitting town, 13, 32; price of flour at (1853), 90n30
Kansas River: ferry on (1845), 313; toll bridge at, 323n10
Keen, Richard A., 118n9, 302n20
Kellogg, Philander, 110, 119
Kelly, William, 107(n34)
Kenneday, Enos, 75
Keytesville, and lawlessness, 7
Kilgore, William H., 292(n11), 313(n7), 326(n26),
Kingsville Company, 191-92
Kinship, precedence of over property rights, 146-47
Kirkpatrick, Charles A., 290n3, 336(n6)
Kitchell, E., 100(n8)
Knight, Amelia, 60n25, 86n18, 116n1
Kuhliwein, Hugo Frederick, 130(n2), 234(n34)
Kunkel, G. S., 297 nn 37, 39

Labor: as payment by contractee mess member, 133; as test of exclusive rights to property, 296, 297 and n4, 298n5, 301, 316, 323, 324; as payment for services, 302 and n22
Lampton, William, 202(n10)
Lane, S. A., 202n10
Langworthy, Franklin, 17(n37), 62(n30), 220(n15), 221(n16), 267n15
Lassen's cutoff: price of flour at (1849), 103-04; starvation at (1849), 226-28, 306, 336, 339, 340, 348, 349, 353-54; and alkaline water, 227; location of, 227; and trouble with Indians, 227, 228; and crossing the Sierras, 227, 228; and appropriation of abandoned property,

268n21, 269-70, 272n7, 350-51
Lassen's ranch, 227 and n12, 228, 339, 359
Law: as defined by lawyers, 4; as understood by emigrants, 9, 10-11, 183-84, 203, 204, 213-15, 251, 265 and n1, 359-61; misconceptions and non-applications of on the trail, 137-38, 146-47; decided by majority in partnerships, 206-07; and prevention of violence on the trail, 212-15 and nn 3, 4; *vs.* social practice, 292
Law, institutions of: at the diggings, 4; lack of on the trail, 10, 183, 184, 203
Law-mindedness: 19th-century American predilection for, 3, 10-11, 13-14, 36, 217, 221-22, 335; at the diggings, 7-8; on the trail, 9-11, 19, 127-29, 147, 150-51, 157, 251, 265-66, 285-86, 360-64; and respect for property rights, 155n19, 165-66, 183-84, 202-04, 246-47, 281, 335, 356, 360-364; and attitudes toward violence, 212-15, 221, 347, 349-50, 355-56; and attitudes toward competition, 320-21
Law of abandonment. *See* Abandonment, law of
Law of supply and demand, as seen on the trail, 98-99, 101-02, 103-04, 109, 289-92, 309, 311n28
Law of survival. *See* Survival, law of
Laws, Robert, xii
Lawyers: as emigrants, 9, 17, 18, 30, 43, 71, 259, 325; lack of on the trail, 10, 11; services of not in demand, 119; attitudes of toward Indian right to compensation, 325, 327; attitudes of toward emigrant appropriation of wild food and animals, 333-34
Leavitt, D. G. W., 31(n3)
Leases, 84
Legal behaviorism: threats to on the trail, 221-22; uniformity of, 265,

242, 249. *See also* Chance
Lyman, Joseph, 89*n*27
Lynn (Massachusetts) company, 257
Lyon, James D., 227(*n*15)

McBride, John Holden, 233*n*29, 315*n*17
McBride, William S., 33(*n*20),93(*n*29), 113(*n*12), 118(*n*9), 233(*nn* 25, 26)
McCall, A. J., 145-46*n*15, 228(*n*20), 336(*n*3)
McCanne, Hugh, 295(*n*28)
McClure, _____ , 260
McClure, Andrew S., 63(*n*36), 309(*n*21)
McConnel, _____ , 190
McCowen, George, 92(*n*7), 131(*n*6)
McCoy, _____ , 204
McDonald, Richard Hayes, 113*n*13
McFadden, Sam, 215*n*4
McGlasken, J., 268(*n*20)
McIlhany, Edward Washington, 149*n*8
McIntosh, Col. _____ , 279
McKeeby, Lemuel Clarke, 339
McKinstry, Byron N., 142-43, 198(*n*2), 229*n*5, 240(*n*16), 276*n*7, 292(*n*9), 294(*n*15), 295(*n*29), 337, 345*n*14
McKinstry, George, 12(*n*5)
McLane, Allen, 99(*n*5), 302*n*22
McLeod, Patrick H., 45(*n*13), 142(*n*4), 300(*n*9), 319(*n*38)
McNeely, _____ , 263-64
McQueen, Angus, 34(*n*27)
Madison Company, 99
Mail station, on the Forty-Mile Desert (1859), 297
Mann, _____ , 83-84, 87
Mann, H. R., 22(*n*19), 62(*n*29), 95(*n*30), 272*n*9, 336(*nn* 5, 9)
Mariposa, and respect for property (1849), 5
Marshall, George, 290*n*3
Mason, Leonard, 5(*n*13), 6(*nn* 14, 16), 185*n*2
Mathews, S., 52(*n*12)
Maxey, James M., 71(*n*10)

Maynard, Dr. David, 121, 122
Meals, price of at Ragtown (1850), 343
Mechanics, as hired hands, 288*n*7
Medicines, 39, 40, 222*n*2; whiskey as, 40, 170*n*8; payment for, 121, 123; as concurrently-owned property, 159; brandy as, 170*n*8. *See also* Opium; Physicians; Quinine
Merchants, on the trail, 17, 105-06
Merriweather, _____ , 141
Mess, eating, 134-35. *See also* Messes
Mess, traveling, 135. *See also* Messes
Messes: and contractual agreements, 84-85, 132-34, 166*n*11, 190-91; food supply of, 39, 189, 190-91, 238, 243, 244, 247-49; and private property, 132, 133, 151, 164-65 and *nn* 7, 8; 247-49; types of, 134-36; as part of company, 137-38, 143, 161*n*7, 187, 189, 352; disputes within, 163-66 and *nn* 6, 7, 11, 12; 170*n*8, 198*n*1, 244; formed at dissolution of joint-stock companies, 177, 179, 180, 188-89, 190-91; and appropriation of abandoned property, 244, 247*n*5, 266
— dissolution of, 155*n*19, 184-85, 190-91, 198, 199-200, 202; within joint-stock company, 161*n*7; causes of, 169, 171*n*10, 193, 201*n*7; and role of money, 198-99 and *nn* 1, 2
— membership of: as partners, 128, 132-36; as contractees, 132-35, 158*n*2, 166*n*11; changes in, 167, 201 and *n*8; controlled by property, 190-91
— property ownership within, 129, 132-136, 151, 154-55, 248-49; con-currently-owned, 76-77, 128, 132, 140, 145*n*15, 160*n*6, 164, 165-66 and *n*12, 179; personally-owned, 141, 164-65 and *n*7, 247-48
Mexicans, hired to track stray animals, 264*n*12
Military, United States. *See* Army, United States

424

Miller, Joel, 254(*n*8), 266(*n*5)
Miller, Martin Wise, 296*n*31
Miller, Reuben G., 258*n*19
Miller, William W., 4(*n*5)
Millington, D. A., 7(*n*24)
Mineral law, east *vs.* west, 359
Mining camps. *See* Diggings, gold
Mining supplies and equipment: carried on the trail, 40, 172-73, 176, 178; shipped around the Horn, 54, 152(*n*3); contracts for hauling, 178 and *n*4.
Ministers, as emigrants, 13, 17, 23, 35
Missouri River: seeing the elephant at, xi; as boundary between civilized and uncivilized life, 8-9; ferries at, 56, 72
Missouri whiskey cart, 106
Moccasins, Indian, sold on the trail, 69, 73, 113
Money: use of and need for on the trail, 32, 70-72 and*n*8, 85, 88, 133, 135-36, 158, 162, 218, 231-32, 291, 310*n*33, 360; obtained by sale of personal property, 69, 86-87, 98-107, 314-15, 339, 340, 343, 358-59; and barter, 71, 154, 158, 311; worthlessness of, 71-72, 101, 104, 242, 243, 245-46; availability of, 94, 111; at Fort Kearny, 106; as payment for services, 116-17, 118 *nn* 8, 9; 121-25, 320 and *nn* 19, 20; and relief funds, 129-30, 294, 360-61; and dissolutions, 185-86, 188, 191, 192, 198-99; as mess property, 244, 248-49; and purchase of food, 244, 310-11, 337, 339, 340, 341, 357-58; subscriptions for, 294; and tolls, 314-15, 322. *See also* Bank notes; Credit
Monroe (Michigan) company, 78, 79
Moore, Jonathan Limerick, 334*n*66
Moorman, Madison Berryman, 21(*n*12), 149(*n*9), 179(*n*4), 262*n*34, 294(*n*19), 343(*n*54)
Morgan, Martha M., 260-61(*n*32), 307(*n*8)

Mormon Crossing of North Platte River, 298
Mormon Island, 5
Mormons: settlements of, 55, 154; ferries and bridges of, 59, 313 and *n*9, 316, 319-20; as traders, 92, 97, 114, 234-35; courts of, 215*n*4; as guides, 226; emigrant attitudes toward, 306, 307; as ferrymen, 313, 315 and *n*20; as thieves, 344; and refusal to sell, 346*n*17
Morton, _____ , 167
Mosquitoes, as trail hazard, 175
Mountain fever, 222. *See also* Sickness.
Mountain men: as traders, 91, 94, 110, 114; as guides, 116-17; as ferrymen, 313, 319*n*37; and violence, 344*n*1
Mount Washington company, 39
Moxley, Charles G., 17(*n*35)
Mules: as hauling animals, 16, 37-38, 42, 45, 54, 55, 287*n*7; as pack animals, 33, 53, 219-20, 237; dead on the trail, 46-47, 232*n*22, 236, 237, 245*n*4, 339; sold by traders, 91, 113, 114-15; and Indians, 110, 227, 332; as private property, 144, 148, 360; as payment for hauling, 302*n*24; as food, 312, 339, 342, 353, 358
— commonly-owned: prescriptive rights to, 148 and *n*6, 149; division of at dissolution, 148, 194
— government: purchased by emigrants, 277-78 and *n*10; reclaimed, 277-78 and *nn* 10, 12
— prices of: in St. Joseph, 31, 32; along the Humboldt (1849), 101; at Fort Laramie (1849), 102*n*2; on the trail (1865), 132. *See also* Horses; Livestock; Ponies; Riding animals
Murphy, Andrew Lopp, 59(*n*20)
Murphy, Patrick M., 9(*n*31), 37(*n*1), 148*n*6
Murphy's Diggings, and respect for property (1849), 5

Murrain ("murram," "murrim," "murrin"), 66n46, 80 and n6
Murray, John, 36(n33), 58n6, 324n14
Murrell, George McKinley, 4(n3)
Muscott, John M., 7-8, 14(n13), 37(n6), 43(n4), 45(n14), 135(nn 15, 16)

Natural resources, rights to and exclusive possession of, 305
Negotiable instruments, 124
Negotiation. *See* Bargaining
Ness, Richard, 267n13
Newcomb, Silas, 25(n34), 26(n40), 97-98(n41), 337(n10)
New York Herald, 172(n12)
Nixon, Alexander B., 177(n1), 178(nn 2, 3, 4), 179 (nn 5, 6), 180(n7)
North Platte River: and abandoned property, 48, 356; and alkaline water, 58; traders at, 91, 92; blacksmith shop at, 94; grocery stores at, 95; drownings on, 229; boats on as quasi-public property, 300-01 and n15; ferries at, 312, 313 and n9, 315, 317, 319. *See also* Platte River; South Platte River
Notes payable, 88, 124-25 and n42. *See also* Credit
Notices: placed on abandoned property, 271 and nn 4, 5, 6; and reservation of ownership, 272 and n9, 274
Nusbaummer, Louis, 50(n51), 292(n13)

Ohio Statesman, The, 245n4
Open range laws, east *vs.* west, 359
Opium, as medicine, 121. *See also* Medicines
Oregon trail: and family emigrants, 11, 25; compared with California trail, 11, 76-77, 83, 85, 128; numbers using (1853), 67n1; hardships of, 56-90, 288n8; and emigrant attitudes toward property, 77-90 *passim;* value of abandoned property

on (1853), 89n27
Ormsby, Dr. Caleb N., 12(nn 6, 7)
Orvis, Andrew, 145
Otzman, _____ , 201n7
Outfits: prices of compared, 32-33; abandoned, 268n21; bartered, 311; sale of, 358-59
Overland market, dynamics of, 98-102
Overland trail: law-mindedness on, 8-11, 292, 336, 356, 359-64; hardships of, 54-55, 115-16, 124-25, 217-21, 228-29, 358; condition of, 218; custom of, 273-74 and n14, 276-84, 352, 354, 362-63; non-emigrants on, 306-07
— routes taken, 287, 288; Gila River route, 43, 49, 225 and nn 1, 2; 272n9, 291n7, 358-59; and Death Valley, 50, 226, 293, 354-55; 1849 cutoffs, 95; Lassen's cutoff, 103-04, 226-28, 268n21, 269-70, 272n7, 306, 336, 339, 340, 348, 349, 350-54; Hastings cutoff, 178n4, 225, 241, 293-94 and n20; northern route out of Salt Lake City, 241-42
Overloading, 38-50 *passim,* 41n24, 53-54, 55, 68-70, 80, 89-90, 99, 110, 160; as problem in joint-stock companies, 171-74, 176, 177-78, 179, 180, 184-85, 186 and n5
Owen, Benjamin Franklin, 260(n29)
Owens brothers, 124
Owners, rightful, 253 and n4, 256; and recompense for return of property, 262-64 and nn 36, 41, 42; 275-76, 280; and claims against good-faith purchaser, 274-80
Ownership: and exclusive possession, 112-13, 145, 285-305, 288n9, 351-54, 360-63; as understood by emigrants, 139, 151-52, 246-47, 249, 251, 252n3, 282, 283, 305; and use of possessive pronoun, 150; and rights to lost or stolen property, 251-64. *See also* Abandonment, law of; Property, respect for ownership of; Property, private, rights

and privileges of ownership of Oxen. *See* Livestock.

Packers: and emigration of 1850, 232, 237; and appropriation of abandoned property, 267*n*13, 273-74; and purchase of provisions on the trail, 346*n*16, 352, 353
Packing: on foot, 33-34, 35, 146, 165-66, 237-38, 339, 342, 348, 352, 360; by mule, 35-36, 39, 49, 53, 78-79, 219-20, 342; from Fort Laramie, 47; speed of, 78, 79, 200-01, 353; reasons for, 78, 221, 273, 291, 339; across Forty-Mile Desert, 145*n*15
Packing companies, 100-02
Pack mules. *See* Mules
Packs, manufactured from cut-up wagons, 101
Page, Henry, 43(*n*5), 46(*n*27), 249
Palmer, Joel, 309(*n*27)
Papea Creek, Indian toll bridge at, 72, 323*n*10
Paramilitary organization, joint-stock company as, 143
Park, Dr. E. C., 205-06
Park, Edmund, 205
Parke, Charles R., 18(*n*41), 137(*n*3)
Parker, Elias, 166*n*11
Parker, William Tell, 43(*n*2), 70(*n*7), 238(*n*5), 275(*n*4), 290-91(*n*6), 311(*n*37), 338(*n*23), 342(*n*48), 345(*n*12)
Parkman, Francis, on emigrant attitudes toward traders, 307*n*10
Parsons, Mary Collins, 321-22(*n*3)
Partnerships: and concurrently-owned property, 128, 130-132, 198, 205 and *n*2, 210-12, 213; informality of, 129-31; definition of, 128, 129, 130, 132, 134, 137, 198; and division of income, 130-31, 132; and mess property, 132-36; and personal property, 141, 204-05 and *nn* 1, 2; 211-12; formation of, 157-58, 165*n*8, 198; contracts of, 183, 208-09; decision-making process

of, 205, 206-07; and violence, 344*n*1
— dissolution of: at destination, 115*n*19, 199-200, 208; attempted, 159; causes of, 161-66 and *n*12, 171*n*10, 183, 200-03 and *n*7, 205-06 and *n*3; 210-12; and division of property at, 162-64, 211-12; problems of, 185, 193, 200, 201-02, 211; and role of money, 198-99; on the trail, 198-204, 206-12; before setting out, 199; as a common practice, 199-200; consequences of, 200-04 and *nn* 10, 12; cost of to departing members, 206-08, 212
Paschel, Albert G., 23(*n*29), 62(*n*33), 96(*n*33), 240(*n*15), 311(*n*37)
Passage, overland: cost of (1852), 287, 288*n*7; methods of payment for, 302 and *n*20, 360 and *n*5
Passage money, demanded by Indians for crossing territory of, 326-28
Passengers: as contractees, 128, 174, 209-10, 302 and *n*20; rights of, 287-88 and *n*9, 303-04 and *n*26
Passenger wagon trains. *See* Wagon trains
Payne, James A., 37-38(*n*7), 93(*n*15), 238-39, 288*n*7, 308(*n*15), 313(*n*5), 324-25(*n*18), 356-58
Peacock, William, 218(*n*5), 231*n*12
Peoria Pioneers, 137-38
Perkins, Elisha Douglass, 42(*n*33), 44(*n*12), 45(*n*15), 53-55, 56, 59(*n*21), 133-34, 164, 184-85, 258(*n*22), 342(*n*48)
Personality clashes, and dissolution of companies, 171*n*9
Phelps, A. W., 203
Philly, James, 105*n*28
Physicians: on the trail, 12, 13, 17, 18, 35, 43, 64, 70, 159, 205, 228, 233 and *n*29, 244*n*17, 290, 302*n*22, 314, 339, 345, 347; as members of joint-stock companies, 119-20, 121*n*29; vendible services of, 119-23 and *n*25; Cherokee as company surgeon, 120*n*20; advertisement by,

121-22. *See also* Medicines
Pierce, Hiram Dwight, 6(n15)
Pike's Peak gold rush, 110, 199
Pioner Line, 113n13, 174, 288n9
Placerville, 245
Platte River, xii; and abandoned property, 45-46; cholera epidemic on (1849), 120; grass on (1849), 232. *See also* North Platte River; South Platte River
Pleasants, W. J., 6(n19), 7(n26)
Plummer, Samuel Craig, xii, 233(n28), 311(n40)
Political clashes, and dissolution of companies, 171n9
Pomeroy, Horace Barton, 116(n1)
Pomeroy's train, 105
Pond, Ananias, 146-47, 269-70
Pond, Horace, 4(n6), 272(n7), 350(n1)
Ponies: on the trail, 15-16, 93; Indian, 146. *See also* Horses; Mules; Riding animals
Porter, Lavinia Honeyman, 315(n15)
Portneuf River, Indian toll bridge at (1853), 74(n27), 323n11
Possession: wrongful, 252-56; *vs.* ownership, 252-66 *passim*, 305; temporary, and claim against abandoned property, 269-70
Possessive pronoun, as indicator of ownership, 150
Potash, at alkali ponds, 59
Potter, Theodore Edger, 324(n15)
Powell, Daniel, 44(n8), 264n41
Powell, H. M., 204-08
Powell, John Wesley, 111-12(n10)
Powell, Walter, 205
Prairie hens, 302n24
Presbyterian company, 171n10
Prescriptive right to corporate property, 147-50 and n6
Price, Hugh Morgan, 11(n2), 42(n35), 59(n19)
Priority rights, 305
Pritchard, James A., 26(n37), 47(n34), 192-97, 263-64
Private enterprise, and sale of water

on the trail, 294, 296-97
Professional men, as emigrants, 17
Promissory notes. *See* Credit documents
Property: traditional American attitudes toward, 9-11, 18-19, 53, 71, 127-29, 141-47, 194, 217, 285-87, 349-54; types of ownership, 11, 127-29, 183, 286; definitions of, 18, 249, 251, 305; value of on the trail, 31, 127-28; variety of on the trail, 38-41 and nn 13, 24; bargain and sale of, 47 and n32, 54, 56, 66-90 *passim*, 69n5, 80n5, 159, 245-46; role of in formation of social units, 66, 78-90 *passim*, 157-61, 189-92; rental of, 83-84, 112, 302; leasing of, 84; and buyer's market, 109; and seller's market, 109; sale of and warranty of soundness, 115-16 and n1; professional services as, 116-25; letter of reference concerning, 125; prescriptive rights to, 147-50 and n6; adverse possession of, 147-50 and n6; forfeiture of in withdrawal from joint-stock companies, 174-76; and dissolution of partnerships, 199-200; found, 260 and n30; socialist ideas concerning, 285
— abandoned: on the trail, 43-50 and n17, 57, 100-02, 160 and n6, 236, 243-44, 247n5, 350-51, 356; appropriation of, 89, 243-44, 249, 258-62 and n30, 265-74 and nn 13, 17, 21; 299, 346-47, 350-51, 355; reclaimed by owner, 252n3, 256-57, 258, 273-74 and n14, 274-84; and doctrine of exclusive ownership, 252n3, 266, 279, 289-91; return of to owner, 253, 256-63, 274-84; recompense for return of, 262-64 and nn 36, 41, 42; 275-76, 280, 305; and claim of prior appropriation, 269-70; instructions for use of, 270-71 nn 4, 5, 6; right of Indians to, 276 and n6. *See also* Abandonment,

428

law of

— concurrently-owned: discarding of, 49-50, 140, 171-74 and *n*16, 177-78, 179 and *n*5; problems inherent in, 55, 140, 145, 158-61 and *n*6, 165-66, 177-85, 207, 214-15 and *nn* 3, 4; 246, 247-48, 249; division of, 72, 134, 159, 162, 171-72 and *n*10, 179, 184-204 *passim*, 206-08, 211-15 and *nn* 3, 4; and personal property, 128-29, 147, 204, 248-49; conversion of to other types of holdings, 147-50, 180, 183-84, 190-92, 214; necessity for, 157-58. *See also* Companies; Companies, joint-stock; Messes; Partnerships

— government: compensation for, 109*n*1; and authority to repossess, 278-80

— left behind: and reassertion of ownership, 260-61, 271-74 and *n*14, 276; guarding of, 269, 271-72, 273; and notices of reservation placed upon, 272 and *n*9, 274

— military: Indian appropriation of, 276-77 and *n*9; surrender of by emigrants, 277-80

— respect for ownership of, 109, 143-44, 146, 335-36, 339-40; in Sacramento, 4; in Stockton, 4; at the diggings, 5-6; on the trail, 9-11, 202-04, 212-15 and *nn* 3, 4; 217; and exclusive possession, 112-13, 145, 285-305, 288*n*9, 350-59, 360-63; and self-preservation, 222-23, 224, 225, 240, 245-49, 344-46 and *nn* 9, 11, 14, 16, 17

— shortages of: effect on prices, 109, 292; and creation of demand rights, 289, 290-92

— stolen: at the diggings, 6; recompense for return of, 252, 253*n*5, 254, 255, 274, 275-76; held in trust for owner, 252-53 and *n*4, 258; and Indians, 252-55; recapture of, 252-56 and *n* 10; emigrant attitudes toward, 252-56, 274-75; owner's

right to return of, 252-60; and suspicion of theft, 253-54, 259-60, 268, 274-75; concealment of, 261, 262*n*34

Property, private, 127-30, 153-56; surplus, 46*n*19, 68-70, 109-11, 141-42, 143, 290, 292; burden of, 56-90 *passim*, 153, 167-69; pooling of for mutual benefit, 66, 84-85, 151, 157-59, 209; purchase and sale of, 69, 86-87, 98-107, 152-54, 209-10, 251-52, 340-43, 354, 357-59; services regarded as, 116-23; held within companies, 128-29, 140-47, 148-50, 169 and *n*7 , 173-74 and *n*19, 180, 195-97; held within messes, 132, 133, 151, 164-65 and *nn* 7, 8; 247-49; guarding of, 269, 271-72, 273, 338; caching of, 273 and *nn* 12, 13; violent seizure of, 299, 301, 344-50 *nn* 1, 9, 11, 14, 16, 17; 356

— rights and privileges of ownership of, 83, 127-29, 215, 239-46, 254, 297-30, 340-41; attitudes toward, 71, 141-47, 221-22, 285-87, 299-305 and *n*15; and respect for, 109, 143-44, 146, 347-49; absolute nature of, 112-13, 145, 285-305, 288*n*9, 351-54, 360-63; and concurrently-owned property, 128-29, 134, 174, 180, 184-85, 192, 204; refusal to sell or share as, 143, 239-46, 298, 299, 305, 340-49 and *nn* 1, 14, 16, 17; 352, 353, 356; and starvation, 143-44, 146, 245-50 and *n*17, 344-46 and *nn* 9, 11, 14, 16, 17; 355-56; and water, 144, 291 and *n*7, 292-97, 305, 340, 341, 354-55; and horses, 144-46 and *n*15, 152-54, 254-55, 272*n*9; and losses, 146, 151, 152-54, 205*n*2, 360-61; *vs.* possession, 252-53, 264, 265-66, 305; assertion of and strength of owner, 253-55, 256, 262, 321-22, 323, 327-28, 351, 354; and demand rights, 262-64 and *nn* 36, 41, 42; 297-98 and *n*4, 302; *vs.* need, 268 *nn* 17, 21; 285,

290, 305, 353-54; and decision making as, 287-88 and n9, 303-04 and n26; destruction as, 289-91, 298-300, 305; and grass, 291-92; and role of labor in determining, 296-97, 316, 319, 323, 324; and game, 297-98 and nn 4, 5; 305, 331, 333-34, 357; and ferries, 298, 312-13, 315-21; and boats, 298-301 and n15; and specially manufactured products, 298-301; collection of fees for use of as, 301-02 and nn 20, 22, 24; hoarding as, 305; and traders, 305-06, 309-12; and Indians, 321-34; and law of east vs. law of west, 359-60

Proprietors: of passenger companies, 287-88 and n9, 303-04 and n26; of boats, 301-02 and n19. See also Ferries, ownership of; Ferrymen

Provisions and supplies: purchase and sale of on the trail, 33, 54, 68-70 and n5, 86-87, 91-107, 109-11, 115-16 and n1, 225, 234-35, 239, 244, 245-46, 248-49, 268n17, 290-91, 314, 338, 339-42, 343, 345 and n14, 345n17, 352, 353, 356-59 and n2; variety of, 38-40 and n13, 41n24, 104-05; amounts carried, 41, 42, 170, 234; abandoned and appropriated, 43-50, 99, 103, 234 and n36, 237, 238, 252n3, 267 and n13, 274; concurrently-owned, 134-35, 140, 160n6, 165-66 and nn 11, 12; 170 and n8, 188-89, 344n9; sharing of, 141-42, 238, 290, 292-93, 305, 341, 343, 357 and n2; and refusal to sell, 143, 239-46, 298, 299, 305, 340-49 and nn 1, 14, 16, 17; 352, 353, 356; shortages of, 165-66, 218, 233-38 and nn 4, 6; 289, 290, 291-92; division of upon dissolution of partnerships, 200, 204; begging for, 237, 238, 239, 292, 338, 340, 342-43, 356-58; as personal property, 239-40, 247-48, 290-91, 353,

354; purchase of on credit, 343, 352; threats to take by force, 344-45 and nn 1, 14; 347-48
— prices of: at Council Bluffs, 90 and n29; effect of supply and demand on, 98-99, 101-02, 103-04, 309, 311n28; on the Humboldt (1850), 112, 239-40, 292, 341-42, 343-44, 345, 357; at Salt Lake City (1850), 235; characterized as exorbitant, 309, 311, 340, 341-42, 343-44; charged by traders, 309-11 and nn 32, 33, 37; on the Sweetwater, 310n33; at Ragtown (1850), 310, 311 and n38, 343; during the 1850 emigration, 310-11 and nn 33, 38; in California, 348, 357; on Lassen's cutoff, 348, 359
— specific items mentioned: anvils, 49, 50; apples, 38; augurs, 39; axes, 50, 365; axle grease, 69n5; axles, 39; axletrees, 39, 103, and n18; bake-oven, 38; bedclothes, 38, 356; beef, 38, 98, 242; blankets, 38, 258; bookcase, 267-68n16; books, 45, 267 and n15, 273; boots, 38; bread, 38, 45, 69, 98, 231 nn 12, 16; 237, 342, 356, 358; brooms, 40; brushes, 40; butter, 38, 96; camp stools, 38; carpenter's tools, 39; casks, 291n7; catsup, 38; chains, 38; cheese, 96, 105; chocolate, 38; clothing, 39, 40, 43, 44, 45, 48, 49, 101, 236, 290, 342, 356; codfish, 38; corn, 231; corn meal, 38, 236, 267n13, 343; feather beds, 49; fish, 38; forges, 49; fruit, 38, 244; games, 40; gourds, 291n7; ham, 38, 244, 357; harnesses, 39, 43; hatchets, 39; herring, 38; hoes, 39; honey, 38; horseshoes and nails, 39, 40, 310n33; India-rubber bags, 291n7; India-rubber rainwear, 39, 258; jewelry, 40; knives, 39; lard, 99; lead, 38, 45, 50; mattocks, 39; milk, 38; mirrors, 40; molasses, 343; nails, 45; nuts, 38; oats, 341; oxbow, 38; ox shoes, 40; peaches,

430

38; peas, 38; picket pins, 38; pickles, 38; pies, 343; potatoes, 38, 357; rope, 38; saddles, 39; salt, 109-10, 290; sausage, 38; saw mill, 46; saws, 39; scythes, 39; sewing supplies, 40; sheet iron, 39; shoemaking supplies, 40; shovels, 39; soup bone, 341; stoves, 38, 46; syrup, 38; tables, 38; tea, 38, 39, 242; tents, 49, 267n14; tinware, 38; tobacco, 105n28, 309; turpentine, 290; utensils for cooking and eating, 38, 46, 267; vegetables, 329; venison, 38, 39; vinegar, 38, 62, 63, 347; wedges, 39; wheat, 231n16; yeast, 38. *See also* Bacon; Beans; Brandy; Coffee; Flour; Hay; Liquor; Medicines; Mining supplies and equipment; Rice; Sugar; Tools; Whiskey

Public domain, Indian territory as part of, 325, 328

Purchasers, good-faith: and claims of rightful owner against, 274-80; of government property, 277-78 and nn 9, 10, 12; rights of, 291

Pushcarters, on the trail, 34, 36. *See also* Handcarts; Wheelbarrowers

Quarrels, as cause of partnership dissolution, 201-03

Quinine, price of at Lassen's cutoff (1849), 109n1. *See also* Medicines

Rabbits, hunting of on the Humboldt, 334

Rafts, 299, 300, 319, 324

Ragtown: traders at, 97-98, 276n7, 310, 311; and 1850 emigration, 237; prices at (1850), 311 and n38, 343

Ransom, paid for lost or stolen property, 254, 255, 264 and n42. *See also* Recompense; Reward

Read, G. W., xi(n3), 61(n28)

Ream, _____ , 190

Receipts, and division of concurrently-owned property, 203

Recompense, for return of appropriated property, 275, 280. *See also* Ransom; Reward

Recruiting of livestock, 82, 94, 113-14, 238, 244, 272, 276n7

Reed, James Frazier, 71

Reid, Bernard, 116n12, 174(n21), 199(n3), 268n17, 288n9

Relief funds, 129-30, 294, 360-61

Religion, emigrant attitudes toward, 19, 20-24. *See also* Sabbath observance

Rentals. *See* Property, rental of

Return to the East. *See* Turning back

Reward, paid for return of lost or stolen property, 254, 255, 262-65. *See also* Ransom; Recompense

Rice, 38, 39, 101; price of on the Humboldt (1849), 102; prices paid for by traders, 109-10

Riding animals, 15-16; prices of, 31; sharing of in companies, 148-49 and n3. *See also* Horses; Mules; Ponies

River crossings: fees charged at, 72-73; hazards of, 314, 315 and n17. *See also* Bridges; Ferries; Swimming of cattle

Road building, as a vendible service, 118 and n8, 301

Roads, private, and tolls for use of, 301, 323n10

Robe, Rev. Robert, 323n10

Roberts, _____ , 354

Robidoux family, as traders, 93

Robinson, Jack, 110-11

Roosters, 353-54

Roots, as Indian food on the Humboldt, 332

Rough and Ready company, 300

Royce, Josiah, 14

Royce, Sarah, 14, 325(n20)

Rudd, Lydia, 223-24

Rudy, _____ , 190

Russle, _____ , 302n24

Rustlers, cattle, 25, 26, 344

Sabbath observance, 20-24; and Sunday travel, 162n2, 171n10, 187
Sacramento, 17, 245; and respect for property (1849), 4
Sacramento Transcript, 238n6, 241(n18)
Sagamore and California Mining and Trading Company: organization of, 175n22, 186-87 and n4; dissolution of, 186-89, 191
Sage brush, as substitute for wood, 219
St. Clair, Arthur, 234(n33)
St. Joseph, Missouri, 8, 13 and n10; prices of outfits at, 32-33
St. Louis, Missouri, prices of outfits at, 32
Sale of goods. *See* Provisions and supplies, purchase and sale of
Sale of personal property to raise cash, 69, 86-87, 98-107, 315, 339, 340, 343, 358-59. *See also* Money; Property, bargain and sale of; Property, private, purchase and sale of; Provisions and supplies, purchase and sale of
Sale of services. *See* Services, vendible
Saleratus, on alkali ponds, 59
Sales, forced, on the trail, 99, 101
Salmon, Indian sellers of, 329
Salt Lake City: bypass of, 153; routes into and out of, 154n11, 241-42, 287; courts at, 162; provisions for sale at, 234-35, 241
Sanford, Mary Fetters Hite, 271(n3)
San Francisco, respect for property in (1849), 4
Santa Fe trail, 54, 55, 204-06
Sawyer, Mrs. Francis H., 308(n15)
Sawyer, Lorenzo, 112-13, 338-39
Scheller, John Jacob, 98(n43), 159(n3), 239n10
Schneider, Charles G., 200(n5)
Scotts Bluff: and alkaline water, 59; trading post at 93, 114, 306
Scurvy, 222, 227, 347

Searls, Niles, 29(n52), 30(n55), 59(n22), 259(n23)
Sedgley, Joseph, 167n1, 186n5, 188(n10), 303-04n26, 340(n36)
Sell-out, as means of dividing concurrently-owned property, 72, 132, 162, 163, 198-99 and n1, 203, 206-08
Senter, Riley, 14(n17), 307(n8)
Senter, W. R., 44(n8), 46(n26), 307(n11)
Services, vendible, 116-25; methods of payment for, 302 and nn 22, 24. *See also* Blacksmithing; Clothes washing; Cooks; Druggists; Ferries; Guard duty; Guides; Hauling; Hired hands; Hunting; Letter carrying; Physicians; Road Building; Swimming of cattle; Wheelwrights
Shackly, as trail vehicle, 131
Sharp, _____ , 254, 255n9
Sheep, 58, 102
Shepherd, James S., 70n8, 121(n28), 340(n35), 342(n51)
Shipping around the Horn, of supplies by companies, 152n3
Sickness: at the diggings, 6; on the trail, 29-30, 218, 222-24 and n10, 227; and law-mindedness, 221-22, 224; on Lassen's cutoff, 227, 228; and 1850 emigration, 233n29. *See also* Cholera; Diarrhea; Dysentery; Mountain fever; Scurvy; Smallpox; Typhus
Sierra Nevada, xii, 92, 245
Slaves, on the trail, 118n8
Smallpox, 222n6, 309
Smedley, William, 266, 309(n23)
Smith, _____ , 279
Smith, C. W., 162-63, 171n9, 201n8, 237-38, 239(n13)
Smith, G. A., 16(n33), 26-27(n42)
Smith, Jedediah, and Death Valley, 226
Smith, John, on the Oregon trail (1853), 56-90 *passim*, 66n47, 69n5, 85n16, 87n20, 88 and n25, 225, 249

432

Smith, Pegleg, 95, 96, 114-15
Snake meat, as food, 220-21
Snake River: ferries at, 65, 74-75 and
n28; and alkali, 79-82; dead live-
stock at, 82 and nn 9, 10, 12; 86n18.
See also Fort Hall
Snelling, _____ , 207-08
Snow, fear of, 224, 226, 230
Socialists, and ideas concerning prop-
erty, 285
Soda Springs, first emigrants at
(1841), 116
South Pass: and abandoned prop-
erty, 48; and alkaline water, 64
South Platte River, and alkali, 58. *See
also* North Platte River; Platte River
Speed. *See* Travel, rate of
Spencer, _____ , 84
Spencer, Hiram, 84-85, 89
Spooner, E. A., 22(n17), 60(n24),
303-04
Stage stations, 252
Stampedes, 104, 168n3, 219, 327
Staples, David, 16(n29), 24(n32),
270(n1)
Starr, J. R., 361(n9)
Starvation: and respect for property
rights, 143-44, 222, 225, 285, 339-
40, 345; fear of, 221, 336-38, 352-
55; on the trail, 224-49, 225 nn 1, 2;
232 nn 21, 22; 340-41, 344-46 and
nn 11, 14, 16, 17; 347-50, 353-56,
357 and n2, 358
— alternatives to. *See* Begging; Borrowing; Force, threat and use of;
Horses, as food; Livestock, as food;
Mules, as food; Packing; Provisions and supplies, purchase and
sale of; Sale of personal property;
Stealing; Turning back; Violence
Stauder, John A., 134(n14), 259n25,
313-14n9
Stealing: emigrant attitudes toward,
91, 252-56, 259-60 and n26, 262n34,
266, 268, 272-73, 344, 345; by Indians, 110, 153, 165, 227, 253-55, 256
and n13, 275, 276-77 and n9, 326,

332, 333 and n61, 334, 346; and
violence, 276n7, 344 and n1; by
emigrants of Indian "property,"
329-34; as alternative to starva-
tion, 338, 339, 342, 345-46 and n11,
355-56, 358, 359; lack of evidence
for, 355-56. *See also* Horses, theft
of
Steele, _____ , 256n13
Steele, John, 311 (nn 39, 42), 312(n43)
Stephens, _____ , 195
Stephens, J. L., 221(n17), 353(n12)
Steuben, William North, 32(n12),
337(n13)
Steubenville Ohio Company, 189-91
Stevenson, _____ , 298n5
Stevens party, guide for, 117
Stewart, Agnes, 82n12
Stewart, George R., 14(n15), 35-
36(n31)
Stewart, Helen, 22(n16)
Stillman, Dr. J. D. B., 228(n23),
339(n28)
Stimson, Fancher, 231(n17), 232(n20)
Stine, Henry Atkinson, 97(n40),
132(n8), 140(n7), 257(n17)
Stockton, and respect for property
(1849), 4
Stray animals, and right of appropri-
ation, 249. *See also* Livestock, aban-
doned and appropriated
Stuart, Joseph Alonzo, 145, 149(n10),
150(n11), 160n6, 161n7, 174n20,
234n36, 258(n21), 277n10
Sugar, 38, 39, 98, 107, 290; price of on
the Humboldt (1849), 101; jointly-
owned and problem of unequal
consumption, 166 and nn 11, 12;
170; price of at California border
(1850), 357
Summers, Joseph A., 292(n10)
Sunday travel. *See* Sabbath observance, and Sunday travel
Supplies. *See* Provisions and supplies
Supply and demand, law of. *See*
Law of supply and demand

Surgeons. *See* Physicians

Survival, law of: *vs.* property rights, 344-50 and *nn* 1, 9, 11, 14, 16, 17; and threat to kill, 345-46

Sutton, Sarah, on the Oregon trail, 79-81 and *nn* 5, 6; 308(*n*14)

Swan, Chauncey, 215*n*4

Sweazy, _____, 201*n*7

Sweetwater River: and abandoned property, 48; and alkali, 63, 78; bridges on, 74-75*n*27; traders and trading posts on, 92, 94-95; packing from, 232; price of horseshoe nails on (1852), 310*n*33

Swimming of cattle, as vendible service, 73, 74, 75, 118

Sykes, Lorin, 84-85

T., Dr., 15(*n*24), 44(*n*11), 47(*n*29), 109(*n*2), 114(*n*17), 144(*n*9), 144*n*11, 310(*n*32)

Taos, traders from on the trail, 91

Tate, James, 60(*nn* 25, 26)

Taylor, G. N., 57*n*5, 86*n*18

Taylor, John S. L., 220(*n*13)

Taylor, John W., 93(*n*18)

Teamsters, 33, 128, 148*n*6, 158*n*2, 162, 287-88 and *nn* 7, 8

Texas Democrat, 39(*n*13)

Thacher, _____, 254, 255*n*9

Theft. *See* Stealing

Thissell, G. W., 105*n*28, 344(*n*55), 346*n*17

Thomas Fork: of Bear River, 66, 69, 73; of Green River, 29

Thomasson, A. H., 93(*n*13)

Thompson, Harlow Chittenden, 70 (*n*8), 253 and *n*4, 255

Thompson, William, 317-18

Thomson, Origen, 28(*n*47), 162*n*2

Thorniley, John C., 34(*n*25), 330 (*n*54)

Threat. *See* Force, threat and use of; Violence

Thunderstorms, on the trail, 229

Thurber, Albert King, 43(*n*1), 176-77, 214

Tiffin Boys, 101-02

Timber. *See* Wood

Tinker, Charles, 191(*n*14), 298(*n*7), 299(*n*8)

Title, transfer of, subject to covenant, 299-301 and *n*15

Title to products of nature, bestowed upon exclusive possessor, 305

Titus, Capt., company of, 101-02

Tolles, James S., 308(*n*14)

Tolls. *See* Bridges; Ferries; Roads, private

Tools, 39, 40, 172; abandoned, 45-46, 48, 50, 160*n*6; prices for in California (1850), 155*n*19. *See also* Mining supplies and equipment

Traders: as livestock dealers, 67-68, 76, 86, 89, 94, 113-15; Indians as, 69, 73, 75, 87, 93 and *n*14, 152, 256, 275-76, 329, 333; business practices of, 69 and *n*5, 87, 91-98, 109*n*2, 110, 113-15, 234, 308-12 and *n*33; and Indians, 91, 94, 110, 113, 307, 308 and *nn* 13, 17; 309; French-Canadians as, 114, 258 and *n*19, 306; emigrant attitudes toward, 305-12 and *n*10; life-style of, 307-09 and *nn* 13, 14, 17; as thieves, 344

— California: in the Sierras, 92, 311-12, 357; at Ragtown, 97-98, 310, 342, 343; haul goods to the trail from the West, 98, 306 and *n*2; on Forty-Mile Desert, 251-52, 276*n*7, 296-97, 310-11; at Lassen's Ranch, 339. *See also* Bargaining; Barter

Trading posts: blacksmithing at, 75, 119*n*18; on Oregon trail, 85; locations of on the trail, 91-98; prices at, 109-10. *See also* Fort Bridger; Fort Hall; Fort Laramie

Trappers, 47, 218, 306; as traders, 91-92, 95; as guides, 117 and *n*4.

Travel: methods of, 33-36; rate of, 169, 171 and *n*10, 175, 178, 180, 187, 224, 288. *See also* Packers; Passengers; Pushcarters; Teamsters; Wagons; Wagon trains; Walkers; Wheelbarrowers

434

Trials, legal, on the trail, 25, 26, 203*n*13
"Tribute," paid to Indians, 325-27 and *nn* 36, 39
Truckee River: trading posts on, 97; prices at, 97, 102; water hauled from to Forty-Mile Desert, 296
Truesdale, C., 97(*n*36)
Trusteeship, of stolen property, 253, 255
Turnbull, T., 92(*n*6), 271*n*5, 296(*n*33), 318*n*32
Turner, William, 232*n*21
Turning back, 33, 103, 137, 218; reasons for, xi, 15, 25, 51, 136, 161, 198*n*1, 222, 230, 303 and *n*26, 342, 344*n*9
Tuttle, Charles, xi(*n*4), 27(*n*44)
Tuttle, Ziba Smith, 8-9(*n*30)
Tyler, _____ , 150
Typhus, 222*n*6

Udell, John, 9(n32), 100(*n*8)
United States Army. *See* Army, United States
United States government: stations of, 97; supply trains of, 111, 112*n*10, 161-62; officials of on the trail, 162; relief party to Lassen's cutoff (1849), 229; statutes of governing Indian relations, 325. *See also* Army, United States; Fort Kearny; Fort Laramie
Upper Mississippi Ox Company, 143
Utah desert, and Hastings cutoff, 241

Vail, _____ , 203
Varner, Allen, 5(*n*10), 33(*n*14)
Vasquez, Louis, 94, 95
Vehicles. *See* Ambulance; Buggies; Carriages; Carts; Handcarts; Shackly; Pushcarters; Wagons; Wheelbarrowers
Vendible services. *See* Services, vendible
Verdenal, John M., 287(*n*6)

Violence: American predilection for, 3; on the trail, 127, 184, 212, 213-15 and *nn* 3, 4; 221, 344-50 and *nn* 1, 9, 11, 14, 16, 17; and boat and ferry tolls, 299, 316-18 and *nn* 25, 26, 32; 322; and starvation, 338, 339-40, 342, 344-46 and *nn* 1, 14, 17; 347-50, 356, 358; and horse thieves, 346; and failure of property owners to anticipate, 346*n*17, 347-50, 356. *See also* Force, threat and use of
Voting: in companies, 171*n*10, 287-88 and *n*9; in joint-stock ventures, 172-80 *passim*, 174*n*20, 186-87, 191-92, 214; in partnerships, 205, 206-07

Wagons, 169, 286-87, 311, 350, 360; variety of property carried in, 38-41; repair items for, 39, 40, 103 and *n*8; and problem of weight, 41-42, 44, 46, 50, 53, 54, 68-70, 80, 87; converted into carts, 47-48, 49, 50, 77, 129; advantages of, 53, 79; on Oregon trail (1853), 56, 64-65, 67*n*1, 77, 83-89; purchases of on the trail, 66, 77; converted into packs, 101; and contracts for hauling, 178, 196, 248-49, 274, 301, 302 and *nn* 20, 24; 351; gambling, 201*n*8; bailment of, 211, 274; fitted up as boats, 298 and *n*6, 313; ownership of and decision to return, 303-04 and *n*26
— abandoned, 45, 146, 200, 268*n*21, 302*n*24, 356; at Fort Laramie, 47-48, 103; on the Oregon trail, 82, 83-87, 89*n*27; claims of owners on, 82-83, 252*n*3, 273-74, 279*n*9; at Fort Kearny, 103; on the Humboldt, 236; on the Carson River, 237; in the Sierras, 245; appropriation of, 266-68 and *n*21, 274; destruction of, 267, 268 and *n*21, 271 and *n*6, 289, 290; notices placed on, 271 and *n*6
— as concurrently-owned property,

37, 147; division of upon dissolution, 202-03 and *nn* 10, 12; 204, 206; within partnerships, 204, 205*n*1
— price of: on the Oregon trail (1853), 87; on the trail (1849), 98-99; at Fort Laramie (1849), 104*n*22, 109*n*2; in California, 155 and *n*19
Wagon trains, 128, 148*n*6, 174, 187, 189, 191; proprietors of, 302 and *nn* 20, 22, 24
Walker, Joseph Reddeford, 91, 117
Walkers, on the trail, 33-34, 35, 36, 232. *See also* Handcarts; Packing, on foot; Pushcarters; Wheelbarrowers
Wallenkamp, Henry, 62(*n*32), 251, 295(*n*24)
Warner, Elizabeth Stewart, 65*n*45
Warranty of soundness, 115-16 and *n*1
Washington City and California Mining Association (Washington City Company), 111, 117, 143, 175-76
Washtenau (Mich.) *Whig*, 70-71(*n*9)
Water, 40, 220, 228, 232; containers for, 38, 39, 49, 291 and *n*7, 296 and *n*31; shortages of, 45, 293-94 and *n*19, 295; alkaline, 58-67 and *nn* 25, 26, 32; 81-82, 235, 339; exclusive possession of, 144, 291 and *n*7, 292-97, 305, 340, 341, 354-55; sharing of, 238, 292-93; barter for, 293; as Indian property, 326-28, 330
— price of: on Forty-Mile Desert (1850), 248, 251, 294-95 and *n*23; on Hastings cutoff (1850), 294
— sale of by traders, 294, 296-97; on Forty-Mile Desert (1850), 251, 294-95 and *n*31; on Hastings cutoff (1850), 293-94; on the Humboldt (1850), 294; on Hastings cutoff (1863), 294*n*20; on Forty-Mile Desert (post-1850), 296-97 and *n*35
Water law, east *vs.* west, 359
Waters, Lydia Milner, 169*n*7, 287(*n*5)
Watts, John William, 95(*n*27)
Waugh, Lorenzo, 308(*n*15)

Way stations, 54-55
Weapons, 149*n*8, 359; at the diggings, 5-6; on the trail, 37, 38, 172; abandoned, 44, 46, 50, 356; and violence, 317 *nn* 25, 26; 344*n*1, 346*n*17, 347-48. *See also* Ammunition; Gun powder
Weaverville, and respect for property (1849), 5
Webster, Kimball, 172(*n*13), 173(*n*16), 217(*n*1), 220(*n*12)
Weight, problem of. *See* Overloading
Wells, Epaphroditus, 137(*n*4)
Welsh, John Pratt, 22(*n*20), 32(*n*10), 75(*n*27), 273(*n*11), 273*n*13
Western Reserve Chronicle, 134(*n*13)
Weston, Missouri, 53, 54
Wheelbarrowers, on the trail, 34, 36, 37, 302*n*20
Wheeler, George Nelson, 100(*n*7), 342(*n*49)
Wheelwrights, and sale of services, 119, 123
Whiskey, 4, 40, 112*n*10, 273*n*13, 317*n*25; emigrant attitudes toward, 20; and trappers, 47; and traders, 98, 309; prices of on the trail, 106, 107, 109, 110; use of for medicinal purposes, 170*n*8. *See also* Brandy; Liquor
White, _____ , 24
White, Dr. _____ , 279
White, Dr. Thomas, 64(*n*12), 326(*n*28)
Whitlocke, _____ , 124
Whitman, Dr. Marcus, 94, 117*n*4
Wigle, Abraham J., 121*n*29, 326(*n*24), 328(*n*41)
Wilkie, _____ , 195 and *n*17, 196, 197
Wilkins, James F., 104(*n*22), 309(*n*27), 313-14*n*9
Wilkinson, J. A., 84-85, 94(*n*20), 265(*n*1), 267*n*14, 297(*n*38)
William Mullin & Co., 105
Williams, John T., 326(*n*29)
Williams, Velina A., 22(*n*22), 323(*n*7), 324(*n*17)
Willow trees, 235, 243, 330. *See also*

436

Fuel; Wood

Wilson, J. S., 163($n3$)

Wilson, Luzena Stanley, 362($n13$)

Wingart, _____ , 69$n5$

Withdrawal petitions, and dissolution of joint-stock companies, 187

Wolcott, Lucian McClenathan, 232 ($n19$), 233($n24$), 237, 313($n6$)

Wolf Creek: Indian bridge at, 322, 323 nn 9, 10; 324, 325; competing emigrant bridge at, 324

Wolverine Rangers, 40, 146, 175, 214

Wolves, 29, 354

Women and children, on the trail, 11, 12, 23, 26-29 and $n38$, 35, 53, 129, 209-12, 237, 259, 351, 354, 360

Wood: shortages of, 29, 219; as Indian property, 325-30. *See also* Fuel

Wood, John, on the Humboldt (1850), 71-72($n14$), 241-49, 294($n14$), 310, 313$n9$, 340-41, 343, 345

Wood, Joseph Warren, 5, 41($n25$), 133-34($n12$), 259($n24$)

Woodworth, James, 35($n30$), 38($n9$), 40, 102(nn 13, 14), 114($n20$)

Wright, Ovin D., 11($n4$)

Yager, James Pressley, 58-59($n12$), 330($n53$)

Youell, _____ , 195

Young, Brigham, 309

Yuba River, and respect for property (1849), 5

Zieber, John S., 327($n37$)

Zilhart, William, 276$n7$

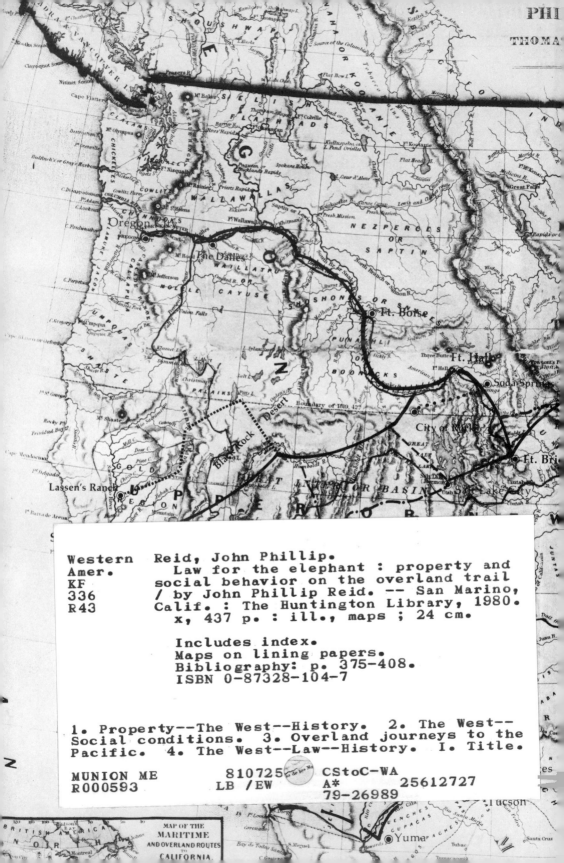